YOU BELONG TO US

A MEMOIR

MOLLY McCAFFREY

To Shea —
Thanks for stopping
by! Enjoy!
Molly
14 NOV 15

MINT HILL BOOKS
MAIN STREET RAG PUBLISHING COMPANY
CHARLOTTE, NORTH CAROLINA

Acknowledgements: A small portion of this book appeared in different versions in *Silent Embrace: Perspectives on Birth and Adoption* (Catalyst Book Press, 2010) and *How to Survive Graduate School & Other Disasters* (Main Street Rag Publishing Company, 2011).

Library of Congress Control Number: 2011923702

ISBN 13: 978-1-59948-520-1

Produced in the United States of America

Mint Hill Books
Main Street Rag Publishing Company
PO Box 690100
Charlotte, NC 28227
WWW.MAINSTREETRAG.COM

For Mom and Dad

Author's Note

Though this is a work of non-fiction and I did interview numerous people who appear in the book about the events that occurred, I was otherwise forced to rely almost entirely on my own memory to re-create events and conversations. I have done so to the best of my ability, but I imagine that other people might remember things differently. Such is the nature of memory.

In addition, I have changed the names of all of the people in the book except for my closest friends and family. I have also altered identifying details, including locations, when I felt it was necessary to protect anonymity.

Though some letters and messages have been truncated, they have not been edited for grammar or punctuation, appearing as they did in their original form—with misspellings and errors still intact. In a similar fashion, though dates precede some letters, they have not been included unless they were provided in the original correspondence.

CONTENTS

Dear Molly,

We've been thinking about you and did try to call you once. I hope all is going well for you and Dave. I know your birthmother is coming to visit soon. It will be an emotional experience, and I will be anxious to talk to you. But no matter what . . . you belong to us.

We love you very much.

Have a great visit and a very special love to Dave too.

Grandma & Grandpa

PART ONE
THE WAITING PERIOD

APRIL 1993-MARCH 2000

I met my biological mother at an airport in Dayton, Ohio, two weeks before my thirtieth birthday. On that cold March morning in 2000, the fluorescent lights in the terminal were buzzing overhead like thousands of tiny bees. *Buzz off*, they were saying. *It's not too late. Get out of here!* But I didn't listen. How could I? The woman who had given birth to me was on a plane headed in my direction. She had told me her flight information, and I had said I would pick her up. We had made an agreement.

Explicitly we had agreed to meet at the airport, but implicit in that agreement was another: from then on, we would be a part of each other's lives. So what kind of person would I be if I just left? If I wasn't waiting—as promised—when she got off the plane, I wouldn't just be abandoning her at the airport. I would be cutting her out of my life. Probably forever. In other words, I would be a bad person, and I had never in my life been a bad person. So I remained in the airport, waiting for a plane from Virginia to arrive. And I tried my best to ignore the buzzing in my head that kept telling me I was making a mistake.

And that's when I began to panic. The bright overhead lights were making me feel light-headed, and my insides had been set on spin cycle ever since we'd left the house that morning. I turned to my husband and said, "I can't do this," as I tried to calculate if there was still time to change my mind.

"You don't have a choice," he said without hesitation.

"Are you sure?" I asked, looking into his watery eyes and hoping to find a way out.

"I'm absolutely sure," he said, not willing to offer me the lifeboat I was so desperately seeking. "It's too late to get out now."

"I think I'm going to throw up," I said.

"You'll be fine," he said, patting my back and raising his head to look for the woman coming toward us, the woman who had given me life.

Almost as soon as the plane landed in Dayton, passengers began emerging into the terminal in a Lazarus-like fashion—their clothes wrinkled and off-kilter, their faces lined with exhaustion, but their eyes bright and happy.

Airport arrivals usually bring me great joy, but that day, I felt no such thing as I watched couples reuniting and parents embracing children. I was too anxious and apprehensive about my own impending reunion for exhilaration. And in my head, I was thinking, *Maybe she won't show up. Maybe she will have changed her mind. Maybe, maybe, maybe…*

But only about two dozen people exited the plane before I saw her.

The first thing I noticed was the sadness in her eyes—sadness and pain. I knew instinctively they were emotions that had been with her for all of my thirty years. But I tried as hard as I could to remove myself from real emotion, not wanting to open up to someone I didn't even know. She still had not seen me—I was hidden in the small crowd of people greeting their loved ones—so I had time to pull back, and when I forced myself to look at her again, through a more distant lens, I saw an image I had not been prepared for no matter how many pictures I'd been sent.

The woman who was biologically my mother was weary and disheveled, like a turtle at the end of the race, as if life itself had robbed her of any vitality. I still remember that she was wearing too-big khaki pants and a lavender-colored sweater set with dark violet flowers embroidered on the surface. Her hair was done in a fashion that seemed to replicate the style worn by senior ladies who go to the beauty shop once a week—much too old for her fifty-one years—but failed on some level, not put together or refined enough to pass for the look she was trying to achieve. And no matter how hard I tried to be positive, to be open-minded, a little voice inside my head said, *Oh, no.*

No, no, no, no, no.

I suddenly realized that, for years, I had been—without even knowing it—creating some fantasy she was unable to fulfill. It will reveal superficial things about me to admit this, but I have to be honest: I was disappointed. The first glimpse of my birthmother in real life confirmed a fear that had been developing since I'd learned the barest of details about her six years before: we had nothing in common. My own wardrobe consisted of black combat boots, jeans, and a faux fur coat I'd bought at Goodwill. We were about as unlike as two people who shared the same genes could be.

I looked at my husband and said, "Is this really happening?"

"Oh, yes, it's happening," he said, never taking his eyes off the woman who shared half of my genetic makeup.

She had seen us by then, presumably recognizing us—as we had her—from the photos we'd sent each other through the adoption agency. And as soon as she did, the sadness on her face was replaced with a smile. A large unabashed smile as if that were the happiest moment of her life, making me hope desperately that it wasn't.

"Hi," she said simply when we were a few feet from each other.

I could hear the trembling in her voice. She was nervous.

"Hi," I said with a smile that was as generous as I could afford considering how confused and disconcerted I felt. *Was this woman really and truly related to me? Why didn't she look more like me? How was it possible that I shared more of this woman's biology than I did with my own parents?* But no matter how uncomfortable I felt, I knew how I was expected to behave at that moment, so I opened my arms and reached out to her.

When I pulled back a moment later, I could see her eyes were filled with tears.

In contrast, I felt almost nothing.

Well, not nothing, but I was fearful and uneasy rather than being moved. And seeing her very real display of emotion made me feel like an awful person. *Why wasn't I crying? Why did I care what she was wearing? Why wasn't I more affected?* But rather than face these difficult questions head on, I shifted the focus away from me.

"Paula, this is Dave," I said, turning to my husband.

Though we had not been in the same room since I was an infant, I knew her name was Paula. She was Paula Tucker by then though she'd been Paula Hurley when she'd given birth to me. I knew her name, her age, how tall she was, and how much she had weighed when she'd gotten pregnant. But I didn't have any idea how I was supposed to act now that I had met her.

Dave and Paula glanced at each other, equally uncertain about what to do next. Then Dave held out his hand, and the two of them exchanged an unnatural shake, not unlike two strangers on a business trip.

I sensed then it was going to be a long weekend.

After all, what do you do with a person you've not been in the same room with since you were born? A person with whom you share a genetic bond even though, for all practical purposes, you've just met?

"Should we get your luggage?" I asked, hoping to diffuse the awkwardness of the moment.

"I don't have any," Paula said, gesturing toward the small rolling bag she pulled behind her, and, again, I was confounded. I'm the kind of person who doesn't take an overnight trip without two suitcases and a carry-on. But Paula had made the most important journey of her life with a wheelie that could fit in an overhead bin. How was it possible we were related?

It was obvious the three of us were a little apprehensive, so we moved tentatively in the direction of the parking lot, making small talk. Paula said the flight from Virginia had been easy and uneventful, but when I told Paula I hadn't flown in three years, she seemed mystified.

"But why?" she asked.

"It terrifies me," I said matter-of-factly. "I know my fear isn't logical. I know it's safer to fly than drive, but it just doesn't feel natural for a one-hundred-ton aluminum tube to take to the air."

"But people do it all the time," she said.

"That doesn't mean *I* do it," I explained.

"But how do you get anywhere?" she asked.

"We drive," I said, glancing at Dave for support before turning back to Paula. From the look of horror on her face, I could tell she was already thinking I was one of the strangest people she had ever met. It wasn't the first time I had encountered a negative response to my unwillingness to fly, but it was perhaps the most unadulterated view I had ever seen of another person judging my fears.

It was clear to me then that Paula held nothing back.

And with that realization came another: I had finally discovered something we had in common.

I had found Paula through the adoption agency that placed me with my parents. The whole process had dragged on for six years from start to finish, so I was pretty shocked when she decided to fly to Ohio for our first meeting only nine months after her identity had been revealed to me—less than a sixth of the time the rest of the search had taken.

It had all started in April of 1993 when I quit graduate school, left my fiancé in Savannah, and moved to Washington, D.C.

I didn't know what I wanted out of life when I was twenty-three years old, but I was certain I wasn't ready to be married. I also knew getting an M.F.A. in graphic design was a waste of money since I didn't need it to get a job. So I packed everything I had in the Honda Accord my parents had generously given me for my college graduation present—including the TV my ex and I fought over before I left and the dog he had never loved the way I did—and headed north.

I wanted to go to a city, a real city not a tourist trap in love with the past. I wanted a city that everyone knew about: a city that made news, a city that inspired people, a city that would inspire me. Even though I'd grown up only forty miles away in suburban New Jersey, New York seemed like too big a challenge for someone who had just failed at two of the most important parts of life—love and school— so I opted for East Coast city number two: Washington, D.C.

I told myself D.C. was safer and cheaper, and anyway my best friend was moving there in a matter of weeks. So after detouring through Indiana to see my parents—who wanted answers I didn't have about why I was leaving everything in my life behind—I headed east, back to the part of the country where I'd been born, back to a question that had called to me all of my life like a still-wrapped present.

Who was I?

I drove into our nation's capital on a glorious May afternoon in 1993 with three hundred dollars in my pocket—seed money my parents had given me to start over. The sun was blazing overhead, and pink, white, and blue azaleas were blooming all the way down Connecticut Avenue as if the streets had been lined with floral bunting for my arrival.

After temping and renting a single room for a month, I landed a full-time job as a graphic designer and moved into a group house with four other twenty-somethings.

My new life had begun.

So there I was—twenty-three years old, single, and living less than thirty minutes from the place of my birth. How could I not think about where I had come from?

Of course, I thought about it. I thought about it all the time.

But I told myself *not* to think about it. And, for the most part, that approach worked. I was content just being young and living life as fully as I could: working late some nights and staying out with my roommates until five a.m. other nights, hanging out with my girlfriends most of the time and going out with all the wrong guys other times.

I was busy with other things.

But when I finally slowed down and caught my breath—about a year later—the same questions were still nagging at me. Who was I and what did I want out of life? Even though I was relatively happy, I was no closer to having any answers.

After living in D.C. for nearly a year, I finally broke down and called the adoption agency during the spring of 1994. I wanted to find out what I would have to do to uncover the secrets about where I had come from. Naively, I'd hoped I could make the call, arrange to have my birth certificate opened, and have all of those secrets revealed to me. But, as it turned out, that was not the case. Like thirty-six other states at the time, Virginia did not allow adoptees access to their birth certificates when they were eighteen.

The only option was to work with the adoption agency, go through the slow process of trying to find my birthmother, and ultimately get her to agree to trade information with me. It was called "mutual consent," but for me it felt like being forced into something I didn't want.

So I waited.

I waited, and I did something most people I knew at the time probably thought was pretty stupid. I reunited with my ex-fiancé.

We first saw each other again in May of 1994: he'd moved back to his hometown of Cincinnati a few weeks before I went to Ohio to visit my maternal grandmother, so we made plans to get together. After spending a little more than a year apart, we were like a couple of dumb teenagers: desperate to get our hands on each other but completely naïve about what it would take to be together in the long run. So instead of worrying about what was wrong with us the first time, we just waded into the warm pool of reclaimed love without concern for the future, seeing each other when we could get to the same state for crazy romantic interludes. And before we could figure out what it would really take to make things work, it was over again, our mad, passionate summer ending with a bitter and angry "don't ever call me again."

After the most significant relationship of my life had failed a second time, I found myself thinking again about what my life was all about and considering the possibility of contacting the adoption agency. *What was the harm in starting the process of searching for my birthmother?* I wondered. If it didn't feel right, I figured I could simply walk away. After all, that was something I had become very good at doing.

The adoption agency required adoptees and biological parents to go through three steps before initiating a search of any kind. The first step was to find out everything the adoption agency already knew—besides names and addresses. This information was compiled in a document called a "Non-Identifying Background Report." The second step was to attend a support group meeting for all of those involved in the adoption process: adoptees, adopters, and biological parents. The third and final step was to participate in a screening interview conducted by the agency to determine if the interested party was psychologically ready for a search.

So in October of 1994, I finally decided to take the first step, filling out the paperwork necessary to generate the report and sending the agency a fifty-dollar check to cover their administrative costs.

Whether or not I knew it then, there would be no turning back.

At first, I thought about the report all the time. *What would it say? Would it tell me everything I wanted to know?* Or would I read it and just feel I needed more: more information, more answers, more everything? But after a few weeks passed, I forgot about it almost completely.

So I was shocked when I came home from work one evening in December of 1994 and found a plain white envelope waiting for me with a return address from Arlington, Virginia—205 N. Thomas Street. I knew immediately it was the address of the adoption agency even though I could not recall memorizing it.

At the time, I was living with my best friend, Tracy, and her future husband. We were renting a small post-war house—a brick rambler with three tiny bedrooms and an equally humble living room, dining room, and kitchen—but it had enough character in the form of glass doorknobs and crown molding that we'd jumped at the chance to live there. Still, my room was so tight I'd bought a loft bed, so I could also fit a desk and futon for out-of-town guests in the small space.

It was unusual to be at home alone on a weeknight, but I was by myself the night the report arrived. The sunlight from the big front window was still bright enough that I could almost see through the envelope to the contents inside. I stood in the living room for a while, just holding it in my hands, measuring the weight of it. The envelope was light, probably only containing one or two pieces of paper, so I knew I had to take my time with it, stretching out the significance of what was happening. My name and address—as well as the return address—had been printed on an old-fashioned typewriter, the stiff serifs making each individual letter look like an important statement.

This is your life.
This is who you are.
This is what you've always wanted to know.

I went into my room, locked the door behind me, and opened the envelope.

CATHOLIC CHARITIES
Non-Identifying Birth and Background Report
Prepared for Molly Ann McCaffrey

You were born on April 5, 1970 in Annandale, Virginia, after an estimated pregnancy of 41 weeks and a labor of 7 hours and 21 minutes. Delivery was normal, assisted by low forceps, with no complications. Your birthmother began pre-natal care in September, 1969. At birth, you weighed 7 pounds 6 ounces and were 20 inches long. Your AP-GAR score (a measure of your physical and developmental wellness at birth) was a 9 on a scale of 1-10. You were slightly jaundiced after birth, a condition that is not unusual in newborns and clears up within a week or two. Your birthmother named you Anne Marie.

At that point, the muscles in my neck closed around my throat as if they were choking me. I could not fathom what I had just read, so I read it again.

Your birthmother named you Anne Marie.

My birthmother named me Anne Marie? What did that even mean? And why would they allow such a practice? I reached up to my neck, grabbing it at the base as if that would help me stay calm. I was suddenly angry, my first sign of what was to come. My birthmother had given me another name? Who, in their right mind, would think that was a good idea? As if I wasn't already confused enough.

Before I read it in the report, it had never once occurred to me that my birthmother had given me a name. Or even that she would've been given the *option* of naming me. Wouldn't that make it so much harder for her to move on? And how was I supposed to feel now that

I knew there was a time when I had not been myself?

I had always loved my name.

Molly McCaffrey.

Not only was it alliterative, it was aesthetically pleasing to the ear. But it also sounded serious. Like my father's name, Mike McCaffrey, it was the name of someone who could get things done. And I had always been someone who could get things done, hadn't I?

I was, in fact, so wedded to my name that I had vowed—at age twelve, after a boy in my seventh-grade class made fun of it—that I would not change my name if and when I married. That day I had sworn I would always and forever be Molly Ann McCaffrey. But here was a document telling me that—for a short time at the beginning of my life—I had been someone else.

I picked up the report again and went on.

On April 8, 1970, you were transferred to St. Jerome's Infant Home for pre-adoptive evaluation.

Transferred to St. Jerome's Infant Home.

That must have meant I'd been taken to this home—St. Jerome's—after I was born but before I was adopted.

I'd always wondered where I had stayed in the weeks between the time I was born and the time I was placed with my parents. Now I had a name, the name of the first place where I had lived.

One of my many questions had been answered.

It was noted at the time that you had a slight rash on your face and that you were a thumb sucker. You were pediatrically and developmentally cleared for adoption by early May. You were baptized into the Catholic faith on May 18, 1970, and joined your adoptive parents on May 22, 1970.

May 22nd.

The day I had met my parents. It wasn't a date I thought about often though it had appeared on the birth announcement my parents had sent to their friends and family.

Penny & Mike McCaffrey
announce the adoption of
Molly Ann
Born 5 April 1970
Arrived 22 May 1970

May 22nd was two days shy of six weeks after the day I was born, and, as long as I could remember, I'd been curious about those six weeks. *What had happened during that time? Who had been with me?* Ever since I was little, I'd treasured a picture of the three of us taken on May 22nd, but the baptism date—May 18th—was new to me. My mother wasn't very good with details, so it was no surprise she hadn't told me I'd been baptized before I was placed with them. In fact, questions about my baptism or godparents had always been met with long pauses and blank stares. I clearly remembered my sister's baptism three years later, but my own had been obscured for twenty-four years.

YOUR BIRTHMOTHER
Your birthmother was 22 years old and single at the time of your birth. Her heritage was English/Irish, and she had been raised in the Catholic faith. She was a high school graduate, a Registered Nurse, and worked in a hospital setting. Her health was good at the time. She was nearsighted and wore glasses. She had a tonsillectomy in 1968 and an appendectomy in 1965. Her interests were sports, reading, and writing poetry. She was described as being 5'6" tall weighing about 125 pounds with light brown hair, brown eyes, and a fair complexion. For reasons of confidentiality, your birthmother entered the agency maternity home in January, 1970 and remained there until your birth.

It shocked me, too, to find out my birthmother had entered a maternity home "for reasons of confidentiality." What could that mean? Why did her pregnancy have to be a secret? Was it just because of the times? Or was there something else that made her want to keep it a secret? I had hoped the report would have answers, but instead, like a good novel, it had raised more questions than it answered.

Your birthmother's father was 56 years old at the time of your birth. He had an 8th grade education and worked as a postman. Her mother was also 56 years old, a high school graduate who worked part time as a secretary. Both parents had mild arthritis. Your birthmother was the youngest of four children. She has a 30 year old sister who was a high school graduate and working as a secretary. This sister was married but separated from her husband. She had a 26 year old married brother who was a high school graduate. He was artistically and musically talented. He worked as a bartender and artist. Her youngest brother was 24 years old and married. He worked for a manufacturing company.

Reading this part of the report was completely overwhelming. I felt like I had entered a Dalí painting, the concrete things I thought I knew about myself becoming fluid and malleable. Gently, I set the report down on my loft bed, which came up to chest, and stared at it, hoping words that seemed nonsensical would make more sense if I concentrated on them long enough. I had believed all my life that my biological mother would have certain things in common with me, especially intelligence and education. But, as it turned out, she came from a somewhat uneducated family and had a father who hadn't even gone to high school, much less college.

This information just didn't jibe with what I knew about myself—that not only was I intelligent, but I was also more intelligent than most of the people I knew. It was a cocky attitude to have, I admit, but it was the truth. Except for a few times when I let social distractions get in the way, I had always done well in school and had always outperformed most of my peers. I loved to read and had been raised to believe I was a bit of a nerd.

On top of that, almost everyone in my family was highly educated, so much so that they considered it baffling when I'd dropped out of the M.F.A. program at the Savannah College of Art and Design the year before. Both of my parents had attended grad school, my father earning his M.B.A. when he was only twenty-three.

Not only were my parents educated, but so were their siblings. All of my aunts and uncles had gone to college and half of them had earned graduate degrees. Both of my grandmothers had attended college for a few years, too, which was much more uncommon for women when they were young than it is now, and, though my paternal grandfather did not, he'd worked a white-collar job all his life. Topping off my impressive family tree was my maternal grandfather: like his father, he'd been an M.D. and a prominent member of the small city where my mother grew up.

So to find out that my biological mother came from a family of people who hadn't attended college and had a father who only had an eighth-grade education was completely jarring and disorienting. If I wasn't the daughter of highly educated parents, who was I?

The other thing I couldn't wrap my head around was why the one-page report ended so abruptly. The last few lines had been typed over the address at the bottom of the letterhead. *Why were they in such a rush to finish?* I wondered. *What were they hiding?* Yes, I understood these reports were supposed to be a simple list of facts, but something about it seemed hurried or unfinished as if they weren't telling me everything they knew. And what I didn't know then was that suspicion would ultimately be proven true.

After I first read the report, I was so confused by the details revealed to me that I felt absolutely no desire to seek any other information about my birthmother. I was adamant about that decision even though the adoption agency had included a flyer advertising the support group I would need to attend next if I continued my search. I told myself I already knew everything I needed to know—my birthmother was obviously very different from me, so much so that I probably had nothing in common with her. The only thing missing was any information about my birthfather, who wasn't even mentioned. The form letter attached to the report explained the birthfather's identity was sometimes not disclosed to the adoption agency, making me believe my birthmother probably didn't even know who he was.

I wouldn't find out how wrong I was for another five years.

In the meantime, my life went on as it had before: I moved into my own apartment in the District, spent a lot of time with friends, started taking creative writing classes, and simply enjoyed my new life as an adult with no real responsibilities. For the most part, I didn't think very much about searching for my birthmother. Somewhere in the back of my head, I knew if I wanted to continue the search, I could, so I tried not to dwell on things beyond that.

I figured there was no hurry.

It was the same feeling I had about my ex-fiancé at the time. *There was no hurry. If it was meant to work, it would.* And I really believed that to be true.

So I have to admit I wasn't completely shocked when—a year and a half later, in July of 1996—he showed up on the doorstep of my D.C. apartment, wanting to get back together. Dave and I hadn't seen each other in two long years—since the summer when we'd foolishly rushed back into things without considering what it all meant—so being near each other again made us feel both lucky and grateful. As a result, our second reunion was more thoughtful. We didn't jump right in like we had before, but over time, we learned to trust each other again. More importantly, we figured out how to make our relationship work.

A little more than a year later we were engaged a second time and making plans to get married and move to Ohio to study creative writing in grad school. That meant I would be leaving D.C. in just six months' time and would be very far from the place where I was born.

All of a sudden there was a hurry.

If I wanted to keep searching for clues about my past, I had to go to a support group meeting next. But that was something I had zero desire to do, which was probably why I let more than two years pass since the time I'd gotten the background report from the adoption agency. During that time, Catholic Charities had sent me three flyers listing the meeting times for 1995, 1996, and 1997, but I had yet to do anything with that information. The support group was for everyone involved in the adoption process, and I had no interest in attending because I couldn't imagine that others would have any wisdom to impart about my life, which I foolishly saw as unlike anyone else's. *What could any of those people possibly know about what I'd been through?* I wondered. *And what could they possibly teach me?* What I didn't get was that, even if they didn't fully understand me or my life experiences, simply watching their faces wilt and crack while they told their life stories would have a profound effect on me.

Ultimately, I had no choice but to attend a meeting if I wanted to move forward. And going to the support group meeting wouldn't mean I *had* to go ahead with the search. It was only the second of the three hoops Catholic Charities made adoptees jump through before initiating a search. I told myself that even if I went to the meeting, I wouldn't be obligated to say or do anything else. I could just sit there, listening, in order to satisfy the demands put on me by the agency. So I figured there wasn't any harm in going. And that's how I ended up driving to Arlington, Virginia, on a cold and rainy night in February of 1998.

I had never been to the Catholic Charities office before. I don't know exactly what I had been expecting. I suppose I had some vague image in my head of a cheerful place where happy things occurred, a place where brightly colored cut-outs lined the walls and sunlight shone in every room, not unlike a kindergarten classroom. I guess I believed any agency that had matched me with my parents would have to be a place of joy. So I was a bit surprised to find that was not the case.

The entrance was on the first floor. When Dave and I peered through the nondescript glass door of 205 N. Thomas Street—an address I'd been thinking about for almost four years—we were surprised to see a buzzer not unlike the kind you'd find on the first floor of an apartment building. We double-checked the address, and then I said goodbye to Dave, who was planning to spend the evening at the public library. After he was gone, I stepped inside the foyer, pressed the buzzer, and announced my arrival to an unknown voice on the other end of the speaker. Once I'd climbed the stairs, I was greeted with a space that looked like any other bureaucratic office. It was run-down and drab and much in need of a makeover. Beat-up file cabinets were pushed against scuffed walls, and metal chairs sat on top of worn-out carpet.

I did not have a good feeling.

A thirty-something African-American woman approached me almost immediately. "Here for the support group meeting?" she asked me.

"Yes," I said, wondering if I had made the right decision, but too nervous to admit my hesitations out loud.

"Just go right in there," the woman said warmly, pointing to a larger room with about twenty chairs set up in a circle.

I entered the space, finding about half a dozen other people—mostly women—scattered around, either sitting in chairs talking quietly or getting coffee from a folding table near the back wall. They offered me short but friendly hellos, but mostly people kept to themselves, and I couldn't help but notice something in the room felt distinctly off, as if there was a general feeling of unhappiness hovering in the air. I assumed that not very many people would show up, but about ten minutes later, every chair was filled.

The woman who had greeted me when I first came in joined us pretty quickly after that, welcoming everyone to the meeting. "We don't really have any rules here," she said by way of an introduction. "Except that we want to give everyone a chance to talk and tell their story. I know we have all members of the adoption triad here tonight, so it will be good to hear from those various perspectives." Then the woman sat down somewhat abruptly and said, "So? Who wants to go first?"

I hadn't known what to expect, but I was shocked when I realized in that moment that the meeting was simply about giving everyone a space to tell his or her story. I understood then what had seemed off when I first arrived: it felt like we were at a meeting for people who had a problem—not unlike an AA meeting or a grief support group—and these people, the people sitting around me, were all in need of help. They were real people whose lives had been forever changed, more often than not negatively, by adoption. The majority of them were birthmothers who were still mourning their loss, and witnessing their pain was the first glimpse I would have into what my own birthmother had experienced. Most of them weren't there because they'd had a positive experience with adoption like I had. Most of them were there precisely because they hadn't. It was a perspective on adoption I had never witnessed before, and it was truly unsettling. One woman in particular told a story about halfway through the night that made me re-think everything I thought I knew about searching for my birthmother.

"I gave up my little girl," the woman began, "when I was only twenty."

I leaned in when I heard this. Twenty was only two years younger than my biological mother had been. Growing up, I had wrongly assumed that only teenage girls gave up babies, but I was learning that women of all ages were forced to choose adoption.

The woman went on. "She was such a little baby, I could hold her with just one arm. Some people told me not to, but I had to hold her. I just had to." The woman paused at that point, playing with a tissue in her hand. I noticed then how disheveled she looked. She wore an oversized sweatshirt, out-of-style jeans, and her hair was pulled back into a loose ponytail with thick clumps of hair falling out on both sides. "Of course, after, I had to go on. Like some of you," she said, nodding at the other women in the room who had already told their stories, "I got married and had more kids. And I tried not to think about my little baby girl. I never forgot her, mind you, but I didn't want to dwell on her. I wanted to live my life."

When she said this, almost everyone in the room expressed agreement in some way, and I found myself nodding along with them, certain that it was better to move on than to live in the past.

"And then, one day, back in—" She paused mid-sentence to count on her fingers. "Well, let's see, I guess it must have been three years ago now. Yes, three years ago, I got a letter from the agency saying my little girl wanted to meet me." The woman stopped then, looking around the circle with a big smile on her face before continuing. "It was the happiest day of my life. I was finally going to find out about my baby, to find out if she was okay, to find out if she was healthy, if she was happy." A woman on the other side of the room let out a little sniffle, and as I glanced around, I saw that several other women were crying too.

They had all been there, they had all been through what this woman had been through.

"No, wait," the woman said abruptly. "I take that back. The happiest day of my life was when I saw her. About a year later. Her name is Jane now," she said, explaining. "She lives on the other side of the country if you can believe it. In Seattle!" The woman seemed shocked by the idea that her daughter could live so far away.

Immediately a picture formed in my head, a picture of Jane from Seattle.

She would be smart, of course. With a name like Jane, she was probably a reader, and she'd have to be worldly if she had somehow made it all the way from D.C. to Seattle, or at least her parents had made it that far. I had a sudden desire to meet Jane, to become friends, so we could share stories about what it was like to be from one world and grow up in another.

"So she flew all the way back here, and I was never so happy in my life," the woman said, pausing and smiling while she remembered the time when she'd finally met her long-lost daughter. "She was only twenty-four at the time, but she was very grown up."

Twenty-four? I was almost twenty-eight, and I still hadn't even officially started the search to find out who my biological mother was, but this Jane had found out when she was only twenty-four. Mentally, I kicked myself for waiting so long. If Jane could do it, why couldn't I?

"I loved spending that day with her," the woman said, letting out a long sigh before she continued. "We had a wonderful time and shared so much, but—" At that point the woman paused again, ducking her head as if she was trying not to cry, and when she looked back up, I could see the tears in her eyes from across the room. "But I never heard another word from her." The woman looked around the circle again, this time with a pleading look in her tear-filled eyes. "I called and wrote, but she never responded," she said, sounding desperate. "I don't know why. I really don't. It's almost like she didn't really want to know me."

It felt then as if I had been punched in the gut. I didn't double over, but my throat and mouth went completely dry.

"I haven't heard from her for more than a year," the woman pleaded, obviously wounded by the experience. "And I just don't understand why she searched for me in the first place if she didn't want me in her life. Why did she drag up all those bad memories?"

Of course, I knew exactly why her daughter had cut off contact. She had never wanted to *know* her birthmother; she just wanted to know who *she* was and where she'd come from. She had never wanted to have a real relationship with her birthmother. She'd just wanted to fill in the blanks of her life. And she probably didn't even think about dragging up bad memories because, for her, those memories didn't exist. She didn't remember her birthmother any more than she remembered her first birthday or her first steps.

I thought for only a second about explaining this to the woman—who was crying softly into her tissue by then—but my mouth was so parched I couldn't have possibly spoken, and I realized, too, that telling her such a brutal truth wouldn't help her as much as it would merely continue the hurt.

I studied that woman a long time. If she'd been twenty when her daughter was born and Jane was only twenty-something by then, the woman couldn't have been fifty. But she looked much older than fifty. Sixty, at least. There were lines up and down the sides of her cheeks and across her forehead as if her pain and sorrow had been drawn over her face with invisible ink.

I never forgot that woman and thought about her for months afterward. She'd taught me that if I searched for my birthmother, I would be reintroducing difficult feelings into her life and causing a whole ocean of painful memories to surface. At that point I felt certain I didn't want a relationship with my birthmother, but merely wanted to know who she was, who *I* was. So rather than rush forward to the next stop in the search process before I moved to Ohio, I told myself I wasn't ready. I told myself I couldn't give my birthmother what she would need in return. I told myself to wait.

So that's what I did.

I waited through the rest of my time in D.C., I waited through our wedding and the move to Ohio, I waited through my first semester of graduate school. But when we were making plans to go back to D.C. during spring break of our second semester, I figured I might as well take that opportunity to complete the third and final step in the search process: the screening interview. I told myself that, even if I did the interview, I didn't *have* to continue the search. I could still wait as long as I wanted after that to give the adoption agency the okay to move forward.

Little did I know that once that train started downhill, there wasn't really much I could do to stop it.

*

Before I sat for the interview, I was asked to write a check to cover the cost of the search—$150 because I was only making five thousand dollars a year plus room and board in my Master's program—and to fill out a lengthy ten-page questionnaire, asking me dozens of questions that were obviously designed to ascertain whether or not I was crazy. Or, if not crazy, at least sane enough to handle the emotional ramifications of a search.

I was smart enough to know I should answer each question carefully, revealing just enough sensitivity to pass the test. For instance, when I was asked to explain my feelings about Virginia's mutual consent law, rather than convey in full detail how angry it made me, I expressed my frustrations in very polite terms:

I actually am not happy about Virginia's mutual consent rule. I think it is unfortunate that I cannot find out who my birthparents are on my own, and ultimately I think the rule should be changed. The rule has, in fact, been the number one reason I've waited all these years to search.

But more than anything, when I re-read my answers on the questionnaire now, I find them incredibly disconcerting. I can't believe how naïve and optimistic and *young* I sounded. Was I really that clueless about what was going to happen? Did I really not understand the gravity of what I was doing? At one point, I was asked to state my goals and expectations for the search, and I wrote:

I have no expectations, to be honest. I imagine a search may be unsuccessful, but I hope that will not be the case. My goal is to find out who my birth parents are, what they have done with their lives, what kind of background they came from and whether or not they are still alive.

I sound so casual about the whole thing—so business-like and impersonal about doing something *incredibly* personal as if searching for my birthmother was like checking items off a grocery list—that, looking back, I have to believe I had no idea what I was getting myself into. Had I really not understood the monumental significance of what I was taking on? Did I really not get how a search would change me?

If I could go back in time, I would take the young woman who filled out that questionnaire, grab her by the shoulders, look her in the eye, and say, *Think about this more! Think about what you're about to do. Because once you do it, you can never undo it. Never ever ever!*

Because I was so clueless about what was happening and how much bigger it was than anything else in my life, it's no surprise that I remember approaching the screening like a job interview: I felt anxious and nervous to the point that I looked forward to having a drink when it was all over, and I didn't understand how much it would affect me. I also had the false sense that very few people passed the interview, and I had to prove the worth of my search to my caseworker, a middle-aged woman named Margaret who had blond puffy hair and wore a pantsuit.

Despite her average appearance, Margaret had an openness in her eyes that gave me some hope regarding what was about to transpire. I realize now it's probably rare for the agency to say no to someone requesting a search. But back then I didn't understand that, so I was on my best behavior, being as polite and professional as I could be when I entered the same rundown waiting room I'd seen the year before while attending the support group meeting. And after I was escorted into her sunny but dated office, I tried to give the answers I assumed Margaret wanted to hear while also being as truthful as possible. That is, until she mentioned something I had never thought about before.

"You should know it's always possible your birth parents have reunited," Margaret said about twenty minutes into the interview. I had been trying my best to sit up straight on the upholstered couch where I was seated, but when she said that, I felt my body sink into the cushions. "How would you feel about that?"

"Reunited?" I asked, momentarily confused. "What do you mean? Do you mean they might have gotten back together?"

"Yes, have you ever thought about them reuniting and even possibly getting married?"

"No, I've never even considered that." I was being honest. I knew a big part of the interview was to determine if I could handle the emotional challenges of meeting my biological family, so I pulled back from being completely forthright and added, "I'm sure it would be fine. Why? Does that happen often?"

"More often than you might imagine," Margaret said. "These things happen."

"I always figured that if a woman gave a baby up for adoption, that meant her relationship with the birthfather had ended." I glanced out the window then, trying to imagine a reality for my birthmother that was different than the one I had created in my head.

"Sometimes it does," Margaret agreed, nodding. "But you know how relationships work. People break up and get back together all the time."

Of course, I knew Margaret was right. Dave and I had been through the same thing—breaking up and getting back together two separate times before we had eventually married, eight years after we first met. And then it hit me: I had never before thought of my birthmother as a normal person who had been in a normal relationship when she got pregnant with me. I'd always pictured the opposite—a drunken night that ended in a crowded backseat with someone she never saw again. I'd always imagined her as the jilted woman.

I had always imagined her alone.

Not long after Margaret introduced the idea of my birthparents reuniting, she gave me a copy of my non-identifying background report in case I had lost it. I hadn't lost it or forgotten a single thing about it, which was why I was shocked when she handed me a document that was two pages long.

I flipped to the second page and scanned the details. The headlines on that page read, YOUR BIRTHFATHER and WHY ADOPTION WAS PLANNED FOR YOU and SUBSEQUENT CONTACT. I could not imagine why I hadn't seen any of it before.

"What is this?" I asked Margaret.

"It's your non-identifying report."

"I've never seen this," I said, holding up the paper she'd just handed me. "This second page. I've never seen it in my life."

"It would have been in the report. I sent it to you back in—" Margaret paused to peer over some papers in her hand. "Back in 1994. Maybe you misplaced it?"

"I didn't misplace it," I insisted, shaking my head. "I would definitely remember if I had ever read something about my birthfather." Then I repeated myself: "I've never seen this in my life." Then I looked down at the paper in my hands and read the words that had been missing from my life for five years.

YOUR BIRTHFATHER

Your birthfather was 22 years old and single at the time of your birth. He had three years of high school and worked as a mechanic. He was described as being 6'5" tall, weighing about 150 pounds with light brown hair, brown eyes, and a fair complexion. He had been raised in the Catholic faith, but his heritage was not noted. He lived with his mother who had raised him and his older brother since her husband left the family. His mother was 42 years old and working as a waitress. His brother was 23 years old, married but separated. He was a high school graduate and working as a house painter.

WHY ADOPTION WAS PLANNED FOR YOU

Your birthparents had dated for 2 years, and your birthmother had hoped that they could be married. Your birthfather told the agency social worker that he did not want to commit to marriage or to be a parent and broke off the relationship with your birthmother. Deciding to place you for adoption was a very difficult decision for your birthmother. She had been very involved with you in the hospital and visited you at the Infant Home regularly.

SUBSEQUENT CONTACT

The agency heard from your birthmother after your adoptive placement, and she was expressing regrets about having placed you for adoption. Her social worker tried to help her work through her feelings about the situation and reinforce her initial decision. She recontacted the agency in July 1971. She was still having problems regarding your placement and had reinvolved herself with your birthfather. She seemed to be depressed. The social worker offered to set up counseling, but your birthmother declined saying she would contact her own physician. There has been no further contact since that time.

—Prepared December, 1994 by M.N.

"Why didn't I get this five years ago?" I asked Margaret after I saw her initials on the bottom of the report. I knew I sounded more accusatory than I should during an interview designed to evaluate my psychological health. But I was angry.

Margaret took the report from my hands, looking it over as if searching for an answer to my question. "I sent you the whole thing," Margaret said. "Are you sure you didn't get it?"

I looked at her directly, and Margaret's heartsick eyes told me she finally understood—of course, I didn't get it. How could I have forgotten something so important?

"So it was my birthfather who made the decision?"

"I guess you could look at it that way," Margaret said. "He wasn't ready. You can't make someone want to be a parent."

I knew that was true, but I still filed away the information for later. My birthfather had abandoned my birthmother. He had abandoned both of us. "What is this part?" I said pointing to the bottom of the page. "What is this about subsequent contact?"

Margaret rolled her chair back across the floor protector to her desk and picked up a manila folder. *My* folder, I realized. "It says that, after your birthmother started dating your birthfather again, they contacted the agency." Margaret paused and looked at me. There was clearly more she wasn't telling me. She studied me for a moment, and then she sighed as if giving in to something beyond her control. "It says they wanted to get you back."

"Wanted to get me back?"

"Yes," Margaret said, glancing down at the file. "They were dating again and wanted to get you back."

"My God," I said, gasping. And, without realizing I was doing it, I imagined my whole life being played back before me—writing every day during the past year of grad school, dancing to Blue Suede with Dave at our wedding, falling in love with him in our college dorm, struggling to fit in during high school in Indiana, growing up with my parents and my sister in New Jersey—I thought back on all of it, my whole life, and realized, that with one simple change of heart, it could have all—every minute of it—been erased. "My God," I said again. "Could they have done that?"

"Well, sure," Margaret admitted, "they could have." Then she paused. She was studying me again, no doubt processing my response for further evaluation. "But they didn't. We didn't let them. We told them it was too late." Margaret paused again and caught my eye before she continued. "We lied."

"Thank God," I said, my eyes filling with tears as I looked to the ceiling. But it wasn't God I had to thank. It was Catholic Charities. It was someone just like Margaret, so I brought my gaze back to her face and said what I really felt: "Thank you. Thank you so so so much."

During the interview, Margaret also told me about her own experience meeting her biological family since she, too, was adopted.

"It's very challenging," Margaret told me. "I don't have much in common with my birth family. They live in the country, and they all smoke. It's really hard when I visit them. I hate the smell of smoke, and I don't have any idea what to say to them. We're very different."

Poor Margaret, I thought. *How awful.*

Naively, I didn't get what she was trying to tell me—that I was likely to have the same kind of experience. That, like her, my birth family might not be as educated or as civilized as I was, that they might smoke, and I might have little to nothing in common with them.

But instead of getting Margaret's message, I focused on feeling sorry for her, never imagining my own birth family would be anything like hers. *They'll be like me,* I told myself. Despite knowing what I already did about their background and education, I believed we'd have other things in common. After all, the report had said my birthmother liked to write and read poetry.

It was possibly the most ignorant I've ever been in my entire life.

Before I left Margaret's office that day, she told me she'd be going ahead with the search process. I had incorrectly assumed she'd need some more time to think about it, maybe discuss it with her peers or her boss. That she would *ask* me if I wanted to go ahead with the search. But none of that happened. Instead, she said, "Okay, I'll let you know if I find anything."

And, for some reason I still don't understand, I didn't stop her.

*

After I finished my interview, Dave and I decided to drive out to the place where Margaret told me St. Jerome's was located. Though, as a child, I'd had the vague sense I had been cared for by nuns, I'd never known where that care had taken place or in what kind of facility. Was it in a hospital? Or an orphanage? It was a source of great mystery for me, another blank I desperately wanted to fill in, and I thought about that unknown part of my life often when I was growing up. So when I'd received the non-identifying background report and found out about St. Jerome's, I felt a great sense of relief simply because I could associate a name, a description, with that part of my life. So as soon as Margaret told me its location, I knew I had to see it.

St. Jerome's was located in a town that, to my great disappointment, sounded average, not extraordinary: Aldie, Virginia. In 1856, the Daughters of Charity had opened an orphanage in Washington, D.C., called St. Jerome's Infant Asylum to support foundlings and infant orphan children. Of course, "asylum" was the kind of word that didn't inspire optimism or confidence, so, in the middle in the twentieth century, the facility was rechristened as St. Jerome's Infant Center, a name obviously more palatable and less frightening to outsiders. In 1964, only six years before I was born, St. Jerome's was relocated to Aldie, about forty miles outside of D.C. Villa Maria—the home for unwed mothers where my birthmother lived from January to April of 1970—was housed on the same grounds as St. Jerome's, and though it's no longer an orphanage, St. Jerome's still provides shelter for children who, for one reason or another, can't live at home.

All I remember about Aldie itself was that it was unsubstantial. I can recall seeing a few farmhouses and many wide open fields though I'm sure there was more there. The St. Jerome's campus, however, is still vivid in my memory.

It was an overcast day: the clouds were low and dark, and a slight drizzle had started to fall from the sky. Because of the weather, the buildings seemed grim and institutional. I don't know exactly what I imagined when I'd first learned about St. Jerome's. I suppose I pictured something more like a maternity ward in a hospital—nurses running up and down the aisles of pink- and blue-blanketed babies. So I was surprised when we arrived in Aldie and found St. Jerome's felt more like a school than a ward. The campus was home to St. Jerome's and Villa Maria as well as a few other facilities; it consisted of several mid-century yellow brick buildings separated by overgrown trees, vast lawns, and nearly empty parking lots. I knew from my mother that the St. Jerome's of the past had included a nursery— with cribs and rocking chairs—and a playground, and I'd learned later there was also a chapel, the same chapel where I'd been baptized before I was adopted. But I couldn't find any sign of a nursery when we walked around the area in the rain.

Though I had never processed it before, while we were in Aldie that afternoon, I understood that living in a home for infants meant I must have spent a good deal of time alone in my crib, the Daughters of Charity presumably having to tend to dozens of babies at the same time. It had never occurred to me that my life had begun in a way that required me to fight for the attention of a few overworked nuns. *Was that why I had always hated to be alone? Because I had spent the beginning of my life on my own? Was that why, even as a teenager, I had always wanted my mother to stay home with me rather than work? Because she was the first person who made me the center of her attention, who put my needs ahead of everyone else's? Was I afraid that if she left, I would be left alone again?* It was a disconcerting idea. Until the moment I visited St. Jerome's, I had thought of myself as lucky, as special, but suddenly I saw that for a time—a brief time, yes, but not an insignificant amount of time—I had actually been very unlucky and very alone.

And that realization has stayed with me ever since.

Years later, after my mother gave me all the papers and articles she'd saved in relation to my adoption, I found a note on which she'd scribbled the directions to Aldie. As I read her perfect script—a formal style of penmanship that matched the way she constructed her sentences—and imagined my parents driving out to that remote campus on a day in May so long ago, I started to tear up even though there was nothing to cry about. I did that same thing a few days after our trip to St. Jerome's when I received an early birthday card from my parents only days after my interview with Margaret.

March 24, 1999

Dear Molly,

As your 29th birthday arrives, we can't help but tell you how proud we are of you. You have a zest for life and abundant thoughtfulness and loyalty to your friends and family. We cherish you and all you are.

We know your decision to search for your birthmother has been a difficult and slow one. We support your decision to pursue it at this time in your life. We caution you not to overextend yourself and not to underestimate the emotional impact both to you and your birthmother. We are the lucky ones because we know your love and feel secure in our relationship with you as parents. No new information can take that away from us. We appreciate the difficult decision your birthmother had to make in 1970. This decision turned into our blessing, and we are thankful to her for the gift.

You seem anxious to know about any information I have and so I'm forwarding these letters, etc., from Catholic Charities regarding our application and process of adoption. . . so many years ago. (We sent baby pictures of both Mike and I and other family pictures.)

Much love,
Mom and Dad

My interview with Margaret had been in March, and yet again I wrongly assumed it would take months, maybe even years, to locate my birthmother after I'd completed that final step in the pre-search process. Margaret's letter—also dated March 24, 1999— officially acknowledging receipt of my $150 payment for the search, claimed that: *We receive many requests for this service and have only one staff person who performs the necessary work. For these reasons, it may take up to four months to initiate work on your case. Additionally, the nature of this work makes it impossible to quote time frames for locating and contacting the subject.*

This explanation made perfect sense to me, and I told myself to settle in for a long wait. After all, I had made my own half-hearted attempt to research the details surrounding my birth while living in D.C.—going to the local library to look up birth records and old newspapers from the month I was born—and come up empty.

Why would the adoption agency's inquiry be that much more fruitful? Some part of me even believed they would never be able to find my birthmother. I had learned from Margaret that was a possibility, albeit a rare one. Or maybe they would find her, but she wouldn't want to make contact. On my pre-search questionnaire, I admitted I knew that was a potential outcome, saying: *I would not be surprised if my birthparents are not interested in contact. I recognize that it would be hard for anyone to go back to something they have already dealt with in their lives.*

It was as if a part of me had already accepted that the search might not yield anything productive. Maybe I was even hoping for that, letting me off the hook of the hard work of finding out where my life had begun.

For that reason, I was completely floored when I got the following handwritten note in the mail from Margaret less than a month later.

CATHOLIC CHARITIES
Maternity Counseling and Adoption Services

4/21/99

Hi, Molly—

Just wanted to let you know I believe I have located your birthmother. I am doing a bit more verification, and I'll be ready to contact her. Could I please have your letter and picture(s) soon?

Thanks,
Margaret

When I read Margaret's words, I was overcome, a shiver running the entire length of my body. It seemed as if the train had left the station, and I was no longer the one driving it.

I had never suspected I would hear from Margaret less than one month after the agency had initiated the search. What had happened to the four months they claimed it would take for the search to begin? They had clearly not waited that long to start looking. I understood then that the four-month line was probably something they said to keep those who were searching from calling every week to check on the progress of the search.

Still, I felt like I had been misled.

I felt like I hadn't had nearly enough time to process the idea of my birthmother being a living, breathing person who would soon know my name.

I felt frightened.

Not long after I received that note from Margaret, Dave and I went to Indiana. My parents were still living in the town where I'd finished high school—Warsaw—and they also had a small cottage on a nearby lake. At the time, we were living in a tiny efficiency apartment on the first floor of a dorm at Miami University—without air conditioning—so we decided to spend most of the summer at my parents' cottage, far away from the stresses of real life, where we could write and study for our Master's exams the next year. It was a peaceful interlude of writing and reading and spending time with my parents except for one thing. It was during that time when I had to write my introductory letter to my birthmother, and I had no idea where to begin.

Not sure what to say, I turned to the instructions Margaret had mailed me. I highlighted what I saw as the pertinent parts of the document—why I was searching and if I felt grateful to my birthmother—but it's notable I didn't adhere to their very first suggestion: *In order not to overwhelm the birthparent, we recommend that the letter be no more than two pages.* My letter was, in fact, more than five pages long. Granted the letter was handwritten on stationery, but still—what had I been thinking? Didn't a longer letter open the door wider for my birthmother? Didn't it make it harder to shut? Why hadn't I just given her a tiny peak at who I was?

Of course, it was because doing so would not have fit my personality, but it still frustrates me now to recognize I couldn't even obey the simplest of rules. I wrote two drafts of that letter—a shorter one that I still have and the longer one I photocopied and ultimately mailed to the adoption agency.

Below is the letter I ended up sending.

31 May 99

After many years of careful thought and consideration, I have finally decided to try to get in touch with you, my birthmother. I have had a wonderful life so far, and I feel I owe much of that to you and your very unselfish decision to put me up for adoption. I have always felt that it must have been a great sacrifice for you, and I really am very grateful.

As I said, I've had a great life. I was very fortunate in my placement as I was raised by two very loving and supportive parents whom I am still very close with. I also have an adopted sister named Katie who is 25 (3 ½ years younger than me).

Except that we moved around a lot (because of my father's career), my childhood was probably pretty normal. We lived in a few different places, but mostly I grew up in New Jersey from the time I was three until I was fourteen and a freshman in high school. After that we moved to Indiana where I finished high school and went to college. Although I participated in many different activities, I was probably most interested in art, reading and tennis. I attended Catholic school until we moved to Indiana because the small town we moved to did not have a Catholic school. I was a good student, and I always enjoyed learning which is why it is no surprise that I am back in school now. After receiving my B.A. in Journalism and Fine Arts from Indiana University in 1992, I worked for six years as a graphic designer. I was in the south for a year after graduation, and then I lived in Washington, D.C. for five years. It was during my time in D.C. that I started to seriously consider searching for you. Over the next few years, I slowly went through the necessary steps to do so. At the same time, I was considering a career in creative writing. I had always like to read, and while in D.C. I started to write fiction. I still enjoyed graphic design, but at a writing instructor's urging, I decided to go to grad school in creative writing which is where I am now.

I decided to go to a grad school in Ohio, far away from the place I was born and Catholic Charities, my link to you. I think it was this that allowed me to see that I did want to contact you, and as a result I found myself pursuing a search after I moved to Ohio. It seems silly to think that I waited until I moved away from D.C. before I started a search, but sometimes that's how these things happen I guess.

I should also tell you that I am married to a great guy named Dave. Dave and I met and started dating in college. After eight years of dating on and off, we finally got married last summer in Cincinnati, Ohio, Dave's hometown. Dave is also a graduate student in creative writing. He has wanted to be a writer since the day I met him, and now he's finally getting the time to write in school. We are both in the same grad program which is kind of nice because it means we get to share things intellectually as well as emotionally on many levels.

I imagine that all of this information must be very overwhelming to you, and I understand you may want some time to think about it all. After you've taken the time you need, I would really appreciate it if you would respond with a letter back to me through Catholic Charities. I think about you often, and I'm very curious about you and your life and of course, your well-being. I really do appreciate that sacrifice you made, and I look forward to hearing from you very much!

Molly

When I re-read this letter now, it seems very formal. I remember how much I struggled when writing it, probably because I didn't know anything about the person who would be reading it. I also didn't want to sound overly effusive since I wasn't looking for that kind of response.

Still, it's hard not to imagine Paula's initial impression of me being bewilderment when she read this somewhat cold listing of my life to date. I also think it's interesting that I invited her to "take all the time you need" to respond. Again, it's clear to me now that I was trying to do whatever I could to slow the whole process down, maybe even avoid it altogether.

I included three photos of myself with the letter—two from college and one from our wedding. Of the two pictures from college, one is a formal portrait taken my sophomore year when I was still in a sorority, and the other is a snapshot with a friend taken during my senior year.

Looking at those photos now, I can't help but wonder why I would send the portrait. Didn't it seem stuffy and aloof? I suppose that, back then, I still had much of my mother in me, so I believed that when you introduced yourself, you did so in a formal way. Thinking about it now, I'm surprised I didn't also send one of the ridiculous name cards someone had given me for my high school graduation. No matter the reason, the message was still the same: I was from money and had lived a bit of an elitist life.

The other college photo showed me in my dorm room senior year with one of my good friends. On the wall behind me is a blue-and-white hand-woven rug and several colorful art posters—one being Matisse's "Les Gétes de la Mer" and the other "Quilting Time" by Romare Bearden, which features a group of African Americans quilting and socializing together. The impression given by that photo must have been clear too. I was artistic. I was liberal. I appreciated the finer things in life.

I didn't even glance at Paula's letter when it arrived just over a month later, instead going straight to the photos.

Dave and I had picked up the mail after eating dinner in the cafeteria one night when we found a large white envelope with a return address of 205 N. Thomas Street.

I knew immediately it had to be a response from my birthmother.

We didn't run back to the dorm, but we walked as quickly as we could, and I was nearly breathless when we got there. *I was finally—after twenty-nine years—going to find out who my birthmother was.* Once we were safely inside the apartment, I bypassed the long letter for the photos. There were four wallet-sized school pictures of four teenagers, one wallet-sized formal portrait of four young children, and two snapshots: one of the same four young children and one of a group of adults.

There was also a color copy, folded in half around what appeared to be an older letter. The color copy included a short note on the left side—written in blue ink directly on the copy—and, on the right side, two yellowed photos of an older woman holding a tiny baby wrapped in a white blanket. The woman's head was cut off, so I couldn't see her face, but I could tell by her conservative button-up shirt and dark skirt—as well as the vinyl chair and patterned drapes in the background—that the photos were about thirty years old. I looked to the handwritten note for an explanation.

Dear Molly,

I always considered you a gift from God and now I feel humbled that I could finally get to know you.

I have enclosed the thoughts that I wrote the day after you were born. I have reread them several times over the years—hoping that you were happy and well and knowing in my heart that God was watching over you.

These pictures were taken the day you were born—my mother was holding you.

I repeated the words in my head... *These pictures were taken the day you were born.*

In my hands, I was holding pictures—of myself—on the day I had been born.

I let out a breath so loud it sounded like I was gasping, and Dave said, "What? What is it?"

"Look," I said. "Just look."

Until that moment, I hadn't even known such pictures existed. I studied the baby in the photos, a baby who was quite a bit smaller than I am in any of the photos my parents have of me at six weeks old. In the pictures from the day I was born, my little baby legs are sticking out from a plain white receiving blanket. They are noticeably long and lean, showing no sign yet of any baby fat, but my face is a round loaf of bread, my bright pink lips and big eyes dotting the surface of my flushed face like artificial decorations.

I passed the color copy to Dave and picked up the folded letter that had been tucked inside it. It was old, stained, torn around the edges, and creased into quarters. After I opened it, I saw the stationery had tiny pink flowers in the upper left corner, and the neat cursive was written only in pencil.

April 6, 1970

The first few hours when I realized that I was pregnant, I experienced both happiness and sadness (if such is possible). I knew that on my part, she was created out of love—a love that I still believe today was shared by him also. Beyond our love for each other though, our thoughts differed. She was conceived, however, and a new life began. Then happiness, anger, tears, peace, frustration, love, bewilderment, content, and fear she came into the world unaware of so many conflicts. She was total joy, peace, and love—her name Anne Marie—Born on April 5, 1970 at 6:24 AM on a bright, sunny Sunday morn weighing 7 lbs 6 ounces, 20" in length and looking very much like me. That first day I guess I was in as much a daze as she was—wondering at what was going on, how it happened so fast, the months of pain and the peace that comes at the first crys of birth. I didn't even know what to do with her at our first visits with each other. I could scarcely believe that she was mine not to mention the realization of the privilege and beauty that accompanied her. Slowly we got to know each other and by the second day I was aware of every move, each line and curve of her body. Gradually I realized that the pains of birth were more of a camouflaged thunderstorm, that contains a chill and a haunting front, but beyond its cover the beauty of mothernature springs forth in rainbows, flowers and the warmth of human breathing. I know now that it was a privilege for me to share in such an experience. As my love grows for her and my hours with her grow shorter I am aware of the emptiness that I will soon experience. An emptiness which will create the bond between us and permit the memories of these past days to stay with me forever. With these memories will also be a continuous prayer that she is experiencing a shared love between a man and woman who will be her parents and that she will have the wisdom to sense this love and build her life upon it. As much as I would like to keep her and watch her grow I know that at present I could not give her such a love and for this reason I surrender her, along with my love for her, and entrust her into God's hands for it was He who trusted me with such a privilege that I might do right by it. A decision which brings much peace and pain at the same time, but hopefully to her it will add much joy and love to her life. I hope one day she will understand all of this and love me in a similar way as I love her.

I felt as if I should cry when I read these words—the ache in my gut was that great—but I didn't. I was too stunned by what I'd read to do anything. So instead of crying, I just stood there, looking over the words so many times that my eyes weren't even seeing them anymore. They were just a blur of gray lines against a yellowed background.

Though I didn't think about it consciously at the time, I do remember now that, when I read that letter, I was awed by my birthmother's ability to accept her decision peacefully, seemingly without bitterness or anger. She'd made it seem so easy, so right. I assumed then that anyone who was so mature and confident must have the inner strength of a saint, a saint who had walked over burning coals or been dipped in hot oil.

I glanced back over the letter, processing the important parts again.

I knew that on my part, she was created out of love—a love that I still believe today was shared by him also. Beyond our love for each other though, our thoughts differed.

It hit me then that my birthmother had been in love with my birthfather when I was conceived. And she had still loved him when I was born.

I thought back on my visit with Margaret—when I'd learned that my birthmother and birthfather had reunited and tried to get me back. For a split second, it occurred to me they might still be together, but I shut that thought out of me head, wanting the truth to reveal itself to me naturally, the way my birthmother had intended. I re-folded the letter, put it back where it belonged, inside the color copy of the pictures from the day of my birth, and went to see what else she'd sent me.

The snapshots, too, had been copied on a color printer—top to bottom. The one on top was of the same four young children who were pictured in the formal portrait. They were sitting on a floral-patterned sofa in what appeared to be their pajamas. Each of the three smiling boys, who I guessed must have been between five and nine years old, looked as if their hair had been freshly washed and combed perfectly into place. The girl sitting between them was about half their size, making her look like a doll, and she had shoulder-length, curly blonde hair and round thoughtful eyes.

The snapshot on the bottom showed seven adults—what appeared to be a family celebrating Christmas since one of them was wearing a Santa hat. After I'd studied it for a few minutes, I felt completely dumbfounded.

I looked up at Dave, my mouth open but as speechless as a mute.

Without saying anything, I went back to the second snapshot to scrutinize it more closely: the family was made up of two middle-aged adults in front and four younger adults in the background, all six of them hovering around an older woman. The middle-aged couple in front was completely mismatched. The man, whom I figured was in his mid- to late fifties, looked like a flashback to another era with a white Fuller-brush mustache, a full head of coarse gray hair, and tinted old man glasses while the woman appeared to be about forty, had a too-short, '80s haircut, and wore a printed turtleneck under a blue snowflake sweater. At first I couldn't tell what was sitting under the collar of her turtleneck, but when I glanced back to the Santa hat one of the younger people was wearing, I figured it out: there was a Rudolph nose hanging on a band around her neck. The older woman in the middle appeared nondescript as was the young woman who had an arm around her: both looked typical for their ages and wore sweatshirts and jeans of some kind. In fact, everyone in the photo was wearing jeans, an incredibly casual look for a holiday photo from my way of thinking. To make matters worse, the three young men standing on either side of the young woman appeared somewhat rough around the edges—like the middle-aged man in front, they all looked tall and muscular and each of them sported dark stubble and thick eyebrows. One of them had a mustache, another was holding a cigarette and wearing a dark knit cap, and the third wore a leather bomber jacket. They looked like the kind of young men who would get in fistfights over spilled beer or lost bets, the kind of men I had never known. The picture was obviously taken in a bar—with a cigarette machine, a small American flag, and a sign listing the "bar rules" on one side of the group and a table littered with empty glasses in front of a paneled wall on the other.

I had been shaking my head the whole time I studied this picture, wondering who these people were and how they could ever be connected to me. Putting the photos aside, I finally went to the letter for answers.

7/12/99

Dear Molly,

I am so excited I hardly know where to begin. I'm sitting in the office at Catholic Charities and have just read your beautiful letter. There are so many words and moments I want to share with you.

Sitting in the office? Did that mean she hadn't even left Catholic

Charities to write back to me? I looked to Dave for an answer to a question I hadn't even voiced out loud, but he'd picked up the two snapshots and was studying them as closely as I had only minutes before. Was she really that eager to write? I asked myself. But when I thought about it more, it made perfect sense.

Of course, she was that eager to write. She had waited twenty-nine years to do so.

Most importantly I want you to know that you have always been in my heart and prayers. Many, many times especially at night I would pray for your well being—that you were safe and healthy. Your letter answered all my prayers for you. You certainly have had a special and fulfilling life with loving parents and a sister.

I too have had a blessed and gratifying life.

In fact I think I have a very special surprise for you which I hope won't be too overwhelming.

This would turn out to be the biggest understatement of my entire life.

Two years after you were born on June 25, 1972 I married your father— Lawrence William Tucker, who goes by L.W.

I cringed when I read the word "father," saying the words, "Oh, God" out loud. Why had she called him my father? Didn't she know that he wasn't my father any more than she was my mother?

And then I looked at the date, June 25, 1972—*Two years after you were born on June 25, 1972*. But I *wasn't* born on June 25th of 1972. *I* was born on April 5th of 1970. Did she have the wrong person? Had there been some mix-up at the adoption agency? Is that why the people in the snapshot looked so vastly different from me? I felt a rush of relief. My heartbeat started to slow: That was it. They had made a mistake. The people in the snapshot were not related to me after all.

But then I read the line again.

Two years after you were born on June 25, 1972 I married your father—

Lawrence William Tucker.

Involuntarily, my shoulders dropped and my eyes closed. There had been no mix-up or mistake. My birthmother had simply left out a comma after the word "born." Once I re-read the line a few more times, I could see her error—she had meant to say *they* had married on June 25th, not that *I* had been born that day. And that's when it hit me: *my biological parents married two years after I was born.*

As soon as I processed that fact, more questions filled my head. *Why had they waited two years? And why hadn't they gotten married when she got pregnant with me?*

I continued.

We have been married 27 years and were blessed with four more children— Willie, Clint, Wade and Jeannie, so you might say you have 3 brothers and a sister.

Three brothers and a sister?

My God, I thought, as I put my hand over my mouth, *what had I done?*

We are very lucky—each of them are special in their own way and have given us many treasured days and night. I've enclosed pictures of them when they were little and one of each of them when they graduated from high school. The one picture is of all of us plus Alice Tucker (Grandmom) at Christmas time.

All of us?

I looked up from the letter and into Dave's face. He handed me the color copy of the snapshots without saying anything as if he knew intuitively what I was asking. I studied the photo again and tried to figure out what she meant. I took a closer look at the words written in the margin. Next to the snapshot of the four young children on the floral sofa, it read "1983 Clint, Jeannie, Wade, Willie"—her four kids, I guessed—and next to the Christmas photo it said, "X-mas 1998. BR: Wade, Willie, Alice, Jeannie, Clint." These names—the back row, I presumed—were written in an X-shape with Wade and Willie on top, Alice in the middle, and Jeannie and Clint on the bottom.

Then underneath that it said, "FR"—front row—"L.W. and Paula"

I went back to the letter: *I married . . . Lawrence William Tucker, who goes by L.W.*

I stopped and thought about what that meant, and then, suddenly, I got it: the man with the bushy white mustache and old-fashioned glasses, the man who looked like he belonged in a Burt Reynolds movie... that man was my biological father.

And that could only mean that the woman next to him, the woman with her arm resting on his back, was his wife.

Frantic to find out if my deduction was true, I flipped to the end of the letter. And on the bottom of the fourth page, I found what I was looking for. My birthmother had signed her name there.

Paula Ann Marie.

Paula.

The woman in the front row.

I pulled out the snapshot and studied the image of the woman in the front row again. She had milky white skin and pinkish cheeks whereas my skin has a trace of olive in it. But, just like me, she had a full face, a wide nose, a big smile under a thin upper lip, and eyebrows that disappeared into a prominent forehead. Though I had been unsure about it before, I knew it for certain then.

The woman with the Rudolph nose and the snowflake sweater was my biological mother. She was the person who had given birth to me.

It took me some time to process this information.

I wanted to sit down, but I had too much adrenaline in my body to be still long enough to sit. I was so confused: the woman in the front row looked too young to be my biological mother. She looked forty, not fifty. She looked... average. And so did her husband. It just didn't make sense. They couldn't be my biological parents. I had imagined Bob Dylan and some older, more sophisticated version of myself, not two people who spent their holidays in a bar.

I understood suddenly that the young people in the Christmas snapshot—and in the other photos—were Paula's four children. And that if they were Paula and L.W.'s children and Paula and L.W. were my biological parents, then that meant these people were my full-blooded siblings. Four people who looked tough enough to beat up my husband with their eyes closed were my full-blooded siblings.

None of it made sense. *Who was I?*

The next line of Paula's letter handed me another huge revelation.

After I received the note from Catholic Charities that you were interested in contacting me I told them about you.

Told them about me? I went back a line and re-read that whole section…

We have been married 27 years and were blessed with four more children— Willie, Clint, Wade and Jeannie, so you might say you have 3 brothers and a sister … After I received the note from Catholic Charities that you were interested in contacting me I told them about you. They each reacted with surprise, but mostly they were very happy and very eager to meet you.

Her kids.

When she said "them," she was referring to her kids. They were the ones who'd reacted with surprise. If they'd been surprised when they found out about me, that could only mean one thing—before she had told them, they hadn't *known* about me. They hadn't known their parents had another child. They had never even known I existed. I looked up at Dave then, shaking my head, as I thought again, *what have I done?*

I had to wait all week-end to contact Catholic Charities and let them know how happy I was and oh yes I do want to meet you and have the opportunity to get to know you and so do all your brothers and sister.

She did want to meet me.

She wanted to meet me, and she wanted me to meet my "brothers and sister."

Nothing could have told me more clearly that she didn't get it. She had no idea how overwhelming all of it was for me. She had no idea I wasn't even close to ready to talk about meeting her, much less her children. She had no understanding about the idea that they would never be *my* brothers and sister.

Just a little about us—I am a nurse in Labor and Delivery at the hospital where you were born—Saint Cecilia Hospital.

Saint Cecilia Hospital.

My God, I thought as I realized I finally knew—for the first time in my life—where I had been born. I took a minute to savor this information.

Saint Cecilia. Such a beautiful name.

I had been born in a hospital with a beautiful name.

But then I re-read that sentence and took in the rest of it. Paula worked in Labor and Delivery at Saint Cecilia. What did that mean? I sighed as I put it together.

It meant that every day she went back to the place where I had been born, back to the scene of the greatest crime that had ever been committed against her. Who would do such a thing?

I too like to write, but never pursued it as a career. I hope I can read some of your writings.

My husband—L.W.—owns a local bar and restaurant with his mother Alice—it has an outside bar where you can sit and have a drink or food outside— it also has an inside bar and restaurant. It's open 7 days/week 7 am-1 am and serves Breakfast—Lunch—Dinner.

Owns a bar? My biological father owns a bar?

It occurred to me then that was probably the bar in the snapshot. Why else would they take their Christmas photo in a bar? But, still, A BAR?????

Your brother Willie works there 5 days/week. He has an apartment of his own and still likes to party. I'm hoping he finds a good woman to help him grow up.

Still likes to party? That sounded like something a mother would say, so I didn't pay much attention to it. But again she had said, "*your* brother." I was beginning to wonder if she would ever understand.

Clint just graduated from college—played a whole lot of baseball over the years and is now working at FedEx as a supervisor. He has an apartment also, now plays a lot of softball and likes to party once and awhile.

Likes to party once and a while. I was sensing a theme.

Wade just finished 2 years of school in Florida for aviation mechanics and is still looking for work in this field.

Two years of school for aviation mechanics—that was two of my biological siblings who had not gone to college. And, yes, I was keeping track.

Last but not least is Jeannie who will turn 18 this August and just graduated from high school. She is quite an individual who I know you will enjoy—she also writes a little but her big activity right now is Basketball. She will be going to Virginia Tech—she received a full scholarship and will be playing basketball for them.

Wade had only gone to technical school, but Clint had graduated from college and Jeannie was on her way, albeit both of them with some connection to athletics. Nevertheless, I sighed with relief. At least two people in Paula's family were educated.

There is so much to tell you—your pictures and letter makes me feel like I've known you all along in my heart. I had recently decided to make a serious effort at finding you. I was afraid I would disrupt your life, so I hesitated. Here you are the one with all the courage.

When I read this part, I could feel the emotions building inside me, the tears forming in my eyes. Finally, Paula had said something that demonstrated some understanding of what I was going through—of how hard it had been to write to her, of how many years it had taken to work up the nerve to do so. Finally.

God Bless you Molly—I hope this is the beginning of a new path in our lives that will add to our life-long family.

> *As I have always—Love*
> *your birthmother*
> *Paula Ann Marie*

And the way she had signed the letter—"your birthmother"—made me feel better too. Maybe she did comprehend more than I had given her credit for. Maybe she did understand she was a stranger to me—my *birthmother*, not my mother—someone I hadn't been in the same room with since I was born.

At least that was what I hoped.

I'd been in such a rush to read the letter—to find out who the people in the photos were—that I hadn't even noticed what it was written on. Paula's letter began inside a blue card and continued on pastel-colored stationery. On the front of the card was a sandcastle and a Victor Hugo quote: *There is nothing like a dream to create the future.* I understood immediately why Paula had chosen such a card. She had been dreaming of hearing from me, of our future, for twenty-nine years.

Dave had been shadowing me the whole time I'd read Paula's letter, picking up each page I put down and responding to my rhetorical questions appropriately—not answering them but letting them hang in the air like slow-moving blimps. What else could he do? It's not as if he had any answers. My birth family was as much of a mystery to him as they were to me.

I put the card down and picked up the color copy again, finally turning to look directly at Dave. "What does this mean?" I asked him.

"I have no idea," he said, shaking his head in a way that told me he was just as confused as I was.

"Do you think I could be related to these people?" I asked, holding out the color copy with the snapshots for him to inspect again.

"It's hard to believe," he said.

"Do you think they made a mistake?"

"Who, the adoption agency?"

"Yes, them."

"No," he said. "I don't think they make mistakes like that."

"So you *do* think I could be related to these people?" I asked him again. I knew I was putting him on the defensive, but there was no one else to confront about my confusion.

Dave lifted the photo and appeared to be studying it. Without answering my question, he said, "You have four full-blooded siblings." He was looking at me by the time he stopped talking, staring into my eyes, some new thought forming in his head. "Do you realize I don't have any?" It was true that Dave didn't have any full-blooded siblings; even though he had an older sister and brother, they were technically only his half siblings because their father had died when they were young, and their mother eventually married Dave's father, who raised them as his own. He was right, of course, but I didn't have the energy to agree with him before he went on. "Until a few minutes ago, you didn't have any. Now you have more blood relatives than I do. How did that happen?"

I didn't answer because we both knew how it had happened.

I had asked the adoption agency to find my birthmother, to find out who I was, and that's exactly what they had done.

I met my husband, David Bell, during our junior year at Indiana University. We lived on the same floor in the dorm but didn't hold a legitimate conversation until I was wandering around Read Hall looking for strangers to photograph for my photojournalism class. We'd only been introduced a few hours earlier—Dave's grip firm enough to impress me when he shook my hand—so after I spotted him across the lobby, I figured he'd still qualify as someone I didn't really know. At the time, he was sitting at a table with his friend Andre, who I'd soon learn was one of the most direct people I'd ever meet.

Andre's interrogation started immediately. "What do you want to take our picture for?" he asked.

"It's for class. I'm supposed to take portraits of strangers."

"But you met me three hours ago," Dave pointed out.

"I won't tell if you won't."

I shot an entire roll of film while we talked, careful not to let

Andre know that three-quarters of the photos were of Dave, who I couldn't help but notice had incredibly smooth skin, wonderfully full lips, and clear blue eyes he was trying to hide behind round glasses. He didn't look like other guys his age: he was thin, he wore gray shorts and a plain white t-shirt—no sign of a logo or catch phrase as if he existed outside of pop culture—and his hair hung straight around his face and down the back of his neck in lovely wisps.

He looked like he was from another time, a time when young men didn't announce their masculinity over a loudspeaker, and as I studied him from behind the lens of the camera I became even more intrigued. But I was careful not to let on about any of this, instead telling the two of them about my class: "My professor claims some students meet the person they'll end up marrying while shooting this assignment. As soon as he said that, all I could think was how something like that would *never* happen to me."

Without hesitating, Andre responded. "For all you know," he said, "you two could end up married." He looked at Dave and then back at me, connecting us with an imaginary line.

When I followed Andre's gaze, my eye caught Dave's, and I felt a surge of something kinetic pass between us—as if we were already connected. It knocked me back a little, and I could feel myself blush as I stood up, moving away from the table where the two of them sat. "I think I have plenty," I said, holding up my camera as an explanation.

"Don't let him intimidate you," Dave said. "He's just compensating for his own insecurities."

Andre was skeptical. "As if," he said simply, but I still felt a sense of relief pass over me. I'd always wanted to find someone like Dave, someone who wasn't afraid to say what was really on his mind, but I never believed I would. The strange thing was that, even that first day, Dave sensed that about me. He tuned into my apprehensions as readily as most guys tune into a football game.

"Don't talk to any more strangers," Dave advised before I left. "They say it's dangerous."

Sometimes I think Dave has always known me, sometimes he even knows what I want before I do. Like with Paula. Dave wanted to know where I came from before I could put words, or even thoughts, around my yearning.

"But aren't you curious?" he asked me when I first told him I was adopted a few weeks after we'd met.

We had walked from our dorm to downtown Bloomington that night and stopped at a local ice cream shop called White Mountain. As I swirled my spoon around the chocolate chip melting in the Styrofoam bowl in front of me, I considered his question. I really *wasn't* curious about my biological mother, but I also wasn't ready to admit any more than that. "I guess I never thought about it."

"You *never* thought about it?"

I tried to explain. "I have a great relationship with my mother. We talk about everything. I don't ever lie to her. It's not always easy, but it works. I don't need another mother."

Dave leaned back in his chair. He was just barely nodding his head as if taking in my words, trying to find some new angle. Finally, he went on. "But what if you're heir to some throne? What if you're a Kennedy?" He paused before continuing. "Don't you want to know?"

After we'd been together a while, Dave would speculate endlessly about who my birthmother might be, sometimes for hours, but I knew his interest was deeper than just wanting to know if I was related to royalty. Slowly, carefully, his interest in my past became my desire. But at first the inclination was his.

Before Dave, the birthmother question was the one I was always afraid to ask.

I imagine it's not unusual for adoptees to feel disoriented and overwhelmed when they discover the identity of their biological mother or father. And I'm sure when they do find out, they begin to question who they are and what it all means—even if they do feel some immediate connection to the people who conceived them.

My sister experienced something similar.

The whole time I was going through the steps of searching for my biological mother, I believed that my sister, Katie, had never made contact with her past. But about six months before I sat for my pre-search interview with Margaret, Katie confessed to me that she had known the identity of her biological mother since she was nineteen.

That meant she had known who her birthmother was for nearly six years and not told me. My parents also knew Katie had found out, and they hadn't told me either. They all claimed telling me would have influenced my decision about whether or not to search myself. And they wanted me to make that decision without being affected by what happened to Katie.

I was horrified when I learned the three of them had kept such a giant secret from me for so long. I felt totally betrayed. I was also surprised and annoyed by the fact that they didn't think I could handle such information and still be able to make the right choice for myself. They each expressed remorse once I told them how I felt, but that didn't change the fact that, for more than half a decade, I was kept in the dark about something very important to all of us.

As it turned out, Katie's biological mother, Theresa, had not dealt with the adoption very well. Theresa was only seventeen when Katie was born in 1973, and her upper-middle class parents pressured Theresa into giving her baby up for adoption even though Theresa wanted to keep her child. For years, Theresa had worried her daughter might not be safe or healthy, that she might have been adopted by bad people or had a difficult life. So, when Katie was nineteen, as soon as it was legal to do so in her state, Theresa filed the paperwork to find out what had happened to her baby. She'd waited nineteen whole years just to make sure that her long-lost daughter was safe, and she wasn't willing to wait a day longer.

Several months after that, the adoption agency put her in touch with Katie. Once Theresa knew her child was safe, she was able to wait until Katie was ready for the two of them to meet in person, which didn't happen for another six years. Now, more than twenty years after first learning about each other, Katie and Theresa have a delicate relationship—crafted out of lengthy letters and short visits. And Katie's backstory still remains more of a mystery. To this day, Katie has never had any contact with her biological father.

I wish I could say things went more smoothly with Paula and me, but, when all was said and done, that couldn't have been further from the truth.

*

It probably didn't help that three months went by before I wrote back to Paula.

Quite simply, I was too stunned to write, almost too stunned to speak about it, though I told family and friends the barest of details . . . *I have four full-blooded siblings I've never met . . . my biological family owns a bar . . . they want to meet me.* I repeated these lines to the people around me rather than face the emotions the letter had stirred up in my soul: fear, confusion, anxiety, guilt—the Grand Slam of unhappiness. And I put off writing back as long as I could. I waited until the last official day of summer had come and gone and then realized if I waited any longer, an entire season would have passed without me responding to the person who had given me life.

I finally wrote to Paula on my sister's twenty-sixth birthday, a full eighty days after I had learned her name.

1 Oct 99

Dear Paula—

I can't believe it is the first of October—almost three months since I received your letter. I just read it over again and I think it's funny that you said I'm the one with the courage to contact you when I've been so hesitant and afraid to write again. It's not that I didn't want to write—I wanted to write very much. I just found myself avoiding such a difficult task. I think I was more overwhelmed than I initially admitted to myself.

Of course I was so surprised when I found out you had married my birthfather! I had a feeling that might be the case when I did my interview with Margaret at Catholic Charities last March, but it's really shocking to find out it's true and that you've had 4 more children together. It's funny because all my life I've always wanted more brothers and sisters, and I'd always hoped that someday I'll have a large family myself. You really are very lucky to have such a big family. It sounds like you all have had such a wonderful life together, and I'm so glad to hear about what everyone is doing. I also very much appreciated all the photos. My only request is that I get some more pictures of you and L.W.

I guess I should tell you a little about what I've been feeling over the past few months. As I said, when I first got your letter I was very surprised to learn about your marriage and my siblings. Right after I was surprised, I was so excited. It honestly felt like, and still does, the best news I've ever heard. I went around telling all my friends and family about the six of you. I talked to Margaret (at Catholic

Charities) that same week, and she said you wanted to talk on the phone. My immediate response was yes, I'd love to talk to you, but then I started to worry about rushing things, which isn't really like me at all—normally I jump into things without much thought and, for the most part, I've found that trusting my instincts has served me well. Now, I feel like maybe I should've trusted myself and just gotten your phone number. I am so anxious to talk to you and meet you, and it really has been very hard to write you. It just feels so impersonal and strange. I wonder how you can really know me through a letter. At the same time, I just have this feeling that you probably feel the same way. The fact that you wrote back right away tells me that you are very interested in getting to know me. I just hope that my delayed response hasn't changed any of that. I feel terribly that I've made you wait so long, and I just don't want to wait this long to talk again. I guess what I'm trying to say is that I think it would be a good idea to talk on the phone soon. I'm really eager to get to know you better, even though I feel like I know you so well from your letters and photos.

As for what's been going on in my life lately I've been extremely busy with school and work as usual. I am working about 20 hours a week as a graduate assistant (which is what pays for my education), and this year I've started teaching one section of English composition. I'm really enjoying teaching—my freshman students are so fun, and they seem so excited to be here. I always think of Jeannie now when I think of my students because they are the same age. I hope she is doing well at Virginia Tech and that everyone else is doing well also. It's funny that she went to Virginia Tech because Dave and I almost went there for graduate school. We both got accepted there, but Miami (of Ohio) just offered us a better deal here. We also came here to be closer to Dave's family who live an hour away in Cincinnati. I know how much it means to him to be close to his parents who are getting much older. They're both 67, and we just want to spend as much time with them as possible.

Besides being busy, life is good. I enjoy school very much, and Dave and I somehow manage to enjoy each other amidst our busy schedules (he works and goes to school too). We don't know what we'll do when we're done here next summer, but I know things have a way of working themselves out.

I just want to say a few more things about your letter and photos before I finish. First of all, thank you so much for all the photos! It's been interesting to look for family resemblances, and to imagine what it's like to have such a big family and brothers! Since I only had one sister, things were relatively quiet around our house, and I always enjoyed visiting our cousins who all came from large, Catholic families. Also, my dad worked all the time so it always seemed like it was just the three of us girls hanging out together. I can't imagine what is was like with three boys in a row! It sounds like they are all interesting and unique. Dave is a huge baseball fan so I imagine he and Clint would have lots to talk about. (We even went to the World Series back in 1990 when we first met!) It was also so fascinating to see the pictures of everyone when they were young and then now when they're all adults. I would love to see more pictures, especially of you and L.W., and in the hopes that you'll send more I'm enclosing some too.

I was also so interested to learn that you work in labor and delivery at the hospital I was born in! I think that says a lot of good things about you as a person—I think it means that you've had a very healthy life which I admire very much considering the huge sacrifice you made for me. I really do appreciate it, and I always have. I think it's because I was raised to believe that you had to love me to do something so incredibly selfless! I really do think it speaks volumes about the kind of person you are that you were so brave and still work at Saint Cecilia! (I didn't even know I was born there until I got your letter!)

I also very much appreciate the pictures of me when I was born and the letter you wrote the day after I was born. I can't even tell you how much that letter meant! I can't believe you were so strong and so clear the day after I was born, especially at such a young age. The letter was really beautiful—immediately I knew where I got my love for words! It really is all so exciting and overwhelming. I really want to talk and get to know you so much more. I have this weird feeling that everything now makes sense, but I keep telling myself it can't be that easy. I know getting to know each other will take its toll on us and everyone in our lives, but I sincerely believe it's worth it and I hope you do too. I look so forward to hearing from you again soon! Please tell everyone I said hello.

Love,
Molly

Since I'm determined to be honest about everything that happened, I must confess there were some lies in this letter—though there were some truths too.

It's true I was overwhelmed and shocked when I found out my birth parents had married and had four more children. But it wasn't true that I was excited about it.

And, yes, it really did feel impersonal and strange to write to my birthmother, but it wasn't entirely true that I was anxious to meet her. More than anything I was terrified about the idea of meeting her.

Of course, it wasn't a lie to say it was "interesting to look for family resemblances" in the photos she'd sent, but it was obviously a nice of way of expressing the truth: I was shocked by how different they looked from me.

And I did not for one second think that "everything now makes sense," but I kept trying to tell myself that it would soon. Little did I know then it was something I would never really believe.

The one brutally honest detail about my emotional state I did include was made painfully clear by my repeated requests: I wanted more pictures of Paula and L.W. I had only received that one photo of them—the snapshot taken at Christmas in that bar—and, in it, they were both small and somewhat hard to make out. Of course, some part of me still questioned if it were even possible for me to be related to them, so I wanted more photos to search further for any common physical traits or characters.

With my letter, I also included a note for Margaret at Catholic Charities, which more adequately conveyed my real feelings at the time.

1 Oct 99

Dear Margaret—

I'm sorry this took me so long. I think it took more to accept this than I realized. I am, of course, most taken aback by my birth parents being married. I am thrilled for them and for me, but I'm also a little hurt. It's hard to swallow the idea that my birthfather didn't marry my birthmother when she was pregnant with me, and I'm afraid it will be hardest to some day meet him. Please don't share this w/ Paula or her family though—I'm not sure why I'm even telling you since it's really the first time I'm putting this hurt into words.

I am very interested in talking to Paula on the phone and meeting her (and maybe her family). I would like to get her phone number if it is okay with you and her at this time. Also, Dave and I are hoping to make a trip to D.C. between Dec 10-17, and maybe we could set up a meeting for then. If you feel this is appropriate to share w/ Paula at this time, please do! I'm also comfortable w/ you giving her my phone # and address too though I'd like to know when we're going to talk the first time so that I can make sure I have time to talk (most evenings I am home). I've included a ton of photos—I hope it's not too much, but I'm very excited about sharing our lives w/ each other. As always, thank you so much for your help and patience.

Molly McCaffrey

Margaret wrote back almost immediately.

Hi Molly:

*Got your letter and pictures and sent them on. Her phone number is (703) ***-****. I know her schedule changes so if you don't get her you may have to try again.*

I understand how you feel, and I am sure she will be able to tell you more about why it was impossible to marry when she became pregnant. From what I remember about our conversation, L.W.'s mother was the issue. Sounds like she was and continues to try to be very controlling. (She does not know about you.) I got the impression she raised them with an iron fist. The father left the family and she had to be the sole support. I am sure she was not a happy person. It was definitely a different time back then. Paula and I are from the same era, and believe me, if I had come home pregnant by my boyfriend... well, I dread the thought. I guess my impression is that your birthfather was young and his mother had him on a short chain!

Margaret

Margaret's response to my note contained another bombshell: L.W.'s mother didn't know about me. My biological grandmother did not even know I existed. Not only had L.W. abandoned Paula. He hadn't even had the guts to tell his mother why.

Though I would never fully understand L.W.'s motives, I did get more answers from Paula's next letter.

10/26/99

Dear Molly,

I can't tell you how happy and excited I was to hear from you again and receive some more pictures of you and your loved ones. I must have read your letter at least ten times the first day and several times since reading it.

My first letter to you was so rushed—sitting in an office at Catholic

Charities—I think I would have tried to tell you my entire life story in one letter if I had enough time, so I decided not to rush this letter.

I had to laugh when you said you've been telling all of your friends about us, because I have been doing exactly the same thing. Everyone has been so supportive and happy—such a change from thirty years ago.

I can understand you being overwhelmed when you received my first letter and hesitant about pursuing this new road in your life. I suppose because I have been praying and waiting for this moment since I left you at Catholic Charities that I can't imagine anything but goodness and love coming from meeting one another.

Of course, just learning that you are alive, well, and happy was an answer to my prayers.

Our children were understandably surprised also, but very happy. Of course they all want to know when they can meet you, but they also understand that there is only one of you and a lot of us.

Actually I believe it would be best for both of us if just you and I meet at first, share some special moments (hopefully a lot of special moments) and go on from there. I'm not sure how we could go about getting together—whatever would be easiest for you. Perhaps Margaret would have some suggestions. I would be glad to come see you if you would like.

I've enclosed a lot more pictures from over the years. Of course seeing our wedding picture and the most recent pictures of us lets you know that we're not as young or slender as we used to be. In the wedding picture we were 24 and 25. I'm now 51 and L.W. is 52.

I have to agree with you—we have been very blessed to have so many children. When I was growing up my biggest dream was to be a wife and mother—nursing just happened to come along as an extra benefit. They have kept L.W. and I very busy. Fortunately I only had to work part time when they were little, but as they got older, so did their expenses so I've been working full time for almost 10 years. I've been working at Saint Cecilia for 25 years in Labor and Delivery.

Each of the kids have been active in sports, scouts, hunting and fishing. Many week-ends (when they were younger) L.W. and I spent running from baseball fields, basketball courts, swimming pools to bowling lanes, not to mention scouts and camping. Of course, school was in there also. Clint and Jeannie pursued sports a little more competitively, while Willie and Wade were more relaxed about sports. Our home seems very quiet now—Willie moved to an apartment last fall with one of his friends, Clint moved last January and Wade was gone for 2 years in Florida studying Aviation Mechanics and is now a certified aviation mechanic. Of course, you know Jeannie is at Virginia Tech. She has a great deal of natural talent for all sports, but seems to shine in Basketball. She's uncertain of what field she will pursue in college, but I'm sure that will come with time.

I found it interesting that you enjoy writing and are pursuing it in grad school. When I was younger I used to write frequently and often thought about taking some writing courses, but I got somewhat sidetracked with family life.

L.W. and his mom (Alice) own a local bar and restaurant (there are two pictures of the restaurant in the album). It's somewhat of a local landmark. It's open seven days a week for breakfast, lunch and dinner and has many motorcycle patrons, especially during the summer. We have become somewhat of a local folklore and we have become well known far and wide because of the outside bar, the motorcycle enthusiasts and our friendliness and our willingness to help others. We were even used for one of the places in the TV series THE X-FILES in one episode a couple years ago.

I could go on and on—sharing moments in our lives with you, but I really want to get these pictures and my letter to Margaret so she can forward it to you. Hopefully, in the near future, we will be able to share our lives with one another in person.

You are right when you say that it is difficult to write or to speak on the phone. After such a long time of waiting, searching and hoping, I believe that it will only be by meeting each other that we will be able to truly understand each others heart. For this reason, perhaps because I am older, have lost family and friends, and know that what we plan for tomorrow may never come to pass, that I am praying that you will find it in your heart to meet with me in the near future.

I must tell you Molly that not a day goes by that I don't say a silent prayer of thanks that such a life as yours was placed in my hands and that I was able to bless others with the miracle of your life.

Love,
Paula

My dominant feeling when I re-read this letter now is that Paula expressed so much understanding and empathy that I can understand completely why I ultimately moved ahead with her desire to meet in person. I was thrilled when she acknowledged I was probably more overwhelmed than she was. She was absolutely right that she'd been thinking about meeting me for thirty years, but I'd only thought about it since I'd gotten her letter three months earlier. In truth, it was a relief to know she understood that the idea of meeting her was frightening because, until that year, I had known nothing about her.

With her second letter, Paula included an entire photo album documenting the history of her family, including one snapshot taken at her wedding. I had desperately wanted more pictures of Paula and L.W., so I could search for a more obvious resemblance, and when I saw that photo—of Paula in her twenties—I got exactly what I'd been seeking.

She looked *exactly* like me.

There had been no mistake. Without a doubt, Paula Tucker was my biological mother.

I was also a little surprised to see the pictures of the bar owned by L.W. and his mother. In her first letter, Paula hadn't mentioned what kind of bar it was, and in that second letter, she'd said it attracted "many motorcycle patrons." But the images in the photo album made the reality of it incredibly clear.

It was a biker bar.

My biological family owned a biker bar.

Some part of me—a big part of me—wanted to stop things from moving forward at that point. If I hadn't known it over the summer, I knew that fall for sure: I didn't have much in common with my biological family. Margaret's words about her birth family came back to me then: *It's challenging… I don't have any idea what to say to them… We're very different.*

I had incorrectly believed Margaret's case was the exception, that most adoptees met their biological parents and had an immediate connection with them. I was astounded by how naïve I'd been and thought often about how I could unlearn everything I had discovered.

Though I was hesitant to take the next step, Paula was not, and Margaret had sent me Paula's phone number with the understanding that I would follow up and call. How could I not do what I had promised?

One of the strangest things to admit is that I don't remember anything we talked about during that first phone call. Nothing. Not a single word.

Instead I remember thinking Paula sounded younger on the phone than I thought she would. I remember being very nervous about calling. I remember not really wanting to do it. I remember standing in our dorm apartment in Oxford, Ohio, and clutching the phone to my ear and thinking, yet again, *My God, what have I done?*

Once Paula and I had talked on the phone, she was more determined than ever to make me a part of their lives, to pull me back into her circle. Not only did she send me an entire photo album full of pictures, she called me on a regular basis and wanted to talk about not only her past but also her daily life. All of a sudden, we were on a fast track to meeting each other, and I still wasn't sure what to make of all of it.

When I had finally reached the decision to complete the interview so I could search for my birthmother the previous spring, I'd only been sure I was ready for that one simple step: finding out where I came from. I certainly didn't feel prepared to be reunited with six long-lost family members in person.

But Paula had other plans.

Knowing what I do now, I understand exactly how she felt. I've learned it's not unusual for someone who gives up a child to feel connected to that child her whole life—whether or not she ever sees the child again. I've witnessed that phenomenon not only with Paula, but also with my sister's birthmother and a cousin of mine who gave up a baby for adoption. Like those other women, Paula never really let go of me. In her mind, I was still her daughter. I was still an integral part of her life and identity. And, despite the fact that she expressed some understanding of my perspective in her second letter, the truth was it almost never occurred to her that she had never been a part of mine.

It's not that I didn't *want* her to be a part of my life. It's that she simply never was. I, of course, had no memory of the nine months during which she carried me or the few hours we shared together in the hospital. The sad truth was that Paula was as unreal to me as I was real to her.

And that was why Paula was so determined to visit: after being apart for twenty-nine years, she wasn't willing to wait any longer to see me again. She was adamant, and even though I tried to stall and make excuses to delay her visit, she was having none of it. I wasn't sure what to think and certainly wasn't emotionally prepared to meet her, but I finally caved, deciding the whole thing sounded harmless enough even though, in truth, the idea was incredibly distressing. I suppose that, looking back, the real reason I gave in was because I didn't have to *do* anything. I didn't have to commit to a course of action. I didn't have to make any plans. I just had to wait for Paula to arrive. And, if I'm being totally honest, I couldn't think of a good reason to say no.

Once I gave in and agreed to let Paula visit, I had even more doubts. *Were things moving too quickly? Was I really ready for her visit?* To make matters worse, the nature of Paula's phone calls and letters changed. Suddenly, Paula wanted to talk solely about herself and her kids. It wasn't unusual to have an hour-long phone conversation with Paula and only discuss what was going on in my life for the last five minutes. I knew Paula, like me, was the kind of person who talked both when she was happy and when she was nervous, so I chalked her endless monologues up to nerves and hoped for the best. But— in February of 2000—when I got the last letter before her visit, I really started to worry Paula was more interested in telling me about herself than getting to know me.

2/5/00

Dear Molly,

It's been very special to me to be able to talk with you on the phone. Sometimes it feels like we've known each other a long time.

It was also a very nice surprise to learn that you and Jeannie have been E-mailing each other and that you actually had a chance to talk. I'm happy for each of you. The fact that you both can share your experiences about college I know will help Jeannie.

Jeannie seems so up and down about college and basketball life. One day she's quitting everything and the next day she's planning her roommate for the next year.

I know she has really enjoyed playing basketball, but she's had a hard time dealing with the head coach. The more I get to know her and the way she interacts with the team and her coaching staff, the more I'm convinced she doesn't belong coaching young people. She has a way of playing head games with her players which leads to mixed signals and loss of confidence with her players.

When you read the articles about Jeannie along with the small highlights you would think the coach is very pleased with Jeannie's overall performance and she would continue to play a fair amount, but since these writeups Jeannie hasn't played more than 3 minutes a game. Jeannie asked her why her playing time is down and she just said that it was the match-up of players, but at practice she blamed Jeannie for their loss to Georgia Tech because Jeannie wasn't ready to come off the bench—needless to say Jeannie was upset because as the write-ups say Jeannie has been playing her heart out.

I want to go talk to the coach and ask her if there's a problem, but Jeannie says it will just make matters worse. The assistant coaches keep telling Jeannie to hang in there, but I know Jeannie is really frustrated. She's considered going to another college next year. I guess time will tell. Even her coaching and auxiliary staff are intimidated by her and says she's unpredictable and a little crazy, but she's still coaching.

The team seems to stay strong—the girls truly help each other which may be why they're playing well.

They just won a big game at Duke University (Duke had been undefeated at home for some time). I rode down and watched the game and then came home all in the same day. It was fun to see the girls play so well. Hopefully the win was a good sign for the second half of the season. I guess you're tired of hearing about Jeannie and B-Ball. I used to play when I was in nursing school. I wasn't near as good as Jeannie, but I had some great times.

Next I have some good news about Wade. He got a job at a small airport in Manassas, Virginia as a airplane mechanic. The pay isn't as good as working at a large airport, but he is very happy. He already moved to Manassas and is living in an efficiency right on the border of the airfield. He's still looking for a better job, but at least he's getting experience.

Of course this now means we don't have anyone living at home—just our dog—Coty.

Lately I haven't been home long enough to miss anyone. My mother-in-law was very sick, so I was either at the restaurant or at the hospital working for the last two weeks. She had the flu and probably pneumonia. She seems a little better, but she can't do all that she used to do, so I've been filling in. Of course she wouldn't go to the doctor's either, so her recovery has been longer than usual.

I have managed to get off the weekend of March 10th so if all goes well I hope to come visit. As soon as I have definite flight times I'll give you a call. If it's OK with you I'm planning on coming Friday afternoon (3/10) and probably leave Sunday morning (3/12). Perhaps you can let me know a hotel that's near you, so I can get a room for Fri. and Sat. night. I don't care what we do—just visiting each will be wonderful. It's hard to believe we are actually going to meet.

Over the years, I've always felt that someday I would meet you, but now that it's actually going to happen it's very hard to believe.

I'm sorry I have rambled so much. I hope you and David have had success with finding a school for next year.

Thank you for your listening ear to Jeannie.

I've enclosed some newspaper clips about Jeannie and another one about L.W., his mom and the restaurant.

Take Care and God Bless,
♡ Paula

When I first read this letter, I found myself more confused than irritated. Why had Paula spent five pages telling me about Jeannie's basketball career? Why had she only mentioned what was going on with me—and the fact that Dave and I were trying desperately to get into a Ph.D. program—in half a sentence on the last page? That spring, as we waited to hear from doctoral programs, was a tense time for us. We were about to finish our Master's degrees and had no idea what we should do after that. We'd applied to three doctoral programs in creative writing but hadn't yet heard back from any of them. If we didn't go to more graduate school, we'd be faced with the daunting task of trying to find jobs with a Master's degree in creative writing. In other words, to find jobs that didn't exist and to start a life that would allow much less time for writing. It was something Paula and I had discussed on the phone, so it was surprising she didn't even mention that issue directly, instead referring to it obliquely at the end of her letter.

I was also alarmed by Paula's admission that she wanted to talk to Jeannie's basketball coach about why she wasn't playing. I had only been teaching at the college level for a year, but even in that short time I'd learned what a bad sign it was when parents tried to get involved in their children's lives at college. It usually meant the parents were trying to live their kids' lives for them, that they'd been coddling their children for years. Was that the case with Paula? Was she coddling Jeannie?

I also had a more superficial objection to Paula's letter. The stationery was a bit unsophisticated—with two hearts in each of the top two corners and three snowmen sitting in a basket in the center underneath the words, "Snowflakes floating gently to earth . . . bring us joy." Why had the woman who'd initially sent me a card with a Victor Hugo quote used snowman stationery for her third letter?

At that point, I felt pretty certain meeting Paula—or any of the Tuckers—wasn't something I should do. Not yet anyway. It was all just too overwhelming. They were just too different. I decided to tell Paula the truth: It was too soon, I wasn't ready.

I had believed, incorrectly, that Paula and I would get to know each other slowly—exchanging letters for a few years and then phone calls for a few more before finally working up to meeting each other in person. In that way, I'd had the false sense that everything playing out between us would take much longer than it actually did.

But Paula had not wanted to be patient. After receiving her first letter, she'd asked Margaret for my phone number. I was completely alarmed when I heard about her request, wondering how I could give my number to someone I barely knew anything about. But ultimately I acquiesced, thinking that talking on the phone wasn't that much more of an invasion of my privacy than writing letters. But almost as soon as we spoke, Paula was making plans to visit. I didn't have the heart to tell her it was all happening too fast for me. So instead of telling her the truth, I did nothing. Instead of letting Paula know how I really felt, I simply waited for her to arrive.

And that's how it happened that right before my thirtieth birthday—nearly seven years after I'd first thought about contacting the adoption agency, but only nine months since I'd learned Paula's identity—my biological mother stepped off a plane in Dayton, Ohio, and changed my life forever.

PART TWO
THE BIRTHMOTHER VISITS

MARCH 2000

After we picked Paula up from the airport, we made the slow one-hour drive back to Oxford, the barren winter fields outside our car the only distraction from the unspoken tension inside. I had no idea what to say to Paula, but she started talking almost as soon as we were on the road, telling us about a friend of hers who had twins with cystic fibrosis.

"The twins are only nine," she explained, "and they'll be lucky to live till they're teenagers."

"Are they in a lot of pain?" I asked, looking over my shoulder at Paula, who sat behind Dave in the driver's seat.

"Not too much yet," she explained. "But their lungs are only going to get worse, and it's possible they'll both need a transplant. I just had a fundraiser for them at the Town and Country Club. We raised over ten thousand dollars in one night."

"Wow," I said as I turned back to the desolate landscape out the front window and wondered if that was a normal amount for such an event. But before I could ask, Paula went on.

"It was a dinner-and-dance type of thing. We served this amazing meal—steak and potato with salad. And we decorated the hall with pink streamers, balloons, and a long banner with the twins' names on it."

I couldn't help but think about how average it all sounded. Steak and potato? Streamers and balloons? How was that any different than any other party or nice dinner? Couldn't Paula have done something more imaginative? It told me Paula's friends must be either incredibly supportive or easily impressed.

Thankfully, I was still facing forward, so Paula couldn't see what I'm sure was a transparent look on my face. She continued: "There were over five hundred people there. Nobody thought I could do anything that big, especially my mother-in-law, but I did. And I did it all by myself. No one's ever raised that kind of money at a single fundraiser before."

Immediately, I doubted Paula's assertion. Even though I knew she was talking about the world she lived in, surely there were fundraisers in D.C., or even Annandale, Virginia, that had been more profitable. But more important than arguing the point was my realization that Paula was prone to exaggeration. And while I formed this thought in my head, she went on, describing the evening in full detail—what people wore, how long the night went, how happy the twins were. The information she was providing was so specific it was overwhelming, and Paula never paused to let me respond. I was trying to take in what she was saying and gauge Dave's response at the same time, but it was all rather hard to process.

Like I said, Dave had been supportive of my desire to search for my birthmother all along. Sometimes it seemed as if he was more curious than I was, but that afternoon I wondered how this new aspect of my life would affect him. Before that day, dealing with my family had been pretty straightforward: he'd always gotten along with Katie and my parents, but how would he feel now that my biological parents were entering our lives? Not to mention four additional siblings.

"It's the worst thing that can ever happen to a person," Paula was saying just as I came back to the moment.

"What is?" I asked, looking over my shoulder at Paula again.

"Losing a child."

I turned back to the front window. We'd left the interstate and were now on a two-lane highway passing through fields of corn that had been harvested months before, the cut stalks looking like the remains of a disaster site. Intellectually, I knew Paula was talking about her friend and the two little ones who had a disease that might end their lives before they were teenagers, but in my gut I sensed that Paula was really talking about herself.

Because, truth be told, Paula had already lost a child.

She had lost me.

And when I glanced to the backseat again, I could see the pain in Paula's eyes as she stared at the scene outside the car, pain I instinctively knew was deeper than worrying about the children of a friend.

That was the second real hint I had about how foolish I'd been to think I could simply look for my birthmother, find out who she was, and be on my way—no entanglements, no commitments. The first hint had been years before when I'd attended the support group. I didn't fully understand it then, but I was slowly starting to learn that Paula had suffered a loss much greater than the void I could ever possibly hope to fill in her life.

When we arrived back in Oxford, I showed Paula where she'd be staying. It was spring break at Miami, and the town was all but deserted. Faculty members were off attending conferences or doing research, most of the undergraduates had fled for home or the beach, and only the cash-strapped grad students were left behind.

So rather than dump Paula at an empty hotel in a strange town, I'd arranged for her to stay in the guest suite next to our apartment. Thanks to my graduate assistantship with residence life, we were living in a similar suite on the first floor of a female residence hall at the time. Our housing was free, but living in a four-hundred-square-foot efficiency was somewhat demoralizing. Our bedroom was so small we could touch the walls on either side when we went to sleep at night. Our living room was exactly as wide as our sofa. Our "kitchen"—no bigger than a walk-in closet—included two appliances: a dorm-size fridge and a one-burner stovetop, forcing us to eat most of our meals in the cafeteria and walk to the vending machines in the basement for ice. It was challenging to live in such a cramped space. Dave worked at a puny desk in the living room, and I'd set up my computer on the table-for-one in the kitchen. We obviously didn't have room for Paula. But since one of the perks of my job was access to every residence hall on campus, it was easy to convince the powers-that-be to let her sleep in the empty suite next door over a weekend when no one but the two of us would be staying in a building as big as Buckingham Palace.

After I showed Paula her suite, I left her alone, telling her to come to our apartment once she was settled. I couldn't imagine it would take her very long given that she'd only brought one twenty-by-fifteen-inch suitcase with her.

Twenty minutes later, Paula appeared at our door with three gifts in hand: a cardboard box full of mementos, a Virginia Tech t-shirt, and a single red rose. The box of mementos she'd lugged all the way from Virginia was almost as big as her small suitcase, and it occurred to me when she presented me with this unexpected gift that she must have packed little else: a pair of pants, a top or two, underwear, a comb, toothbrush and toothpaste. Yet again, I was reminded of our differences.

"I've been saving all this stuff since you were born," she admitted with a smile, one that told me not only was she pleased with herself for keeping the box a secret for so long, but she was also thrilled to finally be delivering it to the person she thought was its rightful owner.

Inside our apartment, we sat down—Paula on the couch and me in the chair across from her, the beat-up box perched on the coffee table between us like a bomb. At Paula's urging, I began to carefully remove its contents: letters, cards, a hospital bracelet, and other mementos from my birth. I was immediately overwhelmed by the lengths she must have gone to in order to save these things for me. Had she really kept the box all that time? Had she really held me so close? "I hid it in my closet for thirty years," she explained.

When I got to the bottom, I saw two old photographs, their white borders worn around the edges. Immediately I knew they were more pictures from before I was adopted, more pictures from my birth.

I picked up one of them and held it in my hand.

"That was taken after you were transferred to St. Jerome's," she explained. "I went to see you there."

I took a deep breath as I processed what Paula was saying. She had visited me—after I'd left the hospital, after she'd signed the papers. She had gone to visit me after she was supposed to have let me go. I was too taken aback to speak. I'd had a hint about this when

I got the second page of the Non-Identifying Background Report from Margaret, but hearing Paula say it out loud made it real.

Paula went on: "You weren't supposed to take pictures," she explained. "But I didn't know until I'd already done it."

Like the color copy of the newborn photos Paula had sent me with her first letter, the baby in the photo I held in my hand was much, much smaller than any other pictures I'd ever seen of myself. "Is that me?" I asked, not sure if I could believe what I was seeing and moved nearly to the point of tears. I'd promised myself I wouldn't cry during Paula's visit, but for the first time in my life, I felt a real connection to the time of my birth and to the days and weeks that followed. For the first time, that period in my life seemed concrete. It was no longer just a story my parents read to me out of a made-up book. It was real. My birth was real.

"I couldn't believe how much you looked like me," Paula said. "None of the others did."

I said nothing, unable to risk speaking since I knew doing so might make me cry. Instead I stared at the picture, looking for evidence of my own likeness. The photograph was yellowed from age, and the infant in the picture was not the happy, healthy baby I was so accustomed to seeing in photos from my childhood. Instead, the tiny creature I saw was shriveled and purple-pink, a mere morsel of the person I would become.

I passed the photograph to Dave, who was sitting on the opposite end of the couch from Paula. Then I picked up the other photo from inside the box, another one of me by myself, taken from a different angle. As I studied the unfamiliar image, it occurred to me then it was odd there weren't any pictures of Paula, but only pictures of me by myself.

"Why aren't you in any of the pictures?" I asked after I was sure I could talk without breaking down.

Paula's head jerked up. That time she was the one overcome. She looked directly at me without speaking, her eyes bigger than I'd ever seen them, and the reality of what she'd been through swept over me like a sudden onset of illness, causing me to shiver the slightest bit. I knew instinctively there was something she was trying not to say. Like me, Paula only stopped speaking when it was too hard to get the words out.

Then it hit me: she wasn't in any of the pictures because she had been alone.

And she'd been alone because her boyfriend at the time—my biological father, L.W. Tucker—had dumped her when he found out she was pregnant. He'd left her to deal with the consequences of their actions on her own. Paula had been all by herself in the world. No one to take her picture. No one to hold her hand.

Paula Hurley met L.W. Tucker when she started seeing his older brother, Roy. Paula and Roy only went out a few times, but it was an unfortunate detail that would forever overshadow both L.W.'s and Paula's relationships with Alice Tucker. I'm told Roy was a tough guy, a bully, and he never treated people well. I imagine playing second string to his older brother all his life was what gave L.W. and Paula something in common: they both didn't know what to do with Roy's cocksure ways. So, of course, it wasn't long before the two of them formed a bond. But dating your brother's ex wasn't exactly the way to bring the family together, and Paula claimed Roy was bitter about the two of them. And on that troubled foundation, L.W. and Paula started a relationship that would forever define them.

Paula was serious about L.W. from the get-go. Many years later, she would tell me the story of the day she decided she wanted to marry L.W., the day in December of 1968 when he came home from Vietnam for the holidays. This was well before the two of them had started dating. Paula, just twenty years old at the time, had been bussing tables at a local restaurant called The Lawson Inn, where L.W.'s mother worked as a waitress. The Lawson was located in an historic home that used to serve as a hotel at the end of an old horse-car line. It was December, and, as Paula explained, the space was decorated for Christmas with greenery and red ornaments and white lights. I imagine it all looked very alluring and romantic when L.W.—in his dress uniform—came strolling into The Lawson like a character in a movie. Paula told me she still remembers the scene: on his way into the dining room, L.W. had to walk down a long hallway lit with tiny white Christmas lights that twinkled off his brass buttons like stars, and that he looked so handsome, so dignified, she fell in love with him right then.

Once they did start dating, it wasn't long before Paula was pregnant. Though the non-identifying background report says Paula and L.W. dated two years before she got pregnant, I learned later that was an exaggeration, and they'd only been together about six months—though it's still unclear if it was even that long. That was the summer of '69, the summer of Woodstock and free love. The rules were beginning to change. But women still didn't raise children on their own as often as they do now. And it certainly wasn't considered acceptable to do so in working-class Catholic neighborhoods like the ones where Paula and L.W. grew up. Sure, plenty of people were sleeping around, but it was still pretty scandalous for a young unmarried woman to get pregnant. The only solution was for L.W. and Paula to get married.

But L.W. was scared.

He'd only been home from Vietnam for a short time and, according to Paula, was too shell-shocked from that experience to be ready for marriage and a family. To this day, Paula claims L.W. suffered from post-traumatic stress disorder, recounting his nightmares and insomnia in full detail every time the subject comes up, insisting it was even dangerous to wake him when he was sleeping and claiming it was his condition that made him run. I can't deny there is a part of me that's always questioned that explanation, but I'm old enough now to know it's impossible for me to ever fully understand L.W.'s decision to abandon Paula.

To complicate things further, during her visit to Oxford, Paula told me L.W. initially questioned my paternity by implying she was sleeping with other men, a theory Paula dismissed with a casual laugh. Years later, I'd also learn that L.W. didn't speak very fondly of Paula behind her back. I heard from more than one person that he used to describe her as the "ugly duckling" who followed him all the way home, leading me to believe that maybe L.W. had broken it off with Paula not because he didn't believe she'd been faithful, but for the simple reason that he wasn't interested in sharing his life with her. Not the kind of honorable behavior you'd hope for from your long-lost biological father, but I imagine it's closer to the truth of what happened—nightmares or not.

No matter the reason, the fact is that L.W. left Paula when she was two months pregnant. He abandoned her. And he did it so completely, so absolutely, that he never told anyone Paula was pregnant when he broke up with her—not his friends, not his brother, not even his mother, who was, in truth, the person to whom he was closest.

For L.W., Paula's pregnancy never happened. It didn't exist.

And neither did I.

So you can imagine how jarring it must've been for him when I showed up thirty years later, wanting to know all the details about everything he had tried to forget. I think it was as overwhelming and incomprehensible to him that I was in his life as it was that his brother was not, and I don't think he ever fully recovered from that shock.

Paula was only twenty-one years old and still a student in nursing school when she became pregnant with me. Her parents eventually kicked her out, and she had no way to support herself, much less a child. It wasn't a pretty picture, but it was typical of what happened when a young single woman got pregnant at that time.

So, four months before I was born, Paula moved into Villa Maria, the Catholic home for unwed mothers where she and dozens of other young women waited to give up their babies to married Catholic couples who were unable to conceive themselves.

"Looking back," Paula said to me during her visit to Oxford, "I realize now I could have made it work. I could have finished nursing school and made enough money to support a child." I noticed when she talked about what could have been, she used the word "child" rather than saying "you" even though she was talking directly to the child to whom she was referring. After knowing Paula for several years, I eventually figured out she would always have that disconnect between the perfect baby she gave up and the unfamiliar adult I had become. "But at the time," she explained, "it seemed impossible."

And what Paula failed to mention during that conversation, what was filling the air between us as we talked like a thought balloon on the verge of popping, was the unstated but unavoidable reality of her attempt to rewrite history: if she *had* kept me, both of our lives—

lives the two of us like very much—would have been drastically different. Not only would we have missed out on experiences we cherish, but we also wouldn't have shared our lives with the people we love most.

We would simply not be the people we had become.

Because not long after I was born, sometime in the year after Paula gave birth to me, she got back together with L.W. And it wasn't long after that when she returned to the adoption agency and tried unsuccessfully to get me back, explaining that she and L.W. had reunited. Though Paula was unable to do that, she eventually got pregnant again. Rather than run, L.W. stuck around the second time and married Paula in June of 1972, just a little over two years after I had been adopted. And then, in December of that year, Paula gave birth to Willie, their second child but the first most people in their lives would ever know about.

I wasn't there when Paula told her kids they had an older sister. But every time I saw them, they talked about what it was like to find out.

After getting the first letter from me, Paula sat them down individually. At the time, Willie was twenty-six, Clint twenty-four, Wade twenty-two, and Jeannie, the youngest, a mere eighteen, only just having graduated from high school. I don't have any idea if L.W. was there for those difficult conversations, but knowing what I do about him, I can't imagine he would've been able to sit through a moment so emotional, so raw.

"I need to tell you something," Paula began with each of them. "And it's going to be shocking."

Every one of them, I've been told, couldn't imagine what was to come next. The first thing they must have thought about was disease. Was somebody dying? But Paula didn't seem like the kind of person who had bad news. She was too happy, too eager to share, for that to be the case. The other possibility was divorce. Paula and L.W. had hit some bumps in the road over the years, but it was nothing to make any of them suspect their parents would break up the family. Still, it would have been foolish not to consider that possibility. Though I don't know any details, Paula eventually told me she'd spent a month in a hospital trying to figure out who she was in her late thirties, and L.W. had dyed his hair and grown a ponytail not long after that. Was divorce the next step in their mid-life crises? What else could it mean when your mother sits you down without your father and says she has news? Of course, there was also the possibility that Paula was pregnant again—except for Jeannie, they had all lived through that kind of announcement. Paula was fifty-one at the time, so it seemed like a long shot, but I'm sure they thought anything could happen. But what they couldn't have expected, what was farthest from their minds, were the words Paula finally announced.

"Your father and I had another child," she said to each of them. "Before Willie."

Jeannie told me she gasped out loud when her mother revealed the news to her. "What are you talking about?"

"Before you or your brothers were born," Paula explained, pausing to let Jeannie process what she was saying. "Your father and I had another child. We hadn't been dating that long, and your father had just gotten back from the war." Paula must have paused again at that point, hesitating in order to wipe away the tears I'm sure were forming in her eyes. Jeannie admitted to me it was an emotional confession. "He wasn't ready to get married, so I had to give the baby up for adoption."

"What?" Jeannie asked. "Why didn't you tell me?"

If I know anything about Paula at all, I know that by that point in the conversation she had probably given in fully to her tears, letting them come without hesitation.

"Mom? Are you okay?"

Paula hadn't been able to choke out a response, but when she looked into Jeannie's eyes, Jeannie saw the same pain I would witness nine months later: giving me up was a decision that had haunted Paula for nearly thirty years.

Jeannie has never been as openly emotional as her mother. Like me, she's tough, a tomboy who never wore dresses as a young girl and doesn't like to cry in public, but I also know her well enough to know, at a moment like that, she would've had a few tears of her own.

"Wait!" Jeannie said suddenly, realizing for the first time that her mother's announcement meant she had another sibling. "Was it a boy or a girl?"

"A girl," Paula admitted with a smile.

"You mean, I'm not the only girl?" Jeannie replied, the exhilaration in her voice apparent even to her overwhelmed mother. As the lone daughter in a house full of unruly boys, it had been, at times, a challenging and lonely childhood for Jeannie. She'd become a tomboy not just because she shunned ruffles and lace, but also because she'd had no other choice. "I'm not the only one?" she asked joyfully. And the smile on Jeannie's face told Paula that everything would be all right.

After her success with Jeannie, Paula told the others, and it was Willie's reply that I've heard repeated the most over the years: "I'm not the oldest?" he asked her immediately, completely skeptical about the introduction of a new sibling and clearly maligned by his reduced position in the family's hierarchy. I've come to accept it's something he'll never entirely get over. To this day, every time I see him, he says, "I still can't believe I'm not the oldest!"

I can't put into words how difficult it is for me to tell you about the rose Paula brought to my door the first night of her visit. I have both superficial and real objections to sharing that part of my story.

On a superficial level, I am simply put off by anything as clichéd, obvious, and common as a single red rose. (Not to mention that red roses are supposed to be used for romantic, not familial, love.) Of course, by admitting I have this aversion to red roses, I am also admitting that I am and always will be a snob about far too many things. I hate any and all clichéd gifts associated with love and courtship: red roses, stuffed animals, boxed chocolates, heart-shaped balloons, tennis bracelets. And if my husband were ever to present me with one of those items as a token of his affection, I think he knows my natural inclination would be to show him the door.

My snobbery doesn't end with romance either.

I hate almost everything I equate with being average or lacking authenticity, which amounts to a very long list of things, including but not limited to chain restaurants, hotel restaurants, buffets, processed food, frozen food, any pizza besides New York pizza, cruise ships, minivans, SUVs, strip malls, strip clubs, adultery, organized religion, mom haircuts, Capri pants with white sneakers, golf shirts, Crocs, animated movies, rom-coms, laugh tracks, voice-overs, reality television, horse-drawn carriages, June weddings, two and a half kids, blond hair, blue eyes (yes, I know I have them), and a whole plethora of things we like to call traditions, including having women be "given away" by their fathers on their wedding day, sending pictures of one's children or pets at Christmas (rather than a picture of one's self), plucking eyebrows, waxing bikini lines, expecting women to take their husband's name when they marry, spending holidays with family you don't even like, and last but not least—going back to romance—expecting men to surprise their girlfriends with a down-on-one-knee proposal. There is simply no limit to how much I hate the ways in which we as a people have become homogeneous. I guess I have always rejected the mundane and always seen myself as unique, which I admit is also, unfortunately, an average thing to do. My snobbery about such things is not a part of my personality I'm always proud of, but it's who I am, whether I like it or not. And I am well aware it is this aspect of myself that some people vehemently dislike about me.

Knowing all this, it's not hard to imagine how difficult it was for me to find out I came from a rather average background. The Tuckers were working-class people who didn't put much value on education, and they spent their money on motorcycles and guns and beer rather than the things I reserved my money for—books and movies, art and music. I won't lie: before I uncovered the identity of my birth parents, I always fantasized about being the child of a brilliant artist or musician. All kids fantasize about having different parents at one time or another, but adopted kids have the license to take it a step further, identifying celebrities who they imagine look like their genetic match.

When I was nine years old, I watched *The Dukes of Hazzard* and daydreamed about John Schneider being my long-lost dad. As a teenager, I started to believe it was Art Garfunkel. In college, I settled on Bob Dylan as the most likely possibility. The only requirements seemed to be that he have curly hair and be famous. While some people have a desire to inherit money, I wanted to have come from greatness.

And when I'm being completely honest with myself, I can admit the reason I yearned for such greatness, for such brilliance, was because, as much as I am loathe to admit it, I was raised in a very typical household as well. Sure, my parents were typical in ways that were, for the most part, wholly dissimilar to the Tuckers, and I clearly got some of my snobbishness from them. But they were average nonetheless. They were average well-to-do Americans: my father was a vice president of a division of a Fortune 500 company while my mother worked part-time as a nurse. They even lived in a suburb with a cul-de-sac at the end of the street. Worse yet: they believed in the American dream.

The other problem with the rose—my real problem with it— was that it came from L.W.

Wrapped in plastic, I suspected he'd picked it up at a gas station they passed when he drove Paula to the airport. I knew I should have appreciated the thought rather than critiquing its presentation, but my disappointment was about so much more than where or when he got it. Unlike Paula, L.W. didn't write after I first made contact with the Tuckers. He didn't write, and he didn't call. It was almost as if, to him, I still didn't exist.

When I talked to my mom after Paula had flown back to Virginia the Sunday of her visit, she was quick to bring up the one subject I didn't want to talk about: L.W.

"Did Paula wonder if you were angry with L.W.?" she asked me over the phone.

I *was* angry with L.W., but I didn't want to admit that to my mother. I was angry with him for breaking up with Paula when she got pregnant, angry with him for abandoning both of us, angry with him for not reaching out to me, angry with him for never telling his mother about me and for letting her believe that he'd only married Paula because she got pregnant with Willie—in effect, allowing his mother to believe Paula had "trapped" him into marriage even though he'd refused to be trapped once and could've just as easily refused again.

From my point of view, L.W. had failed on many counts. But even then I knew my anger was never really about simple indignation.

It was about fear and apprehension. I didn't want to be disappointed when I finally did meet him. I didn't want that reunion to be as difficult as I imagined.

After giving me the rose and explaining it was an important gesture on L.W.'s part, Paula admitted, "My husband isn't comfortable with me being here. He told me yesterday he didn't want me to come." It wasn't unusual for Paula to call L.W. her "husband" rather than calling him by his first name. Even after I'd known them both for years, she still referred to him that way as if the two of us had never met. Though I never understood why, I feared it had something to do with the wall he was trying to keep between us. "I told him he didn't have much choice in the matter," she added. "I was coming to see you whether he liked it or not." Paula laughed, leaning back on the couch for the first time, and I smiled though I felt nothing akin to happiness.

Immediately, I thought about what she had just revealed to me. L.W. didn't want Paula to meet me. Translation: he didn't want to meet me either. "When did he tell you that?" I asked Paula.

She went on: "Last night when he came home from the bar. He woke me up and said he didn't want me to come here."

"He told you that the night before you left?" I asked as another question formed in my head: why would he wait until the last minute to communicate his hesitations to his wife?

Paula shook her head—not because she was disagreeing with me, but because she, too, was mystified by L.W. "My husband isn't very good at being open with his feelings."

Then I remembered something Jeannie had said about her dad. She'd admitted he wouldn't know what to do if he ever met me, that he hardly had anything to say to her, so she couldn't imagine what he'd act like around me. "He talks to my brothers all the time, but he's totally uncomfortable with me," she'd told me on the phone a few weeks earlier. When I thought back on that conversation, my discomfort with the whole situation came to the surface yet again: what would I say to a man who wasn't capable of finding the words for the daughter he'd known for eighteen years, much less one he'd never met, the one he'd never even wanted to have in his life?

*

Though I was confused and apprehensive and even a bit shocked the afternoon of Paula's arrival, when she went back to her suite to change for dinner, I took the time to send an email message to my family and Tracy, assuring them all was well and telling them none of what I was really feeling. I wonder now why I decided to hide my true emotions from them since that's so unlike me. I imagine I simply must have wanted to protect them and put a happy face on Paula's visit.

Fri, 10 Mar 2000 18:15:47

Hi, Mom, Dad, Katie, and Tracy,

I just want to send you all an update of my weekend so far. Paula (my birthmother) got here safely this morning, and things have gone very well. We went to lunch in the dining hall and spent the rest of the afternoon talking and looking at pictures. Right now, we are resting some and are getting ready to go out to dinner in Oxford. We haven't decided if we'll go to Cincinnati tomorrow or not.

I kind of freaked out at the airport before she got here, but since then things have gone well. Paula is very open, and she really does look like me—even though she is skinny. I really couldn't be more pleased with how things have gone so far.

I'll write more later,
Molly

My parents—Mike McCaffrey and Penny Weems—met while they both went to college in Cincinnati. My father attended Xavier University, the same school nearly all of my uncles attended before opening its doors to women; my mother went to Mount St. Joseph College, one of Xavier's sister schools. Though they were almost thirty minutes apart by car, it wasn't surprising that they met, given that the two Catholic schools often held mixers and dances so students could meet potential spouses.

Mom had grown up in Portsmouth, Ohio, a small city in the southeastern part of the state that sits on the Ohio River. Once a thriving port, Portsmouth had begun its decline by the time my mother was born in 1942, causing her to come of age during an era of reluctant nostalgia. Her father was a well-known doctor, and when we visited Portsmouth, it wasn't unusual for us to meet people he had delivered at birth. The Weemses were one of the town's more prominent families and very influential in the Catholic church and high school, so sometimes I felt a bit like small-town royalty when we traveled there for summer and Christmas vacations.

My father has roots in the Midwest as well, but unlike my mother, his family was never fixed to one town since his father often moved with his job as a salesman for International Harvester. Dad was born in Parkersburg, West Virginia, but his parents had moved to Cleveland by his first birthday. The family relocated four more times before he was ten, but spent five years in Nashville when my father was an adolescent. For that reason, he stayed in Nashville to finish his senior year at Father Ryan High School even though the rest of the family moved on to Zanesville, Ohio.

My parents met at a freshman mixer in 1961 but didn't start dating seriously until their junior year of college. They were a bit of an odd match. My mother—who wore a tailored suit and high heels in one of her high school graduation photos and had a trendy shorter hairstyle when she left for college—was a near replica of Jackie Kennedy, but at the time my father, with a buzz cut and dorky smile, looked more like the captain of a high school math team than a suitable husband. Despite their differences, like most young couples back then, they were engaged in the months leading up to their college graduation, but they put off the wedding another year so my father could earn his M.B.A. on a scholarship from Xavier. My mother lived with three other young women during that year after college, all of them working as nurses at Good Samaritan Hospital in Cincinnati. One year later, in 1965 and only one year out of college, my parents were married at Holy Redeemer Church in Portsmouth.

Dad got a job with Standard Oil of Ohio after finishing his Master's degree, but not long after completing the training program, he decided to enlist in the Navy. The situation in Vietnam was just beginning to escalate, and he felt compelled to do his part but also wanted to avoid being drafted. After Officer's Training School in Rhode Island, the Navy took my parents to Athens, Georgia, and then back to Newport for a year before they settled in Annapolis in 1967, where Dad taught economics at the Naval Academy for the next few years. It was a wonderful assignment and the first time he and my mother weren't separated by long bouts at sea. They made friends with other Navy couples, had cookouts and parties, and, I'm sure, spent lots of time trying to get pregnant, though they never managed to succeed. They'd been married for two years when they moved to Annapolis and were disappointed a baby hadn't yet materialized. It wasn't long after that—a year at most—when they decided to contact the Catholic Charities office.

This was before couples like my parents began using fertility treatments. In fact, when my parents did seek medical help for their problem, they were merely told my dad should try wearing boxer shorts, advice my mother still gives when people have trouble getting pregnant.

About eighteen months after contacting the adoption agency, my parents got the news they'd been waiting for. When I was young, my mother used to tell the story of anticipating that phone call. She always claimed she was so anxious to start a family she would literally jump out of her chair every time the phone rang. Just a few weeks before they found out about me, they got a sign things were moving in the right direction when the caseworker from the adoption agency called them to check in.

"Are you getting ready?" she asked my mother over the phone.

"Oh, yes, we're ready," my mother insisted.

"We'll let you know," the caseworker said. "We're looking at some possibilities."

They'd expected a long wait. "It could be years," their caseworker had originally told them. So when word came through about a baby —a baby with eyes as blue as my father's, they told them—only about nine months after my parents had finished interviewing with the adoption agency, they were so overcome with joy that my mother went running door-to-door, sharing the good news. "We're going to get a baby!" my mom told all the neighbors, who must have been both pleased and amused by the petite women who had been trying to get pregnant since the day she'd been married, nearly five years before.

Obviously I don't remember the day my parents came to get me, but there was a photo taken moments after we first met—a photo of the three of us. In that picture, my parents are clearly dressed for the occasion: Dad is wearing a suit coat with a narrow black-and-brown striped tie, and Mom is in a sleeveless pink dress, a matching pink-and-white scarf around her neck and a large white hat with netting on her head. Mom is holding me in her arms, and both of them are looking at me so intently they forgot to look up for the photo, making their eyes appear closed. But my eyes are open wide, staring at the woman who is watching me so attentively. It's as if I know something important is happening, as if I know *she* is important. It looks like I'm wrapped in a receiving blanket, and there's almost no hair on my head, though a giant pacifier is in my mouth. Mom has the biggest smile I have ever seen on her face, and her dark hair curls so perfectly in the middle of her cheek that she looks like a model. My father, his hair sitting in sweaty clumps on his forehead, is so close to her that there is no space between them, and though Dad doesn't usually smile in photos, the smallest grin can be made out on his face. Underneath that picture in my baby book, my mom wrote:

Our first meeting... A very happy day! Welcome, Molly!

There can be no doubt it was one of the happiest moments of their lives.

When I was growing up, my mother talked all the time about what life was like for my parents after I was adopted. She always claimed those first six months were filled with both joy and anxiety as they waited for the final adoption decree to be processed. Mom says, on the one hand, she was thrilled to finally have a baby and wanted nothing more than to take care of me, but that at the same time, she worried constantly something would go wrong with the paperwork and—again—every time the phone rang in their Annapolis townhouse, she jumped, terrified they would get a call saying they had to give me back.

For almost twenty-nine years I'd believed my parents' fears about losing me had been unfounded, but after my interview with Margaret, I knew it was only thanks to Catholic Charities that the call they dreaded never came.

January 28, 1971

Dear Lt. & Mrs. McCaffrey,

It seems a long time from the day you decided to adopt a baby until the final decree of adoption comes from the Circuit Court No. 2.

It gives me a great deal of pleasure to enclose the decree with this letter. A birth certificate should follow in about three weeks. If you do not receive it, give me a call.

You now have all of the rights and duties of a natural parent. Under the state law, the baby will inherit from you in the same manner as a natural child. For your own piece of mind, I suggest that you check your will or make a will, so that if anything should happen to you, your child will be protected.

The enclosed statement covers services and advances made in your behalf.

It was a pleasure to take care of this matter for you and if at any time I can be of further service to you, please do not hesitate to let me know.

Sincerely,

Edward J. Emerson, Jr.

The three of us lived in Navy housing until my father finished his tour of duty in 1971. Though he considered extending his stay in the military, Dad ultimately decided to seek work in the private sector. He accepted a job in sales with Ethicon, a division of Johnson & Johnson, that took us first to Minneapolis and then Portland, Oregon, before we finally settled in Bridgewater, New Jersey, right after my third birthday in the spring of 1973. Though I can't remember much during those first three years, I can remember it was a frantic time of upheaval and uncertainty, packing and unpacking. Things finally settled down when we moved to New Jersey, but another big change occurred when, in October of 1973, my parents got a call from Catholic Charities in Minneapolis. They'd been on an adoption waiting list when we lived there, and as soon as a baby was available, the three of us were on a plane headed to the Land of Ten Thousand Lakes.

I wanted a baby sister more than anything: more than a Barbie doll, more than a bicycle, more than a pony. So even though I don't remember much about my life at that point—I was only three and a half years old—I do have a distinct memory of the moment I met my sister, a recollection that is admittedly encapsulated inside the fuzziness of my youth.

There must've been a whole flurry of events that occurred once we arrived in Minneapolis. We were staying with our former neighbors, and they had a son who was also three and had been my most frequent playmate during our time there. They also had a younger daughter who, while we were there, lost part of her finger when it got caught in a closet door, but I have no concrete memories of our visit with them. I only remember those details as facts listed on a page in my history.

But I do fully recall everything surrounding the moment I met my sister. The first thing I remember is walking up a long flight of stairs to get to the adoption agency. I clearly remember those stairs because I was so put off when I saw them. I had been waiting what seemed to a three-year-old like an unbearably long time to meet my new sister, and those stairs seemed like just one more delay, reinforcing my child-like sense that good things took way too long.

Once we got inside the agency office, we had to wait for a short time before we were introduced to the baby. Again, the waiting seemed interminable. I was, perhaps, the most excited I had ever been at that point in my short life, so I was uncharacteristically quiet, folding my hands in my lap and sitting up straight in the hopes that such behavior would be rewarded with the prize I was so desperately seeking. My parents were similarly well behaved. Like schoolchildren about to go on summer vacation, we waited obediently for the final bell to ring.

Finally, we were escorted into an adjoining room. Off to the side sat a small wooden crib just big enough for a baby to roll over once. Though we couldn't have been more eager, we did not rush across the room, instead moving slowly but confidently toward the crib: even at that young age, I was aware of the healthy family image we were expected to present if we wanted things to go our way. I was barely tall enough to see over the railing, but when I stood on my tiptoes, I was rewarded with the picture of the most perfect little baby—pink and round, her tiny face twisting into a knot of frustration once we'd crowded around her. She immediately began to wail, but I was too enamored to be bothered by her carrying on. To me, she looked like an angel, a wrinkled, little cherub. I let out a gasp, and a second later, my father said, "She's perfect." It was as if the four of us existed inside a warm bubble of joy.

I don't have any children of my own, so I don't know what it's like when a parent first sees her child, but I imagine the emotions are similar to the ones I experienced that day. I loved my sister unconditionally the second I laid eyes on her, and the bond I formed with her that day has never been broken.

Years later, my mother would reveal she had not been as certain as my father and I that morning. She eventually admitted that when she peered into the crib, what she saw was not a perfect little angel but an odd looking baby, a baby with thick and uneven hair and splotchy skin, a baby who was already emitting a squall loud enough to drown out everything else in the room, flaws my father and I could not see inside our love bubble.

After we brought Katie home, life really did settle down, our entire family fulfilling the expectations society had for us—my dad worked all the time, my mother alternated between being deliriously happy and horribly lonely, my sister laughed and cried with the same passion she displayed on that first day, and I longed to be old enough to play outside after dark with an intensity usually only reserved for lovers and criminals. We were, in many ways, a very average American family. And as we settled into a normal routine, my father began his corporate ascent. His rise at Ethicon over the next eleven years was unprecedented: he did invaluable work on the company's development of the skin stapler, proposing that it be disposable, an idea that ended up being extremely profitable; he won a Cleo for his work on the skin stapler's advertising campaign; and at the age of thirty-six, he was named the youngest vice president in the company, allowing us the great luxury of moving into a much roomier home with a pool in the backyard.

A few years before we moved into the house with the pool, Dad had been featured in a full-color print ad for Ethicon called, "Our Man in the O.R.," part of a marketing campaign he helped engineer. By that time, he'd shed all the remaining awkwardness of his youth, his dark hair and piercing blue eyes making him quite handsome. Dressed in an expensive suit, he stood confidently in the middle of an operating room full of doctors and nurses with his hands outstretched in the style of an educator, and there was the sense that he alone held the answers to all the world's troubles. The ad was a success in that it effectively conveyed the message that this man, this company, could be trusted. It was this image that most clearly represented the way I—and many people we knew—saw my father: tall, self-assured, hardworking, successful.

In my mind, there was nothing he couldn't do.

The only real cost for that success was that I didn't see my dad as often as I would've liked—none of us did. He worked six or seven days a week and traveled constantly. But we were raised to believe that was the price for success, not a bad one we were told. Mostly I took it in stride, though I longed to spend time with him and relished the moments we shared with an intense fervor. I even developed an interest in the things he liked to do—running, basketball, fishing, and reading—in order to spend more time with him.

We also both shared a love of dogs—especially down-and-out, needy ones—so on random Saturdays, after a particularly grueling run, we would reward ourselves with a trip to the city-operated animal shelter that sat adjacent to the high school track. The cement block building that housed the pound was as dirty and pathetic as you would expect: the stale smell of urine and the super-potent toxicity of industrial cleanser worked in conjunction with the high-pitched howls of the abandoned dogs, giving me a headache that would often take hours to shake.

As I walked along the cages, I tried not to think about the idea of numbered days, and, for the most part, it never bothered me. Now it seems obvious this look-the-other-way type of behavior was something I learned from my father, but at the time I was oblivious to how he dealt with this cruel reality. I was so happy to be with him and so eager to adopt a pet that I could look past the small imperfections during our time together. Sometimes we would take one of the dogs on a walk. It was on such occasions when I would give in to my emotion and end up in tears, begging to take the animal home as my father led me quickly back to the shelter to return the miserable little pup.

Despite my many pleas, we never did get a dog from the pound. My mother was worried about poorly trained or rabid dogs, and she didn't care for mutts. She wanted a purebred, and eventually that was what we got. Not long after Paula's visit to Oxford, I thought about the dog pound and wondered why we went there so often if we were never going to take anything home. I would have asked my parents for an explanation, but I already knew how they would respond. My father wouldn't say anything at all, pretending not to hear me, and my mother would say I think too much. She'd say my father took me to the dog pound because I liked it—simple as that—and that I should worry about more important things, like my career. I'd eventually interrupt her with more questions, and finally she'd retaliate by telling me I push people too much, attacking me where she knew it hurt most.

My whole life my family has accused me of overthinking things, of interrogating them without reason, and it's always been a sensitive subject, especially since they were the ones who taught me that good relationships were based on communication. But too often what they really wanted was for me to reveal my innermost thoughts and feelings without requiring the same of them. Rather than admit this, they routinely accused me of pushing them to their limit.

"You never give people a chance to finish, Molly," my mother said to me on the phone mere hours after we'd dropped Paula off at the Dayton airport on Sunday. "You are *always* one step ahead of people, finishing their sentences for them and going on to a new thought."

"I didn't do that with Paula. I'm not like that with everyone. Just you. You're family."

"Well, aren't we lucky?"

I knew my mom was kidding, but I also knew she would've preferred to get a pass—like the one I'd given Paula during her visit—every now and then.

Life went on basically the same way for eleven and a half years. We were, in many ways, a golden family. No, none of us was perfect—my dad still worked too much; my mother still sought a fulfilling occupation or hobby to fill the demands of her under-stimulated mind; I was awkward and nerdy, alternating between burying my head in a book and trying desperately to keep up with the confident cheerleaders who were my friends; and my sister, Katie, was fearless to the point of putting her life in danger, a wildfire that refused to be contained: she climbed to the very top of every tree in our yard, swam in the pool until her lips turned blue, roamed the streets of our neighborhood barefoot all summer, back-flipped across our landscaped yard, walked fearlessly across the top of the monkey bars, rode roller coasters until her scrawny legs buckled beneath her, kept a cat inside her shirt while riding her bike, and repeatedly crawled under all the pews at church during Mass. At times, it felt like the three of us—my father, my mother, and me—were the moons circling her planet, waiting for the next tilt in her axis. And people outside the family were as bewitched by her unyielding energy as I'd been on the first day I met her. But, still, I imagine that from the outside we looked pretty close to the perfect "normal" family.

Of course, things couldn't go on like that forever. Our troubles couldn't always be as uncomplicated as scraped knees and unwashed laundry. And at the beginning of 1984, the end of that golden era was in sight. During the middle of my eighth grade year and my sister's fifth, Ethicon wanted to run a feature story on my dad in the company newsletter. Someone decided a family portrait would be a nice complement to the article, and as a result, the four of us were forced to sit through a tedious photo shoot. I was almost fourteen at the time and had just gotten what my friends called "the magic haircut" because it had managed to transform me from a frizzy-haired, nerdy sidekick to a girl who suddenly had the interest of several boys. Despite this, I was eternally awkward, still a tomboy, and felt totally uncomfortable putting on the skirt, sweater, pantyhose, high heels, and pearl earrings my mother had picked out for me.

"Do I really have to do this, Mom?" I asked my mother as she styled my hair with a curling iron.

"Why wouldn't you want to have your picture taken?" my mother asked, not answering the actual question I had posed, a habit she'd perfected since my birth. I'd spent years perching on the stool in front of her dressing table and had plenty of time to figure out that my mother was the queen of avoidance.

"I don't know," I said. "I look stupid." Even though the magic haircut had caused big changes in my social life, I still didn't feel attractive, and the idea of sitting for a family photograph was about as appealing as going to school naked. My insecurities, as usual, were compounded by the fact that, though she had been an odd-looking baby, my sister had quickly become as perfectly adorable as little sisters come.

"Don't be silly," my mother said, sounding as if she'd never heard this complaint from me before. "You look pretty." I knew I didn't look pretty, that only my sister was pretty, so my mother's words only served to remind me that her opinion could not be trusted.

Once we were all assembled downstairs, my anxiety doubled. Katie was already sitting on the floor in front of my father, her long blonde hair wrapping around her neck like a fur stole, and after my mother stood behind his chair and put her hands on his back, I couldn't imagine how I would fit in the picture.

"Why don't you go over on the other side of your mother?" the photographer suggested with a wave of his hand, and I moved sheepishly across the room.

Naively, I assumed the whole ordeal would be over in fifteen minutes, but half an hour later, we were still in the same spots— hands had been moved, heads had been tilted, but by and large we were stuck in what amounted to a living still life.

"How much longer is this going to take?" my father asked shortly, his impatience readily apparent to the three of us even though the photographer seemed oblivious.

"Just a bit longer." It was a vague answer and one we all knew wouldn't come close to placating Dad, who didn't even like to sit in a restaurant eating dinner for thirty minutes, much less stand statue-still for a picture. He shifted in his seat, moving first to his left and then to his right. Katie let out a sigh so long it sounded like an ambulance crying in the distance. I, too, wanted to verbalize a complaint, but it wasn't in my nature. Over the years, I had become the good girl I'd pretended to be the day we first met my sister, the one who would stand there all day if I were told to do so. I glanced at my mother to see if she were revealing any signs of wear, but a plastic smile was the only thing visible on her face, a silent suggestion to the rest of us. It was then that my sister unhooked the buckles of her patent leather shoes and removed them. Her legs—which were covered in white tights and had been tucked neatly under her skirt a moment ago—stuck out in front of her like twin cigarettes.

"Katie!" my mother said, the alarm in her voice causing it to crack. "Put your shoes back on."

"I'm hungry" was Katie's response.

"We're almost done," my mother pleaded. "Just a few more minutes." She smiled at the photographer, giving him a nod that seemed to be asking for his cooperation in wrapping things up. "Will you please put your shoes back on?"

"I don't want to," Katie whined.

My father leaned over and grabbed her shoulder, gripping it so hard I could see the veins standing out on the back of his hand. "Do it!" he barked at her, but rather than follow his orders, she started to bawl. Her cheeks were soon so red and splotchy that any hope of more photos had been completely ruined.

Yes, we were far from perfect.

When the newsletter came out, I felt like the emotions of the day were painted across our faces like headlines. Would everyone know we weren't the model family the whitewashed article made us out to be? But my response wasn't simply about the fear that our imperfections would be revealed. It was also about the fear that they wouldn't. On the one hand, I felt certain people would intuit the truth about us, but, on the other hand, it seemed that we were, as a unit, above reproach—a perfect picture I felt pressured to live up to on a regular basis. At the time I didn't understand that our imperfections were what made us normal, possibly even functional, or at least as perfect as any family can be. I had the false sense there were other families out there, better families, who were able to sit for such a portrait without launching into petty disagreements and snippy remarks.

In that way, I felt like a fraud.

That incident, simple as it was, should've told me our façade was on the verge of cracking. It was about six months later, mere weeks into my freshman year of high school, when my parents told us we might be moving. We'd lived in New Jersey for eleven years—since I was three and as long as my sister had been alive. I couldn't imagine any other life, and, therefore, I felt confident such a change would never come to pass. Not a month later, my father came into my bedroom one morning to wake me and tell me we were moving to a small town in northern Indiana called Warsaw where he had gotten a new job. He talked about all the lakes in the county where we'd be living and showed me a brochure as if he were a travel agent. But before he could finish, I was in tears.

"What's wrong, Molly?" he asked, clearly worried about my response to what he saw as good news.

"Nothing," I said, knowing full well that my non-answer would not satisfy his concern very long. Despite my fears about our imperfections and my own awkwardness, the truth was that I was happy with our lives. In fact, I'd been happy most of my life. I loved New Jersey—with its pizzerias, hole-in-the-wall sub shops, and Jewish delis; its rolling hills and lush woods; its trendy shopping malls and multiplex movie theatres. I loved going to the Jersey Shore every summer and hiking through Hacklebarney State Park every fall. I loved taking the train to Manhattan to see a play on Broadway or to go ice skating at Rockefeller Center. I loved the stories about the Jersey Devil and the songs of Bruce Springsteen. I was a Jersey girl through and through. And, possibly most of all, I loved my Catholic high school, the place I'd dreamed of going for eight long years, the home of the teams I'd rooted for since I'd been old enough to keep score, the community that was so tight they held an event every year called "Spartan Spirit" just to honor that camaraderie.

Not only did I love my high school, I loved my classmates, my teachers, and my new student council position. No, I hadn't made the cheerleading squad that year, but even that had turned out to be a bit of a mixed blessing as some of my non-cheerleading friends told me after I was cut that cheerleading was "stupid" and "not even a real sport." I was, in fact, in love with my life, a life I'd already planned all the way through my high school job and college education. So much so that, the week before, when asked how old I would want to be if I could be any age, I had answered "fourteen," which was exactly how old I was.

But how could I convey any of that to my dad, a man who'd moved every few years when he was a child, a man who saw his career as the most important part of our success? In short, I couldn't. Though that didn't stop me from trying. "I like it here," I said. "I don't want to move."

"Well, eventually you'll like it there too."

"What about my friends?"

"You'll make new friends."

"But school's already started. I can't move in the middle of the year."

"It'll be fine. You'll probably be a little bit ahead of most of the kids there."

"I will?"

"Sure, it's a public school."

"A *public* school?" I had been upset enough when my dad first announced we were moving, but that last bit of information horrified me. From my limited perspective, public school was a place for hoodlums and gang-bangers and drug dealers. No matter what, I wasn't going to a public school.

My father must've read the look on my face because he said, "It's not like it is here. Everybody goes to public school. And there's less traffic and less pollution."

"But it's so far from the ocean," I pointed out.

"There are lakes everywhere. Look," he said, pointing to the brochure. "There are over one hundred in our county alone."

The way he had used the word "our" made me realize a decision had already been made, that no matter how much I protested we were going. "But it's not the same," I said as the tears started again. And then my dad looked at me with the saddest eyes I'd ever seen. I knew he loved me completely and without any hesitation, the way every parent should, but almost as importantly, I knew he liked me. We were similar in many ways: we both loved to get lost in the world of a novel and hang out at bookstores, we both loved to shoot hoops until it was too dark to see the basket, we had both thrived in the classroom and loved to learn and ask questions. Not only had he passed on his love of books and learning to me, he'd also passed on his belief that anything was possible, that I could do anything in life and be anyone I wanted to be—and that being a girl didn't mean I was less capable or less able to do so. To some degree, that made me his protégé, and the look on his face told me I was doing something I'd almost never done before.

I was letting him down.

He didn't need my approval or blessing. I was the child, and he was the parent. But I could sense he desperately wanted it.

"Okay," I finally said, giving into something I was totally uncertain about. It felt as if we were making a deal: it was as if he was saying, *I promise I'll make this work,* and I was standing there, shaking his hand and agreeing to give it my best shot. Unwillingly I was going along, saying, *Okay, I'll make you proud.*

Of course, it was a promise neither one of us had any way of fulfilling.

How could he control how well I did or didn't fit in? How many friends I had? How I was treated in high school? Obviously, he couldn't.

And I didn't do much better on my end. Maybe I didn't give it my best shot. Maybe I gave up too easily. I certainly didn't make anyone proud. No, my days of being the model child were behind me once I left New Jersey.

At first, it was easy.

With my pinstriped jeans and high-heeled boots, I was an immediate attraction in a place where many of the students hadn't been farther from home than Indianapolis or Chicago. Everyone wanted to be my friend. I had always been on the periphery of the popular group in New Jersey, but I'd never before been the center of attention. I suppose that's part of the reason I was so unprepared for the minefields that lay ahead. My biggest mistake was that I didn't think: I didn't think how my actions would play on the big screen of small-town life. I was well equipped to play the part of the well-behaved daughter at my parents' corporate parties, but I had no idea how to play the new girl, how to only reveal what was necessary. Instead, I simply acted like myself, holding nothing back as I had throughout the rest of my childhood. I talked openly about how different everything seemed—including the drinking and sex, which was much more common in rural Indiana than it had been in my somewhat sheltered Catholic school—and it wasn't long before I had made an army of enemies with whom I would battle all the way through graduation.

The first enemy I made—in my first class on my very first day at the Warsaw Freshman High School—turned out to be the most formidable and ultimately the cause of my downfall. Her name was Karli Vaughn.

Karli was in my first-period art class, and we started talking right away. It wasn't long before Karli invited me to sit with her at lunch.

"That would be great," I said, and I meant it. My worst fear at that time was eating alone in the cafeteria. "But I already told Leigh Powell I'd sit with her."

"Leigh Powell?" Karli said, her face contorting into a disapproving grimace.

"Yeah, I saw her in the office when I checked in this morning."

"How do you know Leigh Powell?"

"I met her when I visited a month ago," I said, sure by then that Karli did not approve of my lunch plans and wondering what people must have thought of Leigh Powell. "I spent the day with Stacy Curtis, and she introduced me to Leigh."

"Stacy Curtis?" Karli said, her voice rising to a high enough pitch that the other students at our table glanced over at us.

"Why?" I asked. "What's wrong with them?" The way Karli was acting made me think Leigh and Stacy had been involved in a murder or something equally nefarious, so I was totally unprepared for what came next.

"What's wrong with them?" Karli sneered. "Nothing! They're only two of the most popular girls in the whole freshman class, that's all!" Secretly I was relieved, but I waited for Karli to finish before I made another comment. "So you'd rather sit at the popular table than with me?" Karli said in an accusatory tone.

"It's not like that," I said defensively, so uncomfortable was I about the fact that I had spent less than one hour at my new school and had already managed to offend someone. "It's just that Leigh asked me first."

"Yeah, whatever," Karli said as she turned back to her drawing.

"It would be rude to tell her now that I'm sitting with you," I added, trying to convince Karli logically there was no reason for offense.

"Whatever you say," Karli said. She didn't look at me again, but I could see a smile had formed on her face, a smile that said, *you have no idea what you're doing,* and, even then, I feared she was right.

For the next couple of weeks, my assimilation to our new life went on without incident. I sat with Leigh and Stacy and the other popular kids at lunch, got invited to do enough things after school to make me feel like I fit in, and Karli and I kept talking all the way through our first-period art class. It didn't take long to see for myself where Karli fell in the high school hierarchy. She wasn't unpopular, but she certainly wasn't part of the in-crowd. She was right in the middle—third tier out of five.

And it was also obvious Karli desperately yearned to ascend to the first tier. She constantly asked me questions about what people at my lunch table were saying and doing. At the same time, she kept bugging me to do something with her outside of school. I had become more reluctant about becoming friends with her because she was so needy and cloying and, to be perfectly honest, because she wasn't part of the circle in which I was turning. But she could only be put off so long.

Finally, I agreed to spend the night at her house one weekend in February, a few months after we'd moved to Indiana. Unfortunately, my naiveté worked to put me at a distinct disadvantage that night with Karli.

By that point, I'd been privy to some things that made me realize even public school in rural Indiana was a world apart from the parochial decorum from which I had come. The most memorable incident occurring the first time I rode the fan bus to an away basketball game when a freshman girl gave a freshman boy a blow job in the back seat. That's not to say no one I knew in New Jersey had ever given a blow job, but the difference was that girls who did such things in my Catholic school were either pretty secretive about doing it or risked being shunned and ridiculed by the entire school.

I'll never forget when some of the boys at my grade school spray painted the school parking lot with a disturbing sexually explicit message about one of the girls in my class after just such an incident occurred the year before we moved to Indiana.

The same could not be said of Warsaw.

After said freshman girl blew said freshman boy, her social standing improved rather than suffered. In fact, the whole incident was treated as normal rather than unusual, and so when a boy asked me if I wanted to "go out" on the fan bus a week later, my immediate response was an adamant no. Since I hadn't had much interaction with boys in New Jersey, I was terrified of putting myself in a position I'd regret. And I wrongly assumed everybody in Indiana was giving blow jobs and having sex on fan buses all around the state.

Unfortunately, it was that attitude I took with me to Karli's house that fateful Friday night. I can't remember what else we did— probably ate junk food and watched T.V.—but, after replaying it so many times in my head, I will unfortunately never be able to forget the conversation that transpired in her bedroom.

"Do you think Bethany Banks is a virgin?" she asked me when we were getting ready to go to sleep.

Bethany Banks was someone who sat at my lunch table, someone with whom I was becoming friends. But she was also friends with the girl who'd given the blow job on the fan bus. "Probably not," I said, feeling more irritated than cautious about Karli's constant inquisition about people like Bethany.

"But she's Catholic!" Karli insisted.

"That's true," I said as I thought back to my Catholic school friends. "She probably *is* a virgin."

I can't remember what we talked about next or anything else that happened that night or the next morning, but that conversation is impossible to forget because it wasn't long after that when Karli used the information she'd so cleverly extracted from me that night to elevate her own standing and work her way into the inner circle. Unbeknownst to be me, Karli approached Bethany and told her I'd called her a "slut." Bethany, a Catholic fourteen-year-old who was as worried about her reputation as Karli was about her lack of popularity, was rightfully aghast, and immediately got me kicked out of the in-crowd, taking Karli under her wing as her new confidante and moving her from third tier to first before I knew what had happened.

It was brilliant.

Still, I couldn't see Karli's power play for what it was at the time. All I knew was that I had been completely ostracized. I no longer had any friends—no one to sit with at lunch, no one to talk to after school, no one to work with in biology class because Bethany and one of her other friends had been my lab partners all year, and the two of them dumped me after Karli misrepresented what I'd said. Luckily, a few incredibly empathetic boys took pity on me, by then easily the most unpopular girl in school, letting me join their lab group and sit with them at lunch. But I can say in all honesty that those next few months—months when I was cursed in the halls, threatened in the locker room, and mocked not so discreetly behind my back—were the most difficult of my life.

I don't want to lay all the blame at Karli's feet. Looking back, I can see that being the child of a successful businessman was much harder in a town that depended on that business than it was in a sprawling suburban area like the part of New Jersey where I'd grown up. My father was a superior to many of my classmates' fathers, men who'd worked for those companies all their lives only to be told that an outsider—and from their perspective, an East Coast outsider—would be their new boss. There were bound to be problems. It's just that neither of us, my father or me, saw that at the time. And the life I'd led before we moved was so narrow, so sheltered, that I helped dig my own grave.

There was one day toward the end of the school year—during the time I was Freshman Enemy Number One—when I revealed just how insulated my life had been before I came to Indiana. Again, that incident occurred in my first period art class.

My teacher was talking about a painting that had just sold for fifty thousand dollars in Europe. That amount seemed impressive enough to me, but the other students were awed by the number, oohing and aahing over it like it was a particular impressive fireworks display. Once the teacher had their full attention, she went on: "My husband said, 'If you could just sell one painting every year for that much, we could quit our jobs.'"

Most of the students laughed and nodded in agreement, but I didn't join them. I was mystified. I knew my art teacher and her husband had two kids, and I also knew my father had been checking the salary box that said "$150,000 or more" on the donation envelopes at church for years. Finally, I rose my hand and spoke up. "How could a family of four live on fifty thousand dollars a year?"

A collective gasp sounded throughout the room. I knew immediately I had made an outrageous error. "What do you mean?" my teacher asked. "That's more than enough money for a family of four."

A girl sitting near me interjected: "My dad makes less than that, and there are *five* of us." Her friend rolled her eyes at me like I was an unmitigated asshole. They clearly thought I was a spoiled brat, and why wouldn't they? The idea that I didn't know regular people made that kind of money was absurd—how could I have been so naïve, so sheltered? And why hadn't I known any regular people before I moved to Indiana?

The truth was that I had known plenty of "regular" people in New Jersey. I'd even known plenty of working-class people, had been friends with them, spent the night at their houses or apartments, but it had simply never occurred to me that a vice president at a place like Ethicon would make five times what a teacher made.

Of course, I couldn't convey the reasons for my confusion to my peers that morning. I'm not even sure I fully understood them at that time. But what I did understand was that no one in that room, and I mean absolutely no one, would ever really like me.

After freshman year, things cooled off a bit. I was certainly never popular or well-liked in Warsaw, but I found my way, made friends, and generally got by. Not fitting in meant I skipped as much school as possible and partied pretty hard junior and senior year. My grades were a disaster too, and the straight As I had when I left high school in New Jersey were replaced with Bs, Cs, Ds, and even a couple of Fs—including one from my art teacher sophomore year (who clearly never got over my fifty-thousand-dollar comment). My parents were rightfully unhappy about my performance, but they let it go when I got into a decent college. After that, I did my best to never look back.

That is, until I met Paula twelve years later.

Well, maybe not even then. And maybe it's taken me all these years to formulate a clear connection between my challenges in Warsaw and my challenges with the Tuckers.

On the first night of her visit to Oxford, we took Paula to a local Italian place called Spaghetti's. It was one of those odd restaurants that didn't know what it was. Located in a strip mall, Spaghetti's paired Formica booths and plastic flowers with white tablecloths and votive candles. Still, they served some of the best food we could find in a town as small as Oxford unless we wanted to spend a fraction of our graduate stipends on a single meal.

"What are you going to get?" I asked Paula after we'd all had time to look over the menu. "Everything is good here." I was trying to be positive but was well aware I also sounded clichéd and bland.

"I'm not sure," Paula said with a hesitation in her voice.

"Do you like pasta?" Dave asked her.

"Who doesn't like pasta?" Paula said with a little laugh. "But that's a lot of calories." Paula glanced in my direction after she said those words, but I couldn't tell what she was thinking. "I just need to look at the menu a little bit longer."

"Take your time," Dave said.

After we ordered, I decided to ask Paula about any medical problems that ran in the family.

"There really aren't any," Paula said, shaking her head in a noncommittal fashion.

"None?" I asked.

"You know, now that I think about it, I did have two aunts who had heart trouble. They were both really overweight, obese even." She looked at me again, her determined face clear even in the candlelight, and I understood then she was trying to tell me something. "They both died young. *Very* young. In their forties or fifties. I can't remember exactly, but you have to be careful." At that point, Paula was speaking directly to me, her eyes trained on me like a hypnotist. "You have that in your genes."

If there had been any question about what Paula was saying before, there could no longer be any doubt about her meaning: Paula thought I was fat, "obese even."

I didn't back down from her challenge. "I've never weighed this much in my life," I said. "It's not a big deal. I'll lose it. I've just had a bad year." It was the truth—the stress of graduate school had taken its toll on me in the form of an addiction to soda and potato chips—but I also didn't feel the need to explain all that to Paula, someone whom I had, for all practical purposes, just met.

But Paula wouldn't let it go. "Well, I just think you have to watch what you eat, maybe think about doing something differently."

I was stunned.

Never in my life had my parents told me to go on a diet, but the woman who'd spent less than twenty-four hours with me since the day I was born was already trying to tell me how to live my life.

"I'm not going to worry about it," I said defiantly. "It will work itself out."

"Good," said Dave enthusiastically, suddenly interrupting our conversation and reminding me again why I loved him so much. "I think that's exactly what you should do."

I did my best to forget the implication of Paula's words once our food arrived, telling myself her comment was just a fluke, more indicative of her upbringing and education than her personality. After all, wasn't I the one who'd asked for any relevant medical history? Thankfully, Paula let it go too, and we fell back into small talk after that. I don't remember anything else about dinner that night except that there was nothing significant to remember. Outside of our apartment, Paula kept the conversation mostly light, talking about her kids in ways that would seem perfectly normal to anyone sitting near our table. In fact, I imagine that if anyone in the restaurant had been eavesdropping, they would've had no idea what we were all going through that day.

After dinner, we stood in the cold parking lot of the strip mall and took a few pictures. I didn't get them developed until the last day of Paula's visit, and when I saw the photos, I was shocked by how much we looked alike. Nearly everything about us was the same. No, I didn't inherit Paula's muddy brown eyes, but I feared the deep lines crawling across her skin like flesh-toned spiders would some day be mine.

Once I studied the photos, I realized that, though our dinner conversation wouldn't have revealed we knew each other, it would've been obvious to everyone in the restaurant that we were related. That was an epiphany almost as jarring to me as the one I'd had after seeing the first pictures Paula had sent. For not the first time since I'd known who Paula was, I experienced the same gnawing sensation: How could I be related to someone so different from me?

Hi, Mom and Dad,

I just want to write back and tell you that things are continuing to go well. Last night we went to an Italian restaurant called Spaghetti's (we're getting tired of Kona!), and then we went to see WONDER BOYS. (You should really see it—it was outstanding, and we all liked it.) Everything went very well. I feel as if I have been lucky because besides the anticipation before Paula arrived, it really has been very easy. I feel bad for Katie and Theresa because of how hard it was for both of them. But I realize that I am a different person than Katie, and Paula is more like me and you (Mom) in that she is pretty comfortable with herself and her life. She talks openly about everything that has happened—the adoption, the pregnancies, her family, our family, etc. I guess I shouldn't be surprised because I have always been an open book!

The only thing I think might be hard for her is that this weekend is somewhat intense as we are spending two solid days together. I think we can both handle it. Yesterday, we took a nap in the middle of the afternoon, and that helped. Today we are thinking of going to Cincinnati, and then I think we should make it an early night. Unfortunately, it is supposed to snow here for the first time since January—I hope it doesn't.

Still no word from Ph.D. programs. Hope you guys have a good day. I'll call you tomorrow in the late afternoon/early evening.

Love,
Molly

Re-reading this email message now makes me realize how naïve

I was that first weekend. I was focusing on superficial similarities and differences with Paula when it was the much more complex facets of our personalities that would ultimately lead to problems. Yes, Paula and I are both open, but I would eventually learn that being open doesn't always translate to being tolerant or accepting.

That day we decided to drive to Cincinnati. It was a Saturday, and there wasn't much to do in a town like Oxford, Ohio, on a normal weekend, much less the first weekend of spring break. Spending the day in Cincinnati would likely make the time go faster, and it would have the added benefit of giving Dave's parents, Herb and Catherine Bell, the chance to meet Paula. Though they'd never asked to meet her, I knew the two of them were curious about my biological family, and a part of me wanted the three of them to get to know each other so I could get some much-needed feedback on what kind of impression Paula made. I didn't think my in-laws were the absolute best judges of character—I knew for sure they judged me pretty harshly for living with Dave before we were married—but I also knew them well enough to sift through their biases and prejudices in order to uncover the answer to my most important question: Was Paula normal?

And maybe there was another part of me that saw the lunch as a test-run for Paula. If she did well, I would consider introducing her to my parents. If not, I'd continue to protect them from such an awkward encounter. Looking back, that idea seems ludicrous. Knowing what I know about Paula now, I would never subject my parents to her, but that first weekend, I was still unsure about who she was.

On the way to Cincinnati, we made small talk—mostly about Dave's childhood and his family, who certainly had more in common with Paula's family than my own, at least on the surface.

"What do your parents do, David?" Paula asked him as we drove along the two-lane highway that connected Oxford to the Queen City.

"My mom used to do credit authorizations for Federated Department Stores, but she quit to babysit the grandkids. Dad retired from insurance a while ago and works at Wal-Mart part-time now."

"Well, that sounds nice," she said, and I wondered if she really believed that or was just saying it to be polite. Even someone like Paula couldn't think that working at Wal-Mart was "nice," could she? Maybe I was wrong. Maybe she did think it was a good job. I had grown up without ever thinking about money while Dave's parents had always worried about it, always would. Though I wasn't sure yet, I felt confident Paula had that in common with them.

So it wasn't much of a surprise when we arrived at Dave's parents' house, and the three of them fell into an easy banter, talking with each other naturally at the house and all through lunch. In fact, it felt like Dave's parents were more comfortable with Paula than they were with my parents, whom they'd always gotten along with but had never connected with in any real way. I'm not exactly sure why Catherine and Herb seemed so at ease with Paula, but if I had to guess, I'd say it probably had to do with them feeling like Paula was someone to be pitied or even coddled. After all, she'd gotten pregnant when she was still young and single and basically had no choice but to give up her baby for adoption. From the Bells' very Catholic, very Midwestern point of view, there was almost no worse fate that could've befallen her. And there was no way they didn't think that meant they were better than she was. Absent any vast differences in class, they held the moral high ground. And from that lofty perch, they embraced Paula like a baby bird fallen from the nest. She was broken. She would never be quite right. Only people without any empathy whatsoever would leave her lying in the grass without nursing her broken wing, her broken heart. Of course, that also meant she could not possibly judge them, two people who'd never committed a mortal sin of any kind much less gotten pregnant outside of marriage, two people whose lives were—from their way of thinking—above reproach.

This dynamic was compounded by the one Paula brought to the table. She was, not totally unlike the fallen baby bird, begging for mercy, for help. Anyone who could give her that would gain her eternal gratitude. And that's what the Bells did that afternoon. They gained Paula's gratitude and respect. For as long as I knew her, Paula would always ask after Dave's parents and seem truly interested in my response, an attitude that was a world apart from how she acted when the subject of my family came up. I have very little recollection of what we talked about in Cincinnati that day, but whatever it was, it forever endeared the Bells to Paula.

I do remember that Catherine and Herb were on their best behavior. They were polite, interesting, and engaged. Herb was charming, almost flirtatious, with Paula, and Catherine solicitous. Dave and I had seen them like that before but only when the four of us would do something on our own. The rest of the time they usually fell into the gendered roles they occupied in the family—commanding and silent—so it was sometimes easy to forget that, when they wanted to, they could both be so good with people, so likeable.

I could not have been happier about their performance that day, and later I would learn Dave felt the same way. Letting the Bells do some of the heavy lifting with Paula gave us a much-needed break from trying to figure out what to say to a person whom we barely knew but still had to treat like a close family member.

The only clue as to what lay ahead of us that afternoon was Paula's response to the food. We went to Skyline Chili for lunch because we wanted to give Paula the chance to experience some local culture. Skyline is a tradition in Cincinnati, and West Siders, like the Bells, treat it more like a religion than a food. But Paula was immediately confused by the idea of Cincinnati chili, which is served over spaghetti noodles.

"So is it chili or spaghetti?" she asked after we'd given her a menu, something none of the rest of us required since we'd been there dozens of times and had memorized the few items served.

"It's both," Catherine said as she glanced around, obviously looking for people she knew. It wasn't uncommon to run into friends or family members anywhere on the West Side, especially at Skyline, so I wasn't surprised when her eyes rolled inquisitively over the other faux wood tables and the U-shaped Formica bar.

"It's chili served on top of pasta," I explained to Paula, pointing to the picture on the plastic menu. "But the chili is just made with meat."

"No beans?" Paula asked with a frown. Clearly she was having trouble understanding the concept.

"You can get beans if you want," I told her, glancing at the teenage, ponytailed waitress who I knew would be approaching any second. "But nobody does."

"Why not?" Paula asked incredulously.

"I don't know. They just don't."

"I think I'll just have a baked potato," Paula said, dropping her eyes back to the small plastic menu.

"You can have whatever you want," Catherine said, reassuring Paula unnecessarily as if she were a child.

"You should really try the chili," I said, doing my best to be persuasive but not pushy. "That's what they're known for."

"I don't think I'd like it," Paula said.

"You won't know until you try it," I said, realizing how much I sounded like the mother in the relationship. But my efforts were futile. Paula ordered a potato topped with chili, mystifying us all, and then turned up her nose at the chili's unusual cinnamon-flavored taste, a response that not only reminded us of our differences, but also told us Paula wasn't very open to trying new things.

We had planned to visit the Museum Center in Cincinnati before driving back to Oxford, but the weather didn't cooperate. There was already an inch of snow on the ground by two in the afternoon, and when an ice storm moved into the area, we decided it would be best to head back before the roads became much worse.

The drive home was anti-climactic. Everything we'd looked forward to all day—introducing Paula to Catherine and Herb, having lunch at Skyline, visiting the Museum Center, getting a break from thinking about what to do next—was over. And now we only had a cold, quiet evening to keep us company.

Back in Oxford, Paula convinced us to turn on the Virginia Tech game. Since Jeannie had started playing for the women's team, Paula had become a fan of the entire basketball program despite the fact that she still talked incessantly about how Jeannie didn't get enough court time. So the three of us got comfortable in front of the television and watched unusually talented young men run up and down a wood floor with a large orange ball. I wasn't interested in the game, but I was happy to have another distraction from entertaining Paula. A part of me thought we should be doing something else—

something more interactive perhaps—but Paula and Dave insisted it was fine to just sit and stare at other people interacting for a couple of hours.

While we were watching the game, Paula mentioned the bar. I'd learned about the bar—or "the restaurant" as Paula liked to call it—from the letters and pictures she'd sent me. But I didn't understand how central it was to their lives, to their identity, until I heard Paula talk about it in person.

"Do you like country music?" Paula asked me during halftime.

"Not really," I admitted.

"Oh," she said, pausing. Immediately, I regretted answering the question truthfully. *Was I supposed to pretend to be someone I'm not?* But before I could recant, Paula spoke again: "I was just wondering because we have karaoke."

I looked at her, not sure what she was talking about. The word "karaoke" tapped on my brain like a knock-knock joke I couldn't understand.

"At the restaurant," she added by way of an explanation.

"Oh, yeah." Until that moment, I had all but forgotten about the "restaurant." *Their* restaurant. It's called Tucker's Hideaway, and L.W. and his mother, Alice, ran the place together for years. Even though Paula called it a restaurant every time it came up, food is an afterthought at Tucker's, and it mainly appeals to bikers because—thanks to an unusual grandfather clause—they can pull their motorcycles up to the outdoor bar and have a beer without moving from the leather seats of their bikes. As a result, the place has quite a reputation, drawing bikers from all over the region and attracting patrons the likes of Senator Ben "Nighthorse" Campbell.

When I met Paula, Alice and L.W. were still in charge—with everyone else in the family putting in time at the bar: Paula planned most of the big events, Willie tended bar full-time, Jeannie and Clint pitched in whenever they were needed, and Paula's sister, Sue, was in charge on weekends. In that sense, it has always been a family business.

"We have it on Wednesdays and Fridays, and we all get up and sing." Paula was still talking about the bar, but I was having trouble focusing.

Knock, knock. Who's there? Your mom. Your mom who? Your mom who sings karaoke.

"Do you sing?" she asked.

"No, I can't sing at all," I said, shaking my head emphatically. "Never could." My next thought was it seemed strange that the person who shared half my genes was talented enough to perform in front of a crowded bar. And that realization made me wonder, again, if Paula wasn't my biological mother after all or if there had been some mistake. Maybe I wasn't the product of two people who owned a biker bar. Yes, that had to be it, I told myself. Otherwise, my life just didn't make sense.

But before I had time to fully consider that option, I looked at Paula and saw the uncanny truth: my own face staring back at me. For a second time, I was reminded there hadn't been any mistake. I tried to hide my disappointment and went on as best as I could with our conversation. "Are you a good singer?" I asked her.

"God, no!" She blushed as she spoke and chuckled a little to herself. "I'm horrible. But I don't care. I just get up there and do it. We all do."

Later she showed me pictures of the whole lot of them standing in front of the bar: the karaoke-singing family from Virginia— mouths open, microphones in hand, open beer cans at the ready. Paula explained: "If everybody's there, we all get up and sing 'Family Tradition' together."

I unintentionally cringed. Though Paula looked thrilled, I was appalled. "Together?" I asked, hoping the horror I was feeling wasn't obvious to her.

"Sure," Paula said as if singing together, as a family, was the most natural thing in the world.

It hit me at that moment that the Tuckers were the kind of people Dave and I didn't get: people who work with their families, people who vacation with their families, people who karaoke with their families, people who do absolutely everything with their families. And yet we were quickly learning that they were, in fact, my people.

"Maybe you could visit next summer," Paula added before I could respond. "It's only an hour flight."

"I don't fly," I reminded Paula, my distaste about the karaoke making my response snippier than I would have liked.

"Oh, yeah, that's right," she said, and it was obvious from the mistrusting look she gave me that I baffled Paula as much as she confounded me.

After we dropped her off at the airport the next day, Dave cracked up, remembering the karaoke, and said I'd probably have to sing with them when we visited. Unfortunately, I was unable to see the humor because, in truth, I couldn't fathom how I would get out of it. So instead of laughing, I steeled myself for the moment when I'd have to go to a biker bar and karaoke with my biological family. And despite my attempts to prepare for such an embarrassment, nothing could've readied me for what would eventually happen.

The rest of Paula's visit was uneventful. We went to dinner at the local Chinese/Thai place, the slash guaranteeing that neither was authentic or good. Paula was polite about the lack of dining options in Oxford, insisting several times that she was a roll-with-it kind of person. And after dinner, we went back to our apartment and watched *The Horse Whisperer*, which Paula said was "okay."

"Have you ever seen *Hope Floats*?" she asked us once the movie was over.

I glanced at Dave, and I could see that, after thirty-six hours of being together non-stop, he'd finally run out of the ability to fake it with Paula. He didn't actually roll his eyes at her, but I knew him well enough to know that's what he wanted to do.

"No, we haven't," I said, understanding it was my turn to be polite. "Is it good?"

"Oh, I love it," Paula said. "It might be my favorite movie. I've probably watched it a dozen times."

"Wow," I said, unsure of what to say next since, by definition, I was a person who had no patience for movies that made the boy-meets-girl formula their central conflict.

"I know," Paula said. "It's crazy."

I knew I was supposed to keep the conversation going, but, after a day and a half of doing just that, I too had finally used up my ability to make small talk. I was exhausted.

"I should probably go to bed," Paula said suddenly, and I figured she must have sensed we needed a break. "It'll be a long day tomorrow."

"Can I get you anything?" I asked. "Do you need something to drink...or eat?"

"No, but I should call L.W.," she said.

"Will he be home from the bar yet?"

"Oh, no," Paula said with a chuckle. "He doesn't usually get home till three."

"Three in the morning?" I asked.

"Yeah, I know," Paula said. "But he takes a nap every afternoon. He manages."

It was the exact right way to describe L.W. and Paula's life: they managed, they got by. It was what Dave and I had been doing since we'd started graduate school the year before—we'd been getting by—and I couldn't help but wonder if we would ever move past that phase, or if, like Paula and L.W., we would be forced to catnap and cut corners for the rest of our lives. My parents had both worked hard for many years, but the reward for their diligence had been plenty of small luxuries. Would we be like them? Or would we always struggle?

The three of us were a bit quieter on the drive back to the airport the next morning. I suppose we weren't sure what to say. Paula and I hadn't been in the same room for thirty years. The unspoken question that ballooned between was obvious. Would we ever see each other again? In that way, it felt a bit like we were driving to a funeral. We had made no definite plans though Paula kept pushing us to come visit over the summer. But no matter how hard she pushed, I wasn't ready to commit, so I made excuses about not knowing what the future held, which was, in fact, the truth.

We rode in silence for a little while until Paula brought up the twins with cystic fibrosis again.

"Did I tell you about the fundraiser I held for my friend's girls?" she asked.

"I think so," I said, trying to be polite about it, but Paula must not have understood what I meant because she started describing the event in full detail all over again.

"There must have been over five hundred people there," she began, and, as she went on, I tuned out, looking out the window and wondering how long it would be until the snow would finally melt.

At the airport, Paula protested as she took her glasses off for one last snapshot: "You'll see my wrinkles."

I pretended I didn't know what she was talking about. "What wrinkles?" I asked. "You look great."

We stood under the artificial lights of the terminal, smiling, an arm around each other as if we were old friends.

Driving home from the airport, Dave said it was strange to meet someone who resembled me so much. I knew his words meant more than he was willing to admit. The truth was Paula scared him. Not Paula the person. But the idea of Paula. As long as I'd known Dave, we'd speculated about who my birth parents might be, but once Paula was real and not just an imaginary character we dreamed up as we lie in bed at night trying to fall asleep, he was worried that knowing her might change us. Maybe he was afraid I would become more like her—I'd start getting wrinkles and wearing mom jeans.

And though I was reluctant to admit it, the idea of having Paula in my life scared me too. It really was unsettling how much the two of us resembled each other considering how little we seemed to have in common. Even though I'd already known we looked alike from the pictures she'd sent, I hadn't fully processed what that meant when she first stepped off the plane. But after spending a weekend with her, I began to understand we shared something fundamental, and I had no choice but to admit, not only did she look like me, but she stood like me and talked like me too. In one picture, we appeared to be a perfect match—like one of Paula's sweater sets. But even after she had come and gone, I still felt as if she was as odd and unknown to me as any stranger we could've picked up at the airport the day she arrived.

After we got home from taking Paula back to the airport, I called my mother.

"I can see everything for what it is now," I said when I got her on the line.

"Really?" she asked, rightly skeptical of my ambiguity. "What does *that* mean?"

"It means I was worried I would feel conflicted. That I wouldn't know who my real family is. I used to feel guilty about it, but it's not the same anymore. Now I know you and Paula are two separate parts of my life."

But as soon as I hung up, the guilt returned. Like an earthquake, it overtook me without warning, violently shaking my foundation. *What had I done? How would I ever face my parents again?* I felt—simply and ruefully—like a traitor who had turned on the people I loved most, the people who'd raised me, the people who'd stood by me my whole life, my real mom and dad. Coupled with that feeling was an intense and overwhelming desire to go back in time and erase everything that had happened—starting the search, finding Paula, meeting her, all of it. At the very least I longed to call my mother back and vow to never talk to Paula again. And at the most basic level what I really wanted was to tell my mother I loved her, to tell her she was the only mom I'd ever need.

Unfortunately, I've never been that kind of person—the kind of person who can say out loud, *I love you, I need you, I am part of you.* So instead of expressing my emotions, I swallowed them—whole and unresolved, like a frat boy gulping down a goldfish.

I didn't realize how transparent I was being until Dave asked me what was wrong. Even before he spoke, I could feel him circling, searching me for clues, but I didn't want to give in to his interrogation so soon since I knew he would force me to confess emotions I wasn't yet ready to admit.

"What did your mother say?" Dave finally asked once he realized I wasn't going to volunteer the reason for my unhappiness.

"*You know* what she said," I replied. "The same thing she always says."

"Let me guess. She *said* she was fine with Paula being here, but you don't believe her?"

I didn't respond. I didn't have to. Dave knew he was right. He knew my family as well as I did, and he'd heard our story over and over.

My younger sister and I were both adopted before we were six weeks old. Like kittens. Just old enough to be weaned, but not old enough to remember.

Except we're not from the same litter.

My parents never hid the fact that we were adopted. In fact, they told us the whole story before we were old enough to understand what they were saying because they believed the truth was one of the most important things they could give us. And so they taught me about my birth by reading me *The Chosen Baby*, a children's book about a special little boy named Peter. Of course, Peter was also adopted. Sometimes they replaced Peter's name with mine, and other times it was Peter's story. But before I was old enough to read I could recite the entire book from memory. I always knew I was adopted, and I always believed I was special. I can't thank my parents enough for that gift.

They also said they would support us if we wanted to look for our birthmothers or any other family. They said it, but I never believed it was true.

I believed, instead, that doing so would be uncomfortable for all of us, that it would hurt our special bond. So for many years I never thought about it in any serious way. It simply wasn't an option. I was at least *that* devoted to my parents—devoted enough that I wouldn't even consider the one thing I was afraid would truly wound them.

And when I was a kid, I didn't think about it much at all. My parents told me that only someone who loved her child more than herself could give her up, and I believed them. I still do. And when I was little, I told other kids that I was special, that *my* parents had paid for me.

I must have repeated those words on hundreds of occasions—every time someone tried to make me feel bad about being adopted, which unfortunately was more often than it should have been—but there was one time in particular that has stayed with me all these years.

My mother had enrolled my sister and me in typing and computer courses at the local public high school one summer in the early eighties. She claimed she wanted us to learn skills she saw as mandatory, but I imagine she also recognized that we were getting closer to that age when trouble and temptation lurked around every corner. And she was right to be concerned. I was twelve that summer, just months away from being a teenager, and though my sister was only eight, the two of us had started spending time with two brothers in our neighborhood. Our interaction with them was totally innocent, but from my point of view the fact that my relationship with the older brother hadn't yet become romantic was mere coincidence, and I believed—incorrectly as it turned out—we would soon be boyfriend and girlfriend. Other kids in our suburban neighborhood had also started experimenting with alcohol and drugs, and I'd grown accustomed to watching some of my friends get drunk or high in the woods across the street from our house. Sex was a real issue too. Several of our high school neighbors bragged about their exploits, and two years later, we would know three girls—one in junior high and two in high school—who would get pregnant. At the time, my sister and I were largely immune to these dangers as my sister was very young and I was still too afraid to take any real risks. But my mother didn't know how prudish I was so she hid us in summer school, giving us less time to wander aimlessly around the neighborhood with everyone else.

The parents of two other girls who were the same age as my sister and me—Sarah and Abby Hoffman—must have had a similar idea because both of them were cooped up with us in the stuffy halls of Bridgewater East High School that summer. Thank God, too, because one of the only reasons those classes were tolerable was because we had each other to pass the time with. If I remember correctly, we had typing class first—around ten in the morning. Then we took a break, twenty minutes or so before computer class, to get a snack from the vending machines and gossip about the more troubled kids in our neighborhoods. It was during one of those breaks, long after our friendship had been solidified, that Sarah and Abby found out my sister and I were adopted.

"Why don't you look alike?" Abby, the younger of the two, asked us.

It was a fair question. Though my sister and I don't look drastically different, we don't look that much alike either. Katie has stick-straight long blonde hair, an oval face, and an adorable little nose. She is also quite petite. Back then she was so thin her knees were wider than her thighs. My dad used to call her "the bird" when we were kids, and though I never knew where the nickname originated, I always thought it was because her legs were as delicate as a bird's. On the other hand, even at the age of twelve, I already had curves. My breasts and hips were almost fully developed, and, though my sister said I had thunder thighs, in reality I was perfectly proportioned—so much so that I would soon come to be known as one of those girls who boys would describe as "perfect from the neck down."

It's not that I was ugly. It's that I was terribly awkward and totally uncomfortable in my own skin. I had tea-colored curly hair that I hadn't yet learned to control, a nose that was slightly too large for my face, a long chin that would mostly be corrected when I had jaw surgery in high school, and a prominent forehead. On top of all that, my skin had started to break out. Because of this, I knew my sister liked it when people noticed how little we looked alike, so I wasn't surprised at all when she was the one who responded to Abby's question.

"We're adopted," she announced with glee in her voice.

Sarah's response was immediate: "You are not!"

"Yes, we are!" my sister exclaimed.

"I don't believe you," Sarah insisted, and she was so adamant that I wondered if she and her little sister had discussed the idea beforehand. It was certainly possible given that Sarah and Abby were the opposite kind of sisters. They looked like the kind of siblings you'd see in the Sears catalog—they had the same thick dark hair that fell halfway down their backs, the same topaz-colored eyes, and the same lean limbs. Unlike Katie and me, they were a matched set.

"Why would we lie about something like that?" I asked.

"I don't know," Sarah said. "Maybe you want to trick us into telling other people or something."

I couldn't fathom what Sarah was saying: if we were friends, why would we want to trick them? And why would we want to get them to tell people something untrue about us? "That doesn't make any sense," I said, more interested in logic than any of my peers even at the age of twelve.

"Well, it doesn't matter anyway. What *does* matter is that if you were adopted, you wouldn't be normal. You'd be weird or something."

"What are you talking about?"

"Being adopted is just plain weird," Sarah explained.

"It is not," I argued, remembering clearly what I'd been taught. "Being adopted means you're special. It means that someone loved you enough to give you up and that your parents loved you enough to pay for you." The nervous look on my sister's face told me I was revealing too much, but that had never stopped me before. I really believed that being adopted meant we were special. I still do.

"They paid for you?" Sarah scoffed.

"Of course." I was astounded by Sarah's ignorance about adoption. She had always seemed smart before, but in that moment she lacked any knowledge about something that had forever been straightforward and simple to me. "They don't just hand you a baby for free!"

"That is *so* weird," Sarah said, and with that, Sarah turned on her heel and stomped off in the direction of the bathroom, Abby trailing right behind her and acting as indignant as an eight-year-old could pretend to be. I was convinced they'd never talk to us again, but the next day, it was like nothing had ever happened. And the four of us remained friends as long as we lived in New Jersey.

Sixteen years later, Dave and I were helping my parents clean out their basement when we found a bunch of paperwork from my adoption. Including a receipt for payment. That was the day I discovered exactly how much special costs.

Two hundred dollars.

That's what the adoption agency charged a young couple making ten thousand dollars a year in 1970.

Dave knew all of this—all of our history—and no matter how much I tried to avoid the subject of my mother after Paula's visit, he wouldn't be put off. "So what are you going to do?" he eventually asked me after I'd gotten off the phone with my mother that night.

I realized even if I couldn't call my mom and say the things I wanted to say, I had to do something.

"I'm not sure," I said. "Maybe I'll email her. It's too late to call back." It occurred to me, once I'd said it, that email was actually the best option. It would give me the chance to go over some of the details we didn't get to on the phone and allow me to do so without having to deal with any more of my mother's endless questions.

Dear Mom and Dad,

I just wanted to let the two of you know that everything went great with Paula this weekend. Besides feeling a little like I wanted to throw up while I waited for her flight to come in at the airport, it was smooth sailing. I really can't believe how easy it was.

Yes, she looks a heck of a lot like me, and we have much in common. Paula talks as much as I do, she's just as open as I am about everything (she's totally fine with the adoption and how everything has gone—it's amazing how well-adjusted she seems), and she also tends to lose track of time and run late like I do.

On the other hand, it looks like I got my desire to plan everything in advance from Mom. Paula was content to wing it, but I kept hearing a little voice in my head saying, "What are we going to do next?" Dave and Paula practically had to tie me down to the sofa.

Well, I guess that's all for now. Hope you are doing well. I'll talk to you more soon.

Molly

I considered signing the email, "Love, Molly" like I had the day before. I desperately wanted my parents to know how much they meant to me, how much I loved them, especially since one of my worst fears was that they would read Paula's visit as an attempt to replace them. But since I didn't usually sign my messages that way, I also worried they'd find it unusual. Would they think I was acting strange? Or, worse yet, would they see it as an attempt to alleviate my guilt? Because that's exactly what it would've been. The truth was I've never been the kind of person who signs messages with the word "love" or relies on predictable sentiments to express my feelings. In that way, I'm more like my dad, keeping my most important emotions to myself. Ultimately I opted to leave it out, instead trying to simply be myself, which, until that moment, had always seemed easy.

Dear Molly,

Your dad says hello, and we are both happy for you. You are at a perfect age and maturity to handle meeting Paula now, and I am glad it has worked out for both of you.

We already know from what you have told us about Paula's letters that she has many qualities and talents that you have inherited. She has the ability to feel comfortable around people. She is thoughtful and creative. One thing I would like to ask . . . has she ever played the guitar or a musical instrument? Oops, I think that was Katie's mom.

Molly, I am really glad Dave is with you for support. This is an important time in your life. Relax and enjoy it. It will be over sooner than you want it to be. And yes, there will be many questions that you forget to ask. A lifetime cannot be reviewed in a week end. Enjoy Paula and cherish her and her family.

I hope her flight home was a good one.

With lots and lots of love,
Mom & Dad

On the phone earlier that night, I'd told my mom that meeting Paula had made me realize I was too hard on them. But all I could think when I read her email message was that all my life I'd thought it was *my* birthmother who played guitar.

No wonder I could never carry a tune.

Both my sister and I wanted to take piano lessons when we were young, but, like most parents, Mom and Dad were hesitant about such a big investment. We had a four-bedroom Colonial with a landscaped yard and an in-ground swimming pool, and we vacationed at the Jersey Shore, but for some reason we still couldn't buy a used piano.

After much persistence, Katie and I finally convinced Mom and Dad to let the two of us enroll in piano lessons on a trial basis. For six weeks, we trudged a block up the street to practice what we'd learned on a piano at a neighbor's house. When the trial period was over, my mother kept promising to work on my father about getting a piano, but nothing ever came of it. Except that I can still do scales. And because of all the money my parents saved, we all get to vacation at their Florida condo for free, which even I can admit ended up being worth it.

Paula turned out to be the opposite way with money. She told us during her visit that she gave my biological brother Willie, who was twenty-seven at the time, enough money to buy a car even though he'd been arrested for drinking and driving and that, at the age of twenty-four, another of my biological brothers was still living at home.

My parents had high expectations for my sister and me. They wanted each of us to get a place of our own after college and claimed people who supported their adult children did them a disservice, citing a distant cousin who'd lived off his parents his whole life as evidence.

As it turned out, their tough-love approach worked—both my sister and I have been independent since graduation, never having to call their bluff. In that sense, my adulthood was nothing like those of my peers who came from well-to-do families. There was no trust account to fall back on, no bottomless bank account.

Of course, that doesn't mean there weren't incredible perks to being the daughter of a corporate executive—there obviously were. There was a pool in our New Jersey backyard after my Dad became a VP and a lake cottage not long after he took the job in Indiana. And I can't deny that having parents who paid for college was a tremendous gift. Not only did Mom and Dad pay for our education, they also bought us both new cars as graduation presents. They did that even though my parents had claimed to be staunchly opposed to such a practice right up until the day of my commencement and despite the fact that my grandfather had bought my mother a Karmann Ghia when she finished college. Oddly, I'd been reminded of that fact during Paula's visit.

"You'll never guess what Paula's first car was," I said to my mom when we talked on the phone that night.

She paused to think, and then in an energetic voice began to say the name of her first car: "A Karmann—" She stopped before she'd completed her words.

"Yes, a Karmann Ghia!" I said, forcing myself not to wonder why she'd hesitated mid-sentence. "Isn't that weird?" I was determined to smooth over my anxieties. "You both had the same car."

"We did?" she asked, disbelief in her voice.

"I guess that's something you shared."

My mother was silent on the other end of the line, making me wonder what had caused her to stop talking, what she was thinking. It occurred to me in that moment I had inadvertently compared her to Paula, something I had never wanted to do to either of them. And then the guilt came back to me all over again, and for not the last time, I found myself wishing Paula's visit had never happened.

My mom has a lifetime of memories with me. Good memories and bad memories, exhilaration and exasperation. The kind of memories of which families are made. We've shared forty-five years of being mother and daughter, for better or worse. That's no small thing.

The only thing Paula has that my mom doesn't is the day I was born. One single day that doesn't even hold a place in my memory. And when I think about Paula's visit—and the way she slowly ran her finger along the border of the picture from the day I was born—I know that Paula would have happily traded that one day for all the others.

Before she flew back to Virginia, Paula left a card behind with a small blue box, sneaking the gift into our bedroom when I wasn't looking. Dave was in on the plan. I didn't find it until after I'd emailed my parents. My name was written on the envelope, and there was a little flower drawn next to the scripted letters. I was relieved when I saw the card had a picture of Monet's "Pond Lilies" on the front.

3/12/00

Dear Molly,

Every day I offer a silent prayer of thanks that such life was placed in my hands and that now I am being blessed with the miracle of touching even a part of it.

I felt that perhaps this early birthday gift would be a gentle reminder to you of how much I treasure the gift of your life and hopefully the friendship we will share.

Happy Birthday today and every day.

Love,
Paula

Inside the blue box sat a delicate gold necklace with a Claddagh heart. I couldn't help but think, *if only it were silver.* In the car on the way back to the airport, I had complained to Paula about how my mother could never pick out gifts for me. "She doesn't understand what I like," I said, selling out my own mother for a quick moment of connection. But when I saw the gold necklace, I realized how wrong I'd been. Paula didn't know me any better than my mom. The cards were just a fluke.

After I closed the box and put it away, I thought about how Paula used the word blessed. It was the same way I'd heard my paternal grandmother talk so many times before. "We are so blessed," Grandma always said. My real grandmother, that is. On the other hand, L.W.'s mother—the only one of L.W. and Paula's parents still alive when I met them—never even knew I existed. Alice had been led to believe that Paula was going to a nursing conference the weekend she visited me. Back then, I couldn't accept that L.W. still hadn't worked up the courage to tell his mother the truth, and even today, I still can't fathom it. After all, I was the person who told my parents everything. But L.W., it seemed, hadn't even been honest with himself.

Ironically it was my grandmother's words that stuck with me in the days after Paula left. She'd written me before Paula's visit, and I took out her letter almost every day after she was gone.

Dear Molly,

We've been thinking about you and did try to call you once. I hope all is going well for you and Dave. I know your birthmother is coming to visit soon. It will be an emotional experience, and I will be anxious to talk to you. But no matter what, you belong to us.

We love you very much. Have a great visit and a very special love to Dave too.

Grandma & Grandpa

P.S. Get something you'd like from us for your birthday.

Grandma sounded so sure of herself. So proud. *But no matter what, you belong to us.* I had been worried that Paula's visit would cause doubts for everyone in my family. But Grandma was unshaken. To someone who didn't know her, that assertion may have sounded possessive or proprietary. But I knew she said it only because she was confident about who she was and what family meant.

My birthday was two weeks after Paula left, but she told me I was thirteen days late. No surprise since I clearly inherited my tendency for tardiness from her. As we'd hurried down the airport corridor to her gate only fifteen minutes before her flight home, she'd laughed about how she couldn't remember the last time she'd been to a flight so early.

I didn't see either my mom or Paula on my actual birthday that year. My parents were in Florida for the winter. They're retired and like to joke that they're spending my inheritance.

Dear Molly,

Happy 30th! Please don't be depressed about 30; you're still young and have much ahead of you...we're very impressed to see both you and Dave accepted with funding in two doctoral programs. You both have much of which to be proud. We're certainly very proud of both of you; it's a real achievement.

We're getting into the process of packing to come home but we should be able to make one more visit to Oxford. Let us know when the pressures of studying, etc. subside and we'll work on a date.

Happy birthday again, Molly; and we're very proud of you.

Love,

Dad and Mom

Paula made it safely back to Virginia that night. She called after I talked to my mother, saying I should fly out to see them soon. I reminded her that I don't fly and, just like I do with my mom, said,

"Remember?" before I could stop myself.

I couldn't sleep after talking to Paula. Instead I lay in bed wondering about all the changes that had taken place that weekend. And when the digital clock on the bedside table changed from 2:59 to 3:00, I realized that L.W. would just be driving home from closing the bar, reminding me again how different my life had been from theirs.

Dave and I had just accepted offers to study in the Ph.D. program at the University of Cincinnati, and L.W. had never even finished high school. I was the lucky one. So why couldn't I just forgive him?

Dear Molly & Dave,

Thank you for a wonderful week-end. It was all I expected and more. I feel like we've known each other for years. The two of you seem to share a special relationship. Continue to grow as the unique individuals you are, and I'm sure you will continue to grow in love as one. Be good to each other and love tenderly.

God bless,
Paula

P.S.—the money is for all the phone calls.

Paula's thank you arrived a week later, a twenty-dollar bill falling out of the envelope. "Damn it," I said out loud.

"What's that for?" Dave asked.

"Phone calls."

"How many phone calls did she make?"

"Not twenty dollars worth."

"It's our inheritance," he said.

"Very funny," I said, but I thought about what that word meant, *inheritance*, and I understood then that my birthright had been two-fold: what I had gotten from my parents—a love that never waivered—and what Paula had given me too, a life that could never be repaid.

And for the first time since she'd left, I felt not guilty, but incredibly fortunate.

PART THREE
THE LOST DAUGHTER RETURNS

SEPTEMBER 2000

Once Paula had visited us, it felt as if we had no choice but to visit her and the others in Virginia that summer. Because we were moving to Cincinnati in July, we planned the trip for late in the summer—mid-September, right before the start of our doctoral program—and decided we should spend a week visiting various people in D.C., Virginia, and New Jersey.

That was our first mistake.

It was really far too much to take on over the course of one summer, much less during a single seven-day trip. It wasn't the actual miles but the emotional distance we'd be traveling that was so overwhelming. Still, we were naïve enough to think we could squeeze everything we wanted to do into one big rolling vacation, and we set out for our journey not knowing what lay ahead.

Our second mistake was getting a late start. This was back before we'd perfected the art of getting on the road for a long car trip, and we often wouldn't leave for such journeys until the afternoon, meaning we'd arrive at our destination well past dark—even on summer nights when the sun could sometimes be spotted as late as nine. And our trip east that summer was no exception: we left late and had only traveled two-thirds of the way when the sun disappeared, and we decided to stop for dinner. It had already been an emotional day—because of our slowness and because we were heading toward one of the biggest moments of my life—when we came across a little roadside restaurant called Penny's Diner in LaVale, Maryland.

I had been struggling with my guilt all day. Why, I kept

wondering, did I feel it necessary to make this trip? Why had I even searched for my birthmother in the first place? I loved my parents completely and, therefore, had no void to fill in my life. But I had still insisted on finding out where I'd come from. The entire thing felt selfish and unnecessary, and I had spent most of that day—and, despite how well things had ended with Paula's visit, a big portion of the months since then—beating myself up about my inability to see that earlier.

So when we saw the neon pink Penny's Diner sign glowing in the dark, it felt like some kind of sign. Possibly a reminder of my guilt, but more likely a sign that we were doing the right thing, that my mother was with us—that day and always.

Penny's was a regular marketing mecca, selling t-shirts, mugs, and postcards, and I bought one of the latter for my parents while we waited on our burgers and fries. It was a card I would never mail, but one I kept all these years so I wouldn't forget where my head was on that hot summer night.

29 August 2000

Hi Mom and Dad,

We stopped at Penny's Diner on the way to D.C., and of course we thought of you. You would like it here—it's a lot like Dig's. We miss you already.

Love,
Molly and Dave

Mistake number three was sleeping on an inflatable mattress on our friend Kara's floor for two nights in D.C. Kara is a generous host, but once you've passed the age of twenty-two, it's never easy to get a good night's sleep on anyone's floor, even one belonging to a good friend. It was doable, and we survived, albeit a little bit worse for the wear. But it wasn't the best way to prepare for our first visit to the Tuckers' house. The lesson we learned from all that was not to do anything too taxing, especially something that requires you to lose much needed sleep, right before you meet your birth family.

So when we arrived in Annandale a few days later, we were a little bit tired, a little bit moody. Definitely not the best emotional state for such a momentous occasion. And to make matters worse, nothing could have prepared us for what we found.

We had gotten directions from Paula before our trip, so we went directly to the Tuckers' house when we arrived in Annandale. Paula had told me they lived in the country, so I'd imagined something pastoral and quaint: a hundred-year-old Victorian sitting in the middle of a wide field of corn and basking gloriously in the summer heat.

Instead of finding the kind of farmhouse I'd grown accustomed to in Indiana, the home we pulled up to lacked much in the way of character. The Tuckers' house was set into a slight incline with trees lurking around the perimeter and shading the structure in darkness. I had also imagined that theirs would be the only residence for miles—again, revealing my ability to romanticize their lives—when, in fact, houses intermittently dotted the road on either side. From the front, it appeared to be a ranch, but we would find out later that the attic had been converted so two additional bedrooms and a bathroom could be added upstairs.

We pulled around to the back where there were two cars pointed toward the yard like sentries. The house was situated on a corner lot, and we parked along the otherwise empty street that fenced in the Tuckers' property.

Paula had told us to come to the back door, yet another hint the Tuckers would be different from my own family where no guest— family or friend—went to the back door, whether it be their first visit or their last.

The back door sat in the middle of a medium-sized covered deck. There were a couple of cardboard boxes and a full laundry basket sitting near the door, and if we hadn't double-checked the house number out front, I might have worried we were at the wrong place. I looked at Dave one last time, a part of me hoping he'd suggest calling the whole thing off. But he nodded at the door in a resolved manner, so I went ahead and knocked.

Paula came to the windowed door immediately, and I saw she hadn't changed much in the five months since we'd last seen her. Still, I had yet to grow accustomed to how disheveled she always seemed. Not that I was any model of grooming myself. That spring I had aggravated a knee injury from a skiing accident a few years before, an unfortunate occurrence that kept me off my feet for eight weeks and pushed my weight up to its unhealthiest level ever. Needless to say, my self-esteem wasn't the best that summer, a fact that wasn't making the trip any easier. So even though I sighed when I saw Paula's glasses sitting in a crooked fashion across her nose, I also found myself pulling down my button-down shirt, making sure it covered as much of my too-tight skirt as possible.

"You made it!" Paula said as she opened the door. I could tell from the steadiness in her eyes that any nervousness she'd had during our first visit was nonexistent on her home turf. We were in her house, her world, a place where she felt loved and totally at ease. "Come in!" she gushed, shepherding us through the screen door and into a small dining room.

"I can't believe you're here," Paula said with a generous smile, pulling me into an embrace. She was as happy as I'd ever seen her.

"I can't believe it either," I said. "I never thought it would really happen." It was the truth. After meeting Paula and finding out more about the Tuckers, some part of me never believed we'd actually make the trip to Annandale, that we would put it off indefinitely, hoping to avoid what would certainly be an awkward reunion. But there we were. In Annandale, Virginia. In Paula's dining room.

Adjacent to the traditional-looking dining room was the kitchen—a throwback to the seventies with a linoleum floor, ancient appliances, dark cabinets, and a round Formica table.

"I'll show you the bedrooms," Paula said, "and then we should go. But we have to be quiet because L.W.'s sleeping on the couch."

L.W. Tucker. My biological father.

For the first time, the two of us were in the same place.

As we made our way down the hallway connecting the kitchen to the bedrooms, Paula poked her head into the living room and pointed at L.W., putting her finger to her lips so we'd know to be quiet. Even with his eyes closed, he looked exactly as he had in his pictures—tall, brusque, and manly. He had soapy gray hair just like my grandfather's and the matching gray mustache I'd seen in the pictures Paula sent me. His body was relatively fit for a middle-aged man, a feat probably helped dramatically by his unbelievable height. Paula had told me that he—like all his sons—was six-five. Though he was snoring softly, his square-shaped glasses still sat on his face.

My first glimpse of my biological father, and he was asleep.

I should have been disappointed, but instead I was relieved. In truth, I would have been happy to meet the whole family that way—each of them lying peacefully in their beds while I tiptoed from room to room like Goldilocks checking her charges.

"This is our room," Paula said, forcing me to catch up to Dave and Paula at the other end of the hallway. The master bedroom was pretty average for a house built in the fifties—big enough for a king-sized bed, but too small to include a walk-in closet. The blinds and curtains were shut, making it hard to see much, but I noticed everything was in its place. "And this is Jeannie's room," Paula said, turning to the next door. This room was more light-filled but still a bit dark. "Normally you'd stay in here, but I put you upstairs because the bathroom down here is under construction." Paula nodded at the third door in the hallway, and I peeked inside. The ceiling of the bathroom had caved in, and wet drywall was hanging from above. "Of course, that means you'll have to share with Wade," Paula said with a roll of the eyes, and, though it's always nice to have your own bathroom, I still figured Paula was overreacting.

"It's no big deal," I said.

"I can't take you up there now because the stairs creak, and I'm afraid we'll make too much noise." Paula looked me up and down when she said this. Was she implying *I* was the one who would make too much noise? "I don't want to wake L.W. But I'll show you later. Jeannie and I painted the room last week for your visit."

"You didn't have to do that," I protested.

"I don't mind," Paula said. "I wanted it to be nice."

It was exactly the kind of comment that made me feel overwhelmed with guilt. Paula had clearly cleaned the place from top to bottom, even gone to the trouble of painting. All that for the two of us. For me, really. And I was obviously not worthy of such generosity. Not only was I not sure I wanted to be there, I wasn't sure I would ever come back. It was more than apparent to me Paula should have spent her energy on someone else.

Margaret, who was still serving as our case counselor at the adoption agency, had recommended we all meet her for lunch the afternoon of our arrival. I wasn't sure if that was standard protocol or not, but I knew she wanted to help smooth our transition and make sure our visit was off to a good start.

Paula rode to Arlington with Dave and me, and we made small talk on the way. Looking back, it seems strange L.W. didn't come with us. Wouldn't he have been invited to such a meeting? But at the time it didn't occur to me that he probably should have been there. Even before I'd met him, I'd become so accustomed to his absence that I no longer questioned it.

We had lunch at a packed café, the tables pushed together to accommodate all of the customers, and settled on a small table—more suited for two than four—near the back of the restaurant. Not long after we'd ordered, two well-dressed professionals, a man and a woman, sat at the empty table next to us. Our tables were so close I could have reached over and taken a bite of their food if I'd wanted, and as soon as they sat down, I felt my entire body tense. They were African American, and I already knew Paula well enough to know there might be a problem. On more than one occasion, she'd gone off about the black basketball players at Virginia Tech, so I was immediately afraid she would say or do something inappropriate.

I glanced at Dave and could tell from the strained look on his face he had the same fear I did. We'd both been privy to Paula's rants. At the same time, Paula seemed oblivious, babbling on about the fundraiser for the twins and Jeannie's basketball career to Margaret, whose curious glances told me she'd noticed our anxiety level was increasing.

Our food arrived quickly, and I tried to focus on eating, but I had all but lost the ability to make conversation, so worried was I about what Paula might do or say. My nervousness seemed silly in some ways. I was no more accountable for Paula's actions than she was for mine, but I still felt some responsibility for her.

"Jeannie had to be there at the beginning of August—for practice," Paula told Margaret, still rambling on about Jeannie's life in college when the food arrived at the table next to us, and the man leaned over to ask if he could borrow the salt and pepper.

"Sure!" Paula said with a warm smile, handing the man the glass dispensers. At that moment, I thought we were safe. Paula had clearly seen the couple, so I felt confident she wouldn't say anything to embarrass us.

But I was mistaken.

Because a moment later Paula launched into one of her favorite tirades about Jeannie's roommate. Jeannie had landed her basketball scholarship to Virginia Tech as a result of her friendship with another high school ball player named Valerie, who'd been recruited first and then recommended the coach consider Jeannie for the team as well. That kind of gigantic favor might have caused other mothers to worship someone like Valerie, especially since Jeannie and Valerie were the only white players joining the team that year, but Paula's response to the situation was the exact opposite. Rather than appreciate Valerie's generosity, Paula focused on the fact that she believed Jeannie was the superior player and should've been signed first. She was constantly criticizing Valerie's game, her work ethic, and—most importantly—her choice of boyfriend. Valerie was dating a basketball player from Virginia Tech, and he was black.

"I just worry about Jeannie rooming with someone like Valerie," Paula said to Margaret as if she could read my mind.

I didn't even have to look at Dave to know he was thinking the same thing I was: Paula was going to say something she shouldn't. We'd heard Paula complain about Valerie several times when she'd visited us, so we knew what was next.

"Why is that?" Margaret asked cautiously in between bites of her salad, and I wanted to wave my arms and shout, *Margaret, no!* But it was too late. Paula had the opening she was looking for.

"Well, Valerie hangs out with a rough crowd," Paula said as she shook her head and took another bite of her sandwich. When she was nearly finished chewing, she went on. "She's always spending time with the black basketball players."

I closed my eyes, letting my disappointment fully sink in, and when I opened them, Margaret was looking at me with concern. She had warned me about the many ways in which I might be at odds with my biological family, but I still wasn't prepared for Paula to say something so overtly racist with two black people sitting not much more than a foot away from us. I was horrified but could do nothing more than send sympathetic looks to the other table. I also had trouble reconciling this Paula with the person who had so selflessly given me up.

Paula, refusing to notice the alarm on all of our faces, continued: "She's even dating one of them."

I stole a look at the table next to us, but the couple continued talking as though they hadn't heard Paula or, at the very least, didn't want to admit they had.

"I'm sure they have a lot in common," Margaret said. "You know, because of basketball." Margaret was clearly trying to turn Paula's comment around. It was an argument I'd tried to make the first time Valerie had come up, so I knew it was useless.

"Then why doesn't she date one of the white players?" Paula said with a laugh, oblivious to the fact that no one—at our table or anywhere else—was laughing with her.

"Paula!" I said, finally unable to keep my mouth shut.

"What?" Paula said skeptically. "It's true, isn't it?"

It wasn't true that Valerie should have to date one of the white players any more than it was true that black people shouldn't be served in the same restaurant as white people, but I also knew there was no point in saying any of that to Paula. So instead of telling her she was wrong, I set my fork down on my plate and hoped my behavior would indicate I was ready to go.

After lunch, Margaret lingered with us on the sidewalk outside, probably feeling a tiny bit guilty about the mess we were clearly in. At that point, I finally understood what she had been telling me during our interview the previous year—meeting Paula and L.W. was going to mean having a lifelong relationship of some kind with two people I had almost nothing in common with and might not even like.

"Be sure to keep in touch," Margaret said to me as she gave me a big hug. "You can call any time."

"I will," I said, holding on to Margaret as long as I could and wishing more than anything that Margaret had been my birthmother or—short of that—that she could accompany us on what was sure to be one of the most challenging weekends of our lives.

Paula hugged Margaret next, and then said, "I'll give you a call next week."

"Oh, I know *you'll* call," Margaret said with a laugh before she put her sunglasses in place and walked away, leaving the three of us to deal with the rest of the family on our own.

When we returned to Paula's house, the laundry basket and cardboard boxes we'd seen earlier had multiplied in a pod-like fashion. By then there were dozens of boxes and several piles of laundry scattered around the deck.

"Can you believe this mess?" Paula exclaimed without offering any explanation. Instead, she opened the door, and we followed her. As soon as we got inside, I saw a tall girl standing in the kitchen.

Paula turned back to me with a huge smile and said, "This is Jeannie," waving toward the girl who appeared to be trying to hide behind her. I'd seen pictures of Jeannie and knew she was a basketball player, but nothing could have prepared me for the lanky young woman lurking behind Paula. Even though she was stooped over, I could see she was as tall and slim as a runway model, a world apart from my unmistakable curves and at least five inches taller than either Paula or me.

"Hi," Jeannie said quickly, getting the word out almost without moving her lips. She seemed to not know what to say—or think— about me being there. She hung behind Paula like an overgrown child as if we hadn't already established a connection through email and over the phone. She was obviously nervous, almost distressed, about my being there. I reminded myself she was only nineteen, that it was probably totally freaking her out to meet her long-lost sister, and that she was most likely at a complete loss for what to do with any discomfort or anxiety she felt.

A more controlled person would have responded carefully, thoughtfully, but I blurted out the first thing that came to my head: "Wow, you're so tall!"

Jeannie's eyes lit up, and she didn't hesitate again. This was obviously a favorite topic of hers. "Wait till you meet my brothers," she said, genuinely delighted by the idea. "Every one of them is six-foot-five." I, too, was delighted because I'd found a way to reach a person I'd briefly worried no longer wanted to be reached.

"All of them?" Dave asked.

"Yup, my dad too."

I wondered, not for the first time, why I'd missed out on the height the others had been blessed with. "They told me I'd be tall when I was little," I said. "But I stopped growing around the time I was ten."

"Really?" Paula asked, glancing at me with suspicion in her eyes, obviously surprised. "But you're even shorter than me."

"I'm five-foot-six," I said, correcting her. "Same as you."

"Are you?" Paula said, the skepticism in her voice as obvious as her prejudice had been earlier. "I thought you were shorter than me."

"It might seem that way, but I'm not."

"Well," Paula said, "you wear it differently, I guess."

Paula's words stung. I knew exactly what she was saying—that I was heavier than she was and, thus, *appeared* shorter. The truth was she was thinner than I was at that time, but not by as much as she imagined. In fact, it was obvious I'd gotten my body from Paula. We were both a hair under five-foot-six and could stand to lose a few pounds. But we weren't totally unlike Jeannie either. The one thing the two of us had in common with Jeannie was that she, too, had inherited Paula's posture—none of us knew how to stand up straight.

"Did you see that mess outside?" Paula said, changing the subject to one the look on her face told me embarrassed her a bit. "That's all Wade's stuff. He's moving back in. I told him to clean it up before you got here, but he just keeps adding to it."

"Okay," I said, trying to remember which one was Wade.

Willie was the oldest, Clint came next, and Wade was the youngest brother. I tried to imagine a scenario in which my parents would have allowed me to pile all of my junk on the porch, even if we didn't have an important guest visiting, but I couldn't because I knew moving home after college hadn't been an option, much less leaving all of my stuff out in the open for the whole world to see.

"Why is he moving home?" I asked.

Paula rolled her eyes and leaned her head back as if the answer to my question were written across the ceiling. She glanced at Jeannie and sighed before she answered. "He wants to save money," she said as she shook her head. "I've never known anyone as tight as Wade in all my life. I don't know where he gets it. Not from me! For God's sake, he won't even turn on the lights in his apartment."

"He won't plug the refrigerator in either!" Jeannie said with a laugh, the easygoing person I'd gotten to know on the phone over the past eight months finally making an appearance.

"Why not?" Dave asked.

"He's too cheap to pay the electric bill. Didn't Mom tell you?" Jeannie asked me, picking up an apple that sat on the kitchen table. "Wade is not normal. He's . . . I don't know how to explain it. He's just different." Jeannie took a big bite out of the apple, backing away from us as she chewed.

"But if he doesn't keep any food in the fridge," I asked, "what does he eat?"

Paula didn't hesitate to respond: "He gets three hot dogs every single day for lunch from the hot dog cart outside his job," she explained, laughing a bit to herself as she thought about the strange routine of her youngest son. "He says that's all he needs, but I know he grabs dinner at the restaurant sometimes when he thinks I'm not looking. I'm just glad he got cleaned up, that he's not using anymore."

There were a million questions in my mind—Paula had told me Wade had a drug problem when he was younger though she'd never mentioned any of his other idiosyncrasies—but before I could ask any questions, the back door swung open, and a gangly young man lunged inside. He wore old jeans, a flannel shirt with the sleeves cut off, a dirty ball cap on his head, and a cigarette behind his ear. It was the same uniform, with or without sleeves, that I'd seen on him in every picture Paula had sent me. The only new detail I noticed was that the mullet spilling out of the back of his hat revealed hair that featured the same curls as mine.

It was Willie, Paula and L.W.'s oldest son.

"Hey," he said so softly I almost didn't hear him.

"Hi," I replied, sure that I would have to win him over in the same way I had with Jeannie. But before I could try to think of the right thing to say, Willie stepped forward, his arms extended, and took me into an awkward, if appreciated, hug. He was as tall as Jeannie had promised, and I had to stand on my toes to put my arms around him. After he stepped back, he reached for Dave's hand, and their flexed muscles told me it was a test of sorts. I was immediately glad Dave's handshake was stronger than one might have expected by looking at him.

"Welcome to the family, I guess," Willie said after the introductions were over.

"Thanks," I said.

Willie adjusted his ball cap, and we all looked around the room, not sure what to say next. "Well, I should get down to the bar," he said abruptly. "You got any money, Ma?"

It seemed rude to listen to their private conversation, so I turned to Jeannie and asked when she'd gone back to college.

"Two weeks ago," she said as she rocked back on her heels. She started to tell me about the all-day practices she'd had to endure once she'd arrived, but I was too busy eavesdropping on the conversation between Willie and Paula to pay attention. And when Paula took out her wallet, I was reminded yet again of how different the Tuckers and the McCaffreys really were.

Almost as soon as Willie was out the door, Clint showed up in his place. Wearing a blue-and-white baseball uniform, he seemed totally all-American, the kind of guy who never met a stranger, and that first impression ended up being completely accurate. Unlike his spindly older brother, Clint was more filled out, his tanned arm muscles standing out against his white sleeve like a testament to youth and vitality. The other difference was Clint displayed no sign of nervousness, walking into our meeting as confidently as I imagined he entered any situation in life.

"Hey!" he said in a warm and welcoming voice. "Isn't this wild? I can't believe how cool it is that we finally get to meet you." He held out his arms and gave me a hug more relaxed and natural than Willie's. When we parted, he took another look at me and said, "Wow, you look just like Mom." He turned to Jeannie. "Doesn't she?"

"Totally," Jeannie said.

"This is so wild!" Clint said, and I could tell Clint was going to be the easiest part of our visit.

After Clint went to his ball game, Jeannie showed us upstairs.

The slanted walls in the bedroom where we were staying had been painted a fresh coat of yellow, and a new quilt adorned the bed on the far side of the room. An upholstered rocking chair sat opposite the bed, and a coordinating yellow tufted pillow filled its seat. Jeannie plopped down in the chair and started chatting away as if I really were an older sister home for a visit. I couldn't help but wonder if we would've shared countless conversations in that very room if our lives had gone another way. It all felt so natural with Jeannie I almost forgot we had just met.

Wade's bedroom was located across the hall, separated from ours only by a bathroom and a small hallway. When I'd glanced that way as we climbed the stairs a few minutes earlier, I'd caught a glimpse of a rifle the size of a small child propped in a corner of the room. Not having any experience with guns, I wasn't sure if it was normal to keep one like that in a bedroom. But when I'd worked at the National Crime Prevention Council in my early twenties, I'd learned that the people most likely to die from a gunshot were those who slept in the same house with them, and as a result, the sight of that rifle made me feel even more unsettled than I'd felt when we'd arrived.

We hadn't even finished putting our bags away when Wade appeared in the hallway, looking like a washed-out duplicate of his oldest brother, the only difference being that his skin was untanned, his hair was a richer, darker shade of brown, and his clothes were more clean cut: he wore a short-sleeved button-down shirt and blue work pants. Wade was employed as an airplane mechanic at the time, and he even wore a pocket protector in his shirt. Rather than enter the room, Wade stood just outside it, filling the door frame from top to bottom like a voiceless guard.

"You can come in, Wade," Jeannie said in a tone that betrayed impatience, but Wade made no attempt to move forward. Instead, he looked from Jeannie to me and then to Dave, clearly surveying the scene before he committed to entering it. I was surprised to see that, unlike his sister and brothers, he displayed no discernible emotion on his face. He wasn't nervous or excited as they had been. He was just blank.

"I have to get something," he said cryptically and disappeared down the stairs before we could respond.

After that, Wade came and went while we unpacked our few things and talked to Jeannie. About fifteen minutes later, Wade finally came in the room, settling in the middle of the bare wood floor with his legs crossed. Like a curious turtle, his narrow neck stretched from side to side as the conversation ping-ponged between the three of us. When we paused to catch our breath, he took the opportunity to jump in.

"I like to use this pen at work," he said abruptly, pulling a gleaming silver pen out of his shirt pocket and holding it up for us to inspect. I had no idea where the comment had come from, but I studied the pen as if it were important. Once we'd gotten a good look, he shook it for emphasis. "But they won't let me. They say it's not the right kind. But it's such a good pen! What's wrong with it?"

I glanced at Jeannie just in time to see her roll her eyes at her brother and then looked back at Wade.

"Why won't they let you?" I asked, trying to express an interest in a topic that seemed to have come from another universe.

Wade turned his attention from the pen to me, inspecting my face without trying to hide what he was doing. "Mom says you're my sister," he said suddenly. "Is that true?"

"Wade!" Jeannie yelled, scolding her brother as if she were the older one.

There was nothing anyone could've said to prepare us for a comment like that or for the strange person who sat in front of us. What we'd been told about him—that Wade was "different"—was not even close to what we'd both later admit in private was the reality of the situation. Both Paula and Jeannie had gone out of their way to say the same vague thing about Wade being different, a comment repeated often enough by the two of them that we should have understood there was more to it than that. At the time, we'd taken it to mean he was odd or unusual. Like a goofy uncle or an eccentric cousin. But in that moment it was clear to us Wade was not like others. We would quickly learn he has many of the traits associated with autism: social ineptitude, coldness, paranoia, and obsessiveness. It's possible his condition is a mild form of autism, such as Asperger's, which would make sense given his work as a mechanic, but because no one wants to admit what's so apparent to the two of us, he has never been diagnosed or seen by a professional for his condition.

Still, that realization didn't help me have any idea how to answer Wade's question. What could I say? The truth was I still wasn't entirely sure if I was his full sibling or not. And how could I ever know for sure? I was forced to rely on Paula, to believe she was telling the truth, but could I ever be certain? I was the one who'd asked the same question Wade was asking as soon as I saw the first pictures of Paula and her family. I had expected to feel some connection that would make it clear I shared the genes of the people I was meeting, but besides some obvious physical similarities with Paula, what did we really have in common? Wade, despite his differences or maybe as a result of them, was posing the questions none of us had the courage to admit. Were we really related? Was this really happening?

My mouth had grown dry, and when I tried to speak, no words came out. I cleared my throat and finally worked up the nerve to say, "I guess so" even though, in truth, I was just as skeptical as he was about the whole situation.

Paula had left two gifts for us in the room—a t-shirt advertising the bar and the quilt she'd put out on the bed. I'd told Paula during her visit to Ohio about my mother's homemade wedding quilt and how I wished someone had made one for us when we got married. I'll admit I was more than a little surprised when I realized she'd remembered that conversation.

Dear Molly & David,

We missed your wedding, so we thought we'd give you our congratulations with a comfort of love. May you enjoy your visit with us and realize that you will always be welcome here.

Paula & L.W.
Willie, Clint, Wade & Jeannie

I wanted to be happy about how thoughtful it was that Paula had given us the quilt, but I couldn't get past the fact that, unlike my mother's, it looked like it had been made in a factory. I wanted to be the kind of person who didn't care about such details, but, in truth, I was exactly that kind of person. I was also horrified to see the size of the t-shirt. It was an XXL, two to three sizes bigger than the size I normally wore. And, as a result, I couldn't help but see that "gift" as an insult.

To make matters worse, Paula's request that we "realize that you will always be welcome here" made me uncomfortable. It was hard enough to visit the first time. I wasn't even close to ready to think about a second trip to Annandale. And the fact that Paula had redecorated a room for us made me feel like she was putting expectations on us already, expectations I simply wasn't ready to handle. Nevertheless, I had no choice but to accept the gifts and move on.

After getting settled, we decided to spend the evening at the bar. Unless I counted spying him when he was napping in the living room earlier that afternoon, I had yet to meet L.W., and since his work schedule forced him to sleep most of the day, it seemed like a good idea to visit him in his natural habitat. Jeannie and Wade wanted to drive separately from each other, and they suggested one of us ride with each of them. Immediately, I felt uncomfortable with the idea of riding with Wade, but I also couldn't fathom putting Dave in that position, especially since he's somewhat of an introvert and being in Wade's company might require him to do a good deal of the conversing. But Dave saved me from making that difficult decision when he volunteered to ride with my youngest biological brother almost as soon as the question came up. Later that night, after we were alone, Dave confessed he'd done it to protect me. Since we don't ordinarily fall back on those kinds of gender roles, his actions that night surprised me, but I understood, on that one occasion, he'd felt it was required.

Jeannie and I, as I soon found, had something else in common besides our poor posture—we're both leadfoots—and it wasn't long before we'd left the boys behind in a cloud of dust and Madonna music. As soon as I lost sight of the headlights of Wade's pick-up in the passenger side mirror, I began to worry if I would ever see either one of them again. After all, Wade was the one who kept a rifle next to his bed and had wondered out loud if I was really his sister. I would eventually find out Dave had experienced the same fear.

We arrived in the parking lot of the bar about fifteen minutes later, but it took another ten minutes for Wade's pick-up to arrive. When we went to bed that night, Dave told me that was because Wade meandered along the dark roads at twenty miles an hour like an old man who had lost his confidence behind the wheel. Though he felt pretty sure Wade was always a slow mover, he was never entirely certain Wade wasn't using the opportunity to ask more questions.

Once they were on the road, Wade had turned to him and said, "So…are you a foster child too?"

"No," Dave said, deciding not to elaborate or correct Wade when he said "foster" child. He figured the difference between being "fostered" and "adopted" wasn't going to make much sense to someone like Wade. And he also wondered if Wade even understood that the two of us were married or if he'd somehow gotten the false sense that we were brother and sister. Or did he think that if you were adopted, you had to also marry someone else who had been adopted? Or that adopted kids were just drawn to each other? Either way, it was clear we were as strange to Wade as he was to us. And Dave didn't try to correct that impression. Once he'd lost sight of Jeannie's car, he was more focused on getting to the bar safely than trying to get through to someone who seemed rather unreachable.

That was when Wade went back to the subject of our earlier discussion. "My mom tells me that Molly is my sister," he said, "and I'm trying to believe her, but I'm just not sure."

Dave told me that it seemed to him as if Wade simply couldn't comprehend how he could be related to me if he'd never met me before, that the whole situation was simply beyond his grasp. Rather than try to explain what might have been unexplainable, Dave kept quiet, letting Wade go on, which was how the conversation shifted from me to his job.

"They don't give me enough responsibility," Wade had complained. "They don't ever let me do what I want. My boss yells at me all the time, and it makes me so angry." Dave told me Wade's voice had risen in time with his emotion, so much so that he was almost yelling when he went on. "Sometimes I just don't know what I'm going to do about it!"

Never once did Wade glance over at his passenger while he was talking. Instead, he kept his eyes trained on the road as if he we were the only one in the cab, his voice permeating the dark air between them like a demon.

Dave would later reveal it was at that moment when he began to wonder if he would end up on the side of the road somewhere— abandoned, dead, or worse. He barely knew Wade or any of the Tuckers, and yet he'd found himself alone, on an unlit road in the middle of nowhere, with a young man who kept a rifle in his bedroom and who even his own family considered "different." He described it as a moment of near epiphany: when faced with a potentially life-threatening situation, all he could think was that the moment was interesting enough to warrant the end of his days.

As it turned out, there was no reason for concern. Wade raised his voice and got upset for a little while, but then the moment passed, the two of them traveling in silence the rest of the way to the bar.

It was an ominous start to the weekend.

For many months I'd worried about visiting the bar. What would someone like me—someone who hated to be around smokers and questioned the wisdom of anyone who was willing to wear a tattoo into old age—do in a biker bar?

It was a question that ended up being a moot point because, as it turned out, you do mostly the same thing in a biker bar that you do in any bar. You drink.

But before we could drink, I had to cross the only threshold that still stood before me on that trip: I had to walk in the door and introduce myself to the man who had helped conceive me.

Tucker's Hideaway is housed in a nondescript building that looks like a country roadhouse surrounded by an asphalt parking lot on three sides. It sits along an under-populated portion of Backlick Road in Annandale, Virginia, not far from the intersection of I-95 and the Capital Beltway. If it weren't for the white and red sign that stands fifty feet in the air bearing the name of the establishment, it would blend almost entirely into the wooded hills that sit behind it. As I walked from the parking lot behind the building to the front door, I noticed the structure also had several obvious additions as if it were more of a work-in-progress than a completed project.

As soon as we rounded the front corner, we saw the outdoor bar that made Tucker's famous to bikers far and wide. More than half a dozen old-fashioned stools sat underneath a wooden counter that ran along the front of the building like the tie-rail at an Old West saloon. Though I've been there other nights since then when the parking lot is packed with bikers from the edge of the boulevard all the way to the woods in back, that night there were only a handful of people hanging around—two sat on barstools, and the others stood politely around their parked Harleys as if the motorcycles themselves were participating in the conversation. It was immediately clear that, at Tucker's, Harleys were treated with as much respect as people.

There was also a tall man with a full gray mustache—a man I was almost sure was L.W. Tucker—standing behind the bar with a rag in his hand when we walked up, but he disappeared through the door that separated the outdoor bar from the one inside before we could make eye contact.

"That's my dad," Jeannie said before I could ask. "He's quite a talker, isn't he?"

I'd been raised in a household with a quiet father and was married to an introvert, but it was immediately clear to me that L.W. Tucker was going to give both Dave and my dad a run for their money in the strong and silent department. I knew he must have seen me, must have known who I was, but rather than introduce himself, he had retreated.

When we stepped through the front door, L.W. was down at the far end of the inside bar, making himself busy with the cash register that sat along a mirrored back wall.

Jeannie looked at me and rolled her eyes. She seemed to know as well as I did that he was avoiding me.

"Dad," she called across the bar, and L.W. turned in our direction, walking slowly toward us as he wiped his hands on the towel. "Dad, this is Molly."

L.W. extended his hand across the bar, and I reciprocated. "Hi," I said. There were two reasons for my brevity: I was experiencing the same kind of shyness I always felt around reserved men I didn't know, and I had enough experience with such men to know they didn't want to be the recipient of an overly effusive greeting.

"Nice to meet you," L.W. said in that confident, masculine way that only a man who's watched hundreds of John Wayne movies can do. I half expected him to cock his head and add the words, "little lady," to his greeting. I also noticed that he gave me a real handshake—firm but not so tight it crushed my hand, not like he was compensating for something the way so many other macho men do, but also not the reluctant half-finger grip intellectual men give when they have to shake hands with a woman they consider a threat.

"And this is Molly's husband, Dave," Jeannie said, gesturing gracefully at Dave in a way more appropriate for a game show hostess than a nineteen-year-old jock. It hit me then that Jeannie, almost as much as Clint, knew how to handle herself in awkward social situations. Sure, she'd been nervous when I first walked in the door that afternoon, but that was a momentary setback, one more indicative of her age than her confidence level.

L.W. took Dave's hand into what looked like a much stronger grip than he had given me, a test of Dave's manliness, I presumed. "L.W. Tucker," he said as if we didn't already know his name. Before there was time to say anything else or ask any questions—questions about why he hadn't stood by Paula when she'd gotten pregnant with me or about whether or not he was really my father or about anything at all—L.W. waved suggestively toward the back of the room. "Your mother's in the kitchen," he said to Jeannie as if hoping to send us in that direction and end the conversation. And after such a clear gesture, we didn't hesitate to move toward the back, taking a table next to the swinging door that led to the kitchen.

I'd known for months that L.W. was going to be hard to reach. Jeannie had said as much, and Paula's admission of L.W.'s hesitations about her trip to Ohio made it clear he wasn't going to welcome me with open arms. And just to be clear, that's not what I was looking for. Not then and not at any time. But, even though I'd been forewarned, his abruptness surprised me. It was as obvious to me then as it is now so many years later: L.W. Tucker wanted nothing to do with me.

For the next hour, the evening went smoothly. The four of us ate an unhealthy but satisfying dinner of chicken strips, fries, and cheap beer, and after the kitchen closed, Paula joined us at the long table we'd commandeered for the friends of Clint and Jeannie who were filtering in as the night went on. There were about a dozen of us sitting at the table by ten o'clock, and we talked about random things without ever getting too deep. It was a nice change from the gravity of the earlier part of the day. But it wasn't too much later when L.W.'s mother, appeared, causing my anxiety to skyrocket yet again.

Alice Tucker—affectionately known as "Miss Alice" to her patrons—was the founder and proprietor of Tucker's Hideaway. After high school, Alice Deming had moved to Washington, D.C. from her childhood home in Iowa, presumably to get away from the Midwest. She was working in a restaurant when she met Warren Steele, the man who would eventually father her two sons: Roy and L.W. Though Warren was married—a detail obviously omitted from the Non-Identifying Background Report—he was very possessive of Alice and expected her to be faithful to him. About a year after their second son was born, Warren didn't think L.W. looked enough like him, so he put the baby in the freezer, threatening to kill him over what he presumed was Alice's infidelity. Alice was so frightened by Warren's behavior that she packed up the boys and left D.C., supposedly traveling to Florida before eventually winding up in Annandale in 1950 and changing their last name to her mother's maiden name—Tucker—so Warren would never be able to find them. That was also when Alice began waiting tables at The Lawson Inn, the same place where Paula Hurley would be working nineteen years later when Alice's youngest son came home from Vietnam in his dress uniform one Christmas, causing Paula to fall for him and, eventually, get pregnant with me.

After working as a waitress for twenty-five years, Alice had saved enough money to buy the rundown building in Annandale that would become Tucker's Hideaway. It proved to be a wise investment, supporting Alice and L.W. for the rest of their days. The bar provided them both with employment, income, and in Alice's case, a home: Alice lived in the apartment upstairs for the second half of her life.

I'd learned all about Alice from Paula and Jeannie, so I knew full well that she was the kind of old biddy you didn't mess with. She ate bikers for lunch and chewed on hubcaps for dinner. Paula always claimed her mother-in-law hated her, mostly because Alice accused Paula of trapping L.W. into marriage by getting pregnant with Willie and breaking the family apart, which could have been perceived as the truth since L.W. never really reconciled with his brother after the two of them were married. Paula also claimed Alice routinely criticized her attempts to modernize Tucker's or bring more customers in with special events and, in general, acted like Paula was the worst thing to ever happen to her son. So it shouldn't be a surprise I distrusted Alice before I'd even laid eyes on her.

But more important than my feelings about Alice was the fact that she had no idea I was her biological granddaughter. Paula claimed L.W. never told Alice about me because she'd always expressed disdain for people who put their babies up for adoption. She supposedly equated it with abandoning them, but when I found out she had raised L.W. and Roy on her own, I realized her dismissive attitude about adoption was more about defending her own choices than anything else. Alice had been a single mom in the 1950s—a time when it was considered completely taboo to have a baby on your own. Back then, a woman who got pregnant and didn't have an illegal abortion would almost always give up her baby for adoption. As a result, Alice was an anomaly, and her identity as such must have isolated her from the more traditional members of her community. Except for a sister who lived nearby, she'd spent most of her life alone—just her and the two boys. It was clear to me that was the real reason Alice was so protective of L.W. Not because of any problem she had with Paula, but because if she ever lost L.W.—like she'd lost his father and, to some degree, his brother—there would be no one left.

All of these thoughts and many more were swirling in my head that night when the famous Miss Alice strolled up to our table at

Tucker's, but the most prominent thought in my head was whether or not Alice would recognize me as Paula's child. In the months since Paula had visited us in Ohio, I'd finally admitted to myself that I looked exactly like Paula did when she was younger, and it was hard to imagine Alice wouldn't also see our striking resemblance. That night Paula had sat down at the end of our table after she'd finished cleaning the kitchen, pulling up a chair right next to mine. I figured, side-by-side, the two of us probably looked like mirror images of each other.

"What's going on?" Alice asked when she stopped next to Paula, sweeping her eyes down the long table while she waited for her daughter-in-law to answer. Some might have mistaken her roving gaze for curiosity, but after growing up with one hard-nosed grandmother myself—on my mother's side—I knew what Alice was doing: she was looking for trouble, ready to pounce on anybody who was acting in a way she found distasteful. I found out later that Alice enforced a strict no-profanity policy at Tucker's, and the fact that she could accomplish this in a bar full of bikers said more about her tyranny than I ever could. But her eyes moved over me so fast I wasn't sure she'd even seen me.

"Nothing much," Paula said in a disinterested voice. I'm sure she was as anxious for her mother-in-law to leave as I was, though when I'd asked Paula if we should worry about Alice figuring out who I was, she'd waved away my concern with a nonchalant shrug. No, Paula wasn't worried about me being identified. She was worried about being the target of Alice's scorn.

"Well, I'm going to see what the kitchen looks like," Alice said without ever meeting Paula's eyes.

Paula's tone conveyed exasperation: "Whatever you want," she said with a sigh. It was clear Alice was checking up on her.

And before I knew what had happened, the woman who had given birth to my biological father was gone, the only sign she'd been there a galley door swinging on its squeaky hinges.

"Do you think she recognized me?" I asked Paula after the kitchen door had stilled even though I was pretty sure she hadn't noticed I was alive, much less that I was one of her descendants.

"Definitely not," Paula said with another dismissive wave. "She just thinks your one of the kids' friends." Alice was surely used to seeing Jeannie and Clint's friends at the bar, but it was still hard for me to believe anyone could have missed how much Paula and I resemble each other, especially someone who knew Paula when she'd been my age. But for whatever reason, Alice had been oblivious to my presence.

When I revisit that night now, I feel certain Alice never really looked at me or anyone at our table. She'd been so intent on uncovering wrongdoing or trouble that she'd passed right over the biggest secret of her son's life—even as the human embodiment of that secret sat right under her nose.

The karaoke began after Alice had finished her inspection of the kitchen and made her way back upstairs for the night. It was an event I'd been dreading for months—since Paula's visit to Oxford and the afternoon when she'd first told us that the whole Tucker clan sometimes sang "Family Tradition" together.

As it turned out, my fears were unwarranted.

There was no family sing-along.

No Hank Williams Jr.

No moment when I was dragged up on stage against my will to perform a song about family with six people I barely knew.

No, the awkward moment I had pictured, thankfully, did not materialize. Maybe it didn't happen as often as Paula had implied, or maybe my presence had changed the dynamic of the entire evening. Whatever the case, the event I had worried about for so long was, at least at first, more entertaining than frightening—a welcome reprieve from the small talk we'd been forced to make the first ten hours we'd been in Annandale.

Jeannie was the first to sing.

I would soon learn Jeannie never passed up an opportunity to get up in front of a crowd, and though, like Paula and I, she lacked the ability to hit every note, she was enough of a ham that no one noticed. In fact, she was a born performer—confident, bold, and attractive. A world apart from the person I'd been at nineteen. Her self-assurance mystified me. Why hadn't I had any of her bravado at that age?

One of the reasons I suspected the "Family Tradition" tradition had been skipped as a result of my being there was because the rest of the performers seemed to be following a script: as if it had all been done before. So I wasn't surprised when Paula got to her feet and headed for the stage half an hour later. Before she left the table, she leaned over to me and said, "This is the song I *always* sing. Try not to be too shocked, okay?"

I smiled but was a bit put off by Paula's warning. It wasn't as if I were a delicate flower, and I thought my being there—in a biker bar with people I barely knew—would've clearly demonstrated that. Little did I know that, in the end, I would have to admit Paula had been right to warn me. Because even after all the surprises we'd encountered—after the laundry on the back porch and the guns in the bedroom, after the biological father who hoped to ignore me out of existence and the brother who lacked the ability to understand how I had come to exist—even after all that, Paula still managed to surprise me that night.

Microphone in hand, Paula mounted the stage like a much younger woman and announced her intentions to the audience: "I'm sure most of you have already guessed what's coming next," she said. "I'm going to do an old favorite of mine: 'Ode to My Car.'"

It wasn't a song I was familiar with and I didn't think it fit Paula's personality to serenade something as material as a car, but the crowd whooped and hollered like it was the best thing they'd heard all night. I leaned over to Dave. "What is it?" I whispered in his ear.

"I have no idea," he admitted, his voice betraying his apprehension.

As the happy-go-lucky notes warbled out of the amplifier, I realized that, unlike the other country songs that had been sung that night, Paula's had a reggae sound, but I quickly learned it was no Jamaican anthem.

Before I could figure out any more about it, Paula leaned into the microphone and howled at her audience: "Piece of shit car," she sang, the word "car" blowing across the bar room like a foghorn. She was not as assured or as on key as Jeannie but every bit as brazen, and I can honestly say the crowd went wild. People were hooting at Paula and slapping their tables like a seductive bare behind. A fifty-something woman cursed at them, and they acted like she'd taken her clothes off.

I glanced at Dave, and he offered me a hangdog grin, a look that told me Paula had exceeded even his low expectations, but he was trying his best to play along.

Paula went on: "I got a piece of shit car. That fuckin' pile of shit never gets me very far."

It was the face of L.W. I jumped to next. He was standing in the same spot he'd been all night—leaning against the back bar, his arms folded across his chest in an authoritative fashion. I'd heard all about L.W. and Alice's no-cursing policy, so I was surprised to see a small smile creeping across his countenance. Clearly the rules didn't apply if you were family because instead of stopping Paula's impression of a foul-mouthed sailor, L.W. appeared to be enjoying it.

And Paula went on without the slightest bit of hesitation: "My car's a big piece of shit 'cause the shocks are fucking shot."

I can honestly say I'd never expected to experience a moment like that one in life. It was true I had been spared the awful indignity of having to perform like a trick pony with the Tuckers, a fate I'd feared ever since I had first met Paula, but in that moment—the moment when I heard the woman who had given birth to me, the woman whose genes I shared, tell her titular car it could lick her "sweaty nut sack"—I no longer felt as if I'd avoided even a single iota of humiliation.

In truth, it seemed quite the opposite had occurred: Paula's ballsy rendition of a foul-mouthed song written by a child-like comedian was, in fact, my criminal sentence. Rather than getting a dispensation for my sins, I was instead serving my long-overdue and much anticipated penance.

We were so tired by the time we got back to the Tuckers' house that we got a good night's sleep despite the bizarre events of the previous twelve hours. And thankfully no one woke us any earlier than we would've liked. If we'd been spending the weekend with my family, I know someone would've accidentally banged against our door or the phone would have rung, but the Tuckers' house was as quiet as a monastery in the earliest hours of the day. It seemed no one in their family was a morning person, and I felt more than a little relieved to note something else we had in common.

When we eventually made our way downstairs, we found Jeannie sitting in the kitchen.

"I think we should go out for breakfast," she said rather than offering an artificially cheerful good morning, and I realized Jeannie was our kind of people: down-to-earth and real. "There's nothing to eat here, but I know a coffee shop that has awesome bagels. Mom wants to go too."

"Perfect," I said, happy to have the opportunity to do something we were accustomed to rather than venturing into more of the unknown. After an evening of Harleys and karaoke, a morning of bagels and caffeine sounded like bliss.

At the coffee shop, the four of us talked for over an hour, long past the time it took to eat. It was probably the most relaxed I had ever felt with Paula. It was clearly Jeannie who was putting us all at ease. As I had sensed earlier, she was not only laid back but also the kind of person who made people feel comfortable being themselves. And I wasn't the only one who felt more relaxed with Jeannie. Paula was also different—less anxious and more willing to listen.

Even though Dave was with us, we discussed girly things like makeup and menstrual cycles, reminding me yet again why I was so happy to be in a relationship with a man who didn't bristle at that kind of talk. I had my period that weekend and had to take a small mountain of ibuprofen with my giant bagel to ward off cramps.

"I could honestly eat another one of those," I said after we were finished eating. "You can't get bagels like that in Ohio."

"But you have to be careful," Paula said, "and watch what you eat."

It was similar to the comment Paula had made to me during our first weekend together, and I had the same response the second time as I'd had the first: I wondered why in the hell Paula thought she had any right to tell me what to do. Though I knew my parents had noticed my weight gain and we discussed exercise constantly, the two of them had never in all of my thirty years come out and said I needed to watch my weight or put any pressure on me to diet. It was as if they knew instinctively that doing so would be bad form— unhealthy for me and for our relationship. If anything they had done the opposite: battling me fiercely when I experimented with dieting and fasting as a teenager. Sure, they'd nibbled on my confidence in other less obvious ways, mostly by constantly praising my sister's thin frame, but Paula was trying to take a huge bite out of my self-esteem. What galled me more than anything was how parental she sounded when, in truth, I believed she had forfeited the right to act like my parent the day she gave me up. Of course, I couldn't say any of that out loud, but I could push back against her suggestion.

"When I have cramps this bad, I let myself eat whatever I want."

"You get bad cramps?" Jeannie asked, thankfully changing the subject whether she intended to do so or not.

"The worst," I said.

"Me too!" Jeannie said, as thrilled as she might have been if she'd found out we both like the same kind of music.

"Really?" I asked, wondering for the first time in my life if my grueling periods were the result of genetics rather than simply being caused by bad luck.

"They're awful! I'm doubled over in pain and can't do anything. I spend at least a whole day in bed every month."

"That's *exactly* what it's like for me."

Without thinking, we both looked expectantly at Paula, waiting for her to confirm our unspoken suspicions.

"I used to get 'em bad, real bad, but ever since I got pregnant with you," she said, nodding her head in my direction, "I haven't had a problem. My skin used to break out something awful, too, but after I got pregnant, my hormones balanced out."

I'd had terrible skin and nightmarish periods all of my life, and yet Paula was telling me it all could have been avoided by getting pregnant when I was young.

"Maybe I should get pregnant," Jeannie said with a chuckle, and I didn't tell her I'd been thinking the same thing.

Jeannie whisked us off to the mall for the afternoon, continuing our reprieve from the topsy-turvy world of the Tuckers. I had wanted to visit a Nordstrom during our travels but hadn't had time to do so in D.C. and was shocked to learn there was one not fifteen minutes from the Tuckers' house. It seemed ironic to me that had I grown up in Annandale with Paula and L.W., who appeared totally disinterested in the world of fashion and trends, I would have had easy access to such amazing shopping, but that spending those years with my family had meant that in high school we were nearly an hour from the clothes and goods my mother and I desired. Nordstrom was, in fact, the epitome of my mother's desires. She would ooh and aah every time I mentioned going to one and was always seduced by the piano player and attentive sales people whenever we went together. It was for this reason I thought of my mother when we arrived in Nordstrom that afternoon.

I had been plagued by an overwhelming sense of guilt ever since I'd first learned of the Tuckers' identity, but I noticed that afternoon that those feelings had subsided to some degree over the past twenty-four hours. Once I had seen Paula and her family on their home turf, I understood how little of a threat they were to my own family. No, the feelings of guilt were not gone—and they would never be entirely absent from my life—but they had been seriously diminished by my certainty that these people, though an important part of my life, were never going to be *my* people. They were *never* going to replace my family. And though I had not once suspected or imagined they would, meeting all of them allowed me to understand that on a more visceral level.

Paula had planned a blowout for that night—two kegs, countless bags of potato chips and pretzels, and an unending stream of friends: friends of the kids, friends of Paula's, friends of friends, friends curious to meet the long-lost daughter, friends looking for some free beer, and on and on. It quickly became clear that Paula saw the evening as a way to introduce me to all of the people in her life, but I wasn't entirely sure I was ready for such a big production to be made out of my visit. Still, what could I say? That I didn't want Paula to throw a party in my honor? That I didn't want to meet her friends? I really couldn't say anything unless I wanted to hurt Paula's feelings, and I had no desire to do that. So I smiled when Paula told me about the evening and steeled myself for a night of shaking hands and making small talk. But before I would have to endure being presented to dozens of people I didn't know, there would be another test—an old-fashioned crab bake.

Paula had ordered what seemed like hundreds of crabs and invited her kids and siblings to join us on the back deck of the house for a casual dinner. It was late afternoon when we sat down to eat, the sun still blazing overhead, but the picnic table was situated under the covered part of the deck, giving us some relief from the sun and allowing a gentle breeze to blow through. The activities of the day had relaxed me, and I can honestly say I felt comfortable at the Tuckers' house for the first time since we had arrived. In many ways, it was my kind of get-together—good food, good beer, and, as I would soon learn, good company. Paula had invited the two siblings of hers who lived within driving distance—Charlie and Sue. I sat at the head of the picnic table with Jeannie. Charlie, Sue, and Sue's boyfriend were on the side facing the back of the house while Dave and Clint held down the other side. The seven of us sipped our beers, snacked on rye bread and some kind of dip, and let Paula wait on us. I wouldn't have acted that way anywhere else—not offering to help— but I went along, not wanting to rock the boat.

"I know you've had crab at least once," Paula said to me as she brought more food to the table before turning to Dave. "But you've never eaten crab before, have you?"

"Not that I can remember," Dave admitted.

"Never? You've *never* had crab?" Jeannie exclaimed, clearly unaccustomed to dining with people who didn't have a lifetime of experience with the culinary treasures of the Eastern Shore.

It was the kind of emphatic statement I knew drove Dave nuts, but rather than express discomfort with Jeannie's surprise, he played along, acting just as appalled as Jeannie over his inexperience. "Never!" he said dramatically. "My God, it's like I've never really lived!"

"It's true," Jeannie said. "I've been eating crab since before I could walk."

"We all have," Paula said as she set a second heaping platter of crabs on the newspaper-covered table and squeezed onto the bench between Clint and Dave.

"It's a lot of work," Paula said. "But it's worth it. You'll need a mallet, a knife, and a whole pile of paper towels." Paula nodded at the equipment on the table and speared a crab with her fork, dumping it on my plate. "I'll help you," she said to Dave, "and Jeannie can help Molly."

I knew having someone help him eat his dinner would irritate Dave, too, but I had to give him credit. He had his game face on and allowed Paula to guide him through the procedure with grace and appreciation.

The others started working expertly on their crabs, while Paula and Jeannie dictated instructions to the two of us. I had little understanding of what I was doing, so Jeannie did most of the work, and when I glanced over at Dave, I saw he was letting Paula do the same. Once everyone had gotten to the meat, the conversation began again.

"So," Paula's brother Charlie asked us. "What do you two do?"

Glad for the break from eviscerating the poor crab in front of me, I jumped right in. "We're studying fiction writing in grad school."

"You mean, like short stories?" Charlie asked. "Novels?"

"Exactly," I said, surprised by Charlie's intelligent response since most people had no idea what it meant when we told them we wrote fiction.

"Wow," Sue added, "that sounds wonderful."

As if on cue, Paula said, "Is that for the newspaper?" even though I'd told her on more than one occasion that Dave and I were both trying to sell our work to literary journals and publishers.

"Lit mags, Paula," Charlie said without a trace of disappointment in his voice, and I made a mental note to learn from Charlie's ability to instruct rather than judge. "You've probably never even heard of them since they refuse to sell most of them in the big bookstores."

I was truly dumbfounded. Not looking entirely different from any other middle-aged man you'd see on the street, Charlie had a bushy full beard, the same plastic old man glasses L.W. wore, and a Brillo pad on top of his head. If it weren't for the tie-dye t-shirt he sported that night, he would have totally blended in with his surroundings. But Charlie, it seemed, was one of the few old hippies who hadn't sold out.

Charlie continued: "All those guys care about is money."

"It's just another way for The Man to keep us down," Dave said with faux outrage, causing everyone at the table to laugh. Initially, I wasn't sure if he was making fun of Charlie or agreeing with him, though I knew he despised the corporate takeover of booksellers as much as anyone. In the end, I decided it was a little of both. He was reveling in Charlie's anti-establishment views while also finding a bit of entertainment value in his beatnik persona.

"What do you do, Charlie?" Dave asked, more interested in the conversation than he'd been since we'd arrived.

"Me?" Charlie asked, grabbing another crab from the pile. "Oh, I don't do anything like you guys do. I used to paint, you know, for real. But now I just paint people's houses."

"You still paint!" Paula insisted.

"Yeah, Charlie!" Sue said.

"Not anymore," Charlie said. "Not like I used to. Not like Jimmy." As the only one of Paula's siblings who had moved away from the area, Jimmy was also the only one of Paula's siblings who wasn't present that night. He'd moved to New Orleans years before and didn't often make the trip home. Paula had made him out to be a bit unreliable, but as Charlie implied, they all saw him as the family's true artist. It was Charlie and Jimmy who were supposed to be the genetic link to my own artistic talent. I had picked up my first paint brush before kindergarten and made a study of art from the time I was five until the summer of my twenty-eighth year, just two years before, when I had decided to abandon my job as a graphic designer for creative writing. And meeting Charlie made me wonder if I hadn't inherited more from him than my love of art. Perhaps my progressive outlook on life had been passed down through my genes after all. Was it possible that I might have a real connection with these people?

"Oh, phooey," Sue said, playfully shoving her brother.

"I'm just saying," Charlie argued as he whacked his crab with a mallet. "It doesn't pay the bills."

"It doesn't for most people," Dave said.

Charlie put down his mallet and looked directly into Dave's eyes. "True, my friend," Charlie said. "*Very* true." And it seemed that, in Charlie, we had indeed found a compatriot, a friend.

The other guests started to arrive just as we'd finished clearing the table, pouring absolutely everything—the plates, the shredded newspapers, the dirty paper towels, the empty beer cans, the shaved-clean corn cobs, and the discarded crab carcasses—into a giant trash can as if there were no concerns about the environment, land fills, or global warming.

After an hour of being introduced to people, I felt certain I would never remember anyone. But Paula leaned over and offered a comment that made sure there would be at least one person I wouldn't be able to forget.

"I see that Olivia isn't here yet," she said with a snort.

I didn't have to ask who Olivia was. Paula had told me all about Clint's girlfriend. A local equestrian, from Paula's point of view, Olivia acted like she was too good for Clint. Olivia's family was well off, and Paula always got the feeling they didn't want their daughter to marry a young man whose parents owned a biker bar. I could understand why some people would have such an objection, but ultimately I agreed with Paula: they should no more judge Clint by what his parents did than anyone should be judged by their parents. But at the same time, I judged Paula and L.W. for their affiliation with Tucker's Hideaway, didn't I? It wasn't exactly the same thing, but, still, wasn't that judgment almost as bad as the one Paula thought Olivia's parents were making?

"Maybe she's just running late," I said, hoping that was the case and that Olivia wasn't as superficial as Paula made her out to be.

"Trust me, she's not running late," Paula said. "She knows she can show up whenever she wants, and Clint will still fall all over her. She knows he worships her and takes advantage of that." Paula took another sip from her beer and went on. "She just doesn't see Clint as worthy of her respect."

A big part of me didn't trust Paula's assessment of Olivia. I had heard her criticize Jeannie's roommate and other of her kids' friends before, so how was I to know if her appraisal was accurate or not? If nothing else, I was sure it wasn't objective.

Some time during the dizzying array of introductions, we met a friend of Charlie and Paula's named Dominic. Like Charlie, Dominic had a beard and glasses, and though he wasn't as clearly anti-establishment as Charlie, I wouldn't have been surprised if, at one time, Dominic had hated The Man as much as the best of them.

"Paula tells me you two are in graduate school," Dominic said, not long after we started talking to him. It was a refreshing change from the negative comments we often got from family and friends, who never hesitated to ask us if we'd ever be finished with "college" even though we'd earned our Bachelor's degrees eight years earlier.

"We are," I said, "but sometimes I wonder if it's worth it."

"Of course, it's worth it," Dominic said without hesitation. "You can't underestimate the value of an advanced degree."

"If we ever get jobs," Dave said.

"Oh, you'll get a job," Dominic said with the kind of confidence normally only reserved for parents and spouses.

"We have to finish first," I said. "And we're just starting the Ph.D. this fall. That can take years. We're not even sure we *want* to finish. The only thing we know for sure is there's not a whole lot you can do with a Master's degree in creative writing." This was the truth. Though we were going to start a doctoral program in three weeks, we kept telling ourselves that we could always quit, that studying creative writing wasn't necessarily about the degree as much as it was about finding time to write. My parents hated when I talked that way. They had always foreseen a future when my sister and I had graduate degrees, and they were still irritated I had quit my first attempt at grad school—back when I was only twenty-three and still interested in graphic design—without even finishing a whole year. And, as a result, telling them I wasn't sure if we would ever finish the Ph.D. aggravated them to no end.

"You *have* to finish," Dominic said. "You don't want to do all that work for nothing." This was a somewhat typical response—the kind we got from both my parents and all of the people we knew in academia though other people in our life, less educated people, sent the opposite message: that we were crazy to stay in school so long. Or else they simply acted disinterested, which was Paula's response. But Dominic's attitude was less frustrated than that of my parents and more supportive than the naysayers. In that way, he seemed like a genuinely nice person. And realizing that forced another, much uglier thought into my head: why couldn't someone like Dominic have been my biological father? I had always imagined that the people who'd made me would be both highly intelligent and creative. It was clear that one of the benefits and drawbacks of being adopted was that the adoptee invented these kinds of elaborate fantasies in which long-lost parents were as perfect as Mary Poppins and Mike Brady.

On the one hand, these fantasies could allow a child to see the whole world as available to her in a way that children who are not adopted often don't experience, their dreams sometimes hindered by the accomplishments of their parents. On the other hand, it allowed adoptees to have the false sense that their biological parents MUST have more in common with them than their adopted parents, a fact which is often far from the truth. Sure, I had Paula's athletic body and poor posture, but I had my mother's thoughtfulness and social skills and my father's love of books and critical thinking. What I didn't understand until I met the Tuckers was that, in truth, I was much more like my parents than I was like Paula or L.W., and my fantasy of finding people who looked and acted just like me was just that: a fantasy. And not only did I have to accept Paula and L.W. for who they were, but I also had to accept my parents on their own terms. It's easy to talk about that lesson now as I look back, but at the time it was a difficult reality to accept.

As it turned out, no one would ever be just like me.

The other person who stood out that night was Kalea.

Kalea was Paula's niece and Jimmy's twenty-five-year-old daughter, his only child, and she was visiting from the Virgin Islands where she lived with her mother at the time. Paula had been raving about Kalea all night, and when she arrived, she was as mature and fun as Paula had promised. As soon as I met Kalea, I felt as if I had known her for years. And just as if she felt the same way, she handed me a card that she'd apparently picked out before we'd even met.

Molly,

I have been very anxious to meet you. You are very courageous to come all this way to find all of us. We are all very glad for it. You are very much loved here, even before we've met you!

I hope you enjoy your stay.

Your friend (and cousin),
Kalea

"Kalea's an artist too," Jeannie said after I finished reading the card.

"Like your dad?" I asked.

"Well, I'm not as talented as he is," Kalea said. "But I try." It seemed that Kalea got her modesty from her Uncle Charlie and everyone in the family put Jimmy on a pedestal, a fact that made me wary of their praise. "So what's it like for you to meet all these people?" she asked, shifting the attention away from herself. "To meet a whole new family? Are you completely freaked out or what?"

Kalea's question was the first time that weekend anyone had acknowledged what I was going through. I was obviously freaked out, and I liked that Kalea was smart enough to get that. Of course, that didn't mean I could fully admit my reservations—to her or anyone else at the party.

"It *is* kind of surreal," I said, trying to be as bland as possible in my response.

"I know," Jeannie said with a twisted face, "it totally is."

I had known all along how weird it was for Jeannie and her brothers to find out about me. After all, how bizarre would it be to discover the parents you thought you knew everything about had kept a secret like that your entire life? And that they'd had another child, a sibling you didn't even know existed? That kind of discovery would be more than a little bit off-putting to anyone, and I imagine it was even more of an adjustment for people like the Tuckers who lived a very straightforward, traditional life—a life in which family was the center around which everything revolved.

"How surprised were you when you found out?" I asked Jeannie.

"Are you kidding?" Jeannie said. "I thought it was insane. I just started laughing. I couldn't believe that my parents, my mom, had done something that wild. I always saw them as so straight-laced."

"Exactly," Kalea said. "Not Paula! She's such a goody two-shoes."

"But your dad knew the whole time," I said to Kalea.

"I guess so," Kalea admitted, but the surprised look on her face told me it was a detail she had neglected to process.

"That's what amazes me," I said. "All of these people kept it a secret for so long. Charlie, Sue, your dad." I nodded at Kalea. "Weren't they just dying to tell someone?"

"You know what?" Jeannie said. "I always knew something wasn't right."

"Why?" Kalea asked, stretching the word out and opening her eyes dramatically. The two of us gawked at Jeannie while we waited for her answer.

"Well, I never told anyone this," Jeannie began, lowering her voice, leaning closer to us, and using a conspiratorial tone, "but every time we go to church, Mom cries. Every single Sunday. And I never knew why. Sometimes I would ask her what was wrong, and she would say it was nothing. But I think I always knew something was really hurting her."

Immediately I felt the implications of Jeannie's revelation in my gut. Though I know she hadn't meant to upset me, I still felt like I had been sucker punched. Paula had cried every week? Could it really have been over me?

"And you know what else?" Jeannie continued. "She doesn't do it anymore. I don't think she's done it since last summer."

Last summer.

That was when I had first contacted Paula. It was a time I'd been thinking about a lot over the past twelve months, wondering if I'd made the right decision, especially once I found out the Tuckers were so dramatically different from almost everything I knew. But in that moment, any regret I felt about finding Paula felt supremely selfish. If I hadn't wanted to admit it to myself before, I had no choice but to admit it then: Paula had been waiting for me to make contact all of my life.

And, after all those years, I had finally made what was wrong in her life right.

Kalea was hoping to become a graphic designer, so that was something else we had in common. At the time, I thought I had an easier time connecting with people like Kalea, Charlie, Sue, or Dominic simply because I had more in common with them, but now

I understand it was easier to connect with them because there were no expectations. If I never spoke to any of them again, if we never again crossed paths, it wouldn't really matter, it wouldn't really offend anyone or reflect on our relationship in any way.

But with the Tuckers, there were expectations: expectations of phone calls and visits, of gifts and holidays, of love and support, but most importantly, Paula made it obvious she expected me to make a lifetime commitment to being a member of her family. The pressure to do so was so great, so constant, that I felt as if she'd be sitting me down to sign a contract before I left the next morning. To be honest, it was completely overwhelming and totally confusing. I already had a family. I already had a place where I spent my holidays and vacations, people I called when I wanted to share good news and bad, a house I called home. But Paula didn't seem to understand that. It was as if she expected, after all those years, I would be moving in with them. She had lived in a suspended state of waiting for me to make contact with her, but during that time, I'd had an entire life of my own. And the idea that Paula just couldn't understand that scared me more than anything else in my life ever had.

I was enjoying the party to some degree. I had made unexpected connections with so many people—Jeannie, Clint, Charlie, Sue, Dominic, Kalea—but at the same time I never felt entirely comfortable in the world of the Tuckers. There were lots of people there who hadn't spoken to me, and I could see them taking sidelong glances in my direction, sizing me up and passing judgment. Willie's friends, especially, seemed to keep their distance. And why wouldn't they? I was about to start work on my Ph.D., and these kids spent their nights sitting at the counter at Tucker's, drinking cheap beer and smoking overpriced cigarettes. What they didn't realize was that some of the grad students I knew spent more time in bars than in libraries, and, because of that, I didn't believe being a grad student meant you were any smarter or better than anyone else.

I was also insecure about the way I looked. I had gained thirty pounds in the six months following our wedding, maxing out at an unhealthy two hundred pounds, and two years later, I still hadn't managed to get back to a healthy weight. I was thirty, a normal age to start having issues with my weight, but most of the people at the party were much younger than I was. Willie was twenty-seven, Clint twenty-five, Wade twenty-three, and Jeannie only nineteen, so their friends were still young enough that they could drink as much beer and eat as many potato chips as they wanted without having it show up on their waistline. I knew I seemed like I was from another world and that they assumed I thought I was better than them, which I probably did, but I also knew my weight gave them a reason to look down their noses at me, especially since Paula and L.W.'s other kids were all tan, thin, and buff. And I can't deny it made a formidable situation that much more anxiety-inducing.

Though I felt like a bit of an outsider at the party, I did find one person who clearly wanted to make me her ally: Clint's girlfriend, Olivia. Not long after Olivia arrived, she rushed over and gave me a big hug, pulling me away from the conversation I'd been happily having with Dominic and Dave.

"It's so nice to finally meet you," she said enthusiastically. "Paula has told me so much about you." I wondered immediately if Paula used the same words to describe me that she'd used to described Olivia: spoiled and snooty.

"You too," I said, and I told myself I wasn't being entirely dishonest.

"She said you used to ride horses?"

"When I was growing up in New Jersey, but when we moved to Indiana, there wasn't really a place to do that."

"English or Western?"

"English," I said.

"Me too! I've been riding since as long as I can remember, and I got Savannah, my horse, for my sixteenth birthday."

Thinking about Olivia's parents presenting her with her own horse for her sweet sixteen made me realize how incongruous she and Clint really were. Part of the reason I never had my own horse—never even dared to seriously ask for one—was because of the enormous expense involved, and if *my* parents had scoffed at spending that kind of money, I knew Olivia's parents must have had a lot of money or at the very least been the kind of people who *live* like they have a lot of money.

"I would love to have a horse some day," I said, knowing full well I'd probably never have the time or money to do so.

"Oh, you have to!" Olivia squealed. "There's nothing like it." Though I hated to admit it or to have anything in common with a person Paula disliked so much, I knew Olivia was probably right. In truth, there was nothing like the adrenaline rush of riding a beautiful horse across an empty field. Ironically, the only thing that came close was riding a motorcycle.

"So are you two serious?" I asked.

"Who?" Olivia asked. "Me and Clint?"

"Uh, yeah," I said, shocked she had to ask.

"Clint thinks we are, but we're really not."

"Why not? Do you think you're too young?"

"No, I would *love* to get married. But Clint has no idea what he wants to do with his life. He's just working for FedEx. That's not exactly a real career. And I don't even know how long he'll do that."

So Paula had been right. Olivia had no intention of staying with Clint, who had given me the impression he thought she was The One. My wish for Paula to be wrong about Olivia had, sadly, gone unfulfilled.

Paula emerged from the house a few minutes later with a tray full of Jell-O shots, and I didn't hesitate to take one. I'd stopped drinking beer since I wasn't keen on getting a heavy buzz two nights in a row, but the sideways glances and judgmental looks of some of the guests had me re-thinking that approach.

"Now here's something I've had before," Dave said when Paula stopped in front of him.

"Really?" Paula asked. "I would have thought you'd be more likely to eat crab than do a shot."

"Oh, no, Paula," Dave said. "Jell-O shots are a staple at my sister's house. I was probably twelve when I first had one there."

Paula laughed, but I didn't join her because her response reminded me of something else she seemed unable to remember about us. We had told her many times that our families, both Irish Catholic, drank at every family get together and that Dave's siblings especially liked to have a good time, but Paula seemed incapable of processing that fact. It was as if she thought we were too uptight or too educated or too *something* to ever enjoy a cold beer or let loose. It felt, at times like those, as if she was simply unable to give us any credit. But rather than argue, I threw back a red shooter and then eagerly reached for another.

The rest of the night passed in a blur of Jell-O shots and meaningless conversation. But before it was all over, Paula corralled all of us kids—as well as Kalea, Charlie, and Dave—into the living room for a group picture. By that time, Willie had lost his shirt, and almost everyone was a little bit drunk. A few minutes later, we would all go our separate ways. Paula would start collecting beer bottles and paper plates, a mother to the end. A bunch of partygoers would go pool hopping at a neighbor's house, Jeannie coming home with her torso wrapped only in a beach towel that Paula would pull down revealing Jeannie's pale moon for a *Candid Camera* moment. And eventually, Dave and I, exhausted, would retire upstairs, letting the nearby sounds of the ongoing festivities lull us into an uneasy sleep. But for a few minutes, we were all together, piled on the sofa like the best of friends.

What surprises me most when I study that picture now is how pleased and content we all look. Every single one of us is smiling and flushed with joy. Sure, the beer and shooters clearly helped soften our various edges, but it was more than that. When I look back on that moment, I can clearly recall being happy and even experiencing a sense of belonging for the first time that weekend.

Unfortunately, it was a feeling we wouldn't share for another seven years.

By the next morning, the buzz had worn off.

All of the Tucker kids were still asleep at the hour we needed to get up and get going, and when I peered out our bedroom window, I saw Paula wandering around the yard with a giant black trash bag, collecting the remnants of her children's debauchery. It was the same thing she'd been doing when we went to bed the previous night, and I couldn't help but wonder if she'd gotten any sleep at all. It also hit

me then that it was something my own mother would never do, that
I'd be expected not only to clean up after myself but also to do so
before the night was over.

Downstairs, we declined Paula's offer of breakfast, claiming we
had to hit the road. It was true we wanted to get an early start, but
L.W. was in the kitchen when we appeared with our suitcases. And
there was no denying his presence influenced our decision to make a
quick exit.

Paula insisted on one last picture before we left. A picture of the
three of us—L.W., Paula, and me. That was back when my summer
beauty routine consisted of showering and rolling down the windows
of the car to let my hair dry, so I argued I was in no shape for photos.
But Paula was persistent, and it was soon clear we weren't getting out
of there until I acquiesced.

It turned out my concerns were unfounded because the picture
was so dark that it's impossible to clearly see any of us, which—even
after all that's happened—makes me kind of sad given that it's the
only photo ever taken of the three of us together. The sun was at
our backs that morning, covering our faces in shadow. Despite the
dark exposure, you can still make out our three shirts: I was wearing
a blue t-shirt emblazoned with a commanding image of Shiva, the
Hindu goddess of destruction, while Paula and L.W. sported plain
gray t-shirts that read "Hokies" and "Virginia Tech Basketball"
respectively, a contrast that should've told us in no uncertain terms
there would be trouble in our future. Though our faces are mostly
hidden, Paula's wide smile is still visible. Her emotion appears genuine
but tentative, as if she wants to let herself be happy but doesn't yet
feel comfortable enough to give into that emotion. My own smile
looks more forced, clearly conveying how much I no longer wanted
to be playing the part of the long-lost daughter.

And then there is L.W.

His face is the hardest to see, but I can tell his lips are parted.
Maybe there are even a couple of teeth showing. His eyes are
completely hidden behind his old man glasses, making it difficult to
tell what he was thinking on that September morning. Maybe he was
relieved my visit was finally coming to an end. Maybe he was still
nervous or unhappy about me being there. I'll never know for sure.

But I can say this: the two of us have never looked more alike. We both appear utterly miserable.

PART FOUR
THE LOST DAUGHTER DISAPPEARS

SEPTEMBER 2000-JANUARY 2005

I'd heard stories about adopted children who disappear from the lives of their biological parents after finding them—most memorably in the support group meeting I'd been required to attend before searching for Paula—but the crazy thing was that back then I couldn't even begin to fathom how someone could do something so cold, so uncaring.

That is, until I did it myself.

Dave and I skulked away from the Tuckers' house that September morning the same way we would have if we'd engaged in a drunken one-night stand: we were both embarrassed and uncertain about the events of the previous night. *What had really happened? Had we made promises we couldn't keep? Would we ever even see these people again?*

After leaving Annandale, we headed for New Jersey and the place where I'd grown up, a bedroom community less than an hour's drive from Manhattan called Bridgewater. I'd only been back a handful of times since we'd moved during my freshman year of high school, and my visits there had always been brief, see-everything-in-one-day excursions. And that summer was no exception. We arrived during the early part of the afternoon and left first thing the next day, spending most of those eighteen hours in the car so we could drive by every landmark, school, and neighborhood that reminded me of my youth. Visits to New Jersey were always emotional for me, and that year I was even more overwrought than normal. As I re-lived the best moments of my childhood, I couldn't help but feel I had betrayed those memories by searching for Paula.

If I had really appreciated my childhood and my family, why did I need to find her? Wasn't what I already had enough?

The answer was that it was enough. More than enough. As I would find out once we'd returned to Ohio, our lives were, in fact, overflowing with enough.

Exactly one week after we got back to Cincinnati from our trip east, I sat for my Master's thesis defense in Oxford. That was on a Monday, and the very next day, Dave and I started our weeklong orientation for the doctoral program at the University of Cincinnati. During that week, my friend Tracy visited us for three days, and not long after she left, Dave and I got in the car again for another long road trip: Chicago was our destination that weekend, a mandatory excursion because my sister's baby shower was being held there on Sunday. So we went to orientation Saturday morning from eight until noon, packed the car, drove six hours to Naperville, Illinois, where my sister and her husband lived, had dinner with the family, made food for the baby shower the next day, slept a few hours, went to church with everyone the next morning, made nice-nice at the baby shower, and then drove the six hours back to Cincinnati so we would be home in time to go back to orientation again at eight o'clock on Monday morning.

Classes for the fall term began forty-eight hours later. In addition to taking two graduate classes and a teaching practicum, we each had to teach one three-credit freshman composition course, and because we were newbies, we both got stuck teaching 8:00 a.m. classes that met three days a week. It was an appropriate beginning to what the next five years would hold for us: too much to do and too little time to do it.

Not to mention too little money.

That first year at the University of Cincinnati we were both paid a $9,000 stipend plus the cost of our tuition. Though we found an incredibly cheap one-bedroom apartment for $425 a month, it still wasn't quite enough to get us through a year of books, fees, rent, utilities, groceries, insurance, and gas, which was basically all we spent our money on at that time—besides our weekly trip out on the town for the two-for-one matinee at the local independent theatre and a cheap dinner. Once we realized we weren't going to be able to make it on $18,000 that year, we decided we had no choice but to move into Dave's parents' house. They lived in a small bungalow on the West Side with two empty rooms in the converted attic. The only problem was the house had only one bathroom—and it was on the first floor. One bathroom for four people, two of whom were in their late sixties. It didn't seem like a great way to keep harmony in the family. So, reluctantly, we asked my parents for help.

After I'd dropped out of grad school the first time, my parents told me that if I ever went to grad school again, I'd be on my own. I understood their reasons—a big part of me even agreed with them—but it also seemed silly for them not to help us if they could. After all, we'd both finished the M.A. program in two years, right on schedule and without needing any financial assistance from anyone. For that reason, I thought they might bend.

But when I proposed the idea to them a month before we had to move out of the dorm in Oxford that summer, they weren't thrilled, and we argued for a short time about the possibility of them helping us out. I had asked for $7,000, which would bring our household income up to $25,000 that year. My father balked at that number, tearing apart the budget we e-mailed him and cutting anything extra—from our two magazine subscriptions to the dozens of Christmas and birthday gifts we bought family members every year. When he sent the budget back to me, he said he was willing to give us $2,000, estimating we could get by on $20,000 that year, which I knew would be a nearly impossible challenge. Still, I didn't have much choice but to agree, so a deal was made. For that reason, I was more than a little bit surprised when his letter arrived a few days letter with double what he'd offered.

24 July 2000

To: Molly
From: Dad
Subject: Rent

Molly, I've enclosed a check for $4,000 to be used over the next year to help defray yours and Dave's rent cost in Cincinnati. You might be wise to deposit it *now in an interest-bearing account so that it can be turned into a slightly larger amount. It is more than we discussed. I'd like to see you both get off to a positive start in your new university and Ph.D. effort.*

Love,
Dad

To our surprise, my parents had stepped up and given us $4,000, bringing our annual income to $22,000. It was enough for the two of us to survive if we cut everything unnecessary from our lives— no concerts, no fancy dinners out, no expensive gifts for family, and not much in the way of travel besides trips to Indiana to visit my family—and by some miracle (or maybe the help of our dedicated graduate director), we both got $2,000 raises the next year, making it possible for us to get by on our own after that.

Still, like most new beginnings, that first year in the doctoral program was brutal. Dave worked a second job stocking magazines for extra money, and we both studied seven days a week, cramming in the prep work we had to do for teaching and leaving hardly any time for a life outside of school.

But that didn't mean there weren't other demands on our time. Because, in truth, our social obligations were more taxing than ever. Since we were living in Cincinnati together for the first time in our lives, we were closer than we'd ever been to Dave's family and high school friends, meaning there was suddenly a huge amount we were expected to do after hours and on weekends. In Dave's family alone, there were birthday parties and baptisms, holiday dinners and graduations, communion celebrations and cookouts, not to mention random dinners and get-togethers. We were both thrilled to have the opportunity to do so much with family and old friends, but at the same time, between school and social commitments, we were exhausted.

Of course, graduate school also had its own extracurricular obligations, and we spent countless evenings attending readings, lectures, receptions, and department parties as well as repeatedly driving visiting writers and job candidates to and from the airport. I hear other academics claim grad school was a breeze compared to how much they have to do once they're actually teaching full-time, but that wasn't the case with us. Yes, being a college professor is more work than most people will ever understand, but the demands of such a job are still much easier to juggle than those of a grad student. To put it in terms anyone can understand, there was a hell of a lot going on. So I guess it shouldn't be a surprise that one of the things that suffered was my relationship with the Tuckers.

The first time I didn't take one of Paula's phone calls it wasn't because I didn't want to talk to her, but simply because I was worn out from all the stress of our new lives. That first phone call came only a few weeks after we had visited Annandale, and I figured the Tuckers could be put on the back burner for a while in order for other things to take priority. So when Dave answered the phone and said, "Hi, Paula," I waved at him frantically, whispering the words "I'm not here" so I wouldn't have to talk.

I never intended for it to become a habit. It just did.

The second time Paula called, several weeks later, I felt the same way: too burdened with schoolwork and other commitments to have the energy for what I imagined would be an hour-long conversation with Paula. I did the same thing I'd done the last time, begging Dave to lie and tell her I wasn't home. There were more calls after that, but at some point they all started to blend together, and I lost track of how many times I didn't take them.

It wasn't that I didn't want to talk to Paula, but once I avoided those first two calls, it began to feel like a bigger and bigger hurdle to overcome. As soon as I accepted a call, I'd be placed in the awkward position of explaining why I hadn't talked to her since our visit, why months had gone by since I'd made contact of any kind.

Dave wasn't happy about lying, but at the same time, he didn't understand why Paula wasn't getting the message that I needed some time to myself. Sure, we were overwhelmed with graduate school, but deep down I had to admit there was more than that keeping me from making contact. Our visit to Annandale had been as mind-bendingly confusing as an Escher drawing: totally illogical and impossible to comprehend. In twelve short months, my immediate family had grown from an undemanding table of four to a duplex for ten. We needed time to adjust.

The easiest solution would've been to tell Paula all of this. I'd like to think she would have been understanding about it if I had been more forthright. But that first year, it felt as if space was the last thing Paula wanted to give us. She wanted us to visit at Thanksgiving and Christmas, she wanted us there for birthdays and weddings, she practically wanted us to move in, or at least that's how it seemed when we showed up and found out she had redecorated a bedroom with us in mind. And her desire to have us around all the time frightened both of us almost as much as the doctoral program. We were scared. And getting us to come back was going to be as challenging for Paula as trying to get a squirrel to eat out of her hand.

Like I said, the simple thing to do would have been to tell Paula the truth. But back then I didn't fully understand why I was avoiding Paula, nor was I sure if I ever wanted to see her again. It wasn't that I didn't like Paula or the Tuckers. It's that I didn't understand where to put them in my life. One of the things people don't often talk about in the adoption process is what happens when the child grows up and people inevitably make contact. Who do those people become in the child's life? I tried to tell myself for a while that the Tuckers were kind of like another set of in-laws, but that was far from the truth since I knew all along we would never be opening presents in Annandale on Christmas morning.

Still, none of that was totally clear to me then. *Nothing* was clear. I was simply afraid and nervous and confused. More confused than I can explain. Most people who know me would describe me as the epitome of an open book, but when I am *really* uncomfortable with something, when something makes me *truly* unhappy, I refuse to talk about it at all. I shut it out of my life and pretend it doesn't exist.

And, as much as I hate to admit it, that's what I did with the Tuckers.

Paula rightfully grew more petulant each time she called. Whether she was leaving a message on the machine or sifting her way through Dave's lies, even I could hear the new edge in the voice on the other end of the line. So I was more than a little surprised when she sent us a big package of Christmas presents that year, as would soon become her habit every December.

Paula's biggest asset—and also, like all of us givers, one of her greatest challenges—is her generosity. She likes nothing more than to shower her family and friends with gifts and love. The truth is that she sent us so many gifts over the years I can't remember which ones were in that first holiday package. It might have been the Christmas wreath or the Christmas blanket or the Christmas centerpiece. Or maybe it was a framed picture of the Tuckers or the ceramic bowl with potpourri. It's impossible for me to remember what came that year, but there is one thing I can be sure about: it was a big package with numerous gifts Paula had picked out specifically for us. Whether it was the wreath she sent because she remembered I had been wanting one or the XXL lime-green sweatshirt she sent after I mentioned liking the color, she always put a lot of thought into her gifts.

Still, as hard as she worked to give us things she thought we'd like, she almost always got it wrong. The wreath came a few weeks after we'd bought one of our own, lime green was a color I liked for decorating, not clothing, and I'd never in my life worn an XXL shirt, which was something I'd told Paula more than once.

In that way, she was like most mothers—trying too hard to please and often missing the mark. A few years later, we started going to Florida to see my parents for Christmas every year, and even though I told Paula numerous times we would be away, she still sent huge packages every December that would sit on our doorstep for days, signaling to any would-be thieves in our rundown building that our apartment was empty despite the fact that we went to the trouble to stop the mail and put the lights on timers. And back then—during a time when mixed emotions dominated my feelings about the Tuckers—I saw those shortcomings as evidence of the fact that Paula didn't really know me at all. I'm embarrassed to admit I was actually bothered by the gifts rather than being appreciative of them. And maybe this fueled my desire to avoid Paula. Sure, I still felt incredibly guilty about not talking to her for so long, but I was also frustrated by her inability to take a hint and give me what I saw as an understandable desire for some much-needed breathing room.

*

I honestly cannot remember the occasion when I finally broke down and called Paula, but I know for sure that I did call her that December, three months after our visit, because that's what I wrote in my thankfully meticulous calendar. I have the vague sense we talked only briefly—either because I made some excuse about being in a hurry or because Paula was angry that I had put her off so long. No matter what, I know that nothing significant was said beyond my apology for not talking to Paula sooner.

I made contact. I made my apology. I made nice.

And then I got out.

Paula's frequent calls and my ignoring of them continued, and when Paula called in March of 2001—for probably the twelfth time in a half as many months—it was only two days after Dave's dad had undergone a quadruple bypass. I wasn't home when the phone rang, so Dave, obviously distraught, told Paula the whole story: his dad had started experiencing chest pains on a Sunday morning while working at Wal-Mart and been rushed to the hospital, where it was determined he was on the verge of a massive heart attack and would need immediate bypass surgery. Dave also explained to Paula we were in crisis mode, thinking the situation with his father might smooth things over and force Paula to give us the additional space we needed, but at that point it was kind of like crying wolf the third time: Paula had had enough of being ignored, and her frustrations with me left her no room for sympathy. Almost as soon as he had gotten the words out of his mouth, Paula changed the subject back to her life, talking about things that were of little or no consequence. She never told Dave she was sorry about his dad and never offered to help in any way.

Deep down I'd been hoping to find a way to bridge the gap I'd unintentionally created, and when Dave's father had open-heart surgery, somewhere in the back of my head I was hoping that trauma would give me the opening I was looking for. I saw it as an opportunity to justify the fact that I had been preoccupied with family and friends in Ohio, thus excusing my bad behavior. No, it didn't justify not talking to Paula more than once in six months, but I hoped it would at least help ease her frustration. She couldn't be that angry with me if my father-in-law was in the hospital, could she?

But as it turned out, Paula was, in many ways, already beyond reach. I imagine her cold response to Dave's news was more about me than it was about his father. But back then I couldn't see that. All I could see was a person who seemed more interested in herself than she was in me.

It was a turning point.

I really did feel awful about not talking to Paula for so long and not returning her many phone calls, but I was also angry that, at that time, she seemed incapable of recognizing that we had lives of our own. Dave's father had just been through major surgery, but she was still more concerned with her everyday issues than she was with our extraordinary ones. In the nearly two years I'd been in contact with Paula, I'd often found myself frustrated with her desire to talk more about her life than my own, especially because she often repeated stories I had already heard several times, but this incident was one that seemed leagues more offensive than the others. I decided, in that moment, to pull back even further. I was under no obligation to have a relationship with Paula or L.W. No, I wouldn't cut off contact completely, but I would no longer feel obligated to give everything Paula asked of me. And I would be free from the guilt that had dominated my life since the first day I had found out Paula's name.

Of course, it wasn't that easy.

Sure, the guilt receded, but it never entirely disappeared. For a good while, it was obstructed by my anger: anger about Paula's response to Dave's father, anger about L.W. leaving Paula when she was pregnant, anger about the feeling I got that Paula wanted us to always be around.

And, finally, anger about the newsletter article.

I didn't know Paula was writing an article about me.

But then again, I hadn't talked to her in so long I guess I shouldn't have been too surprised not to be kept in the loop. Still, when a fat envelope arrived in our mail a few weeks after Dave's father got out of the hospital, I was not prepared for what was inside.

Paula had enclosed a long letter dated a month earlier and a folded newsletter from Catholic Charities. The date at the top of the first page of the newsletter said December 2000, so I figured that—given possible delays in printing and mailing—it had taken at least two months for Paula to forward it to me. At first, I thought Paula was including the newsletter simply to keep me informed about the goings-on at Catholic Charities, but a split second later it hit me: Paula had written about us.

As soon as I realized what had happened, my brain flooded with questions: *What had Paula said about me? How had she described our so-called reunion? Had she mentioned how long it had been since we talked?* I felt so overwhelmed by the idea that Paula had told our story without consulting me that I had to sit down at the kitchen table.

Once I caught my breath, I flipped through the newsletter until I was greeted with a picture of myself I had never seen before. As soon as I saw it, my vision began to shrink, vertigo-like, until I could only see the photo in front of me, the rest of the world blocked out by my anxiety. Paula looked healthy and optimistic—not to mention young—whereas I looked tired and cranky and overweight, and more than a little bit older than my thirty years. We looked more like sisters than mother and daughter: Paula was the well-adjusted older sister, and I was the bitter younger one. She had obviously selected an outstanding picture of herself and not given any thought to what I looked like.

I was more than put off. I was outraged.

And what I read after I saw the picture didn't help much either.

PAULA AND MOLLY'S STORY
by Paula Tucker

Thirty years ago, I was blessed with the miracle of life—unfortunately thirty years ago when you weren't married and became pregnant, it was considered a family disgrace, kept a secret, and you were strongly encouraged to place your baby up for adoption. Actually, you weren't offered any choices—it was just what you were expected to do if marriage wasn't an option.

At the time, I was twenty years old, a new nursing school graduate who was feeling inadequate and a failure to my parents. I believed that everyone surrounding me knew what was best for myself and my baby that was growing quietly— unaware of the storm outside. As my baby grew, perhaps because of my faith and my respect for life, I began to feel a strong belief that I had been blessed with a miracle. Regardless of the circumstances, she had been created out of love between myself and her father, and my decision for her future needed to be out of love. I wanted her to experience the love that bonds a couple together, and hopefully, her adoptive parents would surround her with love and guide her gently thru life's journey.

So, on April 5, 1970, in the early hours of a Sunday morning, Anne Marie was born. Indeed, she was a miracle—a gift of life from God. Just as the miracle of her birth and the bond between mother and daughter were ignited, so did the harsh reality of the pending adoption temper the joy I was experiencing.

All too soon, with the single act of writing my signature, the gift and the privilege of her life was given to a couple I hoped would be loving and offer her a better life than I believed I could at this time in my life.

The emptiness and loss I felt that day and for days to come was indescribable compounded by a deep sense of being all alone. As we know, however, life goes on, and so did mine.

As the days and years passed, my life was filled with the usual ups and downs, joys and sorrows. Amazingly (to the surprise and disapproval of some), I rekindled my relationship with Anne Marie's father, who I might add, I never stopped loving. As the story goes, we eventually were married. Once again, we were blessed with four more gifts from God—Willie, Clint, Wade and Jeannie.

Through all of these days, I had my small box of memories (Anne Marie's picture, baby bracelet, diaper, many inspirational readings, and the letter I wrote to her the day she was born). Very few days went by that I didn't wonder how she was, where she was, hope she was happy, and prayed perhaps someday that I would at least see her from a distance, and I even dared to hope I would meet her one day.

As my life's journey continued, I grew more anxious to know Anne Marie, especially so that she might know her brothers and sisters. One day, in July 1999, a letter arrived on a Saturday afternoon from Catholic Charities letting me know that Anne Marie was interested in meeting me. The magnitude of that moment, the memories, the hopes and the prayers all came back along with a great sense of relief which enveloped me.

I practically held my breath until Monday when I could call Catholic Charities. While I waited for Monday, I used the time to share my long kept *secret with my children. Their reactions varied from disbelief, amazement that I had kept a secret for so long, tears, laughter, but most of all they hugged and loved me.*

Catholic Charities sent me her letter. It was warm, encouraging, and forgiving. She told me a great deal about herself, especially that her name was Molly, that she had married David a year ago, and they were both in school for creative writing.

My return letter to her was filled with happiness, excitement and a good bit of information about marrying L.W., her birthfather, and of course, I told her about her four siblings. I later learned that she found all of this a bit overwhelming, and it took her three months to write back! I felt we would eventually be reunited.

Thirty years later, one month shy of her thirtieth birthday, I met my birthdaughter at her home in Ohio. For a while, I felt as if I was dreaming, but gradually the illusion became reality. We spent the next three days talking endlessly about everything. Oddly enough, I felt like I had known her all my life. She even reminded me of myself at times. Could this reunion be any better? Yes, it could!

This past Labor Day weekend Molly and her husband came to our home and met Dad, Willie, Clint, Wade, Jeannie and other relatives and long time friends of our family. She was such a brave soul to meet so many people. She often tells me how welcomed she felt. It was a special, wonderful weekend with people getting to know each other and lots of hugs and kisses. It was indeed a celebration of life and love.

I still feel blessed that God trusted me with the miracle of Anne Marie's life and let her grow below my heart, and then gave me the strength to place her with and into the hearts of her adoptive parents, and finally to return her to me. Heart to heart!

Thank you God for so many miracles of Life,
Paula

As I re-read this article years later, I am surprised by how warm and benevolent—even ordinary—it seems. Because when I first received the newsletter, it seemed just the opposite: self-absorbed, manipulative, even mean-spirited. Feelings that I can see now were more about my other frustrations with Paula than the words in the article.

I was angry that Paula had written the article in the first place.

Back then, I wasn't ready to discuss my experience of meeting Paula and her family, much less have other people read and talk about it. I was also angry she hadn't told me she was writing the article or asked me how I'd feel about her doing so. I couldn't imagine I hadn't been given the opportunity to read it and offer my comments because Paula's white-washed version of events made it seem like we were the best of friends, that everything was perfect, and that our trip to Annandale had been joyful and easy. That misrepresentation of and misunderstanding about how difficult that trip had been for me was especially infuriating.

Of course, it would have been hard for Paula to tell me about the article or get my feedback since I wasn't taking her calls, but, from my point of view, that should have told her it wasn't a good idea— if I wasn't capable of talking to her, how did she think I'd feel if she told the whole world about what was going on between us? In that way, I felt as if my privacy had been completely violated.

But, more than anything, I was angry about some of Paula's comments, which I read as passive aggressive. The first comment that bothered me was the one about what I had included in my first letter to her: "She told me a great deal about herself," Paula had said, and I took this to mean she thought I was self-absorbed and talked about myself too much. That irritated me for two reasons. First, I thought it was an absurd accusation since, even after I had been to the Tuckers' home in Annandale, I still felt like Paula knew almost nothing about me because she never asked about my past or my parents. And, second, I thought it was like the pot calling the kettle black: Paula was the one who talked incessantly "all about herself," not the other way around. In reality, I felt like all she did was talk about herself. And since that was one of my biggest complaints about my relationship with Paula, it galled me to see her accuse me of perpetrating a crime I knew I had not committed.

It also incensed me that Paula had called me Anne Marie in the article. Yes, she was telling her side of the story in the order that things had happened. But my name wasn't Anne Marie. And by calling me by that name for three-quarters of the article, it sent the message that she wanted to erase who I really was—she wanted to erase Molly—and keep alive the way she had always remembered me:

as the perfect and infallible baby she had left behind so many years ago.

For the same reason, I was furious Paula had referred to L.W. as my "father" and, to a lesser degree, that she referred to her children as my "siblings." L.W. was not my father. He had never once acted like a father, not when Paula became pregnant with me and not when he had finally met me thirty years later. He would never be my father. I already had a father. A good and loving father. A real father. And any attempt to ignore or replace my relationship with my real father would always be met with animosity.

Still, my indignation over Paula's hypocrisy and lack of understanding was easily overshadowed by the other comment about how long it took me to write back after we initially made contact. Paula had said "I later learned that she found all of this a bit overwhelming, and it took her three months to write back!" There was no way I could not take this comment as an attack—a subtle one, maybe, but an attack all the same.

In truth, I didn't realize until reading the article that it had taken me a full three months to write back to Paula after getting her first letter, and if I had been in a better place with Paula, I might have felt bad when I learned that. But I was not yet in a position to be empathetic. And from my point of view, it seemed like a only handful of days, maybe a few weeks at best, had passed between letters—and those were the weeks when I was working through the complete shock I felt by the story Paula had told me about getting back together with L.W. and having four more children.

I should have known Paula and L.W. had reunited and married. Margaret had told me that was a possibility during my screening interview, and looking back, I realize she wasn't just testing me. She was trying to tell me something. *You should know it's always possible your birth parents have reunited.* But, despite Margaret's best efforts, I just couldn't let go of the image I had of a saintly birthmother who'd never had a life of her own, especially a life with the man who had abandoned her. If I'm being completely honest, I have to admit that Paula getting back together with L.W. seemed like a betrayal of sorts. If she had really loved me, wouldn't she have never again spoken to the man who'd made her give me up?

Still, I have to confess that as I re-read the article now and remember all of the negative emotions I experienced when I first saw it, I can't help but feel bad for Paula. All those years she waited to find me, and then she had to wait that much longer because I didn't begin to know what to do with all of the love she was trying to give me. In some ways, I feel ridiculous re-counting these emotions now. Clearly I overreacted and didn't get that, despite those one or two comments, Paula's article was totally positive and upbeat. But I simply couldn't see that then. I was too confused and angry to see *anything* clearly.

I was so angry, in fact, that I didn't read the letter Paula had included in her package until a few days later.

2/18/01

Dear Molly,

I am amazed that the last time we actually spoke to each other was early December. Somehow we've managed to miss each other. I spoke with David New Year's Eve—he said you both have been really busy with going to school, teaching school, and celebrating the holidays with family and friends. He said you are both doing well in your new endeavors. I remember the last time we spoke you were having some female health problems—hopefully they have been able to give you some answers and you are feeling better.

As usual, I've been busy with work at the hospital and restaurant along with following Jeannie up and down the East coast for basketball. You probably know they are having a fairly good year. Jeannie has started some games, but mostly has played off the bench—she does play about twenty to thirty minutes. The head coach is her usual crazy self—unpredictable and harassing.

Jeannie is seriously considering switching schools, but as yet is undecided. I enclosed another picture and a couple of articles. Virginia Tech has been on HTS—it would be nice if you were able to see them. Her next televised game is this Sunday—Feb 25th at 1pm. Actually its her last regular season game. The following week-end is the Big East tournament—hopefully they'll make it to the NCAA tourney also.

Wade was layed off this past week from his job in Manassas as Aviation Mechanic—he was somewhat disappointed because he felt like he was doing a good job and really beginning to feel comfortable with his work. He's going to look around Dulles, but if you hear of anything your way let him know—he's willing to travel.

Clint is beginning a new business adventure—he's working at a gym with hopes of buying it in about 6 months if he likes it. He and Olivia are off again at the moment, but everyday they seem to get closer at getting back together.

Willie is still working hard at the restaurant. He's also still working hard at partying and flirting with the girls or should I say women—he is 28. I don't think he'll ever settle down.

L.W. is doing OK. He's been somewhat stressed out with the restaurant and his mother these days. He has managed to get to some of Jeannie's games and we managed to have dinner once and awhile. Instead of life getting easier for us it seems like everyday gets a little harder.

It doesn't seem like it's been a year since we met. I can remember our visit— the snow, talking, the ice—talking—eating—talking—visiting and then talking some more. I reread the letters you first wrote, look at the pictures of our visits and hope that all is still well with us.

Everyone says hell-o—Willie, Clint, Wade, Jeannie, L.W., Me, Kalea, my brother and sister, family and friends.

Hope you got my e-mail from Jeannie and enjoyed my thoughts on our reunion that I wrote down for Catholic Charities.

Hope you are both happy and well.

God bless and love,
Paula

Though I was still really frustrated and put off about the newsletter article, there was no way I could not feel guilty when I read this letter. Paula was going back over my old letters and looking at pictures of us, wondering if everything was okay and if we would ever see each other again. She couldn't have said it any clearer—she wanted me back in her life, she wanted me to make contact. If I hadn't known it before, I knew it then—my behavior over the past half-year had been truly despicable. Not only did I feel overwhelmed with guilt, but I also knew for sure I *was* guilty: guilty of being selfish, of being afraid, of being quick to judge.

I knew then, of course, that no matter how annoyed I was about the newsletter I *needed* to call Paula. I *had* to call her. This was April of 2001, so it had been more than seven months since our trip to Annandale, and except for the one quick call I had made to her in

December, we hadn't talked at all during that time. Still, I understood intuitively that too much time had passed and I had pushed things too far for our conversation to go well. I was angry, and so was Paula.

So, yet again, I put off calling.

I really did intend to contact Paula. But no matter how hard I tried to convince myself to call, I just didn't have it in me. I simply wasn't capable of handling the emotions and guilt I knew would accompany such a conversation. So I did the next best thing: I sent a card.

Paula's birthday is in May, and that seemed like the perfect opportunity to reach out. It might have been smart to send the card on time, but my actions that year weren't exactly the most intelligent of my life. No, I couldn't even get the card out on time. In fact, I didn't even buy it until the day of Paula's birthday and failed to mail it until two days later. I was a model of avoidance. Clearly, I believed if I ignored the whole issue, it would go away.

For the most part, Paula did go away after that.

She stopped calling on a regular basis, and, though we still got packages at Christmas and on my birthday, Paula's attempts to make contact were few and far between. In many ways, I felt like I had dodged a bullet. I had found my birth family, followed through on my promise to meet them, and then I pretty much washed my hands of them. I had never intended to have a life-long relationship with my biological parents, and it finally seemed as if they agreed with that decision.

It would have all been okay except that, deep down, I felt awful about the choices I had made, and as much as I tried, I couldn't stop thinking about how uncaring and truly horrible I had been.

The next few months passed in a blur. Dave's dad was recovering from heart surgery, so we spent a good deal of time helping at his parents' house. By June, school was out for the summer, Herb was pretty much back to normal, and we were at the Bells' house one night—doing our laundry and moving things back to the way they were before the surgery—when the subject of the Tuckers came up.

Because Herb had been forced to spend most of his recovery in the living room—either in one of their two matching recliners or on the sofa where he slept—we had moved the television from the TV room in the back of the house to the front living room during that time. But once Herb was well enough to sit in a regular chair again, Catherine wanted the television moved back to its proper location. Since I was the go-to person for electronics, I was on the floor, unscrewing the coaxial cable from the wall, when Catherine started in with her questions.

"Have you heard from Paula?" she asked me as I tried to detach the TV from the living room wall.

"Not lately," I said to Catherine, who was hovering in the doorway with a dish towel in her hand. Dave had always claimed his parents liked to barrage him with questions whenever he was trying to get something done, and, though I hadn't believed him initially, after three years of marriage, I knew the two of them had the uncanny ability to find the most inappropriate times to begin a conversation.

"Do you think you'll ever see them again?" she asked, and I wondered—not for the first time—why she asked me about the Tuckers more than she asked after my mom and dad.

"I have no idea," I said with a sigh. "I try not to think about it."

"Why?" Catherine asked. "Is something wrong?"

"No, nothing's wrong, but they're not my real family so I don't spend too much time thinking about them." This wasn't an outright lie. It was true I did my best not to waste precious time thinking about the Tuckers at that point in my life. But it was just as true I spent too much of my time thinking about why I shouldn't dwell on them or training myself not to do so. The whole not-thinking-about-the-Tuckers thing was, in fact, pretty time-consuming.

I fully expected Catherine to continue with her interrogation, but something about my answer—it had been a pretty cold and dismissive thing to say—must have told her it was a closed subject because, after that, she walked away.

Later, when I went down to the basement to move a load of our darks from the washer to the dryer, I noticed a line of caked-on grime had appeared around the bowl of the washing machine and wiped it clean with a towel. It wasn't the first time I'd encountered a dirty washing machine. Ever since I'd moved out of my parents' house after college, I'd been forced to rely on laundromats and the generosity of family members with washers and dryers, and in that time, I'd been shocked to see that not everyone kept their laundry rooms as immaculate as my mother did. In fact, for the first eighteen years of my life I had lived in a house where everything—the washer and dryer, the fridge, the microwave, the bathroom sinks, the yard— was kept in pristine condition, partially because we had a cleaning person in every other week but also because my mother was particular about her surroundings and believed—like June Cleaver, whom she'd grown up watching on television—that a clean house was a good house.

Before college, I falsely believed all mothers were as conscientious as my own. It wasn't that I hadn't visited houses that were different than my own as a child because, of course, I had. It was that I hadn't *lived* in those houses, I hadn't experienced what it was like to be stuck using a dirty washing machine or microwave for more than just a few hours. Or maybe I was just too young to care. But after college, something changed. I became aware of the fact that some people didn't worry about cleanliness as much as my mother did, some people didn't think it was worth all the trouble. And as I scrubbed the scum from the Bells' washing machine, I remembered the rust stains in the Tuckers' sink, the dust and hair on their baseboards, the laundry on the back deck and thought, not for the first time, how unfamiliar I might have been to myself if I had grown up as Anne Marie Tucker.

Though the first year of the doctoral program was a disaster from start to finish, the second year was not nearly as difficult. Yes, we were still working all the time, but it no longer felt unusual. Because many college instructors have two- or three-day-a-week schedules—teaching on either Tuesdays and Thursdays or Mondays, Wednesdays, and Fridays—most people don't realize that anyone who teaches a college course is most likely working all day, seven days a week with the possible exception of one drunken weekend night at a local bar or, in our case, at the movie theatre. Whether I've had one class to teach during a semester or five, I've always found there are never enough hours in the day to get everything done. From the day the semester begins until the moment finals are collected, the schedule is a grueling, never-ending grind of trying to stay on top of the endless sea of papers, exams, exercises, memos, e-mail messages, committee meetings, midterm grade reports, and class notes. And teaching as a graduate instructor was no exception. If anything, it was more challenging than teaching after finishing the Ph.D. because we still hadn't learned the shortcuts necessary for grading fifty-plus papers in one sitting.

On top of our regular commitments, I took on another one, serving as the assistant to the composition director. It was probably the wrong choice for a person interested in being a creative writer, not a composition scholar, but I was honored to be offered such a prominent position in the department and was thrilled to be working so closely with one of my favorite professors. One of the first things I had to do in that new position was help run the orientation for new graduate instructors in September. Because of the timing of orientation, my plans to visit our friend Kara, who had relocated to New York that year, had to be moved to August. It ended up being a fortuitous change because, had I not rescheduled my trip, I would have been in Manhattan the day the Twin Towers fell. I wouldn't have been in any danger because Kara lived out of harm's way in the East Village, but it still seemed as if fate was on my side.

As it turned out, I was home on September 11th, trying unsuccessfully to prepare for the orientation that was to begin two days later. Instead of working, I spent most of my time, like everyone else, glued to the horrific events unfolding on television.

It ended up working out for the best that I had to go to New York earlier in the summer—not only because of the attack, but also because a family friend was getting married that weekend. If I had gone to New York in September, I would have missed his wedding, which is how I ended up going to the D.C. area for the second September in a row. The only difference being that Paula didn't know I'd be there.

I was obviously dreading the trip because it meant I'd have to make a decision about seeing the Tuckers. But there were other reasons I felt anxious too.

First of all, the wedding fell during orientation, which meant we would have to drive to D.C. and back in one weekend.

It was also happening only days after September 11th. It just didn't feel like the right time for two people to start a life together. I felt certain, too, that the groom, whom I had known since childhood and had become a big shot investor, was making a huge mistake by marrying someone he hadn't known very long and appeared, at least from the outside, to be after his newly acquired wealth, a suspicion ultimately proven true when she left him a year later.

And, of course, there was the issue of the Tuckers. If we were going to be in D.C. for less than thirty-six hours, was I obligated to call them? Was it awful to go to D.C. without telling them?

Dave and I found ourselves in a similar situation to the one we'd been in the previous year when we'd gone through orientation ourselves: we had to travel right in the middle of that hectic time. But, that year, since I was training others rather than being trained myself, I was able to leave town about eighteen hours earlier—right after orientation finished on Friday at four. As soon as we wrapped for the day, Dave picked me up, and we headed east, driving into the night and not arriving at our hotel in D.C. until around two in the morning.

The wedding was at four o'clock the next afternoon, leaving us about six hours from the time we woke to the time we had to be at the church. That meant it was conceivable for us to visit the Tuckers. But did we want to? And was it right?

My parents had also made the trip to D.C. for the wedding, and the idea of contacting Paula with them in town felt like a true betrayal. And though not telling her about our visit could clearly be considered a betrayal as well, my loyalties were obviously with my parents. So instead of visiting the Tuckers, we spent the morning working out and then had a late lunch with the two of them.

Lunch seemed fine on the surface, but inside I was a complete wreck. Even though we were miles away from Annandale, where L.W. and Paula lived, I still felt as if they might walk into the restaurant at any moment. I've never cheated, but I imagine the way I felt that afternoon is comparable to the way someone in the midst of an affair feels—I was sure I was about to be caught.

My parents didn't seem to notice, and once we finished lunch, the feeling disappeared. Still, I'll never forget what it was like to sit there and imagine that at any moment my two sets of parents could be in the same room—inspecting each other, inspecting me, and trying to convince themselves I still belonged to them. No, there was never any danger my parents would lose me to the Tuckers, but that didn't stop me from agonizing over them considering that possibility. In fact, sometimes it seemed as if all I ever did for years was worry about the whole thing with Paula hurting their feelings.

Of course, the awkward moment I feared so much never came to pass. We went to the wedding and, except for the fact that most of the people we knew were questioning the bride's intentions, the rest of the day went on without much excitement. In order to get back to Cincinnati at a decent hour on Sunday, we had to leave as soon as we got up the next morning. And that's how I ended up spending an entire weekend in D.C. the Tuckers never knew anything about.

Well, that is, at least until they read this book.

While we were living in Cincinnati, we spent our Thanksgivings with Dave's parents, the four of us usually alternating between celebrating the holiday at Dave's brother's or sister's houses. But that year Dave's sister was going to be out of town visiting her in-laws, and his brother was having his wife's family over for dinner. Normally we would have Thanksgiving at Catherine and Herb's house in that situation, but as it had only been eight months since Herb's bypass surgery, we decided to have them over to our apartment. We had a small place by other people's standards—a one bedroom with average-sized living and dining rooms, a galley kitchen, and a bathroom we could barely turn around in. But after living in our dorm apartment in Oxford for two years, our average one-bedroom seemed more than roomy enough to host a turkey dinner.

So we invited Herb and Catherine over for the holiday as well as two other students in our doctoral program, both of whom lived too far away to go home—Seung Hee had come all the way from Seoul to attend grad school at the University of Cincinnati, and Natalie

Larrew had moved from California, so her son could be near his father, an Ohio native, while she was in school.

All of my life I had looked forward to hosting holidays as an adult—maybe because we had lived so far away from family when I was growing up in New Jersey—and in the fantasy I had created, I always imagined we would invite people who had nowhere else to go. I suppose I bought into the idea that holidays were as much about community as family, a notion I'd picked up from my maternal grandmother and one that fit well with my personality. For this reason, I was thrilled to be having six people over for Thanksgiving that year and spent hours cleaning the apartment, planning the menu, decorating the table, and preparing the food. I had even taken out the vintage dishes and Kosta Boda vase we'd gotten as wedding presents three years before, running to the park across the street at the last minute to cut a few branches from a red chokeberry tree for the center of the table.

By the time everyone arrived, dozens of candles and the smell of turkey had transformed our rundown apartment into an inviting space, though the table was so crowded we had to move the vase to the floor during dinner. The food turned out surprisingly well even though we'd never made a turkey before, and Catherine and Herb were outgoing and friendly, Herb flirting mercilessly with Seung and Natalie while Catherine asked them questions about their lives. It was when we were talking about Natalie's two-year-old son that the issue of adoption came up.

"Where is he tonight?" Catherine asked Natalie politely.

Natalie had been about to take a bite out of a turkey leg, but she put it back down on her plate to respond. "He's with his dad," she explained. "And his grandparents. They all live here."

"Oh, that must be hard," Catherine said, a sad expression forming on her face as she spoke.

"What?" Natalie said, clueless about what Catherine was trying to imply. "What must be hard?"

"To be away from your little boy on a holiday."

Natalie let out a small laugh. "Oh, no, honestly I don't mind. It's good for him to get to spend time with his dad, and I'm happy to have a night off." I was relieved Natalie had handled Catherine's pointed question so effortlessly, and I hoped Catherine would note that not everyone felt the need to live the same way she did.

"Yeah, but to have to share him," Catherine said, "and split up your time."

"Yeah, sure," Natalie said with some hesitation creeping into her voice.

"I know because my sister was divorced. It's so hard on everyone, especially when there are young children."

The entire table came to a standstill at that point. The clattering of silverware against dishes stopped as we all looked to Natalie for a response. Her eyes had gotten bigger, her lips were parted, but she was holding it together. I was pretty sure I wouldn't have been able to do the same in her situation.

"Natalie is doing an excellent job making it work," I said, doing my best to put things in a different perspective. "After all, she moved here so her son could be near his father."

Catherine went on, ignoring my attempt to focus on the positive. "Of course, it was different with my sister. Her kids were adopted," she said. "And that's not the same."

As soon as the words were out of her mouth, I stood up from the table, not even bothering to put my fork down and knocking the vase—still sitting on the floor—over with my foot as I did it.

The sound of breaking glass caused everyone to shout at once— "Are you okay?" "What happened?"—but Dave's voice was the only one that reached me through the commotion.

"Did you hurt yourself?" he said, jumping to his feet and reaching out for my arm.

"I'm fine," I said. "It's fine."

"What happened?" Catherine asked again.

"It's nothing," I said. "I broke the vase."

"Oh, no!" Catherine squealed. "That was one of your wedding gifts, wasn't it?"

"I know," I said. "It's fine. I'll just clean it up."

"No," Dave said, still holding onto my arm as if I were in danger of falling. "I'll do it. Just sit down. Are you sure you're okay?" he asked me. I could feel his eyes on me, but I knew if I looked at him, I'd start to cry.

"We can replace it," Dave said. "We can get another one."

I finally worked up the courage to glance up at him, and he caught my eye, pleading: *Please just let it go. Please don't say anything.*

"It's fine," I said. "It's no big deal. I'll survive." And I knew I would. After all, Catherine's words were nothing new. They were just one more indication that most people would never understand me.

As long as I had known Paula, she'd been badgering me to go to one of Jeannie's basketball games. Sometimes she would go so far as to suggest I meet her at a game several states away from where I was living. She would ask me not-so-subtle questions like, "How many hours are you from Kansas City?" or "Is it very far from your place to Alabama?" as if she had no understanding of the geographical makeup of the middle of the United States, fly-over country as some people, including Paula, saw it. It was an issue she had raised so often that I felt obligated to go when Jeannie's team was playing only fifty miles away at the University of Dayton the week after Thanksgiving.

I'm not sure how I found out about the game. Paula and I weren't communicating very much at that time—maybe she wrote me a letter or left a message on the machine, or maybe she'd mentioned it long before we'd fallen out of touch. Regardless, that was how I found myself in Dayton one cold November night in the fall of 2001 watching my biological sister play basketball.

I should've known by then that my faux fur coat wasn't the way to go when seeing one of the Tuckers, but back then it never occurred to me to question the message my wardrobe might send. At the time, I only owned one winter coat and one good pair of winter shoes, so I put on my cold-weather uniform—including my black combat boots—and headed north, naively believing everything would go just fine. I didn't want to go to the game alone, but Dave had to teach that night, so a friend from school went with me.

When we arrived, my friend Julia and I were surprised to see the gym was virtually empty. Only about fifty spectators were in attendance, spotted around the ten-thousand seat arena like clusters of stars. I had never been to a women's basketball game before and had incorrectly presumed the gym would be at least half full. Still, the sparse crowd allowed us the freedom to sit anywhere we wanted, so Julia and I clomped down the endless concrete steps until we were directly behind the nearly empty Virginia Tech bench. All of the players were warming up on court, and, for a moment, I worried I wouldn't recognize Jeannie or be able to pick her out from the other players, but it only took a few seconds for me to locate her, the name on the back of her jersey an immediate reminder why I was there: by blood, I was a Tucker.

"That's her," I said to Julia, pointing to the tallest blond on the court.

Because of Paula's insistence that I go to a game if the team ever came within a few hours of Cincinnati, I suspected Jeannie knew I was going to be there. But just to be sure, I had emailed her the day before, letting her know I was making the trip. Despite this, nothing about Jeannie's demeanor that evening indicated she had seen me even though Julia and I were the only ones sitting anywhere near the team bench. Still, I immediately had the sense Jeannie knew I was there because the space felt suddenly charged as if there were a current of electricity running across the hardwood floor between us.

So it seemed pretty strange when the team gathered around the bench after the warm-up, and Jeannie didn't even look in my direction. And it seemed even stranger that she continued to do so throughout the entire two-hour game even though I was sitting less than ten feet away from her. I felt certain she knew I was there but was clearly choosing to ignore me.

At first I pretended not to notice. "Maybe she didn't see me," I said to Julia, and, like any good friend, Julia agreed: "Maybe not."

But by the time halftime rolled around and the players headed for the locker room—Jeannie never once turning her head in my direction—it was painfully obvious she was trying to pretend I wasn't there. Julia and I discussed explanations for Jeannie's behavior the whole time the team was gone. Maybe she wasn't allowed to talk to people while she was playing, maybe she simply didn't want to be distracted from the game, or maybe—and this was, of course, what I really believed—she was ignoring me because that's what I had been doing to Paula for fourteen months: ignoring her, hoping she would go away. I was certain Jeannie's coldness was not about the game, but about my behavior. And as much as I wanted to believe I didn't deserve it, I knew I did. Jeannie was being standoffish on her mother's behalf, and I understood then something that had never occurred to me before: if I didn't have a good relationship with Paula, I wouldn't have one with Jeannie either.

The second half of the game continued the same as the first. Jeannie didn't so much as glance my way, apparently believing if she made eye contact with me, she would have to acknowledge my presence, something she was evidently not willing to do. So Julia and I sat and watched the players throw the ball back and forth like well trained children, and I grew even angrier with Paula. What had she said about me? Had she told Jeannie to ignore me? And, if so, why had she been so adamant about me going to one of Jeannie's games? Didn't she know it was a sacrifice to take one night off from studying to make the drive to Dayton? To put gas in the car and pull Julia away from her own obligations?

More importantly, I wondered if I should try to make contact or just leave. But I didn't feel comfortable leaning forward and tapping Jeannie on the shoulder while the game was in progress, so instead I just waited, certain that when it was all over, Jeannie would have no choice but to turn around and talk to me. Of course, if I were being honest with myself, Jeannie's behavior would've told me no such thing would happen, but, instead of admitting what was really going on, I naively believed it would all work out in the end. And that's why I was not only surprised but also completely gutted when the game ended and Jeannie headed for the locker room without even glancing behind her, sending the message she had no intention of talking to me at all.

I was not only hurt. I was irate.

I had taken the time and money to drive to Dayton, and for what? So I could be ignored? So that Jeannie could reject me right to my face?

Still, I couldn't leave. I was too angry for that. I didn't want to let Jeannie win so easily. If she wanted to hurt me, I was going to make her admit out loud that's what she was trying to do. I was going to make her say it. So I got a hold of one of the team managers and asked her to tell Jeannie I was waiting for her to come out of the locker room and talk to me. The young woman was clearly nervous, her eyes darting around the empty gym like a trapped animal as she edged off the court and away from me. She told me, sheepishly, she wasn't sure Jeannie would have time to do that. It was clearly an excuse, and I understood then that she—and possibly everyone else on the team—knew about me. Maybe they all knew who I was and that Jeannie was trying to blow me off. It even seemed plausible that she'd recruited them in her attempts to snub me. Still, I was persistent, telling the manager how far I'd traveled and pushing her to do the right thing. In the end, it worked because the girl fled down the long tunnel to the locker room, and, a few minutes later, Jeannie appeared in the same spot where the girl had disappeared, her head held high as if she was more than confident of her ability to handle our dispute.

When she got close enough, she spoke. "Hi," she said casually as if she hadn't just spent the night ignoring me.

"Are you allowed to talk?" I said, wanting to get right to the point—was she going to blame the team for her behavior or was she going to own up to it?

"Yeah, I guess," she said. "I mean, I don't have much time. Like five minutes."

Five minutes. That's what she was willing to give me. When all was said and done, I would have spent about five hours driving to Dayton, watching her play, and driving home, but she was only going to give me five minutes of her time.

"We have to catch the plane," she said by way of explanation.

"The plane, right," I said. "You didn't talk to me the whole game. I thought maybe you weren't allowed to talk."

"No, it's not that. I just wanted to concentrate."

"I thought maybe you were angry with me," I said, and then, not willing to play games anymore, I added, "you know because I haven't talked to your mom in so long."

"No!" she insisted, her palms up as if she was trying to explain, to make me understand. "I'm not angry. It's nothing like that. It's just that—" She hesitated. "Coach has been all over me."

Years later, I would understand that Jeannie was a master at avoiding confrontation, but in that moment, I only knew she wasn't going to cop to her real feelings. I thought about pushing her further, seeing if I could get her to admit the truth, but instead decided to back off, leaving well enough alone. I knew she had been avoiding me, I knew she didn't want to see me. Her behavior the entire night had told me that as clearly as any words could have. So, instead of discussing what was really going on between us, instead of discussing what really mattered, we made small talk. She told me what was happening with everyone in the family, and I told her what was up with school. And, ultimately, we parted amicably, not making any plans to see each other again but not spitting in each other's faces either.

The evening had gone nothing like I'd hoped.

Some time after Jeannie's basketball game, I stopped thinking about the Tuckers. Or at least I told myself I wasn't thinking about them. Sure, they were always in my head—buried underneath the enormous pile of other stuff I had to worry about: teaching, studying, writing, living up to the expectations of family and friends, losing weight, working out, living life. I did such a good job of convincing myself I wasn't thinking about them and that they weren't a significant part of my life that I didn't make any contact whatsoever with Paula for another six months. And then it was only to send her a birthday card, which I felt obligated to do.

Sure, she still tried to call every once in a while, but we simply stopped answering the phone, letting the answering machine tell us if it was safe to pick up or not. I just didn't have the courage to talk to her. And though I often thought about calling her back—even going so far as to put it on my list of things to do every month—it never happened. Instead, I sent birthday and Christmas cards, which seemed like the least I could do, and Paula did the same, the latter of which she'd send with what seemed like more elaborate gifts every year. And every year those gifts would sit outside the door of our apartment for weeks while we visited my parents. And every year I would feel an overwhelming mix of anger and guilt when I returned to find them on my doorstep despite the fact that I'd made it clear to Paula in my thank you letters that she shouldn't send anything over the holidays.

And somehow, without even realizing it or wanting it to happen, just over four years—yes, four years—passed without me speaking one word to the woman who had given birth to me.

It might be the single thing I'm least proud of in my life.

PART FIVE
SHE TRIES AGAIN

JANUARY 2005-MARCH 2007

Anger dominated my emotions toward Paula during most of those four years, but after all that time passed and the anger faded, I found what I was left with was my own guilt. Had I really been the person who searched for my biological family and then cut off all contact with them? Was I really that cold, that unforgiving?

Right around that time, a friend told me about an essay he had read in *The New Yorker* called "The Mistress's Daughter." It was a piece by A.M. Holmes, a writer who had also been adopted as an infant and, like me, met her birth parents many years later. I remember clearly that I felt something akin to righteous indignation when I read about Holmes' decision to stop talking to her birthmother. It was a decision she had made because of the difficulty of having a relationship with a demanding mother figure whom she had almost nothing in common with, and I was certain Holmes was being unfair, even selfish. Couldn't she see her birthmother had done the most selfless thing a person could do? She had given up her own flesh and blood, so her child could have a better life. Couldn't she see that not appreciating such a generous gift was simply wrong?

But then it hit me.

I had done the same thing.

It was certainly the easy way out. If I didn't see Paula or talk to Paula, my life was less complicated. There were no questions about my identity, no additional demands on my time, no disappointments or frustrations about how different we were, no resentment about the fact that Paula seemed to want her life and her family to be the center of our relationship. But was it right?

The answer was no.

No, it wasn't right. And deep down, I had known that all along. But it had taken "The Mistress's Daughter" to help me see that. The truth I could no longer hide from was that I had made a mistake with Paula almost as big as the one L.W. had made with us so many years before.

When I finally realized that, I didn't do anything about it. Instead of immediately trying to fix my mistake, I spent the next few weeks letting it settle inside me like an unhatched egg. I needed time to process this new understanding of my actions and the situation with Paula. I couldn't just call her up and tell her I had been wrong. And even if I could, how would that conversation go?

Hi, Paula, it's Molly. I'm so sorry that I've completely ignored you for the past four years, but I just figured out what an ass I've been, and I want to apologize.

No, I couldn't apologize over the phone for years of mistakes any more than L.W. could make up to Paula for what he'd done to her with a rose wrapped in plastic. I also couldn't say any of that because, if I did, what would be next? Another weekend at the Tuckers' house? More time together? Or maybe it wouldn't go that way at all. Maybe Paula would be so angry she would lash out at me.

In truth, I suspected the latter would never happen. I believed Paula was far too interested in having me in her life to retaliate. But I couldn't be sure she wouldn't betray how much I had hurt her, and I was not prepared for that kind of naked emotion.

So rather than act, I did the opposite. I did nothing.

And I waited.

In the back of my head, I knew we would be heading back east eventually. In fact, we were scheduled to go to D.C. for a conference the very next month. I didn't know if I would be ready to contact Paula so soon, but I was pretty certain I would be ready at some point in the not-so-distant future. As it turned out, that moment came just a few weeks later.

*

At the time, Dave and I were in our fifth and final year of the doctoral program, finishing up the dissertation and searching for jobs—for one or both of us, anything to live on after the graduation day we had been dreaming about and dreading during the five long years since we'd met Paula. Over the course of our studies, Dave had become more interested in mainstream fiction, probably as a way of resisting the academic obsession with literary writing. Sure, we both loved the classics—Shakespeare, Woolf, Hughes—but we also loathed the elitist attitude of most academics, the attitude that literature was best appreciated by the educated. Instead, we believed great stories were ones that inspired regular people, not just those in the ivory tower. Though we both had that response to grad school, the feeling was much more pronounced in Dave, who was desperately searching for his voice.

And that was how he ended up at Borderlands, a "boot camp" for writers—that is, mainstream thriller writers. He was tired of feeling like he wasn't learning anything concrete about writing and wanted to study with people who were reaching the masses. It was only a three-day conference, but he hoped to uncover more about what real people were reading than he'd learned in the seven years it took us to get through all of graduate school.

As it turned out, Borderlands was based near D.C.

As always, it took us a whole day to make the drive, but unlike our previous treks east, we got an early start. Our ability to get on the road at a decent hour ended up being fortuitous as we encountered more setbacks on that trip than ever before. The first occurred before we'd even left Cincinnati when our rental car began making a funny noise. Not wanting to risk trouble, we stopped at an Enterprise location just outside of Cincinnati and traded one rental car for another.

Not long after that, it started to snow. What started out as flurries would eventually become a full-blown blizzard, but we would be out of Ohio before the worst of it hit. Nevertheless, enough snow fell that we needed to use our washer fluid to clear the windshield, which would have been no big deal except that as soon as we did that, the engine light came on. And that's what led us to stop a second time—

in Columbus, Ohio—to exchange our rental car again. Making that trade was easy, but it was starting to feel like we were living inside a video game where obstacles were constantly being thrown at us in an obvious attempt to slow us down.

"Do you think the universe is trying to tell us something?" I said to Dave, who was driving through a bad part of Columbus at the time, navigating the snow and an unusual number of jaywalkers.

"Maybe," he admitted. "But we've come this far. I'm not giving up now."

I had been worried for months—as long as we'd known we were going to Borderlands—that the trip would be difficult for me on an emotional level, but what I couldn't have foreseen was that it would also be so challenging to get there and that everything, mother nature included, would be working against us. Looking back on it now, I have to wonder if fate really was trying to tell us something.

We finally arrived at the conference hotel around eight, ten hours after we'd left home and two hours longer than it should have taken us to get there.

I hadn't decided if I was going to call Paula or not, but after we had dinner and were settled in for the night, I found myself looking up her number and punching it into the keypad of my new cell phone before I could reconsider.

My heart raced as the phone rang in my ear. I couldn't imagine what Paula would think. I hadn't talked to or seen her in years, and yet there I was, calling her from a hotel that was only a short distance from where she lived.

There are certain people in life who never feel very far away no matter how long you go without talking to them, hovering under the surface of your consciousness like emotional submarines—your parents, your spouse, your siblings, close friends—and for me, at that time, Paula was in that group as well. Even though we hadn't talked in nearly five years, when I heard her throaty hello on the other end of the line, it was as if it had only been a few weeks since we'd last spoken. The sound of her voice was that familiar to me, and the gravity of what I had done by re-initiating contact hit me like a torpedo.

"Paula?" I said cautiously.

I had expected Paula wouldn't know who was calling, but immediately she said my name, almost as if she had been expecting my call.

"I'm so glad you called," she said without hesitation, not a trace of hostility in her voice. I hadn't been sure what to expect—anger? disgust? judgment?—but I suppose I had never expected Paula to be happy to hear from me. I had thought, for sure, there would be some resentment in her voice.

But if there was resentment there, she was hiding it well enough that I couldn't hear it. And I honestly believe if she hadn't sounded happy to hear from me that day, I don't think we would've ever seen each other again. In her voice, rather than judgment I heard acceptance, and part of the reason I had stayed away so long was because I feared her reproach. If Paula could deal with me dodging phone calls and avoiding visits for more than four years, it told me she could also accept me on my own terms, that she understood I had a life of my own, and I had to live that life no matter how much she wished I could live the one she had imagined for me.

I have a cousin who put a baby up for adoption, and over the years we've talked about her son from time to time. During these conversations it's clear to me that she'll never let go of him. That for her, he will always be alive in her heart. He'll be learning to walk and going to school and becoming a young man. And those pictures she has of him in her head will be as real to her as her own life. I know now that most mothers who put a child up for adoption feel that way—their children never stop living a full life in their heads because that's the only way they can cope with their overwhelming sense of loss.

And I knew, by then, Paula was typical in that sense. She had constructed a life for me—a life, a name, a personality—and when she'd met me five years before, she had never imagined I wouldn't be the person she'd created in her head. That was what made it so difficult for us to fit into each other's lives. She had wanted me to step into the picture she had imagined for me, and I'd wanted her to step into mine. Of course, that could never happen. The pictures we'd created were fantasies that fulfilled our wishes but never considered anyone else's. So when I heard Paula's voice on the other end of the line—accepting, benevolent, even warm—I sensed that she finally understood this. She finally understood she had to take me as I was—Molly, *not* Anne Marie—or not have me at all.

Paula and I talked for about fifteen minutes and decided to get together the next day while Dave was at the conference. I had already made plans to meet friends for lunch in Georgetown, but I promised to go to the Tuckers' house in the early evening.

As I was walking back to the hotel after lunch the next day, it hit me what was about to happen. I was going to see the whole Tucker clan for the first time since our initial visit. Nearly four and a half years had passed, and they'd all had plenty of time to get used to the idea that I was related to them—if not in the traditional way, then at least by blood. And because of the way Jeannie had acted in Dayton, I knew they'd all probably felt some ill will toward me over the years. Who did I think I was, after all? From their point of view, I had made contact with their beloved mother, disrupted all of their lives with the insane announcement that I was their long-lost sister, and then dumped them like a forgettable one-night stand. Was I crazy to try again? To open up all those old wounds? What if they attacked me?

I'm not sure why, but I was certain I had to face them all again. I had to accept the consequences of my actions. Maybe it was the guilt driving me to do it, but I sensed it was more than that. I needed a resolution to the drama I'd been feeling ever since Paula had first stepped off the plane in Dayton. I needed to know I'd done the right thing.

So rather than worry about what might be waiting for me, I embraced what was ahead. I went back to the hotel room and changed into what I thought of as a Tucker-friendly outfit—something I could wear to the bar but still feel like I was being true to myself: a white V-neck t-shirt with a shrunken gray jacket, jeans, and my beloved cowboy boots. On the way to Virginia, I was listening to one of my favorite CDs when a song I loved came on: Badfinger's "No Matter What." Not straight up rock 'n roll, but rock with a little bit of country and a little bit of metal added in equal measures. It was a hybrid of some kind, a song that appealed to both people with glasses and people with mullets. And, as I sang along at full volume, I realized that, maybe, that's who I was: a hybrid of the world I grew up in and the world I came from. Sure, I was more nerd than biker, but I had some of that in me too. Just a little bit. Just enough to know it was there. After all, I was a girl who'd had a motorcycle license at sixteen, a girl who fixed everyone's VCR, a girl who drank Miller High Life and shunned craft beer. And I hoped reminding myself of that fact would put me more at ease when I crossed the border into Tucker country.

No matter how much I psyched myself up for my visit, I was still a bit shocked when I made the transition from my world to theirs for the second time in my life. That night hunting gear was scattered around the porch and cases of beer were lined up by the back door. It almost seemed more redneck than I remembered.

I knocked and, through the window of the door, saw a flurry of women inside. Paula had told me a bunch of her friends were having their hair done at the house that night, but I had not steeled myself for a crowd and the performance it would surely require. Still, I put on my best smile and was ready when Paula opened the door.

"Come on in," Paula said as she stepped out of the way. I could sense everyone was watching me. I understood intuitively that I was something they had never seen before. A person who had grown up away from her family. A sideshow freak. But as soon as I crossed the threshold, I turned to Paula, and she hugged me, maybe longer than she had ever hugged me before. A part of me knew right then everything was going to be all right, and maybe I'd known that even before I'd arrived.

Something was different.

Paula was different. She was more open, more accepting, than I'd ever seen her before.

Still, I knew my toughest audience was yet to come—Jeannie and her brothers.

Luckily Jeannie was occupied when I got there, sitting in the middle of the kitchen with a towel draped around her neck as a woman I had never met folded strands of Jeannie's wet hair inside pieces of tin foil. Definitely redneck. It was safe to say I had never had anything done to my hair anywhere but inside the sanitized walls of a salon, much less a kitchen.

"Hey!" Jeannie said as soon as she saw me. "I can't believe you're here!" She spoke with the kind of genuine enthusiasm reserved for family members and old friends, and I sensed that as long as Paula was happy, Jeannie would be too. And with this realization came its twin: the gut feeling I'd had in Dayton had been right—I could not have Jeannie in my life if I didn't have Paula too.

Don't get me wrong. It wasn't that I didn't want Paula in my life; it's that I still wasn't sure what that meant. I already had a mother I loved, and for that reason, Paula could never be my mother. And, though I already had a sister, I'd never worried about having enough room in my life to accommodate another one. In fact, I had known from the moment I met her that I wanted Jeannie to stick around.

"Molly, this is Deanna," Jeannie said, gesturing with her head at the woman who had her hands in Jeannie's hair. "Deanna: Molly."

Deanna offered me a short hello, and I could tell right away she didn't trust me. She gave me the same artificial sneer I'd seen so many times before from anyone who assumed I came from more money or education than they did: her smile was plastered in place, but her eyes told me I'd best watch my back.

Jeannie jumped in before I could say anything else. "Deanna's so good with a blow dryer she can make me look like Claudia Schiffer. Well, Claudia Schiffer with a real ass." If I'd forgotten why I liked Jeannie, I remembered then. She was one of the most entertaining people I'd ever met.

"Jeannie!" Paula said, though I knew Paula's objection was more for show than anything else.

"What?" Jeannie said. "I have a real tushie, okay? Have you seen it lately? It's as big as a fully risen moon." Jeannie leaned over to the side and slapped her butt for emphasis.

Everyone laughed, and I couldn't help but join them. Somewhere in the back of my head I was thinking that maybe Jeannie's body was becoming a little bit more like mine than it had been several years before when she was nineteen and as lean as a greyhound.

"Oh my God," Paula said. "You're embarrassing me, Jeannie."

But even though she said this, she smiled with everyone else. Then she turned to me and said, "Have you met Amy?" as she gestured toward the young woman leaning against the stove.

After we exchanged the briefest of hellos, I turned to Paula and said, "No, I don't think we've met before."

"Amy is dating Clint," Paula explained. "I don't think they were dating the last time you were here."

I had met one of Clint's girlfriends during our first visit, but at that moment I couldn't remember if it had been Amy or someone else. All I remembered was that, though I hadn't disliked her, I could tell the two of them would be better off if they broke up. I was pretty sure Amy was not the same person, but it'd been so long I couldn't be absolutely sure.

"When were you here?" Jeannie asked.

"Uh—" I said, hesitating. I knew exactly when I'd last been there—four and a half years before—but I was reluctant to admit it out loud.

"I think it was before Clint and I were together," Amy said quickly.

"Are you sure?" Jeannie asked skeptically. "It seems like you've been together forever. I can hardly remember what life was like without you hanging around all the time."

Amy punched Jeannie playfully. "I'm pretty sure it was before I knew Clint." She sounded a little bit nervous, and I understood intuitively that she knew full well she'd never met me before. And, of course, she would've remembered if she had. It's not every day you meet your boyfriend's long-lost sister. Still, Amy was smartly playing along, not wanting to remind everyone of a time before she'd been in their lives.

"What year were you here?" Jeannie asked me, unwilling to let the subject go.

I could see I'd eventually have to answer her question—whether I wanted to or not—so I decided to come clean. "I think it was the summer of 2000." I glanced at Paula, but her face betrayed no irritation at how long it had been since my last visit. Instead she just looked a little bit out of it.

"Was it *that* long ago?" Jeannie said, not realizing how

uncomfortable it made me to put it in words.

"Yeah, it's been a while," I said. "We've been busy with school and everything." I offered that excuse even though I probably didn't need to. No one seemed to be looking for an explanation or interrogating me about my absence, but I still felt the need to say something.

"Well, if it's been that long," Amy said, "Clint and I *definitely* weren't together."

And then Paula said what everyone had been trying not to say: "I think he was with Olivia then."

I glanced at Amy to see if hearing the name of Clint's ex-girlfriend—the name of someone we all knew he'd been crazy about—bothered her, and even though she tried not to show it on her face, I could see in her eyes that Olivia still scared Amy a little. It was then that a detailed picture of Olivia came back to me—the girl with the perfect blonde hair and the big eyes, the girl who rode horses and came from a family with money, the girl who thought she was too good to be a Tucker.

"Wasn't she pretty full of herself?" I asked in a mock innocent voice, knowing full well I could win over Amy and everyone in the room if I were right.

"Hell, yeah, she was," Jeannie said immediately.

Paula snorted, adding, "She always thought she was too good for Clint."

I understood I was using Olivia to improve my own standing, but I couldn't help myself. The truth was even though I'd liked talking to Olivia and felt some kinship with her feelings about the bar and the whole Tucker scene, I had also bristled at her attitude and how it made me feel about mine. Did she really think she was better than them? Did I? It was one thing to admit you didn't feel entirely comfortable with people, but it was another to say something akin to "I love this person, but his family is beneath me." I would've never even considered choosing the person I wanted to spend my life with based on his family. And I also knew Clint was a catch—he was fun and attractive and smart and hardworking and, as a result, far better than someone as superficial as Olivia deserved.

The irony was that I learned later that Amy came from money

too, but the mixture of fear and longing in her eyes told me she would never leave Clint. Even if he brought with him the worst people on earth, she'd stand by him. I knew then that Clint would be lucky to have her.

"Wonder what she'd think of what Clint got me for Christmas," Amy said with a laugh, and immediately Jeannie and Paula joined her laughter, allowing Amy to regain some of her position in the room.

"Oh my God," Jeannie said. "I think she'd have pooped her pants."

"She wouldn't have been happy," Paula said. "That's for sure."

"Why?" I asked. "What did he get you?"

"He got me a Winchester twelve-gauge," Amy said proudly, and when I gave her a confused look, Jeannie jumped in: "It's a shotgun." This caused the four of them to laugh at my ignorance as if the funniest thing in the world was a girl who didn't know her guns. Sure, they were laughing *at* me, but at least they were laughing, at least they were enjoying me being there. And that was fine with me.

When I looked back at Amy, she was still smiling, and I knew what she was saying: *this is why I'm the one for him, this is why I'm better than Olivia.*

"He got you a shotgun?" I asked in a skeptical tone. "For Christmas?" I hadn't intended for my comment to be humorous, but they all laughed again.

"Cool, huh?" Jeannie said to me with a nod when she'd caught her breath. Though she didn't explain, I knew exactly what she meant. Wasn't it cool Clint had found a girl he could buy a shotgun?

"Yeah, but wait a minute," I said. "*Why* did he buy you a shotgun?" I felt compelled to ask even though I knew I could, at any second, turn everyone against me if I acted too self-righteous.

"So we can go goose hunting together," Amy said.

"You hunt geese?" I asked, trying as hard as I could not to betray my squeamishness about the subject.

"Hell, yes," Jeannie said. "Amy's parents own, like, a million acres on the Eastern Shore. We all go out there. It's a blast."

I really have no problem with people hunting if they eat what they kill, but I worried the Tuckers wouldn't have the same caveat. "Do you eat the meat?" I asked tentatively.

"Absolutely," Jeannie said. "It's amazing. You've got to try it."

"Sounds great." I said this in all honesty, though when the following year I would see Jeannie wearing a baseball hat that said, *If it flies, it dies,* I would still feel a bit discomfited by their casualness about shooting birds right out of the sky.

"It's a complete blast," Jeannie said again. "You should come with us some time. You'd love it."

Everyone looked at me, and I knew I had to be careful not to say the wrong thing. "Hmmm," I said, "I'll eat whatever you catch, but I think I'll leave the hunting to you guys." And for some reason, that comment caused the kitchen to go up in laughter again as if I were the most hysterical person they'd ever met.

About an hour after I'd been there, a waifish young woman bounded through the back door like an intruder. She was wearing army green carpenter pants and a tight black t-shirt with a black leather jacket. Her head was shaved, making her eyes stand out, doe-like, against her emaciated face.

"Hi, Misty," Paula said unenthusiastically. "This is Molly." And then, turning to me, added, "Molly, this is Willie's girlfriend."

I glanced in Misty's eyes, but they darted to the floor before I could catch them. With her head down, I had a clear view of her new hairstyle—a buzz cut courtesy of her neurosurgeon. Paula had been telling me all about Misty before she arrived. Misty had been dating Willie for a few years, and the two of them had had a baby boy that fall. Continuing the tradition started by Paula and L.W. of giving their son L.W.'s middle name, Willie and Misty had named their baby William Tucker Jr. I also knew from Paula that Misty was only twenty-one, eleven years younger than Willie, and that she'd recently had brain surgery for an aneurysm. "Hi," I said, not sure what to say to a twenty-one-year-old who'd nearly lost her life and already had a baby to take care of.

Misty barely answered, nodding at me as if she had no voice.

"How are you feeling, Misty?" Paula asked, introducing the one subject I figured Misty didn't want to discuss.

"Fine," Misty said shortly, kicking the toe of her boot against the linoleum floor.

"What did the doctor say?"

Misty glanced up, her big eyes catching mine for just a second before she turned her attention back to the floor. "He said I'm okay."

There was a brief silence as we all watched Misty, waiting for her to say more. Then, after a few uncomfortable seconds had passed, Jeannie spoke up.

"You should tell Molly about the night they came to get you."

"Oh, yeah," Paula said, encouraging Misty to speak. "You should." Paula and Jeannie were acting like Misty was a child who needed to be goaded into talking to adults even though she herself was a mother. But I said nothing, figuring it was best to let them work it out on their own.

"What is there to say?" Misty said, looking at everyone in the room for the first time. Her words sounded defensive, but there was also a sliver of a smile on her face. "I fell down. I had a seizure. They didn't believe me."

"What do you mean?" I asked, sure everyone else in the room knew what Misty was talking about and that her story was for my benefit.

"Yeah," Jeannie said. "It was insane. The paramedics honestly thought she was drunk. While she was having a seizure."

"It was right here," Paula said, pointing at the linoleum floor. "In this very room."

We all glanced at the floor as if looking for evidence that might give away what had transpired. There was nothing there, but as I studied the worn-out tile, I suddenly saw it all happening—Misty falling to the ground, her tiny body convulsing angrily against the hard surface of the floor, the police rushing into the kitchen, searching for someone to blame. I looked back to Misty, her eyes were on me then like she knew I was watching the whole thing play out before me. But when I caught her eye, she turned away, brushing her fingers through her crew cut like a teenage boy trying to look cool.

"They just assumed," Paula said to me, bringing me back to the present, "Misty was drinking."

"Well, who could blame them?" Amy added. "There were a couple of twelve-packs sitting by the back door and a bunch of animal skins hanging from the porch." And though Amy didn't say it, I added Misty's profile in my head—immature, gaunt, single mother. Of course, they had assumed she'd been drinking. Or worse.

"They thought they knew everything about us," Jeannie added.

"But they didn't know us at all," Paula said, and I sensed that she would never understand how the world saw her or her family.

After Misty left, the five of us spent the evening in the kitchen, Paula and I catching up on each other's lives as we watched Deanna work her magic on Jeannie and Amy's hair, the two of them glowing a bright blond before the night was over. A few hours after I got there, Paula suggested we order pizza, but I pretended not to be hungry because of the ridiculous snobbery I've had about pizza as a result of growing up outside of New York.

"I had a huge lunch," I explained.

"Where did you go?" Amy asked with what seemed like genuine interest. A girl who wanted to know where I had lunch? That was someone I could like.

"A Thai place in the District," I said. "It was amazing, but I ate way too much."

"You don't want *anything* to eat?" Paula asked in a concerned voice.

"No, I'm okay." I knew it was dangerous to decline the offer of food. Mothers like nothing more than to feed their brood, but I also knew that if I turned my nose up at their Papa John's, that would be an even bigger insult.

"You're not trying to lose weight, are you?" Jeannie asked. "Because you look amazing."

"Yeah, I love your jacket," Amy added, and I knew that in Clint's girlfriend I had found a kindred spirit.

I could feel my face redden. Their comments were so in contrast to the ones Paula had made about my body in the past that I found myself unsure about how to respond, but I managed to at least get out a cautious thank you.

Then Jeannie added: "And those boots kick ass!"

"Like them?" I said with faux humility. "I got them in New York ten years ago, and they're my favorite pair of shoes in the whole world." It was the truth, and I was thrilled that I could be honest about loving something the Tuckers loved too.

"I didn't think you were the kind of person who wore cowboy boots," Jeannie admitted, and I knew right then I had won her over too. Sometimes I think everything would have been different if I had only worn my cowboy boots the first time I went to see the Tuckers.

"Yeah, well, I guess I'm a *little bit* country," I said.

"But you still don't like country music?" Jeannie asked, surprising me by remembering something I'd confessed years before.

"Not really," I said. "Is that awful?"

Paula saved anyone from answering that question by changing the subject back to my weight. "You really do look good," she said, looking me up and down as if I were for sale.

"Have you lost weight?" Jeannie asked.

"Yeah, I've lost about twenty pounds since you last saw me."

Then Paula went on: "I remember you said you'd never weighed as much as you did when I met you, but I can't believe how different you look."

My throat clenched a little. I'd always felt Paula judged me for my weight, and though her comment was meant to be a compliment, it was hard not to see it as a backhanded one. *You look great! And so different than you looked before when you were such a whale!* But rather than give into my insecurities, I ignored them and went on, determined to make it clear that my previous weight had not bothered me. "Yeah, that was just because of my knee injury."

"Bum knee?" Jeannie asked.

"I tore my ACL when I was twenty-six."

"Oh my God!" Jeannie said. "I have knee trouble too!" Jeannie sounded so excited that you'd think we were talking about something else we shared—like my love of independent films or Jeannie's penchant for scented candles—but I knew from experience that connections like these were treasured more because they were so hard to find. Like the day Jeannie and I had found out we'd both suffered from difficult periods all of our lives, discovering we both had bad knees that night allowed us to feel that much more connected. "So how did it happen?" she asked.

"Oh, it was so stupid," I admitted. "I was skiing in West Virginia, and like a complete idiot, I was trying to keep up with two hotshot boys who were moving a lot faster than I was. While I was racing to catch up with them, I slid on the tiniest patch of ice. I've had much bigger falls in my life—falls when you tumble down the mountain like a piece of laundry in the dryer and think you're going to die or at least lose a leg. But it was that one little slip that did me in. I ended up being rushed down the mountain in a ski patrol sled. It was humiliating." I knew full well it was unnecessary to go into so much detail, but I also knew doing so would bolster my image in the their eyes and help counteract the fragile image I feared the Tuckers had of me. I even hoped they'd see me as a little tough.

"Holy crap," Jeannie said. "That is so cool." It was the exact effect I'd been hoping for.

"My knee's been a mess ever since then. Unfortunately, I reinjured it right before I met all of you—doing yoga of all things— and then spent three months sitting on the couch with a bag of potato chips feeling sorry for myself." Again, I told the truth. For some reason, I felt more comfortable being myself that night than I ever had with the Tuckers. "The worst part for me," I said, going on, "is that I never know when it's going to come back. One wrong step, and I'm done for."

"I know exactly what you mean," Jeannie added.

"You know," I added, "when I was growing up, my parents always acted like I was the brainy one and my sister was the athletic one. But after meeting all of you, I realized I'm more athletic than I thought. I used to think I wasn't very good at sports because I never played varsity or went to the state championships like my sister, but when I got older I realized most people don't even *play* a sport in high school. At least I did that." I was vaguely aware of the fact that I was sharing even more than I had intended, but I wasn't even thinking about what I was saying at that point. The words were just coming out.

"Your parents told you that you weren't athletic?" Amy asked, her wide eyes telling me she was simultaneously horrified and astonished.

"Well, they never said it like that. And I wouldn't say they didn't see me as athletic. I would say they didn't see me *as* athletic as Katie.

She always seemed to be good at everything—swimming, gymnastics, snow skiing *and* water skiing, climbing trees. She was a *big* tree climber. And I was never as good at any of those things as she was. It never came naturally to me. Later, I realized there were plenty of sports, all the eye-hand coordination sports, I was better at—tennis, basketball, softball—"

Jeannie jumped in: "Those are all the ones *we're* good at."

"Yeah, I get that now," I said. "But when I was a kid I felt like I couldn't compete. I still played sports, but I never thought I would be any good at them. I always thought I should focus more on school and books."

"And wasn't that true?" asked Paula.

"Well, sure, but if I had grown up in a different way, maybe I wouldn't think that. It just makes you realize how much your environment shapes you."

As soon as I'd admitted that, I knew I'd gone too far. No one said it, but the rest of my thought lingered in the air like an ominous alternative to the life I'd lived. If I'd grown up a Tucker, I wouldn't be a writer. I'd be a high school tennis coach or a bartender. Maybe even an art teacher. But not a writer and certainly not someone about to finish a Ph.D. in English.

"That's so weird," Deanna said. I'd forgotten she was in the room and was surprised she was listening. But when I looked at the others—their faces as slack as zombies—it was clear she spoke for everyone. Sarah and Abby Hoffman had been right: Not growing up with your biological family was weird. Being adopted was weird.

I was weird.

After the pizza had been finished and Jeannie and the other girls were discussing the rest of the night, Paula suggested we go down to the bar. "L.W. will want to see you," she said.

Would he? Sure, he might feel obligated to see me, but would he really *want* to see me? It was a question I still wasn't able to answer.

"Sure," I said because that was what I'd signed up for—see everyone, make amends. At that point, I really had no choice.

"And Willie will be there. Wade, too, if I call him."

"How is Wade?" I asked Paula.

"Not good," Paula said. "He's using cocaine again."

I could literally feel my jaw drop. Still, I was surprised how much her answer knocked me back. Though I had never really known what to make of Wade, I hadn't expected that answer. Wade had a drug problem before I met the Tuckers, but after things got out of control, L.W. and Paula stepped in, insisting he go to rehab until he was clean. I'd figured once he'd gone to all that trouble, he'd never fall off the wagon again. But I was wrong.

"And he's living with some prostitute in a motel," Paula said.

"What?" I said.

"Yeah, I know." And Paula didn't have to explain: she knew how shocking it was for me to hear because she was shocked too. "He owns a brand new house with four bedrooms, but he stays in a fleabag motel."

"Why doesn't he live in the house?"

"He rents all the rooms out. Thinks he can have it paid off in ten years that way." It was a familiar story—not vastly dissimilar to the one I'd been told about Wade not using electricity in his apartment during my first visit with the Tuckers. If I hadn't been completely sure about him before, I was then: Wade wasn't quite right.

"Have you tried to get him help?" I asked, knowing I was crossing a line I might not be welcome to acknowledge was there.

"I ask him to get help every time I see him." Paula looked into my face then, frowning. "He won't listen. He thinks he's in love."

Paula's plaintive tone told me how horrified she was by her son's behavior. Was it possible she was as uncomfortable with some aspects of her life as I was? Had I misread her ability to love her children unconditionally as enabling them? Was there a difference?

"Don't give up on him. He figured it out before. I bet he can do it again."

Paula didn't answer. She just shook her head. And I knew she had lost whatever hope she still had.

Even though it was only a few degrees above freezing, L.W. was standing behind the outside bar when we arrived, his arms folded just as they'd been the last time I'd seen him there. He didn't meet my eye but glanced at Paula before he went inside through the swinging door that connected the two bars. Nothing had changed. L.W. obviously did not want to see me, and by then, I wasn't sure I blamed him.

Paula stopped outside to talk to a few of the regulars. It was almost eerie how little things had changed—a few stray bikers sat on stools while a couple more stood next to their bikes, hardly enough people to drink a case of beer—and it made me wonder how the place stayed afloat. Inside was more of the same. No more than five people were sitting at the tables around the room, and only two people were pulled up at the bar, a virtual ghost town.

Paula looked at her watch and then at me. "Are you hungry?" she asked. "You must be hungry."

I hadn't expected Paula to guess I was, at that point, famished. By the time the pizza had arrived at the house, my stomach had begun to quake with hunger, and when I saw several people had gotten subs instead of pizza, I realized I could've ordered something else without offending anyone. Watching the others dig into their giant sandwiches and greasy pieces of pizza was almost painful, but I put on a brave face, something it seemed Paula had noticed. I was immediately aware this was a different Paula than the one I had met almost five years before. This was one who was aware of my needs—both physical and emotional, almost maternal—so when she asked if I was hungry, I didn't think about denying it. "I'm starving."

Bar food is not my favorite thing in the world, but by then I was happy to take Paula up on her offer of chicken fingers and a small salad made of iceberg lettuce, food I would normally avoid.

She sat with me while I ate, and though I can't remember any of the specifics of what we talked about, I can remember this—it was one of the more enjoyable conversations we ever shared. There was nothing tense or difficult about our interaction that night. It was just the two of us talking, getting along. For all I know, maybe that's why I don't remember it.

The entire time L.W. was in the background—hovering, watching us, watching everyone, waiting for trouble to break out, I imagine. I knew he had his eye on us, but I didn't care as much as I had in the past. I suppose some part of me had accepted that L.W. and I would never be able to connect, to relate, that he would never fully accept the role I played in his life.

Fortunately, that was not the case with everyone else, so when Willie showed up a little while later, I was greeted with a mischievous smile and a warm, if awkward, hug rather than the cold reception I had gotten from L.W.

"Congratulations on being a dad," I said by way of a greeting. "That's so exciting," I added because I knew that's what you were supposed to say even when the couple was unmarried and you had no idea if they'd be together a year later.

"Thanks," he said as he shrugged and ducked his head in an aw-shucks manner. As if it were required of him, Willie wore his usual uniform—jeans, flannel shirt, and a hooded sweatshirt. "I didn't really do anything, but it's kind of great." Then he took out his wallet and showed me pictures of a toddler who looked remarkably like his father.

"He's cute," I said looking from the photo to L.W., who was still behind the bar.

"He's a good boy," Paula said with a smile before she started clearing my dishes from the table. After he put his wallet away, I followed Willie to the bar, where we sat together on two stools near the end farthest from the door, farthest from where L.W. was standing at that time. Was it possible Willie knew his father wasn't comfortable around me? Was it possible he didn't?

After L.W. had brought us our drinks—domestic beer for both of us—Willie turned to me.

"I still can't believe I have an older sister," he said. He'd made the same comment the first time I'd met him, and it would turn out to be something he would put out there every single time we met. For Willie, being the oldest was a crucial part of his identity. The oldest, the first, the namesake. And when I was around, he no longer held so much position in the family. Willie needn't have worried. I had no intention of usurping his authority, and I have to give him credit—he never acted threatened by me, just mystified more than anything. *How was it possible I had come before him?* he seemed to be wondering. He was as baffled by that question as L.W. was by my presence in the bar that night.

"I know," I admitted. "It's really strange."

"It is, isn't it?"

In some ways, Willie and I are the most distinct. We are almost nothing alike. Wade, though odd, is a bit of a nerd who likes to read and understand how a piece of machinery works, two things I've always enjoyed. As for Jeannie and Clint, they felt like old friends the day I met them. Truthfully, I have a good deal in common with the two of them. We're all outgoing and talkative and friendly, we're all people people. We all have the ability to make others feel comfortable with us, to make them feel like we're really listening. And then there's our wild side, the side that allows all of us to get up in front of an audience and make fools of ourselves, the side that lets Jeannie serenade a bar packed full of drunks, the side that gives me the courage to stand on a stage and read my innermost secrets to strangers. We're all a little bit crazy, yes, but never so much that we cross the line. Our craziness is always within the bounds of what's considered normal. We're not dangerous. Just fun.

But Willie and Wade don't have that quality. They don't really turn it on in front of a crowd. The two of them keep to themselves for the most part. Wade is basically a loner while Willie is a one-on-one guy. Able to make the person sitting next to him feel as if she is the center of his universe, he's a charmer really. It's something he has in common with the rest of us, but his aloofness still sets him apart. He also lacks the ability to know when he's gone too far—whether it's on a motorcycle or with a bottle, a fact evidenced by more than one run-in with the law—and, in that way, he was more like Wade than the rest of us.

No, it appeared that, on the surface, Willie and I were worlds apart, but as I sat with him that night, it occurred to me that one of the things we shared was disbelief, skepticism. It was something I'd seen in him five years before, but not something I'd consciously processed. I realized then that, like his Uncle Charlie, he was appropriately suspicious of the facts as they were presented, and rightly so. After all, it was a little hard to believe the two of us—one of us wearing flannel, the other an outfit copied from a magazine—could come from the same parents or share the same genes. And I liked that about Willie—his unwillingness to accept things at face value. Not only did he question things the way I did, he also, more importantly, *enjoyed* questioning them, got off on it. So we sat there, reveling in our disbelief about how the two of us, out of all the people in the world, had come to be sitting next to each other at the bar of the man who'd sired us.

It wasn't long after that when Wade showed up, thinner than I'd remembered and pale to the point of appearing sickly, a shadow of his former self. Immediately I thought of what Paula had told me earlier—the cocaine, the prostitute. That was where I wanted to get off the Tucker train. But I couldn't blow off Wade, could I, if I wanted to keep things good with everyone else?

Wade sat down on the other side of me, and Willie got up right away as if taking a cue. Did he, too, want to stay out of Wade's way?

After Wade said hello, I got a good look at him. It wasn't hard to do since he almost never returned my gaze. He did appear extremely pale, and, as always, he seemed painfully shy—so shy he kept his head ducked, like a dog that had been kicked too many times—but he didn't seem altered to me, at least not more so than the last time I'd seen him. Wade had always seemed off, but he never seemed high per se, just out of it as if his head was always somewhere else.

I could sense I'd have to be the one to initiate conversation, so I picked an easy topic. "What are you reading?" I asked him. I'd seen the paperback shoved into the back pocket of his pants when he walked in the door. If he was a dope fiend, he was the most well-read one I'd ever seen.

Wade removed the book from his back pocket, holding it out to me for inspection as if answering my question was too difficult a task for him to take on.

"Is it any good?"

"It's okay," he said, turning his head toward me but not looking at me directly.

A second later L.W. showed up, put a glass in front of Wade, and filled it with the soda gun. Wade, it seemed, wouldn't be getting drunk on L.W.'s watch.

Wade caught his father's eye, but neither of them spoke, two mutes silently communicating. I wondered briefly if I should say something to L.W., make a peace offering of some kind, but he was gone before I could speak, much less decide.

I felt a hand on the back of my chair and turned around to see Paula standing behind our bar stools. "Hi, Wade," she said sweetly. "How are you?" She patted her son on the back and stared at him until he responded.

"Okay" was Wade's only reply.

"You remember Molly, don't you?" Paula spoke as if he were a child, and I bristled at her condescension even if it was well intentioned. Yes, Wade wasn't quite right, but he wasn't stupid either.

"Sure," Wade said curtly as if he agreed with me—his mother was selling him short.

Paula nodded at the empty bottle in front of me. "Do you want another?"

I wanted another beer at that moment probably more than at any other time in my life. But it was nearly a thirty-minute drive back to our hotel in D.C. "I have to drive."

"You sure?" Paula asked, and I nodded, hoping to end the discussion there because I really didn't want to be told I could safely get behind the wheel if I had another drink or two when I knew for sure I couldn't.

"Well, I'll let you guys talk," Paula said. "I'm going to finish cleaning up in the kitchen."

"Can I help?" I asked.

"No, you stay here and talk to Wade."

Paula's comment made me wonder if it was unusual for Wade to get quality time with a family member. Jeannie had scoffed at the idea of seeing him earlier when she found out he was coming by the bar, and I felt certain he was largely left on his own more often than not.

I turned to Wade just in time to catch his eye before he looked away. "I guess it's just us."

"Yeah."

His book was still on the bar. "Do you like thrillers?" I asked.

"Yeah," he said, thumbing the corner of his paperback.

"Dave writes that kind of stuff, you know?"

"I don't really read those," he said, moving his hand from the book to his ear, scratching an unknown itch. I wondered if I was the source of his irritation.

"No?" I said with mock innocence even though it was hard to

be patient with someone who, like a three-year-old, was being intentionally obstinate. "Well, maybe you'd make an exception?"

"I doubt it." He smiled and let out a little laugh as if he was embarrassed by his admission, but said nothing to correct it.

That line of questioning had come to its natural end, and I wasn't sure where to go next. I glanced down the bar and saw that L.W. was conversing with someone there. He was happy to talk to a customer, but not to me and not to his own son.

"I heard you bought a house," I said to Wade, trying again to find something to engage him.

Wade nodded, and I took that measly response as an invitation to continue.

"What's it like?"

"It's just a house." Wade laughed nervously. He clearly didn't like to talk about himself.

"It's pretty big, right? Four bedrooms?"

"It's not that big," he said. "But it cost $350,000." Wade smiled at me then, his eyes twinkling like a child's. He was bragging.

"You're kidding," I said even though Paula had hinted earlier that Wade's house had been in the three hundreds. "Where you'd get that kind of money?" As soon as I'd said it, I knew it was an inappropriate question, but Wade didn't seem to notice.

"I saved a long time, and then I rented out the rooms."

I knew that too, but he was talking, so I went with it. "To whom?"

"What?" Wade said, glancing in my direction with a look of irritation.

"Who rented your rooms?"

"Just people who answered an ad. I don't know." Wade turned away from me and scratched his ear again. I was toiling away on my Ph.D. for about $14,000 a year at that point, but my biological brother Wade—a cokehead living with a prostitute in a motel, who at the very least had Asperger's Syndrome—owned a house that cost a third of a million dollars, and he wasn't paying a dime on his mortgage. Was he smarter than I was? Or at least less ignorant about the way the world worked?

We sat in silence for a few minutes while I contemplated Wade's financial coup, and finally he turned to me, again not looking directly at me but generally facing my direction.

"Are you really my sister?" he asked me, not for the first time. When he had originally posed that question to me—five years before—I had been confused by it. How could I not be his sister if his mother said I was? But by then I suspected what he was really asking was something different: Was I his *full* sister?

"That's what your mom says." I wasn't sure if he'd pick up on what I meant. Of course, Paula was my biological mother. Anyone could look at us and see that was the case. But I just had to trust Paula when she said L.W. was my father. Once I'd put it out there, however obliquely, I half expected Wade to look at his father and ask him if it were true, but he showed no sign of wanting to interrogate anyone but me as if I were the one who was lying, a con artist who went around duping families into believing she was one of them. "Do you believe her?" I finally asked.

"I don't know," Wade said a little too loudly. I had irritated him, and I could see suddenly that he was more jumpy, more nervous, than I'd realized. Was that the coke?

L.W. called to us from the other end of the bar. "Everything okay, Wade?" L.W.'s voice was stern, authoritative.

"Yes," Wade snapped in a voice that told me he was tired of being under his father's thumb.

I studied Wade again as he sipped his soda through a straw, but it was clear he wasn't going to risk looking in my direction a second time. He had retreated back to the world of his thoughts, lost to me yet again.

Paula emerged from the kitchen twenty minutes later, looking more worn-out than usual. It was only ten-thirty, but it felt more like three in the morning after everything I'd been through that day, the somber mood of the bar echoing my feeling of fatigue.

Wade and I hadn't spoken for some time, making Paula's presence a welcome one.

"What are you kids up to?" she said even though at the ages of thirty-four and twenty-seven, we were no longer kids.

"Not much," I said. "Actually, I should get going."

"Already?" Paula said, but before she could close her mouth, a cavernous yawn escaped. She was tired too.

"It's been a long day."

Paula cocked her head at me, and I worried I'd said the wrong thing.

"I walked to Georgetown earlier and then—"

"I forgot about that," she said, and I felt like I'd sidestepped a landmine. "You're probably exhausted."

"I am."

"Can you come by tomorrow? We could go out for lunch."

My throat clenched. I had promised myself I only had to do that one thing—see the Tuckers one night, and then, depending on how it went, I could go from there. Admittedly, it had gone well, and things felt mostly different. But Paula's request scared me back into my shell a bit.

"Isn't it supposed to snow?"

"Sure," Paula said, and, in her tone, I could sense her implied question: *And?*

"I mean, a real snowstorm. Like two feet or something."

Paula was studying my face as if still looking for an answer to her question. I could tell exactly what she was thinking. *Could she trust me this time? Was I ready?* I had no idea if I was ready to play a real part in her life or not. All I knew was that I was only capable of doing what I had agreed to do—spend the evening with them—without committing to anything else. I needed time to consider whether I was prepared to take on anything beyond those few hours. And Paula's request to see me the next day made me worry she wasn't ready either, that she wasn't equipped to have the kind of laid-back relationship that was all I could give her. She had seemed like a new person earlier—more accepting, less demanding, more in tune with my needs—but maybe I had read too much into that. Maybe she still wanted me to be her daughter, something I could never do.

"Let's talk tomorrow," I said. "Okay?"

Paula took the hint and backed down from her position of aggression. "Okay, that sounds good. Call me when you get up. I know you're not a morning person."

"No, I'm not," I said, but what I was really thinking was that it might have been the first time Paula had actually remembered something about me.

A full-blown blizzard hit the East Coast that night. The greater metropolitan D.C. area got around a foot of snow—less than other places, but enough that I didn't think it was even possible to make the drive to Annandale, much less to do so safely.

I called Paula not long after I saw the drifts of snow covering the sidewalk outside my window like a miniature mountain range.

Paula's voice was enthusiastic when she picked up, so I shouldn't have been surprised when she asked if I could come over that afternoon.

"There's a foot of snow outside," I said, not able to hide the skepticism in my voice as much as I would have liked. "I don't think I should drive in this weather."

"That's nothing," she said. "The boys have driven in worse. They can come pick you up."

I knew her comment was meant to reassure me, but instead it had the opposite effect: it scared me. The last thing I wanted was to ride in a souped-up pick-up truck along a snow-covered interstate with one of my biological brothers, two of whom were likely to have been drinking. Or worse.

"I really don't think *anyone* should be out on the roads."

"It'll be fine," Paula said again, so I knew I had to be firm.

"I'm just going to stay here and work. I have to prepare for class on Monday, and my dissertation is due in two weeks."

"Are you sure?" Paula asked.

In that moment, I *wanted* to be able to say I wasn't sure and that I was willing to brave the roads to see her, but the truth was I had no desire to leave the safety and comfort of the hotel where I knew I would have the ability to sit in front of the picture window and work in peace and quiet all day. I also knew I was unlikely to bend about driving in the snow—by myself or with anyone. It just wasn't a risk I was willing to take. If I hadn't seen the Tuckers the day before, maybe I could have been talked into it, but since I had, the urgency to reconnect with them was no longer there. On top of that, I had promised myself I would take things slowly with the Tuckers—do a little at a time rather than everything all at once in an attempt to settle into a more laid-back relationship with them. Still, I had no desire to let Paula down either, so it was with reluctance that I said, "Yes, I'm sure."

"Well, what about breakfast tomorrow?" Paula asked, catching me off-guard.

"Maybe, but I don't know what time we're leaving."

"Just think about it," Paula said.

"I will," I said. And then it occurred to me what Paula was after: reassurance. That was something I could give her. "And we'll be back again. I promise."

"Okay," Paula said, but I could tell she wasn't sure she could believe me. And, unfortunately, I knew exactly why she felt that way.

I spent nearly an hour in the parking lot that morning, cleaning the snow that had accumulated on our car overnight. By the time I went back inside, my jeans were completely soaked, and the skin underneath them was pink and raw. Sure, I was cold, but more than anything, I was invigorated. I've been a lover of a good snowstorm all my life, and after my workout in the parking lot, I was high from the endorphins. The truth was that I was also happy to have been relieved of making an actual decision about what to do with my day—whether I should spend it with the Tuckers or stay at the hotel working. It wasn't that I didn't want to see them. It had *never* been about not wanting to see them. It was just that when I did see them, I experienced a blitzkrieg of emotions—guilt, fear, confusion—that I often found simply overwhelming. I had made it through the previous night without any internal injuries, and I was reluctant to risk another day in the demilitarized zone of someone else's family.

After changing my clothes, I realized how hungry I was. So hungry my hand kept moving to my stomach in an unsuccessful attempt to quiet the growling inside. I needed to get something to eat. There was the hotel restaurant, but if I went there, I risked running into people from the conference and having to make small talk. Plus, I'd have to shower and make myself presentable, something I didn't have the energy to do before I ate. I was faced with an ugly realization: if I wanted to get something to eat that didn't come from room service, I'd need to leave the hotel. And if I left the hotel, then why couldn't I visit the Tuckers? Of course, I could argue that was a much longer journey—thirty minutes instead of five—but some part of me suspected that was an excuse. A good excuse, yes. But still an excuse.

Then again, for all I knew, the roads would be impassable, and I wouldn't even be able to consider the trip to Annandale. My only option was to venture out and see what I found.

As it turned out, the roads were pretty bad but not completely treacherous. Two tire tracks had been worn through the snow along each side of the street, and if I'd slowly followed those tracks all the way to Virginia, I probably would've been fine. I'd gotten my driver's license during my junior year of high school when we lived in northern Indiana and, as a result, had learned how to handle winter roads. As one of my Indiana friends had put it, driving a car in the snow wasn't vastly different than driving a boat—to some extent you had to let the car take you where it wanted to go, guiding it through rough waters rather than controlling it, taking slow easy turns rather than sharp distinct ones, and never expecting to be able to make a complete stop. As I walked across the four-lane street in front of the hotel, it occurred to me that if the roads there were passable, that meant the highways were probably clear. I could have driven to Annandale if I wanted. Yes, it would be risky, but not as risky as I had implied to Paula. Still, for some reason, I felt reluctant to leave the safety and solitude of the hotel.

Thirty minutes later, I got to work, putting the faux wood desk in front of the picture window in our hotel room and eating my lunch while I plunged into revising the dissertation and grading a few of the papers I had brought along. I worked like that for hours, until it was dark enough that the scene outside had turned an eerie shade of blue, the parking lot lights bouncing off the snow in violet-colored discs. My back hurt by then, and I needed a break. I thought again of making the drive to the Tuckers but decided to go to the hotel gym instead. Was I avoiding them? Was this more of what I had been doing for five long years? I wasn't sure, but by the time I got back to the room after my workout, the parking lot had frozen over, a virtual ice skating rink. I wasn't going anywhere, whether I wanted to or not.

The time of our departure arrived before I could fully consider the consequences of my decision the previous day. I had to shower and pack the car by eleven to avoid being charged for another day. Dave was still conferencing all morning, and by the time I talked to Paula, there was no time for breakfast or anything else.

"So you're leaving?" Paula asked.

"In about thirty minutes," I admitted.

"Maybe you can come back this summer. You could just fly in for a weekend."

"Well, I don't fly," I said, trying my best not to care that was a detail about me Paula couldn't seem to remember. "But we'll try to visit again. We're graduating in June, and I don't even know where we'll be living after that. If one of us gets a job, we'll move wherever we have to." I expected Paula to balk at that statement—after all, one of her sons had turned down a job forty-five minutes away because it was too far from home. But she ignored it and went on.

"What about the conference?" Paula asked. "Will you come back next year?"

Oddly, Dave and I had discussed the idea the night before. He had enjoyed his time at Borderlands so fully and gotten so much out of it that he was already making plans to come back the next year. "It looks like we might."

"Good," Paula said. "At least we have that to look forward to."

"Yes, we do," I said, and though it wasn't ideal—I still knew I had let Paula down by not visiting the day before—it was an improvement. Paula finally seemed to be accepting that I had other commitments, a life, and I left D.C. that day with a bit of hope about our future.

Back in Cincinnati, I felt renewed. It was our last semester in the doctoral program, and once the dissertation was finished at the end of January, all I had to do was teach one class and try to find a job, leaving me plenty of time to write. Of course, looking for a job at the university level is a massive undertaking that begins in August and often doesn't wrap up until April of the next year. For the second year in a row, Dave and I had sent out literally hundreds of applications. Still, it was a heady time. Writing every day was cathartic, and we were both excited about what was to come—even as we were feeling more and more anxious about it all the time.

The only problem was, like everyone we knew, we weren't having much luck on the job market, landing only four first-round interviews between us before March. Four first-round interviews that didn't lead anywhere, much less to a second interview. Time was running out.

As usual, we were heading to Florida to see my parents for spring break, so Dave decided to take a chance and follow up on a one-year job teaching freshman composition that he'd applied for at Rollins College in Winter Park, Florida. It was a risky move. We'd been warned many times to never contact a school before they contacted us, so Dave's decision to do so was completely unconventional. But it was March: we were graduating in June and had nothing on the horizon. We were desperate.

For some reason, the search chair at Rollins responded positively to Dave's email message and set up a phone interview with him the day after we arrived in Florida. Dave has always been able to turn it on when he needs to, so it was no surprise that went well, and the search chair invited him to come to campus a few days later.

Rollins College is located in Winter Park, possibly one of the most beautiful neighborhoods in the whole state of Florida. It has tree-lined streets, a picturesque lake, and an adorable shopping district with amazing boutiques, decadent restaurants, and a Hemingwayesque hotel. As soon as we drove into town and saw our accommodations, we never wanted to leave.

Dave aced the interview the next day, and he felt confident he would get an offer. That night we were sitting in bed, talking about moving to Winter Park—what it would entail, how soon we should do it, and, mostly, how happy we were to be leaving Ohio for a warmer climate—when our cell phone rang.

It was an Ohio number but one we didn't recognize, and it was pretty late—ten o'clock—for a call from someone who wasn't immediately recognizable.

After Dave answered, he covered the mouthpiece and said, "It's Eric."

Eric Goodman had been one of our professors in our Master's program at Miami University and was still a good friend. But I had no idea why he'd be calling us at ten o'clock on a weeknight.

Dave and Eric talked for a while—about fifteen minutes—while I sat there unsuccessfully trying to figure out what they were discussing. When Dave hung up the phone, he turned to me and said, "You're honestly not going to believe this, but he just offered us a job."

"What are you talking about?"

"Remember the job Dave Kajganich had when we were there? The visiting job in creative writing?"

"Sure."

"Well, he wants to know if one of us will take it next year."

"You mean, he wants to *interview* one of us?"

"He claims he doesn't have to interview because it's a visiting job. And he's offering us the job, said he doesn't care which one of us takes it, and maybe we could even share it, but we have to call him back tonight and let him know if we're interested." Dave spoke so quickly that I knew he was trying to get it all out as fast as he could.

"Are you kidding?"

"I know," Dave said. "This is insane."

"Completely," I agreed.

"I mean, here we are—in Florida—about to get an offer from Rollins, and he calls us like this out of the blue."

"Did he know we were here?"

"He had no idea."

"What did he say when you told him?" I asked.

"He said he understood, but he still has to know something tonight."

"What the hell?" I said. "What are the chances we'd get this call tonight? While we're here?"

"Zero to none."

"What are we going to do?"

Dave shook his head at me, disagreeing with the answer we both wanted to avoid. "I want to move here, to Florida."

"Well, so do I, but can we turn down a creative writing job for a job teaching freshman comp?"

"Hell if I know."

Things went back and forth like that the whole ten minutes we debated the pros and cons of the two jobs, but ultimately we called Eric back and told him that, of course, we were interested. We didn't know it then, but it would end up being a fateful decision, one that would keep us in Ohio against our wishes another year and play a crucial role in helping us move on to bigger and better things.

4/2/05

Dear Molly,

I would have liked to have written sooner, but the older I get the less time I seem to have for myself.

It was a wonderful surprise to be able to visit with you. I'm sorry about the weather interfering without getting together on Saturday.

We've had some exciting days as of late. As you know Wade bought a home last year, but in the last month Clint bought a new home, Jeannie is buying a duplex home on a very quiet street and Willie just got accepted for a small home near the restaurant. All and all we've have three people moving at the end of May – early June.

I know you spoke about moving to California. It sounds exciting, especially knowing all the snow you get, but I have to say that would be a major change and so far away—maybe you should consider a visit. Whatever your decision it certainly be an adventure.

As I said, having the opportunity to spend some time with you are treasured moments. It was always my prayer from the day you were born that someday I would have the privilege of at least meeting you. Being able to share moments together is a gift from God.

My only regret is that you missed being around Willie, Clint, Wade, and Jeannie. Each of them are special unique individuals and again I have been blessed. They each touch my heart in their own way.

Perhaps someday you'll discover the love of motherhood.

Hope your day is filled with love and friends.

Love,
Paula

P.S. Let me know if you move. I enclosed a couple of pictures.

Paula's letter made me laugh and made me feel a bit sad too.

It was funny because we had just decided, against our wishes to some extent, to stay in Ohio for the foreseeable future and because I have no idea how Paula got the idea we might move to California. Maybe that was something I threw out during our visit in January. It was, after all, something we always talked about—like many people, we had dreamed of moving out west for years—and we had applied to several jobs in California. But we were nowhere near making it happen. Or maybe I told her, on the phone or in a letter, about Dave interviewing for a job in California. But it seemed strange, then, that she would tell us to visit first given that we'd both been there more than once. I figured Paula had just gotten confused and tried not to be irritated about her telling us what to do.

More importantly, what Paula wrote about my biological siblings made me sad. I agreed with her that they were all unique—almost unbelievably so—and special in their own ways. And I only wished I could find a way to spend more time with them, especially independent of Paula and L.W., a reality I knew could never happen. I also felt a tinge of annoyance when Paula told me, "Perhaps someday you'll discover the love of motherhood." I had never considered not having children and always told her that we planned to have kids. So why was she saying "perhaps"? Did she think there was some doubt about it?

Despite my mixed emotions about Paula's letter, I decided to focus on the positive: we were getting along just fine, corresponding on a regular basis (though unfortunately I didn't keep copies of any of the letters I wrote to her during that time), and not driving each other nuts. Things had moved forward. I told myself to focus on that and not worry about the small nuisances that came with having Paula in my life.

The three months leading up to graduation were some of the easiest of our lives. Sure, we were still teaching and doing last minute edits on our dissertations, but we were only teaching one class each, the editing was mostly complete, and the hard part was, in many ways, over. We had never planned to finish the Ph.D., always saying it was just a way to have time to write, but suddenly, it was done, surprising us both.

Graduation itself was a surreal experience. We'd regretted not attending the ceremony when we received our Master's degrees, so we were committed to fully participating in it for our doctorates and had been planning our graduation party for years. Throughout my entire time in the program, I'd told anyone who would listen that we were going to have a huge bacchanal—a real rager with unlimited amounts of drugs and alcohol that would go all night and leave us with hangovers we'd regret for the rest of our lives. But when the time finally came, we settled on something more traditional: a backyard party right before the ceremony. We didn't have a yard of our own, but our good friend Bob let us hold the event at his house, just down the street from our apartment building. We invited all of our family and friends and sat around drinking beer and eating sandwiches in the hours leading up to the doctoral hooding ceremony that night.

It was all pretty low-key until my parents decided to make a toast.

Our dissertation director had shown up with a bottle of champagne to mark the occasion, and without our consent, my parents took the opportunity to speak. I remember being more than a little nervous when they got everyone's attention.

The two of them were standing on the top of the small stoop that led into the back of Bob's house like a king and queen receiving their subjects. It hit me just then that I'd done something they'd always warned me against: I'd invited people from school to socialize with people from my personal life. Mom and Dad had repeatedly advised me to never mix work with family, but that's exactly what I'd done. For years, I'd considered that rule ridiculous, an overly prudish approach for people who always played it safe to the point of not having any fun. But in that moment I finally understood the wisdom of it—because I had no idea what my parents were going to say. I had no way to keep them from embarrassing me in front of my peers. It was disconcerting.

They started innocently enough, my mother speaking for the both of them: "Mike and I are so proud of Molly and Dave for all of the hard work they've done over the past five years—all of the long hours they've put in, the sacrifices they've made, the enormous effort they've exerted."

It was beginning to sound like my mother was going to give another one of her my-daughter-is-so-great speeches, not totally humiliating but a little on the embarrassing side.

"In fact, it is quite a feat to get a Ph.D.," my mother said theatrically, making me wonder where she was going. "So we wanted to get them something deserving of that kind of huge accomplishment."

At that point, my whole body tensed. What was she going to say? What kind of gift could be worthy of our "huge accomplishment"? I was terrified of what was to come next, but there was no way to stop what was happening.

"And that's why…" Mom said, pausing for dramatic effect. "We got them…" She took another long pause then, lifting her arms for emphasis and obviously trying to titillate her audience about what was to come next. There were about thirty tipsy people standing in Bob's backyard at that point—some more drunk than others—but for less than a second no one moved and no one said anything as they waited for my mother to finish her sentence. It seemed almost certain that my parents were about to make some grand gesture—a car, a house, something big—and I didn't know if I should be horrified or delighted. Finally, she went on: "A twenty-five dollar gift certificate to Skyline Chili!"

My mother made this announcement with great enthusiasm as if she really were giving us some huge gift, and the whole backyard went up in laughter. My parents had entertained a yard full of academics, a group that I myself had failed to entertain on more occasions than I'd like to admit. I was both shocked and relieved.

But her joke stayed with me. And when Dave and I were driving to campus for the ceremony an hour later, I was still thinking about it. What was it that had made it so funny? Was it because people thought my parents were well-off or that I was spoiled? I had no idea how they'd know the former, and the latter hadn't been true since I was twenty-three and had to learn to support myself. But before I could answer that question, we were there—at the hooding ceremony—lining up in the hall outside the arena where the ceremony was being held, all the doctoral candidates looking like blushing peacocks in their bright red University of Cincinnati regalia.

*

I've always had an amazing relationship with my parents. I thoroughly enjoy their company and feel certain we provide each other with unconditional love and support. But for a long time there was one thing that never felt right between us. I never really felt as if they thought I'd made it. Yes, I had been supporting myself since a year after I finished college, but for some reason it never seemed like they'd processed that fact.

On top of that, my parents were never able to get over the fact that I'd quit grad school the first time. I had only been twenty-two when I started, and it didn't take long for me to figure out it was a waste of time and my program wasn't exactly a stellar one anyway, which was probably why I was admitted at the last minute over the summer. So rather than keep wasting my parents' money—they were footing the bill that time—I dropped out after two quarters. To me, that made perfect sense, but they didn't see it that way. Instead, all they could see was that I was quitting, and they had always abhorred quitters. I didn't worry about it too much since I knew I was making the right decision and had only enrolled in the program because I was too afraid to get a real job. I figured my parents would eventually understand that too because, to their credit, they've always allowed me to make my own choices. Even when they didn't agree with those choices, they accepted them and didn't constantly harass me about them like I know some parents do.

Despite this, they never fully let it go, and when I started grad school a second time—six years later—they were constantly worrying about whether or not I would finish. *Are you keeping up with your work? Are your grades good? Do you think you'll graduate?* When I think back on it now, I can see they feared the same thing would happen all over again. It was something they didn't need to worry about. I hadn't quit grad school the first time because I wasn't doing well. I had quit because it wasn't the right place for me. But my parents have never been the kind of people who understood the notion of quitting something before it was finished—whether it was a good decision or not.

But the Tuckers were different.

As long as they could stay in Annandale, they were risk takers. They would walk away from something if it wasn't working. And no one in the family would think twice about it. It had been a bit of a risk for Paula to carry me to term and give me up for adoption. Sure, abortion wasn't yet legal, but it was possible. And by going through with the pregnancy, Paula was risking the judgment of her friends and family. She certainly lost L.W. when he found out she was going to have the baby. And it was even more risky for her to give L.W. another chance after their first attempt at a relationship had failed so miserably. What if he got her pregnant and deserted her a second time? Then where would she be?

Though I firmly believe most of my personality was learned from my parents, that is one thing I believe I got from Paula: my ability to take risks, to do something that may at first appear dangerous. I love my parents, but they always play it safe. They buy houses based on how they'll resell, they invest in companies that have a history of doing well. When they were young, they chose professions that were most likely to land them jobs.

Being a writer is risky. You could spend years writing and never publish a word, never make a cent off all the time invested. But, for me, to not write, to not create something, is to not live. Maybe that's what Paula felt too. Was that why she chose to have me when she could have taken a different path? I could have asked Paula that question at any time, but I didn't really have to. I already knew that's why she did it.

But after I earned my doctorate, something changed with my parents: the way they saw me, the way they treated me, changed. Not only did they respect me as a person, but they respected what I had *accomplished* as a person. I can't say our whole relationship was altered because we've always been positive and open, but the tenor of our interaction changed just slightly, just enough that I noticed it. No longer did they interrogate me about my life because they were worried about my choices. Once I finished graduate school, their interrogation was more about their interest in my life than their concern.

I have to give my parents credit—even before that day, they had always allowed me to find my own way in the world. No, they didn't like that I quit grad school the first time or stopped going to church during college or lived with my husband before we were married, but they let me make my own decisions. In that way, they had something in common with Paula: they loved their children no matter who they were.

We decided Dave would be the one to take the job at Miami because I wanted to finish the novel I'd been revising since I'd finished my Master's thesis, and, after we made that decision, life became much easier. Dave taught three classes a semester the next year and made almost three times what either of us had made in graduate school. We stayed in the same apartment in Cincinnati, which meant Dave had to commute almost an hour both ways several days a week, but it also meant our costs didn't increase. For the first time since we had started grad school seven years before, we took a deep breath and relaxed.

Writing full-time agreed with me for the most part. The only trouble was that I was pretty lonely the days Dave went to Oxford. Like Paula and my mom, I've always been a people person, which is kind of strange given that I've chosen such a solitary profession for my life's work. I combated my loneliness by spending time working at a nearby coffee shop with friends and meeting with some of my peers to get ready to go back on the job market. Even though Dave had the job at Miami, it wasn't a permanent gig, which meant we had to re-start the whole process of looking for work as soon as the school year began. Despite this, we didn't feel as frantic as we had the year before. No, Dave's position wasn't permanent, but it was renewable for up to five years, so we applied for a few jobs here and there but didn't even come close to sending out the hundreds of applications we had sent out in years past. In fact, we probably only applied to twenty jobs. This also meant we were picky, only considering jobs in parts of the country that might appeal to us on the East and West Coasts.

Looking back, it's obvious we should have examined some of those locations more carefully, but, at the time, we were just choosing states that stuck out—New Jersey, New York, Pennsylvania, California, Oregon, Washington, Colorado, New Mexico, Florida,

North Carolina—and not processing that some of the schools where we applied were located in the cultural backwaters of otherwise desirable states. The only thing that was notable was that we didn't apply for any jobs in Virginia: yes, my night with the Tuckers at the beginning of the year had gone well, but I still wasn't ready for any more than a long weekend together, which was exactly what I got the next January.

The passing of Miss Alice—founder of Tucker's Hideaway, mother to my biological father, and grandmother to my four biological siblings—in December of 2005 was a big deal at Tucker's Hideaway. Hundreds of motorcyclists rode in her funeral procession, pausing in front of the bar, so her soul could slip out of the hearse and float back into the building she had called home for thirty years.

It was a ceremony that would repeat itself fifteen months later. Though, at the time, no one knew what was to come.

I didn't go to Alice's funeral. I wasn't even invited to attend. At the time, that was more of a relief than anything else because I didn't want to go. But looking back now, it probably should have told me that my relationship with the Tuckers would always be conditional. There would always be limits to when and how I would be included in their family. But I was too concerned with keeping my own boundaries in place to notice they were establishing some of their own.

Dave had been so pleased with the people he met and the feedback he got at the first Borderlands workshop that he wanted to go back for another round, and that was how we ended up on the road back to D.C. for a second January in a row, one month after Alice Tucker died. Unlike the previous year, the drive was uneventful with none of the obstacles we'd experienced the time before. The weather was even nice enough to allow us to eat our packed lunch outside—at a rest stop just east of the Ohio-West Virginia border. It was the kind of thing my parents never did when I was growing up, so I enjoyed having a picnic on the side of the highway more than most people, a choice that set a laid-back tone for the rest of the trip.

Another big difference: Paula knew we were coming before we arrived, which clearly lessened my anxiety.

I'd made plans to get together with Paula the night of our arrival—a Thursday—so after Dave and I got something to eat for dinner, Paula, Jeannie, Clint, and Amy came to the hotel to pick me up. Dave and I met them in the hotel driveway, and there was a moment of awkwardness when they first arrived—almost like we just weren't sure what to make of each other or whether or not we should be spending time together. But that brief moment of apprehension was gone so quickly I almost wondered if I'd imagined it. Dave said hello to everyone, and then I said goodbye to him for the evening, so he could head to the hotel bar to start networking.

Clint was driving a huge SUV, again reminding me of how disparate we were—Dave and I were about as likely to drive an SUV as we were to play a round of golf—but somehow cruising along in Clint's virtual tank didn't feel good old boy as much as it felt moneyed. As I would find out the next night when I visited his cavernous McMansion in the suburbs, Clint had made it. He was flush. Real estate was still booming in early 2006, and Clint—who had become a realtor since I'd last seen him—had the goods to prove it: the showy SUV, a house so big there were several unfurnished rooms, and a flat screen television that was as big as a small automobile. All of this made me feel as if something had changed.

Don't get me wrong. I have never been the kind of person who cares about money, and I've always prided myself on that. My friends have come from all walks of life—all cultures, all religions, all ethnicities, all classes—and if I were going to select relationships based on money, I certainly wouldn't have ended up with Dave, who grew up in a working-class part of Cincinnati in a family that often struggled to make it to the end of the month. No, I don't judge people based on how many zeroes they have in their bank account, but that didn't mean it hadn't always felt like money was something that separated the Tuckers from me: for most of my childhood, I had grown up with either a swimming pool or lake in my backyard, a convertible in the driveway, and a closet full of Guess jeans and Limited sweaters. I had also always known I was going to college— and probably grad school too—and that my parents would pay for at least the former, but I knew that wasn't how Willie, Clint, Wade, and Jeannie had been raised. We were pretty close to being on opposite ends of the economic continuum. I imagine that's a typical problem for adoptees. It's certainly more common than it being the other way around. But that doesn't make it any less awkward or easy to hide. When I traded photos with Paula, I was amazed by the image the pictures of my childhood seemed to create. In almost every snapshot, I'm wearing an adorable and pricey Polly Flinders dress, and every single one of my hairs is combed exactly into place. But in the Tuckers' pictures, all of the kids—including Jeannie—are running around in cutoff shorts and t-shirts, a ragtag but adorable group reminiscent of the Little Rascals.

That may be why, when I was finished with college and on my own financially, I felt more comfortable with myself than I ever had before. No longer was I the daughter of well-off parents. I was just myself. Maybe that's why the Tuckers made me so uncomfortable: when I was with the Tuckers, I wasn't just Molly. I was the child of a retired corporate executive who was married to the daughter of a prominent doctor. Just like when I was young, I was seen through the lens of my parents, which made me uneasy.

But as I climbed into Clint's monstrous SUV, I began to let all that go and hope the Tuckers would finally be able to see me just as myself.

We went to a place called Stetson's because they had two things the Tuckers wanted: wings and karaoke. I would've thought they got enough karaoke back in Annandale, but apparently Jeannie wanted more because, as soon as we walked in the door, she went to the stage to put her name on the list of singers.

After we situated ourselves at the bar and Paula ordered a round of beer and wings for everyone, I asked Jeannie what she was planning to sing.

"'Turn Back Time,'" she said without hesitation.

"Do you mean 'If I Could Turn Back Time?'"

"That's what I said," Jeannie insisted, laughing at me as if I were slow.

"The song by Cher?" I asked, still not sure what she meant.

"Really?" I had seen Jeannie sing during our first visit to the Hideaway. Admittedly, she was a natural performer who did an amazing job belting out her favorite country tunes, but I just could not imagine her pulling off something as challenging as Cher. No matter how dissimilar we were, Jeannie still had my genes, and musical ability wasn't something that came with that package.

"You don't think I can do it?" Jeannie responded with a smile. She had clearly picked up on my doubts.

"It's a difficult song, and we aren't exactly gifted in the singing department."

"Oh, I can do it," Jeannie said without hesitation. "I've sung it before. And I'm going to bring the house down."

I should have known by then that Jeannie was the kind of person who could do anything she set her mind to doing, but, a few hours after our arrival in D.C., I was still re-acquainting myself with her confidence and marveling at the fact that someone with her kind of swagger was biologically my sister.

An hour passed before Jeannie was called to the stage, and during that time I talked to Paula while a few of Clint and Jeannie's other friends showed up. Unlike some of our previous conversations, the one we had that night was remarkable only because of how effortless and unmemorable it seemed. There was none of the artificiality or awkwardness that always seemed to be present the first year we met, and Paula didn't say anything that made me look over my shoulder and wonder who was listening. Instead we simply talked about what had been going on the past year—for the Tuckers and for me—which was something else that seemed different.

Paula was interested in me.

It occurred to me then that maybe I'd been too hard on Paula in the past. Maybe it was difficult for her to ask about me because finding out about the life I'd had before only reminded her of what she'd missed. My sister finally met her biological mother, Theresa, when Katie was twenty-five, six years after they had first learned about each other. In preparation for that meeting, my mother and I put together a photo album capturing much of Katie's childhood, so she could share it with Theresa. But when she did, Theresa was overwhelmed with emotion, ultimately giving into her tears and having to leave their reunion.

Katie was shocked. She had thought—we had all thought—that Theresa would want to learn about Katie's life. But when presented with a life that had happened without her, Theresa had crumbled, unable to face what she had missed.

Was that how Paula sometimes felt when I talked about my past? I'll probably never know. I'd have to ask her to be sure, and those are the kinds of tough questions that often lead to trouble. It's hard enough to fold another family into your life, much harder to do so in such an unflinchingly honest way. So for the time, Paula and I stuck to the superficial because that's what was working for us. It's strange to admit that because I have never been the kind of person who enjoys superficial relationships, but it often felt too overwhelming to do otherwise with the Tuckers.

When the emcee finally called Jeannie's name, the people sitting around her hooted and stomped their feet, a sideshow unto itself. Jeannie strutted up to the small stage at the end of the bar like a celebrity, Melissa Etheridge crossed with Mae West, all hip and ass and brash exuberance and, most importantly, not an iota of self-consciousness. Her jeans hugged her curves in all the right places, but she was tall enough to simultaneously appear thin. She whipped around when she hopped up on the stage, offering the room full of revelers a thousand-dollar smile. "Okay, y'all," she said. "I'm going to do 'Turn Back Time.' My—uh—sister over there thinks I can't do it." Every time Jeannie or any of the other Tuckers called me their sister, I flinched involuntarily, and that night I hoped none of the dozen or so people who looked in my direction had noticed. "But what *I* want to know is what do YOU all think?"

Jeannie's friends exploded with a stream of affirmation.

Hell, yes, you can!

Oh, yeah!

Go, Jeannie!!!

The song began with a pared-down introduction, just a few staccato pulses of the electric guitar paving the way for the vocals to enter, and Jeannie nodded her head along with the beat. When it was time for her to release the first words, she delivered like a rock star. Her voice bellowed across the bar perfectly in tune, sending me a message I would have been foolish to ignore.

I don't know why I did the things I did. I don't know why I said the things I said. Pride's like a knife—it can cut deep inside. Words are like weapons— they wound sometimes. I didn't really mean to hurt you. I didn't wanna see you go. I know I made you cry, but, baby, if I could turn back time, if I could find a way, I'd take back those words that hurt you and you'd stay.

I can't remember much else about that night. It's possible I got a little drunk, which isn't hard for me to do. It's even possible I had fun. And why wouldn't I? I wasn't driving, and for what might have been the first time ever, I felt comfortable hanging out with the Tucker clan, like they were old friends rather than the people whom I didn't know where to put in my life.

The next morning led to breakfast at the bar followed by a girls' day with Jeannie and Amy. I had already spent some time alone with Jeannie on our first visit to Annandale five years before, but I still wasn't sure if she was happy about me being back in her life. I wanted to believe she'd forgiven me for ignoring Paula all that time, but the memory of her behavior at the basketball game in Dayton was still in my head, knocking on the door of my soul like a vagrant trying to get in.

Still, there was no sign of the person I had seen in Dayton that weekend. Jeannie was nothing but welcoming, so it didn't surprise me when she asked if I wanted to see her new house.

Because Clint had been doing so well in the real estate business, Jeannie had moved into that line of work as well, as a mortgage broker. It wasn't as dramatic or profitable as selling real estate, but it still paid relatively well. So well she'd been able to buy a three-bedroom townhouse. When Jeannie told me she'd bought a place of her own, I didn't know what to say. At the time, she was twenty-four years old, two years out of college and only recently employed full-time. At thirty-five, I was eleven years her senior and had seven years more school and two more degrees under my belt as well as six years of job experience. But nine months before, Dave and I had been barely able to make the rent on our rundown apartment. We were certainly nowhere near ready to buy a house. Or so I thought anyway.

When we arrived at Jeannie's townhouse, it only got worse. I had imagined a small, cramped two-floor space in a crowded neighborhood, the kind where other grad students lived when we were in Oxford, but the townhouses in Jeannie's neighborhood were three stories tall and spread out with good-sized yards between every other one. No, they weren't huge or ostentatious like the million-dollar townhouses sprouting up in the tonier neighborhoods of Northern Virginia, but they were clearly bigger and nicer than the bargain basement units I had been imagining. When we walked up to the front door, I kept saying the same thing over and over: "I can't believe you live here."

"I know," Jeannie said enthusiastically. "Isn't it great? I love it."

"It must have cost a fortune," I said.

"Oh, I got a great deal. Only two and a quarter."

Two and a quarter was a figure I knew no bank would even think about giving us, but I didn't bother telling Jeannie that.

When we entered the living room, I saw that the square footage wasn't quite as spacious as it seemed outside. Still, it was large enough that two oversized sofas and a big TV cabinet barely filled the room, and the adjacent kitchen and dining room were massive, boasting a trendy island and tall windows overlooking the attached deck and wide backyard. If I hadn't been sure before, I was certain by then: Jeannie was living better than I was.

The upstairs bedrooms were a little tighter than the first floor, but Jeannie's master was roomy enough. I was so obsessed with taking in the size of the place that I almost didn't notice there was a body under the covers of her bed—a body of a man with no shirt and, though I couldn't see under the sheet, I worried nothing else either. He was face down, his dark hair splayed across the back of his head like the tentacles of a spider.

"Kenny's still asleep," Jeannie said. "But you don't have to worry. Nothing can wake up his fat ass." Jeannie kicked the bed as she said it, and Kenny barely groaned. The outline of said ass was visible under the sheet, and even without seeing it directly, I could tell it was a bit plump. And for that matter so was his naked back, and I wondered what Jeannie, who was in tip-top physical condition and perfectly adorable, saw in him. She had told me the night before that Kenny played on Clint's baseball team, and her brother had set them up. I made a mental note to knock a point off Clint's otherwise unblemished record. It occurred to me then that Jeannie was the kind of sister who would do anything to please her favorite brother. And dating Kenny not only pleased him, it allowed her to spend more time with him, a double bonus.

Jeannie had failed to tell me much more about her relationship with Kenny, so when we were back in the hallway outside the master bedroom, I asked her if they were living together.

"Kind of," she said. "I guess. I mean, he's fun. We have a good time together. We hang out with Clint and Amy all the time."

Her words confirmed my suspicions: Jeannie was with Kenny because he fit in with her family, and it was easier to be with him than it was to be alone. And when we made our way down to the half-finished basement, I saw more evidence to bolster my theory that Jeannie was just playing house: a fold-out futon, a foosball table, a tiny trampoline, a TV hooked up to a PlayStation, and a fridge full of beer. Though Jeannie had a grown-up house, she was still a child.

Amy met us at a restaurant near IKEA, so we could do some shopping after lunch. It was the first time I had ever done something with Jeannie and Amy without Paula, L.W., or any of the boys, and it was the most normal I had ever felt around any of the Tuckers. If I had wanted to, I could have imagined that it was just like any other lunch I might have had with a couple of my girlfriends back in Cincinnati. We drank wine and ate too much food and talked and laughed about what all women talk about: sex. It was cathartic and, during those lively ninety minutes, I understood that Jeannie and Amy were more like me than I'd ever realized before. They were witty, intelligent, and entertaining—the kind of women I love. And I sensed that as long as my relationship with Paula stayed in a good place, I could count on them to provide me with a source of comfort while I tried to work my way through the whole biological family fiasco.

But only a handful of hours after I was finally starting to feel comfortable in the world of the Tuckers, I found myself in another awkward position: dinner at Clint and Amy's with Paula, Jeannie, and several of Amy's relatives. I had learned long ago—definitely during my first visit to Annandale but possibly when I was even younger—that people outside of the adoption circle don't really know what to make of adoptees and their various families. I'd learned that from Sarah and Abby Hoffman, I'd learned it from my mother-in-law, and I'd learned it from Paula and Jeannie's hairstylist who sneered at me like I was a freak during my last trip to Annandale. Despite that, I was still surprised when I walked into Clint and Amy's house for dinner that night and was greeted by some of Amy's family members like someone they should be afraid of.

I've never been a minority. I'm white, and I grew up Catholic in suburban New Jersey, which is kind of like saying I was a white flower with a yellow center in a sea of daisies. But I've dated men who are not white, and as a result of that experience, I've become familiar with the look some people offer to those they perceive as different. They try their damnedest to smile and be welcoming, but underneath that smile, you can see the edges of their mouths twitching, their eyes jumping around the room for someone, anyone, to settle on besides you, the person who challenges their previous ideas about identity.

And then there are those who don't try to disguise their discomfort at all. When those people see you, their top lip stretches up toward the middle of their cheek, creating a severe triangle that says, *You are a square peg who doesn't fit in the round hole I've used for everyone else I've ever known.*

Amy's family was in the former group—they tried to hide their discomfort, but I could sense it was there. They didn't know what to say to me, and they didn't know how to act around me. I'm not saying Amy's family didn't mean well or didn't try their best to welcome me. I'm merely saying it was difficult for them because they really didn't know what to make of a woman who didn't meet her biological family until she was thirty, a woman who—as far as they could tell—was raised by complete strangers, a woman who might as well have been raised by wolves for all they knew.

Normally, when you go to a friend's or relative's house for dinner and meet someone you know, the conversation is pretty standard: "Hi, I'm so-and-so. How do you know Amy?" But as soon as I would answer that first question—"Her boyfriend is my biological brother"—I knew I'd have problems. People don't know what to make of someone who refers to her sibling as her "biological brother."

In truth that conversation never happened because Amy's family already knew about me: "the girl who disappeared." That's what I was to Paula. Or "the girl who I never knew existed." That's what I was to Clint and all of his siblings. I feared that for L.W. I was "the girl he thought he got rid of." No matter which options of those Amy's family had adopted, I knew immediately I wasn't "the girl who was like everybody else." And maybe that was fitting since I had never been that girl.

Not long after we arrived at Clint and Amy's, Amy become preoccupied with cooking and getting everything ready. I tried to help, but mostly felt like I was in the way. The result was that I was kind of on my own when her family started showing up a little while later.

I'm not going to lie: they greeted me like I was a rabid animal. "Hi," they said shortly with that twitchy, nervous smile before darting away—to the kitchen, the sofa, the bathroom, anywhere to get away from me.

I set the table and helped make the salad and was all too aware that no one had shared a complete sentence with me. They weren't ignoring me, but they weren't including me either. When there was nothing left to do but lurk in the corner like an awkward teenager at a junior high dance, I decided to slink over to the sofa where *Star Wars* was playing on the giant flat-screen. That was back in 2006, before enormous TVs became as commonplace for Americans as toasters, and I thought immediately of Ray Bradbury's fourth wall, a device allowing the well-off to choose passive observation over human interaction, which was exactly what I was doing.

Still, I sat on the leather sofa with some of Amy's younger relatives, letting a film I'd loved almost my whole life take me to another place and time. And when I stepped back and looked at the scene from the outside—at the massive plasma TV, the overstuffed leather sofas, the imposing stone fireplace, the state-of-the-art kitchen—I realized, yet again, that another one of my biological siblings was more well off than I was. It wasn't long after that when Luke Skywalker closed his eyes and used only The Force to fire a missile into the exact right spot at the center of the Death Star, a planet-shaped space station built by a man he didn't yet know was his biological father. And as I watched Vader's brainchild explode into a million tiny bits of steel and fire, I felt more than a little of Skywalker's righteous indignation.

When I woke the next morning, I decided I needed a break from the Tuckers and did laundry for four hours before going to see them. Back in Cincinnati, we still lived in an apartment without a washer and dryer and had to go to a laundromat or a relative's house to wash our clothes, so I'd brought our dirty clothing with us to the hotel in D.C., where there was a laundry room on every floor. Sure, I was using that chore as an excuse to spend half the day alone. Even though Amy's relatives hadn't offered me a warm welcome, Friday had passed without any major trauma. Despite that, I still wanted some time to decompress and process everything that was happening. Paula, of course, wasn't thrilled. She wanted me there—with her and her family—every minute we were in the greater D.C. area. She even reminded me they owned a laundromat—right next to the Hideaway, a fact I had fortunately forgotten before I begged off to do laundry. Still, I stood firm, reminding myself I needed to maintain my boundaries or risk becoming as overwhelmed as I'd been five and a half years before.

In some ways I ended up regretting that decision. The halls of the hotel were dark and lonely, and I had to lug the laundry basket all the way to other end of the building to reach the small room where I fed quarters into the washer and dryer almost as fast a slot machine. But, in other ways, I was glad for the time alone—time to regroup, to remember who I was.

I had agreed to visit Willie at his house later that afternoon with Paula. I feared Willie's house would be like Jeannie's and Clint's— more evidence that everyone in my biological family was doing better financially than I was—but the reality was Willie was living in the kind of house we probably could have afforded in Cincinnati when we finished grad school. He lived in a three-bedroom row house with a big front porch in a transitional neighborhood. But when we drove up, the first thing I noticed was something we would never have in common: the Confederate flag was flying out front like a beacon telling me to walk away.

I thought about doing just that, but with Paula in the passenger seat next to me, I wasn't sure what I could say to smooth over my retreat, especially since part of the reason we were there was so I could visit Paula's only grandchild.

Willie and his fiancée, Misty, had had their son, William Tucker Jr., a little over a year before and became engaged shortly thereafter. The three of them were living together, but Misty wasn't home that afternoon.

"She works part-time," Paula said as we were walking up to the front porch. "And the rest of the time she's out partying with her friends."

"I thought she couldn't drink . . . because of the aneurysm."

"Well, she's not supposed to, but that doesn't stop her. It's like she doesn't want to be here. She always wants to get away. It's as if she doesn't realize she's a mom now and can't go out every time she feels like it." It wasn't lost on me that Paula had once been in Misty's position, and I wondered if her criticism of her son's fiancée was more about jealousy than anything else.

The house's main stairwell came right up to the front door, greeting us like a welcome mat. When Willie let us in, he gave me one of his standard hugs—standing a few inches away from me as if keeping me at a safe distance, but still giving off a good deal of warmth and sincerity, sending the message that he really did want to embrace even if he wasn't totally comfortable committing to it. He was standing up straighter than normal, and his posture told me he was pleased to have me there, a witness to what he saw as his success.

After we crossed the threshold, Willie passed William Jr. to Paula, a hand-off I sensed had happened many times before. "Want to see the place?" Willie asked with a smile, knowing I would agree.

The two small rooms at the front of the house appeared unused, but the back—the family room and kitchen—was decorated simply with toys. Plastic toys, wood toys, blow-up toys, wind-up toys. Balls and animals and dolls. It looked more like a giant playpen than a home.

"We need to get some real furniture in here," Willie said as he leaned on the kitchen island.

"No," Paula said. "It's fine." Immediately I recognized Paula's talent for enabling her children. "It's good for William Jr. to have room to run around and play." As she spoke, she glanced at the boy, who she had plopped down on the floor in the middle of his kingdom.

"I'm sure he loves it," I said.

Willie and I left Paula with the baby and climbed the stairs to the second floor. Upstairs, there were three small bedrooms with high ceilings.

"Wait till you see this," Willie said, beaming as he opened the door to the master.

Inside, I was greeted with a Tudor four-poster bed with mirrors on the underside of its wood canopy. The wood had been painted black, and, along with the mirrors, the dark color gave the bed a very bachelor-pad appearance, which was obviously incongruous with Willie's new role as fiancé and father. The bed was so large there was barely room for Willie and I to stand at the foot, and we crowded there, taking in the elaborate structure that was the place where he and Misty lay their heads every night.

"Wow," I said. Willie's ear-to-ear grin told me I was supposed to be impressed, and I wasn't sure what else to say to something so elaborate. I tucked my head inside the frame and inspected the mirrors—they were square and had been obviously glued there.

"Only cost me four hundred dollars," Willie said.

"Wow," I said again, wondering why Willie would spend money on a bed built for a king when he still didn't have any furniture in his family room.

"But it's worth way more than that."

"I'm sure it is," I said, and I meant it though I feared the paint and mirrors had devalued it more than a little bit.

"I had to take the whole thing apart and put it back together to get it in here."

"That must have taken forever."

"Yeah," Willie said. "And then I painted it."

"It wasn't this color originally?"

"No, it was just a dark brown wood. I wanted something sleeker."

I inspected the carvings along the posts while I tried to think of something to say.

"Misty hates it."

"She does?"

"Yeah, she won't even sleep in here."

I was shocked, but I told myself not to let it show, instead doing my best to plaster a look of empathy across my face.

Willie continued: "She sleeps across the hall with William Jr."

I knew I was supposed to say something to make him feel better, to let him know it was okay his fiancée was no longer sharing his bed, but all I could think about was the sparseness of the tiny bedroom across the hall with its bare walls and the simple quilt on the bed. "Well, lots of new moms have to do that, I bet."

"Yeah," he said right away as if that was the answer he was looking for. "William Jr. is up every few hours. I could never get any sleep if he were in the room with me."

"I'm sure," I said, nodding in agreement though a question was forming in my head—if Willie had a bed made for a king and William Jr. had a room with enough toys for a prince, what did Misty have? And was that why she had no desire to be in her own home?

Eventually we wandered outside, so I could see Willie's toys—a motorcycle and a four-wheeler. Again, I wondered at the wisdom of buying recreational vehicles when the house needed furniture, but it wasn't a concern I'd even consider putting into words.

It was an usually warm day for January in Virginia—almost forty degrees—but I still shivered in the wool coat I'd bought at Goodwill the year before to give me other options than faux fur. Willie plunked William Jr. onto the seat of the four-wheeler, holding the kid in place like a stuffed animal.

I laughed at the image before me: a baby straddling an off-road vehicle.

"He likes to go fast," Willie said, "just like his daddy." Willie put his hands on William Jr.'s, lifting them to the handles and making a noise like a speeding car, so it looked like his son was revving the engine.

It was the first time I had seen Willie act so proud of his son, and I was happy to see him that way. At the same time, I wondered what it was like to grow up in a family that expected you to like exactly what they did: fast motorcycles, muddy four-wheelers, beat-up trucks, shotguns, goose hunting. What if William Jr. rejected all of that? What if he was more interested in reading Hemingway than riding Harleys? Would they accept him?

I had grown up with far fewer expectations. It was one of the great privileges of being adopted. No one in the family expected you to be like them because they knew there was no genetic link. Instead everyone waited to see what you would grab first—the ball, the crayon, the toy car, the book—in a kind of let's-see-what's-next game of chance. If you were good at sports, great. If you liked to read, that works too. There was never any pressure for me to be like my parents or anyone else in the family. The assumption was that my sister and I would find our own way, and, for the most part, we had. It was liberating to be raised in such a laissez faire environment, but I knew full well that most people didn't have that kind of freedom.

"Where do you ride this thing?" I asked Willie, realizing as soon as I had said it that my irritation was coming through in my voice. I knew I sounded impatient, but I had used up most of my energy trying to pretend that I understood Willie's life. I knew if I weren't careful, I'd say something stupid. And I didn't have any desire to hurt him.

"Up there," he said, pointing to the hills behind his house, and I followed his hand as it moved across the horizon. "Sometimes we ride around all night, come back covered in mud just in time for breakfast."

"Not this time of year?" I said, skeptical.

"Sure," he said. "Down a six-pack, and you're ready to go."

Paula let out an uncomfortable laugh. She had been standing near the back of the yard, and until then, I hadn't been sure if she was listening to our conversation or not. She caught my eye and smiled, but I didn't smile back at her. My ability to pretend was simply gone. *This is your legacy,* I thought as I studied her. *This is what you've created.*

"Don't worry," Willie said. "I don't get on the road like that. Not anymore. Been there, done that. I sure as hell don't want to go back." He chuckled then as if it were funny to learn from experience.

"Oh, yeah?" I said, wondering if he was talking about the DUI—his third—Paula had already told me about.

"Yeah, had a hell of an accident. My helmet slid down, blocked my vision. Couldn't see a damn thing. It was fucking scary. Ended up getting banged up all to hell. I almost died. I'm never doing that again."

I looked back to Paula, who was pretending not to listen by then. This was a story she couldn't brush off with an uncomfortable laugh. Her oldest son had three DUIs. He had almost died. Probably come close to killing people. Behind Willie, I could see the Confederate flag again, waving madly in the winter wind as if it were trying to speak.

"What's with the flag?" I asked Willie, well aware I sounded truculent, disapproving. I was so frustrated I might as well have said, *What's with the DAMN flag, asshole?*

"Oh, that," he said as he waved his hand dismissively toward the front yard. "It's nothing. It's just to keep the property value up."

"Really?" I asked, but I meant it rhetorically, not expecting an answer, and Willie seemed to understand that because he didn't respond. What I really wanted to say was, *Do you know how selfish that is? Do you know what that does to people?* But instead I said, "Well, we better get going" and started walking toward the car, glancing over my shoulder at Paula, so she would know it was time to leave.

From Willie's house, we went right to the bar, and I could not have been happier to see a tall glass of cold beer set in front of me. A free glass of beer at that. It was one of the first times I'd been glad that my biological family owned a bar and no one would wonder why I wanted a drink in the middle of the afternoon. In fact, in the land of Tucker, it was perfectly normal to have one at that hour, which is not to say that my parents would have raised an eyebrow if I had done the same on a Saturday afternoon in their home but just that it was more commonplace in a family whose livelihood was made off beer and chicken fingers.

It was the first time I had seen L.W. that weekend, and he acted as he always had: he nodded at me in a curt fashion and then went on his way. L.W. was like a ghost to me—someone who moved through my life, haunting me but never engaging—and he always would be. I'd already accepted that was all our relationship would ever entail, and, to be honest, I really didn't care. I'd basically written him off.

Paula busied herself with matters in the kitchen while I sat at the bar by myself. Charlie was supposed to be arriving soon, and I was more than a little excited to see him. Of all the Tuckers, he was the one who I felt really understood me, who really shared my values and beliefs. No, he hadn't followed his dreams of being an artist, but he did understand what it was like to have those kinds of dreams and how difficult and dangerous it was to go after them. After all, if you failed, you would have nothing—no career, no money, and most importantly no respect. If you failed at your dreams, you were not a failed writer or a failed painter. You were just a failure. And a fool on top of that because you'd been naïve and stupid enough to think you could be unique and better than everyone else. No, I didn't blame Charlie for not going for it because I got it.

But for some reason, I hadn't been blessed with Charlie's prudence. Instead, I had been given a gigantic share of hutzpah—more than any one person should have and enough that I had kept writing even though I hadn't published anything since 1999. This was also the reason I was back in Annandale a third time, trying to make things right with the same people I'd been unable to comprehend the first time around. But Charlie was different: he was someone I'd understood from the get-go. So when he walked in the door—a little less steady on his feet than I remembered but still a few years from walking with the carved cane that would later become his signature—I uncharacteristically jumped up and greeted him with a hug. Charlie inspired that kind of affection in me.

"How are you, kiddo?" he said nonchalantly as if it hadn't been nearly six years since I'd seen him. And indeed it didn't feel like that long with Charlie. It felt more like days or weeks since we'd last conversed.

"I'm okay," I said. "I really can't complain anyway."

"And David?"

"He's well. He's in the District—at a writing conference."

I sat back down on my bar stool, and Charlie pulled out the one next to me. As soon as his butt hit the seat, L.W. appeared, putting a cold beer in front of Charlie before disappearing outside again.

"So you're both still writing?" Charlie asked after taking a sip of his beer.

"Absolutely," I said, knowing Charlie would understand that I was saying I hadn't given up, that I desperately hoped I never would.

"Good, good," Charlie said. "I hope it works out for you both." That kind of comment might have seemed artificial in someone else's mouth, but I knew Charlie was being earnest. I also knew something was bothering him because he took a long pull from his drink before he continued. "The country's in shit shape, though, isn't it? And this war—" His voice trailed off, but I understood what he meant.

"No doubt," I said before I took another drink of my beer. "It's been a hard time."

"I know it," Charlie agreed.

I let out a little laugh, not because what Charlie said was funny, but because of how surprising it was to be sitting in the middle of Tucker's Hideaway, surrounded by good old boys, and hear Charlie admit that he got it.

Just then Paula appeared, her hands on both of our shoulders as if posing for a picture. "You two ready for another?" she asked as she glanced at L.W., signaling for him to join us with a jerk of the head.

I desperately wanted another—an ice cold tonic that would help me forget everything—the war, the flag at Willie's house, the night ahead of me. But I still had to drive into the District to pick up Dave for dinner. I'd promised Paula he'd come to the bar to eat, and I knew myself well enough to know I'd be in no shape to navigate eight-lane freeways and roller coaster off-ramps after a second beer. "I've got to pick up Dave," I said, wishing more than anything I could afford one more beer as L.W. approached.

"Oh, you can have one more," Paula said with a smile that told me she thought I was being ridiculously cautious. She glanced at L.W. as if he looking for his support, but, as usual, he was closemouthed.

"It's only a fifteen-minute drive," she said, underestimating the time and pushing me to do things her way. Charlie had turned away from me and was facing the bar, sending the clear message he wasn't getting involved in our discussion.

"I can't do it," I said firmly and, when I saw Paula's face drop, added, "I'll have one later. Don't worry. I'm coming back."

I knew there was a chance Dave would bail on dinner. I'd told him the night before how important it was for him to see the Tuckers. After all, unless you counted the five minutes when Clint had picked me up at the hotel two nights before, Dave hadn't seen them in almost six years, since that fateful visit when on some level we had decided—whether we knew it at the time or not—that we might never go back.

But he was also adamant that he spend as much time at the conference as possible, especially since it meant face time with some of his heroes, including David Morrell and Tom Monteleone. I didn't want to deprive him of that experience, but I also knew it would look funny if we came to D.C. two years in a row without him making an appearance at the bar. He had never fully committed, so I wasn't sure how he would respond when I showed up in front of the hotel. For that reason, I was surprised when he jumped right in the car and didn't try to get out of it. Rather than ask if he was still game, I pulled out of the drive and headed back to Annandale, hoping it was too late for him to change his mind.

"We won't stay long," I said, knowing that had to be what was on his mind. "We'll have dinner, you can make nice with everyone, and then we'll get out of there. I'll have you back here in less than two hours."

"Ha!" Dave said, his typical response whenever he thought I was proposing something he saw as undoable.

"I'm serious," I said, glancing away from the road, so I could catch his eye. "Two hours tops."

"The drive alone is going to take us more than half an hour." He didn't sound irritated. Just resigned.

"Right—half an hour for the drive, and an hour and a half for dinner."

"It'll be forty-five minutes there and back at least."

"Fine," I agreed. "Forty-five minutes for the drive and a little more than an hour for dinner."

"We'll see," he said, though his tone indicated how much he doubted it could happen.

The bar was almost empty when we arrived. The few bikers who'd been standing out front that afternoon had fled for warmer environs. Inside, L.W. was still behind the bar, but there was no one for him to serve except for Charlie and Paula who sat side by side in the same spot where I'd left them over an hour before, the red-and-white bar signs casting an ambient glow over the empty room. But rather than making the space feel hollow, the lack of customers made it feel cozy, as if we were finally in Paula and L.W.'s true home.

Dave and L.W. shook hands when we walked in the door, a greeting Dave said was noteworthy only because of its normalcy: L.W.'s shake wasn't too weak or too firm, his words weren't too cold or too warm, his greeting neither too short nor too effusive. He was just average. And when Dave told me that later, I was confronted with the reality that L.W. treated men differently—with more respect and civility—than women. At that point, L.W. had never looked me in the eye, and he'd always been cold and short. The opposite of normal, he rated far below average in his ability to connect with the child he had fathered almost thirty-six years before.

Paula, on the other hand, was always eager to connect. From across the room, her voice rose to greet us: "I set up a table for you," she said.

I walked in her direction, so I wouldn't have to shout. "You didn't have to do that," I said.

"I wanted to," she replied. "I wanted this to be special for the two of you." It was an odd comment and one I didn't fully understand until Paula escorted us to the table. There were the expected plates and silverware, but there was also a lit candle and a flower in a plastic vase as if the two of us were going on a date—strange choices given that we were there to visit them, not spend time with each other. "L.W.'s going to make you his favorite," she added. "Crab Imperial."

I looked at Dave quickly, hoping he'd be happy with what Paula had decided we were going to eat. It was bad enough he'd had to leave the conference to come along. I would have hated if he'd also had to pretend to like something he didn't. But to my surprise, he jumped right in: "Great," he said. "Sounds delicious."

"You like crab, right?" Paula asked, too late for us to admit otherwise without hurting her feelings.

"Of course," Dave said loudly, turning the volume up on his personality so that Paula wouldn't question us further.

"Yeah," Paula continued, "L.W. said he wanted to make it for you."

"He did?" I asked, unable to hide the skepticism in my voice. It was the first time in my entire life L.W. had expressed a desire to have anything to do with me, much less do something *for* me. Was it possible, I wondered, that he was finally reaching out?

"It's his specialty," Paula explained.

Right then, a man in a beat-up leather jacket and chaps walked in the door. Paula's attention immediately turned away from us. "I'll be back in a minute," she said and headed toward the corner of the bar where L.W. was smiling and talking to the customer.

After Paula was far enough away that she couldn't hear me, I turned back to Dave. "Can you believe this?"

"You mean the way they're acting? The romantic table? And L.W.?"

"Yeah," I said. "It's weird, right?"

"It certainly isn't their normal way of doing things," Dave admitted.

I glanced over at Paula and L.W. They were leaning together in a conspiratorial fashion. Then L.W. waved his hand at her as if dismissing her. Paula must have been following orders because she headed straight back for the kitchen.

"What's going on?" I asked Dave.

"I have no idea," he said. "But I feel like I'm being courted."

"I know. It's kind of creepy."

Just then Paula returned to our table with an announcement: "L.W. wants to teach you how to make Crab Imperial," she said.

"Who? Me?" I asked because I was still feeling a bit incredulous about L.W.'s new willingness to acknowledge my existence.

"Yes, you!" Paula said with a laugh. "Who else would I mean?" As she spoke, L.W. passed behind her without stopping, still a phantom to me.

I looked at Dave for help, but he just raised his eyebrow. I knew he wouldn't be volunteering to take my place.

"He doesn't have to do that," I said to Paula, but she could not be dissuaded.

"Of course, he doesn't *have* to do it. He wants to."

I peeked at the swinging door that led to the kitchen. It had a porthole at the top, a small window into the mystery behind the wall that had always separated me from the inner workings of the place. I was pretty sure I didn't want to breach that wall, to find out what happened on the other side. But how could I explain that to Paula, a woman who had no boundaries in her life unless someone else imposed them on her?

"All right," I said reluctantly without getting up from the table.

"Okay, just go on back," Paula said, nodding toward the kitchen. "He'll show you what to do."

I glanced at Dave one last time, wondering briefly if I'd ever see him again, if I'd make it through what could only be described as one of the most daunting experiences of my life.

L.W. was waiting in the kitchen. A young, dark-haired woman stood next to him chewing her fingernails.

"This is Christie," he said gruffly without ever telling Christie my name. "She just started, and she needs to learn how to do this too."

"Hi," I said lamely because L.W. was already onto other things, pulling a large silver mixing bowl down from the shelf above the stove and nestling it between several ingredients that were already neatly lined up on the work table.

"Now," L.W. began, but he paused before he continued, taking a second to look me directly in the eye. He glared at me the same way my maternal grandmother would—like it was a warning more than a communication. *You better be listening*, his look said. It was the first time I had ever felt the heavy weight of his attention on me, so I took in a deep breath and stood as tall as I could, like a student in front of the teacher. Next to his six-foot-five frame, the top of my head barely reached his shoulders, but I held his gaze as he went on. "The first thing you do is make sure the oven is hot enough. If the oven isn't at the exact right temperature, the whole thing will be ruined. This is crucial," he said to me and then turned to Christie: "Don't mess this up."

"Okay," Christie said meekly, so I didn't have to.

"Next you put all the ingredients in the bowl—first the crab. Fresh crab," he added. "Never from a can."

I nodded, so he would know I was listening.

"Then the mayonnaise and Worcestershire." He didn't measure anything, simply eyeballing his ingredients as he worked. "Then the Old Bay and the mustard." A brilliant shower of spices rained into the bowl

"You don't need a recipe?" I asked.

"Been making it as long as I can remember," he said, barely pausing to respond. "Never once used a recipe. A little salt and pepper. The egg is next. Beat it thoroughly before adding." L.W. picked up a small bowl containing the egg and whipped it like a professional, flipping it into the larger bowl in one swift motion.

"Is it written down anywhere?" I asked. "The recipe? Or is it some kind of family secret?"

L.W. looked up from his work, peeking at me from the corner of his eye. "Now be quiet and pay attention," he said, his voice revealing his irritation. "No more questions."

Though I didn't take a physical step back, I did so emotionally. L.W. had silenced me. My whole life I had been taught that questions were good, the sign of an inquisitive mind, not something to be brushed off like an annoying gnat. But L.W. didn't take questions. He gave orders. And he expected people to follow them.

I glanced at Christie, who was also standing up straight, trying to please L.W., to let him know he had her full attention. She hadn't breathed a word unless responding to him directly. Sure, she was his employee, but she seemed more like a minion. And that's when it hit me—if I had grown up with L.W. as my father, I wouldn't have learned to ask questions, to have a natural curiosity about my surroundings and the world. Quite simply, I wouldn't be me. I would be a woman who was afraid to speak. A woman who was better seen and not heard because that's what he would've expected of me. No, Jeannie wasn't the type to sit quietly in the corner, but she also didn't challenge her father and lacked the confidence to do so with those in authoritative roles. Was that why she'd struggled in school? Was that why they all had?

My own father had asked for my respect, but he had not demanded it, which was clearly what set him apart from other, more authoritative fathers. He had also welcomed discussion, even encouraged it, and I was never happier than when the two of us were weighing an issue, breaking it down into manageable parts and putting it back together again like a puzzle that needed to be reconfigured.

But in that moment, I knew L.W. had never done that with Jeannie: he'd never sought her out intellectually. I knew because of what he was doing to me—shutting me down on an intellectual level, saying, *Turn it off and do what I tell you.*

I didn't turn it off—my mind was laying on the gas and taking the corner on two wheels—but I did keep my thoughts silent after that, removing myself from L.W.'s way, emotionally if not physically.

L.W. gave no indication that he knew what was going on inside my head. Instead, he continued with his instructions: "When the ingredients are thoroughly mixed, spoon about a quarter of it in here—" He pulled a small dish off the counter and help it up to the lip of the mixing bowl, filling it with the crab mixture and wiping the knife across the top like it was a cake. He did the same with another dish and then grabbed a jar, gently shaking it over the top of both dishes. "Just a few bread crumbs." I was aware that if a stranger had been eavesdropping, L.W. would have sounded more like a world-class chef than the owner of a bar, but standing in front of him—in a dark kitchen next to an old blackened stove—I could not make the same mistake.

L.W. pulled the door to the oven down in one quick motion. With as much force as he used, I figured it would flip back up and hit him in the hand, knocking the two small dishes he was holding to the floor, but the door obeyed him as well, bouncing a bit when it was fully open but finally falling back into place. He slid his work on a shelf and without turning to the two of us, said, "Under the broiler.

Fifteen minutes exactly or it'll be ruined." He closed the door to the oven and reluctantly looked back at Christie and me. I thought for a second he might ask if there were any questions, but instead, he just wiped his hands on a towel and said, "That's it" as if any follow-up would be a waste of breath.

When I'd first learned the Tuckers were my biological family, the predominant feeling I had, besides shock, was luck. I felt lucky my parents had found me, rescuing me from what I saw as alien territory. The Tuckers had been raised to love things—guns and motorcycles— and though, admittedly, I was raised to love things too—things like designer jeans and pretty shoes—I was also taught to value ideas and analysis. They believed they only had each other, but I'd been taught I would meet new people all the time, that life was about changing and growing. But that night, as I stood in the kitchen of the Hideaway watching my biological father stare me down, I understood I'd been even luckier than I had originally thought. It wasn't just about the education or even the money. It was about perspective.

My parents had taught me to see the world as a place where I would be welcomed rather than a place from which I should shrink, a place that embraced intellectual curiosity rather than shunned it, a place where I could do anything a man could do, be anything a man could be, a place that was in direct contrast to the world L.W. Tucker lived in. And that night I spent in the kitchen with him made me realize I can never thank them enough for that gift.

When I returned to the table, I wanted to tell Dave immediately about what had happened in the kitchen, but I saw no way of doing so without being overheard. And I was so turned off, so irritated, by L.W.'s behavior I knew if I tried to talk about it, I would lose my temper as I detailed the ways in which he had failed me—yes, as a progenitor, but also as a person—and the ways I knew he also must have failed Jeannie and Paula their whole lives and even the boys, though not to the same extent. But I couldn't risk an outburst with Paula and L.W. only a few feet away.

"Everything okay?" Dave asked after I sat down and moved the candle back and forth over the tabletop.

"Absolutely," I said. "What could possibly be wrong?"

"Oh, boy," he said.

"Why are you saying that? Don't I seem happy?" I asked him as I pulled a fake smile across my face.

"You seem like you're trying really hard to look happy, but you're not quite pulling it off."

Just then Paula arrived at our table with two small dinner salads and a basket of rolls. "I hope you're hungry," she said.

"Starving," I said enthusiastically, offering Paula a huge smile in the hopes she would be satisfied and go away.

That must have worked because Paula said, "Okay, I'll let you two get started. Your Crab Imperial will be out soon." Then she walked back to the kitchen.

"My God," I said under my breath. "She acts like it's caviar made for the Queen."

Dave laughed. It was a loud, full-throated laugh, and I knew he was enjoying watching me come unraveled while also blowing off some of his own steam. After he calmed down, he finally spoke: "What's going on?"

"I do *not* want to talk about it here."

"That's fine. I'm simpatico. You can tell me later."

"Great. Now just eat your salad and act happy, so we can get out of here." By way of demonstrating, I stabbed my fork into the iceberg lettuce that sat in front of me.

Dave unwrapped his silverware from its paper napkin enclosure, but didn't use it right away. "Aren't you coming back here after you drop me off?"

"Yes," I said after I finished chewing. "But I need a break from the reality that is L.W. Tucker, Misogynist Number One."

"Wow," Dave said. "You make it sound like he's in the Taliban."

"Not quite, but he's not as far off as you might think."

"Great," Dave said sarcastically, no longer laughing but shaking his head as he moved the food in his salad bowl around without eating any of it and reached for a roll.

"You don't have to tell me. I'm the one who lived it."

"I know," Dave said. "I'm just tired."

"Me too. Like you, I've been on stage all afternoon. Only I had to do it with the Tuckers, and you got to do it with people you admire."

"Okay," he said, "I'll do what I have to do, and then we can plot our escape."

A few minutes later, while we were still eating salad, Paula showed up with our dinners—the famous Crab Imperial and a couple of baked potatoes. Dave displayed his best smile and used the artificial voice I knew he reserved for people he couldn't stand: "Paula, this is too much! You've really outdone yourself! You shouldn't have!"

"Thank you, David," Paula said. "That's so nice of you to say."

I stopped eating so I could watch Dave perform, and when he stole a look at me, a tiny glimmer in his eye, I knew what he was saying: *Don't worry. I've got this.*

On the way back to the hotel, I gave Dave a play-by-play of what had happened in the kitchen.

"You really are lucky," he said when I explained how L.W.'s actions made me see my own father's behavior as even more open-minded than I'd previously realized.

"I know," I said. "But just think about what this means: my dad is the more liberal one in this pairing. He's the feminist."

"You always say you're the product of their upbringing."

"Yeah, but I had no idea . . ." I trailed off as I struggled to find the right words. "I had no idea what it would be like to grow up with someone who wasn't like that, someone who believes women should keep their mouths shut and defer to men. It really pisses me off."

"It should. It pisses me off, and I wasn't even there. Just think about what that did to Jeannie, think about how it could've changed her life if she'd grown up with a dad who valued women's opinions."

"Exactly. I always believed my ideas had value. I always believed my words were worth hearing. But tonight . . ." I paused again, remembering how L.W.'s actions had me feel.

"Tonight you got a different message."

"Yeah, and it made me certain I want nothing to do with him."

After returning Dave to the hotel, I had to find a way to calm down, to not take my anger with L.W. out on everyone else at the bar. I didn't really have time to go up to the hotel room or drive around since I'd told Paula I'd be right back. So I did the only thing I could do, the same thing I did when I didn't know what to do with my unchecked emotions in high school—I rolled down the windows and turned up the radio, belting out whatever song came through the airwaves and letting my hostilities escape into the cold night air like untamed spirits.

It turned out to be a good idea to leave my issues on the side of the highway because when I got back to the Hideaway, it felt like a small celebration had begun: the whole family was there, drinking and talking and getting along—Jeannie, Wade, Clint and Amy, Willie, Charlie, and Paula—and, yes, L.W. was still around, but he spent the night busying himself with customers outside rather than dealing with his lively family. I wasn't sure what had caused so much joy, but I had to wonder if it was the fact that my visit was coming to an end, relieving everyone of some of the pressure we'd all been feeling about how things would go. No matter the reason, the rest of the night was easy, and I relaxed and enjoyed the feeling of being around people I was only getting to know but who were still somehow a part of me.

Even though I was at the bar until after eleven, Paula made me promise to come back the next morning for breakfast. I knew Dave would be busy until at least noon when we had to check out, so I figured it would be easiest to fulfill my obligation to Paula before packing the car for our trip home. When I'd left the night before, everyone was high on the evening, all of them saying they'd meet me for breakfast at nine, but as I drove back to Annandale at the same time people were heading to church, I suspected they'd probably flake out, opting for sleep over greasy eggs and bacon in a smoky bar, which was what I would've done if I'd felt I had a choice. Because of that, I wasn't surprised when I walked in the door and saw only Paula and her sister, Sue, standing behind the bar and Charlie sitting in front of it.

"Well, good morning," Sue said, walking to the end of the bar to give me a hug, and Paula chuckled as if her sister had said something funny. Sue had sent me birthday and Christmas cards every single year since the day I'd met her nearly six years before, and for that reason, like Charlie, she'd earned a special place in my heart.

I said my hellos, giving Charlie a hug too, and sat down at the bar.

"How you feeling?" Paula asked me once I was settled on a stool next to Charlie.

"Me?" I said, confused by Paula's question. "I feel fine."

"Really?" she said. "You were pretty drunk last night."

"Paula," Sue said, "don't interrogate the poor girl."

I looked at Charlie, wondering what he was thinking, but he only raised his eyebrows at me in response. Instead of cashing in on Sue's attempt to save me, I turned to Paula, determined to set the record straight. "I only had two beers after I got back from driving Dave to the hotel."

"Is that all?" Paula said. "Well, you seemed pretty loose, seemed like you were having a good time."

"We all did," Charlie added with a grin, clearly trying to diffuse any tension. "It was a lot of fun."

"That's what I heard too," said Sue.

Things had gone so well the night before—and, in truth, the whole weekend despite my frustrations with L.W.—that I let Paula's comment go even though I didn't like the implication she was making: that I must have been drunk if I was enjoying myself or was fun to be around.

The truth was, until the night before, I *had* needed more than two drinks to relax around the Tuckers, but something had changed, some kind of wall that had previously existed between my biological siblings and me had finally come down. And I wasn't all that eager to put it back up, so I avoided a fight with Paula, knowing from experience I would have to keep things right with her if I wanted things right with them too. "It was a great time," I admitted, not a lie but also not the whole truth.

"Good," Paula said. "I'm glad you got to know each other better."

"Yeah, me too," I said, and I meant it. Though I'd never felt an urgent need for more siblings, when I met Jeannie, Wade, Clint, and Willie, they filled a void I hadn't known was there. Even though it wasn't what I wanted or needed from them, some part of me always imagined that's what it would feel like when I met Paula and L.W., but it never had. It had instead felt that there was nowhere to put them, that the space in my life I allotted for parents was already full and, in truth, always had been. No one could replace my parents or even stand beside them.

"Jeannie and Clint said they're coming, but..." Paula paused to let out another chuckle. "But I don't know." I wondered what was funny to her—that they'd probably be hungover or that I'd be let down. I suspected it was the latter, that there was a part of Paula that wanted to see me have my feelings hurt. Either way, it said something unflattering about her.

"I figured it was unlikely they'd get out of bed," I said. "I had trouble getting here myself."

"Well, it's pretty early," Paula said, looking at her watch.

But just then, the front door opened, and Jeannie rolled in, wearing jeans, a Virginia Tech sweatshirt, and a baseball cap that read "Team Tucker" across the front, her boyfriend Kenny trailing behind her like a bodyguard. "Oh, man," Jeannie said to all of us. "I can't believe I'm awake."

I laughed, but not because her misery was amusing to me as much as because she was entertaining. She shuffled up to the bar, her head hanging low, and slid onto the empty stool on my other side, putting her elbows on the bar and her head in her hands. Kenny offered me a short, polite greeting and bypassed us for a video game sitting on the end of the bar.

"Can I please have some water?" Jeannie said without lifting her head, peeking out between a web of fingers.

Even though Sue was technically the one manning the bar that morning, Paula picked up a glass and filled it with water, setting it in front of her daughter without comment. Jeannie took a long drink, and I glanced at Paula to see what she was she thinking, but her nonchalance told me Jeannie's behavior was nothing new.

After Jeannie put the glass down, she turned to me. "I bet you feel fine this morning."

"I do. I mean, I'm tired, but I didn't drink enough to get a hangover. I had to drive."

"Jesus, I wish I could say the same thing," Jeannie said, letting out a long unhappy moan.

"Well, what does everybody want to eat?" Paula said, interrupting.

Jeannie's hangover didn't cause her any hesitation: "I want a cheese omelet with potatoes and toast. Oh, and jelly. And coffee."

I was shocked by Jeannie's mammoth order, but Paula didn't blink. "What about you?" she asked me.

I had always hated traditional breakfast food though I could handle a pancake in the morning when I was forced to eat breakfast in a restaurant. But if I asked for a pancake and they didn't have them, I worried that would call to mind some notion of me as a prima donna, a notion I had worked hard to erase. Though I wasn't an egg person, I knew I could tolerate eggs with enough cheese to obscure the taste of them, so I followed Jeannie's lead. "I'll have the same thing," I said. "But no coffee."

"Charlie?" Paula said to her brother.

"I'll just take some more of this stuff, Paula, thanks." Charlie held up his mug and tapped it.

Paula didn't ask her sister if she wanted anything, and as I watched Paula disappear into the kitchen, I found myself hoping Sue had eaten when she opened the bar that morning. When I finally turned back around, I noticed Jeannie staring at me.

"No coffee?" Jeannie said skeptically as if I'd told Paula I'd like some crack with my eggs. "Are you crazy?"

"That is crazy," Charlie agreed as he took another sip from his mug.

"I'm not a coffee person," I admitted.

"I'm not either, but after a night like that, I'll do anything to recover." Jeannie took another long drink of her water, and Sue refilled her glass before stepping outside, presumably to see if there were any new customers. At the same time, Charlie excused himself to go the bathroom, leaving me alone with Jeannie, who turned to me then and said, "But, damn, it was a good night, wasn't it?"

"Yeah, it really was."

"We need to do it again sometime," she said, which struck me as funny since Jeannie was in the middle of suffering through the consequences of her actions but still wanted to do the whole thing over again. "Wait—do you like to ski?"

"Yeah, I love it."

"You should go skiing with us next weekend," she said. "We're going to Deep Creek. That would be so awesome."

"I'd love to," I said, "but we've got a ton of work to do. We've been away since Wednesday. I have a feeling it'll take me a week to catch up."

"Oh, that sucks. Well, maybe next year. If nothing else, you have got to come back for Clint and Amy's wedding. It's going to be epic."

"Definitely. But they're not even engaged yet, are they?"

"No, but they will be soon," she said. "I know it. They're perfect together."

As if on cue, the door at the front opened again, and Amy stepped inside. Her hair was damp; unlike Jeannie, she'd gone to the trouble of showering and applying makeup. Still, she was dressed more casually than normal—in jeans and an oversized sweater—and looked just the slightest bit tired. Clint was behind her, and he wore the same hat as Jeannie.

"Okay, we're here," Amy announced with faux enthusiasm as the two of them walked over to the bar. "Barely."

"Nice hat," I said to Clint as he approached.

"Oh, this," he said, removing it and studying the lettering on the front as if he didn't even know what was on his own head. "Haven't you seen these?"

"I don't think so."

Jeannie jumped in: "Oh, you've got to see the back. Check it out," she said as she turned around, Clint pointing to the words embroidered around the image of a goose in flight.

"If it flies," he said dramatically, "it dies!"

Jeannie swiveled back to us and high-fived her brother.

"Oh, God, you guys," I said. "That's awful."

"What's awful about it?" Clint asked matter-of-factly. "We eat what we kill."

"Okay, that's not so bad, but still . . ."

"So what you're saying is," Clint began, "you're not going with us next time we blast some geese out of the sky."

"Not a chance. I guess I'm a hypocrite. I'll eat it, but I don't want to see you kill it."

"You know what I said, Clint?" Jeannie began. "I said she should come skiing with us."

"Oh, yeah, that would be awesome," he said. "Do you ski?"

"Love it. Maybe we can do that next year."

"I cannot wait to hit the slopes," Clint said.

"You can't go this year?" Amy asked me.

"I wish. Being away this weekend is going to put me way behind as it is. And I didn't do an ounce of work while I was here."

"It's good for you," Jeannie said.

"I know," I said. "I probably needed it."

Just then I heard Paula's voice call out from behind me. "When did you get here, Clint?" she said as she moved toward us with two big plates of food. "How long have you been sitting there?" Paula asked again.

"Like five seconds," Clint said.

"You should've told me. I would've made you some breakfast."

"Ma!" he said in a mock irritated voice. "I just said, we've only been here five seconds."

"Well, can I get you something to eat?" Paula asked. "An omelet?"

"No, Ma, don't worry about it. I'll get it." Clint headed toward the kitchen, glancing over his shoulder before he left. "Pancakes, Amy?"

Amy didn't hesitate: "Yes, please. Lots of pancakes!"

About an hour later, breakfast was long finished, and I knew I had to leave or risk not getting out of the hotel on time. But I also wasn't sure how to extricate myself because I always felt like leaving the Tuckers was misinterpreted as rejecting them, especially when I had no definite plans to return. Still, I had no choice. "I should probably get going."

"You're leaving already?" Paula asked.

"We have to be out of the hotel by noon," I said. And then just in case Paula planned to invite us back that afternoon, I added, "And then we have a nine-hour drive home. It's going to be hell."

"Wow, that sounds like hell," Jeannie said. "You don't fly, right?"

I smiled to myself when I realized Jeannie had remembered something about me Paula often didn't. "Not for a long time."

"That would really suck."

"Oh," Amy said, "it won't be that bad. You'll be able to talk to Dave. You've barely seen him all weekend. It'll be fun to catch up on everything you've done."

"That's true," I said, realizing Amy was right, which reminded me again how much I liked her.

"Will Dave be coming back to that conference next year?" Paula asked, suddenly changing the subject.

"I don't think so. I think he's put in his time here." As soon as the words were out of my mouth, I hoped they wouldn't be misconstrued. I hadn't meant Dave had put in his time with the Tuckers, but I worried it sounded that way.

"You'll just have to go skiing with us sometime," Jeannie said.

"Next year," Clint added. "Deep Creek Lake. You'll love it."

"Okay, I'll try."

"And that other thing we talked about," Jeannie said with a wink.

"What's that?" Amy asked.

"Oh, nothing," Jeannie said. "Don't worry your pretty little head about it."

"We've got to take a picture before we go," Paula said.

"Really?" Clint said. "Do we have to?"

Paula frowned at him. "It won't take long. I promise."

"Okay," Amy said. "Everybody up."

We all stood reluctantly and waited for more directions from Paula, who already had her camera in her hand: "I want to take it out front."

"Let's get this over with," Clint said with a laugh, but I knew he wasn't that unhappy about having his picture taken, that he was objecting more out of obligation than true frustration.

And in the photo, that seems to be true of all of us. We look relaxed and happy, if a bit worn-out from our raucous time together. Almost as if we were a real family. Misty showed up at the last minute, too, handing her son to Paula for the photo before turning away from the camera, and William Jr.'s brand new gold-and-red Winnie the

Pooh slippers are almost as bright as the sun that morning, which is nearly blinding those of us in the front row. Nevertheless, we are all smiling—Paula, Sue, Jeannie, and I displaying the same big, toothy unassuming smile that must have been handed down to us from a people who never learned how to pose for the camera. In contrast, Amy stands behind us with the boys, her head tilted just slightly to one side, making her head come in at her neck so perfectly she looks like a catalog model.

But it's also notable that this photo paints a completely new picture, a more contented picture, than the one created by the photo taken at the end of my first weekend with the Tuckers five and a half years before—the one in which Paula looks nervous, I seem apprehensive, and L.W. appears miserable. I didn't know where L.W. was that January morning, but I was sure of one thing: the picture was better without him.

Dear Molly,

Hope your trip back home was restful. I know my kids give everyone a run for their money—they wear the best out.

I'm afraid I really wasn't myself this past weekend, but I want you to know it was special for me to just see you mingle and enjoy Willie, Clint, Wade and Jeannie, as well as their friends and of course William Jr. It is a gift to me that you are beginning to know each other and hopefully be friends.

Have a great spring and much success with your writing. Perhaps you can send me one of your stories.

Take care and God bless.

Love,

Paula & L.W.

P.S. You'll be getting a surprise package in the mail. Something I saw and thought of you—enjoy!

Paula's letter arrived a week or two later. I had no idea what she meant about not being herself. Usually I could figure out what Paula was trying to say—even when she didn't just come out and say it— but when I read her words that afternoon, I was at a loss, especially since she'd seemed a good deal like the Paula I knew during my visit. The only real difference I noticed was, just like the year before, she seemed to be doing a better job understanding I was no longer her daughter and that I wasn't going to become a regular, everyday part of her life, which provided me with a great sense of relief.

It seemed she finally got that I had a family of my own—especially parents who were a big part of my life—and didn't want to change that. So, from my point of view, I couldn't have been happier with Paula. Yes, she still sometimes seemed sad or regretful about the decision she had made to give me up, but she also seemed fully aware that if she hadn't made that decision, her life might not have turned out as it had. And it was a life she treasured very much, one she certainly wouldn't risk changing just to have me play a more active role in it.

On the other hand, the other comment she made—about getting closer to Willie, Clint, Wade, and Jeannie—made perfect sense to me. That had been the most positive aspect of the trip for me. Despite our differences, I really enjoyed my time with them. I wanted to be a part of their lives. No, I would never be as close to them as I was with my sister, but I was hoping we could still have a bond of some kind. And I believed the weekend had laid the foundation to let me have that kind of relationship with all of them.

And, of course, I hadn't missed that Paula didn't mention anything in the letter about L.W. The two of us had interacted more than we ever had in our lives, but that experience didn't even warrant a footnote in Paula's summary of the weekend. Still, that made sense to me. She was avoiding a touchy subject, and I would've done the same if I'd written to her about my visit. Nevertheless, it reinforced my belief that L.W. continued to be unhappy about having me in any of their lives.

But I wouldn't think much about any of that for months—over a year, to be honest. Instead, I became immersed in the present tense of our lives, which meant figuring out what we were going to do the next year.

Dave had the option of staying at Miami in his visiting position another four years, but that also meant every spring there would be a question about whether or not the university would fund his line. Our sense was they would always come through. Money was an issue every year, they told us, but it almost always worked out. Nevertheless, it was an awful way to live—not knowing if your job would be there a year later. And that spring was pretty anxiety-ridden in that sense.

Word around the English department was that the visiting positions in creative writing might be cut, making us even more concerned about the future. So when we both got email messages a month later, in March, from St. Andrews Presbyterian College in North Carolina—asking if we'd be interested in interviewing for the fiction writing position there—we didn't hesitate to say yes. Though we'd both been asked the same question, only Dave agreed to do the interview since we thought his chances of getting it would be better than mine. And once he wrote back to the English department chair, she said she'd be in touch soon, which we took to mean a few days, maybe a week. But after that initial email exchange in early March, several weeks went by without Dave hearing anything. At that point, we worried the job might have been filled or the search canceled.

In the meantime, we got word that the funding for Dave's job was going to come through, and his schedule was set for the fall semester. Once we got that good news, we decided we needed a change. Even if Dave's job would be the same, we could relocate to Oxford, allowing us to feel like we'd finally moved on from the doctoral program and life in Cincinnati. It was also a decision that meant Dave would no longer have to commute to work and I would be able to pick up some classes at Miami on a part-time basis. So rather than sit around waiting for St. Andrews to call about an interview, we hunted for a place to rent in early April.

Oxford was, and still is, a student-centered town, so it was hard to find something affordable that wasn't trashed or adjacent to loud neighbors. But we finally found a small house within walking distance of town. We knew the place would go fast, so we filled out a rental application the same day and were approved the next. The only question was: should we sign a rental contract without checking with St. Andrews first?

We hadn't been able to stop thinking about St. Andrews or give up on the dream of a tenure-track job—something permanent, something that would allow us to feel more settled and secure. We would have just picked up the phone and called to find out what was what, but doing so was supposedly considered taboo on the academic job market. Still, if we didn't contact them, we'd be making the decision for them by signing a one-year lease in Oxford. We spent a whole day weighing our options. And when we finally determined we had nothing to lose, we bit the bullet and Dave sent an email message to the English department chair at St. Andrews, asking if they still wanted to set up an interview. To our great surprise, the chair wrote back less than twelve hours later and said they would love for him to interview, wondering how soon he could do it.

And that's how we ended up driving to Laurinburg, North Carolina, one week later. As I mentioned, we'd been selective about which jobs we applied to that year, trying to pick locales that would appeal to us in some way rather than just applying to every job in the country. But when we mapped our trip, we were surprised to see Laurinburg was incredibly isolated—at least an hour's drive to a city—something we didn't know was possible in North Carolina, which we'd always associated with the mountains and the ocean. As it turns out, there's a whole swath of rural country there that exists between these two ideals, a no man's land where the grass won't grow and the sun provides more irritation than warmth. And that's where St. Andrews is located.

Still, we tried to look at the positives and imagined such a place would mean fresh local produce and family-run diners. We wouldn't know for months we were wrong about both, but after arriving in Laurinburg, it was clear it wasn't the kind of place that inspired optimism.

The entire town was about two square miles—with three blocks of abandoned downtown buildings on one end and a few strip malls on the other. Our hotel was adjacent to one of those strip malls, and the morning after our arrival, I walked around the parking lot, gawking at what could only be described as low-rent discount stores. There were, in fact, six distinct dollar stores in Laurinburg, a town of ten thousand. Soon after our arrival, we also learned there were only two sit-down restaurants—the restaurant at our hotel, McDuff's (I've already mentioned my disdain for hotel restaurants), and a Mexican place called Mi Casita, pronounced "Mi Casitas" by the locals.

Still, that was all yet to come, and after our check-in at the Laurinburg Comfort Inn, we didn't have time to discuss how impoverished the area seemed when we drove into town, nor did we discuss the fact that our hotel sat next to two small strip malls that appeared to make up the whole of Laurinburg. Maybe we were afraid if we admitted those observations out loud, we wouldn't be able to take them back. Until we put words to what we'd seen, it was more like a bad dream than a concrete reality. And we had more important things to worry about anyway—we were having dinner with the English department chair that night.

As luck would have it, I not only had my period, but it was also the one day a month when my cramps were so bad I was forced to alternate between throwing back twelve hundred milligrams of ibuprofen and clutching a hot pack to my gut. I wasn't thrilled about taking so much medicine before I went to such an important dinner, but I had no choice unless I wanted to start rocking back and forth at the table like a savant. So, while Dave called the department chair to let her know we'd arrived, I took my Advil and ironed my clothes, keeping the heat of the iron as close to my abdomen as possible.

Though there were two sit-down restaurants in town, the department chair—Charlotte Allen—told us to meet her at the No. 1 China Buffet, which was about five blocks from where we were staying, halfway between our hotel and downtown on a stretch of road that featured nearly every major fast food restaurant in America. It seemed that what it lacked in formal dining, Laurinburg made up for in fast food.

As I've said, I'm a snob about way too many things, and one of them is bad Chinese food. So when we pulled into the parking lot of the No. 1 China Buffett and saw a rundown building with only about two-thirds of its red letters lit on the sign out front—right next to one of the Dollar Stores—I knew it didn't bode well.

Inside No. 1, there were paneled walls, green Formica tables with matching chairs, and vertical blinds, all of which surrounded three massive buffet tables. Dave and I had been avoiding buffets ever since our first trip to Vegas and a $3.99 prime rib buffet that stretched the length of a hotel, making us feel like animals at a trough. That night in Laurinburg was going to have to be an exception, so I put on my biggest smile and walked into our future.

The dinner wasn't all bad, and the company—the English department chair and two other faculty members—was, in fact, so outstanding that before the night was over we found ourselves seriously considering living in a town that would require us to choose between a run-down Chinese buffet, a bland hotel restaurant, and a local Mexican chain no one knew the name of when dining out.

When I woke the next morning, I could feel something wet around my legs and my stomach, almost as if I had peed my pants. I knew immediately that I was bleeding, but I was not prepared for what I found when I stood up and looked back at the empty bed. Across the sheets was a bloodstain as big as a small child.

It was a frightening sight we would see again—just over two years later—when we finally left North Carolina for Kentucky, and I lost so much blood that the front seat of our car was nearly obliterated by it. That morning, at the hotel in Laurinburg, we had no idea what had caused me to bleed so heavily, but we would eventually find out my uterus had become home to dozens of fibroid tumors, and I'd need to have a partial hysterectomy, saving us from ever having to make the decision about whether or not we wanted to have our own children. But at the time, we still didn't know what was to come, so we rolled the sheets up in a ball, put them in the bathtub, and told ourselves it wasn't a sign.

The next day was Dave's official interview, and I'd made plans to look at houses with a realtor in the morning and visit our friend Meredith—who lived only an hour away—in the afternoon. It's always risky to look at real estate before getting a job offer, but I didn't have much else to do and really didn't want to make another round-trip to North Carolina to do so. I also wasn't sure if I'd move to such a small town if I couldn't find a decent place to live. So the next morning I spent three hours with Pamela Sands, probably the only person to ever sell a million dollars worth of real estate in a town as depressed as Laurinburg and a person who could have sold

Waterford crystal to the homeless.

Pamela showed me a handful of houses in our price range—only one of which had potential but also needed a lot of work—and by noon, I was frustrated, wondering what I'd do if we couldn't find somewhere decent to live. There were basically no houses to rent in Laurinburg at that time, and renting an apartment was out of the question. I had been adamant that, at the age of thirty-six, we deserved more than a galley kitchen and a shared wall. I wanted to feel settled, not waylaid, which was how I'd felt all my adult life.

"How about we look at something just a smidge out of your price range?" Pamela suggested. "I know a house that I think would be perfect for you."

"Definitely not," I said without hesitation, knowing that even the range I'd given her would stretch our budget to its limit. But Pamela didn't listen, which was probably one of the reasons she was so successful.

"It's exactly what you're looking for—big windows, lots of light, screened-in porch, plenty of space, but also plenty of character. Just humor me. I really want you to show it to you, so I can get your opinion on it."

I don't remember agreeing to see the house, but I do remember the light flooding into the main room in a way that seemed almost celestial, washing me in a warmth I hadn't felt since we'd arrived in Laurinburg. Pamela had been right. It was exactly what we were looking for.

A few hours later I drove the sixty or so miles to Florence, South Carolina, to see Meredith, who had started her doctorate at Miami the last year we were in the Master's program there. Meredith had taken a job at Francis Marion University, so when I found out we were going to be in Laurinburg that week, I was determined to make the two-hour round trip to see her. What I hadn't known was that the first part of the drive would be so inviting. The two-lane highway connecting Laurinburg to I-95 cut across soybean fields as vibrant and lush as any I'd ever seen in Indiana and took me past rustic barns and charming plantation-style houses. It was the kind of rural America I had pictured—but not found—when I'd first learned of

Laurinburg. And when I came across it, just a few miles east of town, I thought for the first time, *maybe I can do this.*

By the time I got back to Laurinburg that night, I was pretty sure I could do it. Pretty sure, but not certain. No, Laurinburg was no cultural mecca—just the opposite—but the people we'd met were smart and interesting and incredibly welcoming. No doubt they knew the only reason anyone ever took a job at St. Andrews was the people, and they were selling that part of the job—the people part—hard, as I would eventually learn they always did.

When I got back to the hotel room, I found a note Dave had left for me.

Molly Sue—
   I got back at 5:30. Everything went very well. Charlotte said they should decide by the end of next week. She also said it went "beautifully" and that I seemed to fit in well. The Dean said you could probably adjunct, and Charlotte said the same thing and then hinted at a tenure-track job opening in a couple of years. I am very exhausted from acting happy all day. Come to McDuff's around 7:30 or 7:45 or whatever.
                                                    I love you—
                                                    Dave
   P.S.—They pay 80% of moving expenses. The Dean acted like I would make more than I make at Miami. I got you a present.

I'd planned to join Dave for the last part of his day-long interview—a poetry reading on campus that night—and when I met him and some of the other faculty members at the hotel restaurant, I was relieved to see they were drinking. Not only drinking, but having fun and letting loose a bit. Since the college had the word "Presbyterian" in its name, one of our fears had been that the climate would be more teetotaler than convivial, but we couldn't have been more wrong about that. (St. Andrews—which we would later learn the students dubbed "Camp St. Andrews" because there was so little homework they felt like they were at sleep-away camp—was a party school to its core.) That was when I decided we could make it work if we had to. And as we drove to the reading and heard the seductive sounds of the college's champion pipe band rolling siren-like across the pastoral campus, I realized I might even want to.

Once we admitted to each other that we were open to—maybe even optimistic about—taking the job at St. Andrews, the real work began: waiting to hear if Dave got the job. Charlotte had told him he'd know something in a week. Of course, we didn't believe it would happen that fast. Not knowing anything about the fact that St. Andrews operated in a much less orthodox way than other schools— and knowing full well that a job search at other universities could mean weeks or even months of waiting while other candidates were interviewed, votes taken, credentials checked, and paperwork processed—we worried that we wouldn't hear anything for far too long. And we were still hoping to get the rental house in Oxford if the St. Andrews job didn't pan out. As a result, it was a tense time of mixed emotions, of excitement and anxiety.

But a week later, just as Charlotte promised, we got the call. And as soon as Dave saw the call was from North Carolina, he looked at me and said, "This is it. I got the job."

I had no idea how he knew, but he did. And when he answered the phone, it was the Dean offering him the position. A tenure-track position for him. A few classes for me. Not enough money to shout about, but just barely enough to buy the house Pamela had shown me. And not just money but everything else. Benefits. Retirement. Moving expenses. The works.

We had finally made it.

Our initial adjustment to Laurinburg was easy.

We moved at the beginning of the summer—almost three months before we had to start work, so it felt like we were on vacation. A long, leisurely vacation away from all of our previous concerns. Sure, we were writing every day, but we were doing it in a house that was more than twice the size of our apartment. In that sense, it felt like we were just starting our real lives. We were thirty-six—most people were well into their real lives at that point—but, for us, it felt like a beginning. Like we were finally adults. When you wait that long to get somewhere and make so many sacrifices to get there, it's a much bigger deal when you arrive.

Most people we knew—even our closest family and friends—had no idea how hard it was for us to make grad school work. Since we started when we were twenty-eight, a time when most people are moving up rather than downsizing, it felt like we had failed in some ways. In Oxford, we lived in an apartment the size of a hotel room, and even after getting a slightly larger place in Cincinnati, we still spent every minute worrying about having enough money to pay the rent and buy groceries. We always made less money over the summer and would have to pick up extra jobs—stocking magazines, reviewing books, teaching summer school, working in the writing center—to make it, but I will never forget that during those summers, we had an even stricter budget than normal. A budget that allotted twenty-five dollars a week for groceries for the two of us. It was doable, but it wasn't easy. It meant we ate a lot of beans and rice, a lot of pasta with tomato sauce. It meant we grabbed a free meal whenever we could—at local happy hours, at the houses of family and friends, at receptions on campus. It was a horrible way to live, but we kept telling ourselves it was worth it. We'd soon be free. We'd soon be doing what we dreamed of doing: writing and teaching other people to write. And doing something that fulfilling meant it was worth it to spend seven years subsisting on ten-pound bags of rice and dial-up internet.

I will always remember that during our Master's program we didn't have a freezer. Not having a freezer obviously means you can't buy frozen food, but, more importantly, it means you don't have any ice. After going two years without ice, I will never again take another ice cube for granted. Every time I go to my freezer and push a button, only to have solid cubes of frozen water fall into my glass, I feel lucky. The same goes for laundromats. Every time I use our washer and dryer, I am reminded that the whole time we lived in Cincinnati, we had to lug all of our dirty laundry—awkward laundry baskets and all—down a flight of stairs, out to our car, and up the street to the laundromat. If you've ever cleaned your clothes at a laundromat—and I hope you have—you know it's not the kind of environment that attracts the best clientele. In fact, it feels very much like you've entered a forgotten world, a place where people go when they have nowhere else to be. Our new house not only had an ice maker, but also a laundry room, all the things my bio-siblings had had—two of them without a college education—for years.

To celebrate our new adulthood, we began nesting. We took down curtains, painted rooms, and bought furniture. We'd never been the kind of people who knew how to tile a floor or wire a light socket, but we did become the kind of people who went to the hardware store every other day.

Another reason it felt like a new beginning was because it was the first time in a long time when we hadn't lived near family. For the previous eight years—two in Oxford and six in Cincinnati—we'd been within a short drive of everyone in Dave's family. On the one hand, we'd loved being so close. Dave had always wanted to live near his parents as an adult. But after eight years of celebrating birthdays, holidays, baptisms, and graduation parties with the whole family, it started to feel more like work than play.

I'm sure there are people who could spend every Sunday with family and never grow tired of it, but we are not those people. Don't get me wrong—we didn't regret living in Ohio as long as we did, but we also didn't mind moving on to something new. I'm sure plenty of people will have problems with me admitting that, but deep down, most people know it's hard to sustain that kind of involvement over the long haul. We missed our family in Ohio, but we also loved having so much time to ourselves. In that sense, that first summer in Laurinburg almost felt like a honeymoon—a time when we were solely focused on each other.

That's why it shouldn't be a surprise we finally broached the baby question.

We'd always wanted to adopt. Partly because of my family and partly because it made sense to provide a home for a baby who didn't have one. I knew from experience it could be a win-win situation. It allowed us to contribute something to the world while also getting something back: a child. It was what we'd always planned to do, so it was never a question for us—when we were ready, we would adopt. We had even given a name to our unborn child—Indiana—and talked about it so openly that it wasn't unusual for one of our seven nieces and nephews to ask us, "When will Indiana be here?"

But when I had my annual checkup in Laurinburg that December, the doctor who examined me gave me a hard time about it, claiming I should just get pregnant and give up on the whole adoption thing. We'd looked into adoption several times over the previous few years and were shocked to see how expensive it was. At ten to forty thousand dollars a pop, private adoption wasn't something we could afford, so we knew if we went ahead with it, we'd have to adopt through the state, which meant being trained as foster parents and waiting years for a baby that might never come. I was almost thirty-seven, and the doctor told me it was my last chance. I had never considered getting pregnant and wasn't at all open to the idea, especially after the doctor discussed our options.

"But isn't it risky?" I asked the doctor when we talked to him after the exam. "I mean, at my age."

"It's not that risky," he said. "You have about a one in two hundred chance of the baby being unhealthy."

"One in two hundred?" Dave asked. "Is that what you said?"

"Well, it's actually a little better than that right now," the doctor explained, producing a chart that outlined the numbers. He pointed to my age and slid his forefinger down to three numerals: 275. There was a one in 275 chance that my baby wouldn't be healthy if I got pregnant before I turned thirty-seven in four months. And about a one in two hundred chance the year after that. And it went down to one in one hundred if I waited until I was forty. The numbers dropped at an alarming rate after that. I'd had no idea timing was so important.

Of course, there had been less than a one in one thousand chance that anything would've gone wrong if I'd gotten pregnant when I was twenty, the age Dave and I were when we met. But nobody tells you that when you're twenty years old and a junior in college. Instead they tell you how *not* to get pregnant. Not that I think twenty-year-olds should be going out and getting pregnant, but it was still surprising to learn having a baby at twenty was much safer than having one at forty after having spent so many years being led to believe the opposite was true.

"Those are pretty good odds," the doctor insisted. "And, of

course, we'll do an amnio. If something abnormal shows up, you can just terminate."

"Terminate?" I asked.

"Yes," he said, not clarifying because he knew he didn't have to.

I was speechless—not because of what the doctor was saying, but because of *how* he was saying it. Like getting an abortion was as simple as buying a loaf of bread. I turned to Dave with what must have been a shocked look, hoping he could explain to the doctor that I wouldn't be able to go through with what he was suggesting. After all, Dave had been in my life for more than sixteen years at that point. He knew me better than anyone, so it's no surprise he turned back to the doctor and said, "We probably wouldn't feel comfortable doing that."

The doctor was nonchalant: "It's your decision, but the odds are good." Then he took a long look at me before he went on. "For now. If you wait much longer, you won't be so lucky."

As soon as we were in the car, I said what we'd both been thinking: "Can you believe that guy?"

"I know," Dave said. "Like ending a pregnancy is an easy decision."

"Exactly."

I glanced out the window and studied the empty fields on either side of the car. The soybeans and cotton were long gone and only empty stalks remained, making the landscape look like a never-ending sea of twigs. I hadn't wanted to go to a male gynecologist. In fact, I'd never been to one before, but the wait to see a female gynecologist in Laurinburg was more than six months. I'm sure not all male gynecologists are so nonchalant, but it did make me feel disinclined to visit that particular doctor again.

"Do you want me to get pregnant?" I asked Dave suddenly. "Do you want to have a baby the old-fashioned way?"

"No," he said immediately. "We always said we'd adopt, and we will."

"Are you sure?"

"Of course, I'm sure." Then he looked at me. "Why? Aren't you?"

"I'm sure that's what *I* want to do, but I don't want to wonder if I've pushed you into something you don't want."

"You know that's ridiculous."

"I know," I admitted. "But then why does everyone else think we're crazy?"

"Because people are stupid," he said, and I laughed because he said that every time we were confounded by the world around us.

Once I started thinking about babies and adoption, I, of course, started thinking about my own life. It had been seven months since I'd called the Tuckers in May to tell them we were moving to North Carolina. I still remember Jeannie was thrilled, saying something about how we were finally coming back to the East Coast. Of course, what she didn't know was that Laurinburg, North Carolina, wasn't anything like the East Coast and was, in fact, far less cultured than Cincinnati. But from her point of view, North Carolina was a lot closer to Virginia than Ohio, which was all that mattered. It reminded me of something Dave's mother had said to us once. After finding out we would be applying for jobs in all parts of the country once we'd finished grad school, she suggested we try the post office so we could stay in Cincinnati. As if it were more important to live in Cincinnati than it was to get a job in our field or, for that matter, to use our education. I'd long known the Tuckers had the same outlook on life. For them, it was better to be close to home than to have a good job. Or even to be happy.

When L.W.'s mother, Alice, died the year before we moved to North Carolina, there was an outpouring of support in the biker community. People had claimed Miss Alice was like a second mother to them, insisting she would be "sorely missed." There was also some question about whether or not the bar would be the same place it had always been.

But before anyone could become too concerned about that issue, another, more pressing problem took center stage. Only weeks after his mother's death, L.W. was diagnosed with terminal lung cancer.

Paula told me the news when I called her that December.

"Are you coming to that conference again?" she asked.

I didn't want to say no to a woman whose husband was dying, but I couldn't lie and risk getting her hopes up. "No, not this year," I said, falsely implying we might be doing it again another year.

"Oh," Paula said. "Okay."

I knew I had let Paula down, but I also hoped the new and improved version of Paula—the one who let me live my own life—would accept things as they were.

Since our visit to D.C. in January, I had only talked to Paula twice, but after I found out L.W. was sick, I felt like I should check in more often, so I called Paula again in January of 2007, just a month after I'd learned of his illness.

It was late when I called—probably around nine—and Paula sounded surprised to hear from me at first. But it didn't take long for her to bounce back, returning to her role as the wife of a dying man.

"My husband has cancer," she said after our hellos. No matter how many times I talked to Paula, no matter how many years I knew her, L.W. was always her "husband." Never just "L.W." I've never been sure if that's because Paula thinks I can't remember who L.W. is or if she is simply one of those people whose identity is so wrapped up in being someone's wife that she feels the need to take every chance she gets to remind people of her marital status. I used to think it was the former, but the more time went on, the more I learned about Paula and L.W. and their past, the more I honestly thought, even feared, it was the latter. Without L.W., Paula felt she was nothing. With L.W., she was wife/mother/partner. That's why she always referred to L.W. as "her husband." That's why she hadn't written him off—as so many women would have—when he refused to marry her after she got pregnant the first time. Because from the get-go, from that moment when she first saw him at the Lawson in his dress uniform, her identity was so wrapped up in his that she didn't know who she was without him. It's an idea so counter to how I was raised and who I am that it pains me to admit that, for many years, my biological mother was the woman behind the man.

"I know, Paula," I said. "You told me." I wish I could say I was surprised Paula had forgotten she told me about L.W., but I wasn't. Not in the least.

"I did?" she asked.

Rather than answer, I asked a question of my own: "How is he?"

"He's not good," she said. "It's Stage Four. I don't know how much longer he'll live."

"God," I said. "I'm really sorry to hear that. Is there anything I can do to help?"

"No, we're just trying to keep him comfortable now."

"Well, that's good."

Our conversation didn't go much further than that. The same facts were repeated over and over, the same expressions of sorrow and regret, and I wondered if there was some small part of Paula that was validated by the attention and the fact that she finally got to play the part of the grieving wife and mother, a role that had been stolen from her when she lost me so many years before.

The next I heard about L.W. was an email from Jeannie a few weeks later.

Hey Molly:

I write once again with not the best of news. It's not going so well with my Dad. The cancer has spread. It's in his other lung, the liver and now in his brain. He's doing radiation…wants to fight till the end. Which is very admirable but he doesnt have much time.

My mom has been meaning to either call or write you regarding but it's been so much right now. I offered to let you know.

I'm sorry to write with bad news. I promise to have better news somewhere along the line. If you need to talk to my mom, 703-***-**** is her number and mine is 703-***-**** and Clint's 703-***-****.

It sucks…but everyone is handling it together.

Saw pictures of the new puppy. So cute.

> *Take care,*
> *Jeannie*

I wrote back immediately.

I hate to hear this, Jeannie. I will call you tomorrow or Wednesday at the latest if I can't get my prep for Wednesday done tomorrow night. Should I ask to speak to your dad when I call there? Will he want to talk or would he rather be left alone?

I hate that you are all going through this. I have done nothing to help you through it, and I feel awful about that. As you said in December, even though I don't see you that often, I think of you all the time and feel very close to all of you. You are always with me even when I'm not there. In a way, knowing all of you has changed my life.

*Take care of yourself, and don't hesitate to call. My home number is 910-***-****.*

> *Give my love to everyone,*
> *Molly*

When I re-read my email message now, all I can think is how naïve I seemed, asking if L.W. would want to talk to me. At this point, I realize it was a strange question to ask a man who never wanted to see me, much less talk to me. But back then I had the incorrect sense he might want to say something to the child he'd given up, the child he'd abandoned.

Of course, I was wrong. He wanted nothing to do with me. But I still hadn't fully processed what that meant. I still hoped—more for L.W. than for myself—that he would end his life without any unfinished business, leaving his soul free of any issues that might unnecessarily tether him to this world and prevent him from making a seamless transition to the next.

Molly, you coming into our lives has helped us more than you know. We do consider you family and it's amazing to be able to know you.

I'm not sure if my dad will have strength to talk. Ask for my mom if you call the house and she'll guide you a little bit better than i can on that situation. I'm sure he'd love to hear your voice but I'm not sure on his strength level.

We think of you all the time. I'll save your number and I hope to hear from you sometime this week. I'm staying at my parents house tonight. My mom is going to suck it up and work...change of scenery will be good for her.

> *I'll talk to you soon.*
> *Jeannie*

Jeannie said they did consider me family, but I knew, too, that inclusion had its limits. They wanted me to be there when they needed me to celebrate or mourn with them, but they also never included me in private family matters—like when making decisions about L.W.'s health or the future of the business. And I had no doubt I was not in Paula's will. Not that I wanted to be. Not that I wanted *anything* from them. But I did want it noted that when they said I was a member of the family, they only meant up to a point. A point determined by them, a point that suited them, a point that allowed them to take more than they gave. Again, at the time, that was fine with me. I wasn't looking to be an active part of their family, but I also hoped they wouldn't make demands of me that are only made of family. I just didn't think they should have it both ways.

I put off calling Paula as long as I could again and finally dialed her number a couple of weeks later at the end of February when we were driving home from spending the day in Raleigh.

"All the kids were here last night," she said. "They all came to see him."

"That must have been nice—to have everyone together." It wasn't lost on me that when I said "everyone," I was excluding myself. But I hoped Paula wouldn't realize that.

"It was," she said. "It was nice."

"I'm sure." I didn't know what to say next. I hoped Paula would go on, but her next comment surprised me more than a little bit.

"He knows he doesn't have much time left. We all know. So we talked about all of it, about everything," she said, and I felt my throat clench. *Everything?* "We talked about all that we've accomplished—with the restaurant, with the kids."

I was almost too afraid to speak. Was Paula leading up to something? Had L.W. mentioned me? About the decision he'd made to leave her? I desperately wanted him to say something about it—more for Paula than for me, but, really, for all of us. I wanted him to say he knew he'd done both of us wrong. I wanted him to admit it. I was afraid if I spoke, I would jar Paula out of her memory, but I also felt like I had to do something to get her to say more. "Really?" I said, encouraging her to go on.

Paula continued: "L.W.'s had a good life. He said he feels like he lived a good life. He said he has no regrets."

I was too stunned to speak. *He had no regrets? How was that possible?* I wanted to tell Paula I didn't know what to make of a man who said he had no regrets on his deathbed, dying of lung cancer, even though he'd smoked and worked in a smoke-filled bar his whole life. A man who said he had no regrets even though he had abandoned his wife when she'd gotten pregnant, a man who had lied to his mother about that choice, a man who let his mother think his wife had trapped him into marriage, a man who made fun of his wife behind her back, a man who couldn't talk to his children, a man who thought women should be quiet and listen.

I wanted to say all of that.

But I didn't say any of it, instead leaning my head against the passenger window. The glass was cold, effectively cutting the heat and intensity of my anger. Paula paused for a moment before she went on. Did she know what I was thinking? Did she know why I wasn't talking?

"He feels like he's ready to go on to the next stage, he's ready to be with God. We all told him it was time."

I said nothing.

I wasn't about to let Paula think I believed L.W. should have no regrets. I wasn't going to say something polite that implied some kind of tacit agreement with L.W.'s deathbed proclamation. Doing so would've just been too easy. It would've been wrong. It would imply that, when nearing the end, all sins could be forgiven even if one didn't ask for forgiveness, even if one didn't admit wrongdoing. As much as I hate to admit it, I just wasn't that kind of person. I wasn't that generous or that forgiving.

Paula must have sensed my unwillingness to allow L.W. to cheat his way into a positive take on his life because she started making excuses. "Nobody's perfect," she said. "But he's a good man. He has a good heart. He means well."

Again, I could not agree with Paula's words, but I knew by then I had to say something or risk insulting her. "Uh-huh," I said, gripping the handle on the passenger door like it was a safety valve I could pull to escape. I was too angry to keep talking, but I knew if I just ended the conversation there, I might offend Paula beyond repair. I also risked her guessing my true feelings. And, despite my contempt for L.W., I couldn't do that to Paula, a person who had, after all, chosen to give me life at great inconvenience to herself. So I made small talk for a few minutes—expressed my sympathy—and got off the phone as soon as I could without suspicion.

I never did talk to L.W. that night. I didn't know it then, but it would be his last chance to express regret. A chance he had missed.

Five days later, L.W. Tucker—the man with whom I shared half of my genes—died.

He died at 3:30 in the morning with his wife and four of his children gathered around him. He was only fifty-nine years old when he died.

But he had no regrets.

March 04, 2007

On March 1, 2007, LAWRENCE WILLIAM TUCKER, of Annandale, VA. Loving husband of Paula Tucker; devoted father of William, Clint, Wade, Jean, and Molly. Loving grandfather of William Jr. Long time owner of Tucker's Hideaway and a proud Vietnam Veteran. Relatives and friends are invited to call at the CUNNINGHAM TURCH FUNERAL HOME on Sunday from 3 to 5 and 7 to 9 P.M. and to attend services at St. Michael's Roman Catholic Church, on Monday at 10 A.M. Interment private. In lieu of flowers donations may be made in Tucker's name to the Annandale Boys & Girls Club, 4216 Annandale Road, Annandale, VA or the Northern Virginia Therapeutic Riding Program, 6429 Clifton Road, Clifton, VA.

I, on the other hand, did have regrets.

For seven years, I had regretted using the adoption agency to find out the identity of my biological mother. It occurred to me too late that I should've hired a private investigator to uncover that information. I didn't have the money at that time, but I could've gone to my parents for help. In fact, it was probably an idea we discussed at some point. But my parents always worried I was too young or wasn't ready for such a huge emotional undertaking, so I didn't feel comfortable pushing the issue. And who knows? Maybe they were right. What I am certain about is that, knowing what we all know now, I'm sure they would've been happy to go back in time and pay for a private investigator to avoid all the drama that has occurred over the past fifteen years. But, back then, it would've been a hard sell.

And I feel the same: if I could go back in time, I would handle things differently. If I'd been able to find out who Paula and L.W. were—without them finding out about me—I could have been more in control of our relationship. I could have gotten to know them as people, rather than as estranged parents. I could have devoted as little or as much time as I wanted to them. And I could've walked away without hurting anyone or feeling guilty about that choice.

It's something I will always regret.

Still, there are things I don't regret.

I don't regret knowing my biological siblings are people I genuinely like. To this day—after all that's happened—I can say that with all honesty. They may no longer like me. But I do like them.

I like that when I talk to Willie, I feel as if I'm talking to an old friend. I like how easy he is to be around. I adore Clint's larger-than-life personality, which reminds me of my beloved brother-in-law, Jack. I appreciate how sweet Wade can be, and I'm glad he sees things I do not. I like that both Jeannie and Clint know how to act in any situation, and I have a strong admiration for their confidence. And, finally, I love that Jeannie and I had an immediate bond.

I don't regret knowing these people. And I don't regret liking them.

I only wish I believed they would still say the same about me.

All along, I had worried about the issue of the funeral. Would I have to go? Would I want to? And what would it be like if I did? Would I feel like a member of the family or an unwelcome party?

The truth was I didn't want to go. I didn't want to make the trip, and I didn't want to suffer through the awkwardness of pretending to mourn for someone whom I still felt a lot of hostility toward.

On top of that, L.W. died one day before we were supposed to go to Florida to see my parents, which was something Dave and I did every year at Christmas and spring break. The only time we'd missed that trip—the first year they spent in Florida—was the year Dave's father had quadruple bypass surgery a week before spring break. Though it had been a last-minute decision, we had never regretted cancelling our trip that year to stay in Ohio with Herb.

But I worried I *would* regret going to the funeral of a man I was pretty sure wished I had never existed. If I went to L.W.'s funeral, I would be sacrificing time I usually devoted to my family, and since I was living in North Carolina then, farther from Indiana than I had in years, it would be harder than normal to make that time up. I just didn't want to lose something with my real parents to do something obligatory for a person who chose not to have me in his life.

But I was terrified Paula would insist I attend, making me feel an extreme amount of guilt about my desire to skip the funeral and head to my parents' Florida condo, which was across the street from the beach, a trip that would look like a fun vacation to most people even though that wasn't the reason I was going. Some part of me felt certain that going to Florida was too selfish, but another part of me, the part that eventually won, couldn't fathom going to the funeral of a man who despised me and pretending like I cared.

I haven't kept a journal in years, but every once in a while I write something in my calendar to help me remember what I was feeling on a certain day. Here's what I wrote the day L.W. died:

I just found out that my biological father died at 3:30 a.m. this morning. I feel very, very, very strange about it, and I have no idea what to say to anyone, especially the rest of the biological family. L.W. and I had the weirdest relationship, so this is all very confusing. He was the most uncommunicative person I have ever known, and the most patriarchal man I've ever had in my life. So why do I feel sad? You know, being adopted isn't weird at all, but knowing your biological family is the weirdest thing in the world.

After hours of worrying over what the right thing to do was, I made the decision that I could either go to the funeral or Clint's wedding the next summer, but doing both was simply too much to ask. I called Paula to tell her and was even more confused by her response.

"Oh, you don't have to come to the funeral," she said when I told her I was struggling to choose between L.W.'s funeral and Clint's wedding. "It would probably be weird if you came to the funeral anyway."

Weird? What did that mean? Yes, I thought it would be weird if I went to L.W.'s funeral, but why did Paula think that? Did she know something I didn't? Or did she really not think of me as part of the family? Still, I was more relieved than anything else. I wouldn't have to go the funeral. I wouldn't have to pretend to mourn. I wouldn't have to give up time with my parents. And any discomfort I felt with Paula's comment about it being weird was erased by what she said next.

"And I really want you to come to Clint's wedding. It will be a celebration. I want you to experience that with us."

It was the healthiest thing Paula had ever said to me; she wanted to celebrate with me, not mourn. And I hoped it represented her attitude about our relationship—which I believed was moving from the anger stage to the acceptance stage—as well as a point of understanding since Paula finally seemed to get that I didn't have to be everything to her, that I didn't have to do everything she expected the others to do. She seemed to finally get that our relationship would be unique in that way, that some things would be uncomfortable for us and it was okay to say no sometimes. It was as if she understood we both needed boundaries.

I felt like I'd been given early parole on a life sentence, and that really was cause for celebration.

PART SIX
All's Well That Ends Well

For better or worse, we headed to Annandale for Clint's wedding four months later, in July. In the time since L.W. had died, our lives had been turned completely upside down, and, at that point, we had no idea where the world was taking us.

The semester had ended predictably enough: we read finals, submitted grades, said our goodbyes, and then headed south. We'd decided to spend the first month of that summer in Florida at my parents' condo, where we could write without interruption or, more importantly, the fear of being pulled back to campus for a random meeting or extracurricular event. (We had been strongly advised by other faculty at St. Andrews to spend our first summer away from Laurinburg to send the message we weren't available during that time.)

Like good snowbirds, my parents had already flown north for the summer, so we had almost no distractions in Florida. We sat at our makeshift desks—the kitchen and dining room tables—writing and, from time to time, looking out to the Intercoastal for signs of life. At night, we'd sometimes treat ourselves to dinner out or make our way to the local bookstore or catch a movie. But for the most part, we wrote. For hours and hours every day we wrote. It was a summer tradition we had started in grad school and one that still continues to this day. For us, summer means writing—all day every day.

For that reason, it should be no surprise we were deliriously happy during that month in Florida and started hatching plans to build on that happiness. So much had been going right. During the spring semester, I had been offered a full-time job at St. Andrews—teaching and running the college press—and, more importantly, Dave had sold his first book to a small publisher in Indiana. For the first time in our lives, we would have more money coming in than we needed to pay the bills, and we started fantasizing about what we'd do with all that extra cash. No, we weren't going to blow it all on material goods, and, of course, we did want to pay off some of our debt, but we also wanted to indulge in a few luxuries. Like every other American, we wanted a flat-screen TV, but beyond that, we weren't sure what else we desired. We had a house and a car, so we didn't know what other small amenities would make our lives better.

But then one night, we were driving home from the movies in the rain, and I turned to Dave and said, "I think we're ready to adopt a baby. We can finally afford it. What are we waiting for?"

"I guess we can afford it," Dave said without taking his eyes off the road.

"We can. For the first time. So why didn't we think of this before?" I was staring at him, wondering what was in his head.

"You haven't even started your new job yet. We've only known about it for two months."

"That's true. But why wasn't it the first thing we thought about? Why didn't I go to the interview, thinking, 'If I get this, we can afford to have a baby'? It's weird that it took us this long to figure that out."

"We had a lot on our minds. The end of the semester, all that grading."

I knew he was right, but it still didn't make sense to me that we hadn't thought of it before. We'd been talking about having kids for seventeen years at that point. Why hadn't we acted on it? "Are we sure this is what we want?" I asked.

"Don't you want it?" Dave said, looking over at me for the first time since the conversation had started.

"Yes," I said. "Do you?"

"I think so," he said.

"It's what we've wanted as long as we've known each other."

"Then let's do it."

I was relieved he was saying yes, but also not convinced that we were ready to have a baby. I looked out the passenger window and watched the raindrops pelting the ground in a wave of tiny explosions. It had rained almost every night we were in Florida, so driving around in bad weather had started to feel like a sign of another day passing. "Are you sure?" I finally said.

"As sure as I'll ever be," Dave said, glancing at me again and putting his hand on my knee. "Are you?"

"I guess so. Is anyone ever sure?"

"Most people don't even plan it," he said. "We're way ahead of the curve."

A week later we were at a family reunion talking to my parents when the subject of babies came up again.

"Now you can finally get ahead and start saving some money," my mother said in reference to the fact that we were both going to have full-time jobs in the fall. My dad and Dave were in the room with us, but the two of them weren't really participating in the conversation, pretending to watch a basketball game on TV even though I could tell they were both listening.

"Yeah, maybe," I said. "But we might be ready to adopt. That's going to be expensive."

"Adopt?" my mother said. "But what about your career?"

I glanced at Dave, but he didn't say anything, turning his attention back to the game in an attempt to stay out of the discussion. "I can work and have a baby," I said. "I don't have to choose." I looked in my dad's direction and saw that, by then, his eyes were on me, not the game. He'd always told me I could do whatever I wanted in life, but I wondered then if he really believed it.

"Are you sure?" my mother said.

"Of course, I'm sure," I said, but I really wasn't. Yes, I knew it was possible for a woman to do both, but could *I* do both? Was I that kind of person? Dave and I had let a friend talk us into taking on a puppy a few months before, and we hadn't made it thirty-six hours before we realized we didn't have time for a dog and had to give the puppy back. If we didn't have time for a dog, how could we have time for a baby? "Besides," I added, "it's always possible we won't even stay at St. Andrews, so I may not even be working full-time in a year or two."

My dad jumped in then: "Why wouldn't you stay?"

I looked at Dave. "There are lots of reasons—the teaching load is heavy, there are too many extracurricular commitments, the buildings are falling apart, they expect us to be there all day every day..."

"Isn't that normal?" my mother asked.

"What?" I asked.

"To go to school every day?" my mother explained.

"No," I said. "And it makes it very hard to get any writing done."

"They also don't want us to publish," Dave said suddenly, and I was glad he spoke up. I knew my parents would take our concerns more seriously if they came from him rather than from me.

"What do you mean 'they don't want you to publish'?" my dad asked him.

"They weren't happy when I got my book deal," Dave explained. "They acted like it meant I wasn't spending enough time on my teaching."

"Were you?" my mom asked.

"Of course, Penny," Dave said with conviction. "We both work very hard at our teaching."

My dad interrupted again: "But you both have full-time jobs starting in the fall," my dad said, looking back to me. "Right?"

"Yes," I said.

"And you'll both have all the benefits of a full-time job? Health insurance, retirement, all that?"

"Yes," I said, agreeing even though I knew exactly where he was going.

"Well, then, you'd be crazy to leave that," my dad said with a big laugh. Not the kind of laugh that means something is funny, but the kind of laugh that says, *You're nuts!* "Do you know how hard that it is to find? For both of you?" My father was acting the way he always did when he thought I was saying something crazy. He was leaning forward, elbows on his knees, eyes open as wide as they would go. He wasn't buying it, and he was imploring me—with his words and his actions—to reconsider what I was saying.

"Dad, you don't have to worry. We're not going to quit unless we get something else."

"But what if they find out you're looking?" he countered.

"They won't," I said, knowing full well there was no way I could guarantee that didn't happen.

"If they find out you're looking," he said, "you could ruin all the good will you've worked so hard to create. I think you have a pretty good deal there. Why would you give that up?"

"I know, Dad," I said. "But we're not giving it up. Not unless we get something else. Dave's first book is coming out in January. It's a good time for us to look. And we'll be careful about making sure no one finds out. Besides, who knows? We may not leave at all. We just want to see what's out there. If we apply for anything, we'll be very picky about it—just the places where we want to be."

"I'm just saying, you have a good thing, and you'd be foolish to let that go," my dad said, shaking his head at me and turning his attention back to the television. I had made my case, so I let it go. I couldn't have guessed then how little we all knew about what the future really held.

We had decided in Florida to wait until we got home to look into the adoption question more seriously, so we could continue to focus solely on writing while we were away. Looking back, that should've been a sign something else would always come first. Because just a few days after we got home, we were called to campus for an emergency meeting of the faculty and staff.

I got the email message while I was at home. Dave was at the doctor, so I called him immediately. We had no idea what the meeting was about, but by the time Dave left the doctor's office, it had already started, so he went directly there without coming home to get me. It was our first year, so we didn't know if emergency meetings in the middle of the summer were a normal occurrence at St. Andrews or not.

While Dave went to campus, I sat at home wondering what the hell was going on. And I didn't find out until a whole hour later when he was walking out of the meeting. He hadn't even left the building when he called me.

"We lost our accreditation," he said, and I could hear the fear in his voice already. "It was revoked by SACS."

"What?" I said. "How is that possible?"

"I have no idea."

We'd been told during Dave's interview the year before that St. Andrews was on probation with SACS, the accrediting agency for colleges in the South. But at the time, we were assured it was no big deal. That it had nothing to do with academics but was merely a problem of a little debt, so we didn't have to worry about it. Naively, we believed what we were told and took the advice we were given, not thinking about it again until the day we found out we were no longer working for an accredited college.

"What are we going to do?" I asked.

"We're going to get the hell out of here," he said without hesitation.

Immediately, I knew he was right.

The college spent the next several months—that whole summer—working to get an injunction against SACS to keep their accreditation in place while they fought the decision in court. Though they won that battle—and accreditation was temporarily re-instated right after the start of the fall semester—most of the faculty started looking for work elsewhere. Even our boss, Charlotte, told us to play it safe and go on the job market.

That summer as we began the arduous process of putting our application materials together for the fourth time in as many years, we avoided the discussion of babies, adoption, and the future, focusing instead on CVs, references, and application letters. But it wasn't long before we were forced to admit the painful truth: we couldn't very well start the process of adopting a baby if we didn't know if we'd have jobs in a year or even that fall. So we made the decision, again, to put off starting the adoption process until at least one of us had a reliable job. Everything we had planned that May— the baby, even the flat-screen TV, all of it—would have to wait.

We didn't know then it would be a fateful decision since it would be the last time we would ever seriously consider having children, ultimately concluding that, unless one of us gave up writing or we won the lottery, kids would not be in our future.

Around that time, Laurinburg began to seem unbearable. Maybe our patience with it was wearing thin because we knew we might be leaving. Or maybe we were just angry with everyone associated with Laurinburg and St. Andrews, having felt like we'd been deceived about a problem that was much bigger than we'd been led to believe.

St. Andrews, as it turned out, wasn't just a *little* in debt. They were twenty-five million dollars in debt and only had a fourteen-million dollar endowment. St. Andrews was like the guy who has ten credit cards and owes five thousand dollars on each of them, but is only working at Taco Bell.

They were never going to catch up.

Of course, that only added to our frustration. How could they have brought us there—to a bankrupt college in an economically depressed community—knowing how tenuous things were? Wasn't it irresponsible, even unethical, to lure people to Laurinburg, allow them to buy houses, put their kids in school, and set down roots if they knew that at any moment the whole place could be shuttered?

The good news was that the more disgruntled we got, the more motivated we became. We worked furiously to make ourselves attractive to potential employers, going back to our old habit of applying to almost every job in the country. We did limit things a bit more than we had when we were still in grad school—we only applied to creative writing jobs and skipped the jobs in composition—but that's ultimately how we ended up at Western Kentucky University.

I still remember when we first read the WKU job ad, we looked at each other and said, "Western Kentucky? Where is that?" I had interviewed for a job at Western Illinois University a few years before and learned how isolated that school was. After living in Laurinburg for a year, we weren't that interested in another job in the middle of nowhere. But we also didn't want to be unemployed. So we printed the application materials, sealed the envelope, and crossed our fingers that we wouldn't end up living in another Nowheresville, USA.

To our surprise, Bowling Green, Kentucky, turned out not to be Nowheresville. It's a city—a small city, but still a city—with plenty of restaurants and shopping and even two multiplexes. And, though there could be more culture, there is *some* culture—there are plays and concerts and bookstores and farmer's markets and art shows and roller derby bouts and that doesn't even get into the cultural events on campus. Needless to say, it was a huge step up for us.

But I sometimes wonder—if we had never lived in Laurinburg, would we see Bowling Green the way we do? Would we see it as a vital place full of opportunities if we hadn't lived in a place that, for all practical purposes, had none? I'm not sure we would. And I feel confident we wouldn't appreciate the little things that make a place like Bowling Green so much better than the patch of ice in the Arctic Sea of the South that is Laurinburg, North Carolina.

But the job offer from WKU was still seven months away when we drove to Virginia that July for Clint's wedding. At that time, everything was still uncertain. We had no idea if we'd have jobs, if we could afford a baby, or where we'd be living in a year. It was a time characterized by insecurity and tumult, meaning probably not the best time to meet three hundred of your biological brother's closest friends.

Still, there were a few things we did to minimize the challenges of such an undertaking. Unfortunately, like our first time meeting the Tuckers, we would be seeing them on another whirlwind trip during which time we'd also be visiting both of our families. But that summer we went to see the Tuckers first, before we saw anyone else, so that we'd have plenty of energy to deal with any unpleasant emotions. In fact, that summer, we decided to start in Annandale with the Tuckers, then head to Ohio to see the Bells, and finish in Indiana with my family because we knew that what was required of us would diminish as the trip went on. We also did something else we didn't do on that first visit: we stayed in a hotel. That was crucial because we were visiting people going through one of the most emotional experiences of their lives—a wedding—and like any wedding, things were bound to spiral out of control.

Even though I'd been to Annandale two Januaries in a row—in 2005 and 2006—something about that trip, my fourth visit with the Tuckers, felt different. It felt more real somehow. It might have been because Dave was going to be with me the whole time and it might have been because, for the first time since our initial visit in 2000, there was going to be a party, a massive party at which I feared Paula would again strut me around like a prized thoroughbred. My last two visits had been much more mellow—just hanging out at people's houses or the bar. But this time there would be hundreds of people gathered to witness Clint and Amy's union, and I worried they would be hoping to see a reunion as well, a reunion between a mother and daughter. It was a show I wasn't interested in putting on, but it was one I also knew was expected of me.

So I made sure I was prepared.

During the drive, Dave and I talked about all of the possible contingencies—would Paula be asking us to stay longer, would anyone be angry about me skipping the funeral, would Paula say something about my weight? We discussed all of the possibilities, inventing ways to cope with every potential disaster scenario. It was our attempt to keep the peace I had worked so hard to create.

We were ready.

I was ready.

After we checked into the hotel and changed our clothes, we headed to Paula's house for the rehearsal dinner. When we pulled onto her street, there were dozens of cars lining both sides of the road.

As we approached the yard, the sun was just starting to set in the distance. White lights were strewn along the back deck, and against the backdrop of the newly orange and pink sky, they looked like tiny stars. There were people everywhere—gathered on the porch, milling around the property, and sitting at a grid of newspaper-covered tables in the center of the lawn.

Paula saw us as soon as we entered the yard, and she quickly walked over to us, a beer in one hand and a crooked smile on her face. "Oh, you're here," Paula said, surprise in her voice and a flicker of judgment in her eyes, when she saw us moving in her direction. "I didn't think you were going to make it."

I was shocked. Paula and I had spoken just two days before, and I'd confirmed we'd be at the rehearsal dinner then. She'd also told me to arrive any time that night, that there was no hurry. But the scene before us made it clear we were late. Everyone was either finished eating or just about to finish, chewing on their last bites of food or tossing back the rest of their drinks and staring curiously at us as if we were interlopers.

Still, I was prepared for that kind of glitch. I had practiced my responses in the car, so rather than say what I wanted to—*I told you we would be here*—I delivered my line: "I know, but I'm so happy we could make it," I said, falsely implying that our being there was a spur-of-the-moment decision. As I glanced across the yard and saw tables strewn with desiccated crab carcasses and empty beer bottles, I decided to add a last-minute addition to smooth over that tiny hiccup: "I'm so sorry we're late."

As soon as I said that, Paula's face changed from confusion to joy, the wrinkle in the middle of her forehead vanishing with her distrust. "Oh, that's okay," she said. "It's no big deal. We're just glad you're here."

I didn't completely believe what Paula was saying—that she didn't mind we were so clearly late. At the same time, I didn't think she was being intentionally disingenuous either, so I decided to let it go.

"Now, let's find you somewhere to sit," Paula said.

Just then, Jeannie ran up—a beer in her hand to match her mother's, a golden tan on her face. "Oh my God, it's so great you made it. Clint will be thrilled," she said, leaning in to give me a half hug with her free hand. Then she turned to Dave and said, "Hey, good to see you. It's been too long."

"No kidding," Dave said. "But the only thing I have to do this weekend is drink."

"And dance," I said, turning to look at him. Dave and I had an agreement—he would dance at weddings but nowhere else.

"Do you like to dance?" Paula asked.

"Uh," Dave said, laughing uncomfortably. "Not really."

"But you *are* going to dance tomorrow, right?" I asked.

"We'll see."

"You better," Jeannie said, her enthusiasm reminding me again how alike we could be. "I'm going to be all over that dance floor."

"Jeannie," Paula said, interrupting, "Stop gabbing and help me find a place for David and Molly to sit."

"Uh, okay," Jeannie said. "Impatient much?"

"Well, for God's sakes, they just drove all day! I'm sure they're hungry." Then Paula turned to us. "You like crab, right?"

It was a strange question given that, from the looks of things, that was all that was being served, but Dave jumped in to save me. "Of course, Paula," he said, his delivery as practiced as mine. "We had it the first time we were here."

"Oh, that's right," Paula said.

"Wow, that was a long time ago," Jeannie added. "I was like, what? Twelve?"

"Nineteen," I said, not even having to think about how old Jeannie had been the first time I met her. In some ways, for me, she would always be the energetic nineteen-year-old I'd first met seven years before.

"Oh, yeah," Jeannie said. "It was right after I started my second year at Virginia Tech."

"You were so nervous about college," I said.

"I was?" Jeannie asked.

"Yeah, but I knew you'd do well."

Jeannie laughed, lifting her beer to her mouth but not taking a sip. "I don't know if I did well, but I did graduate."

"That's all that matters," Paula said, patting Jeannie on the back.

I stretched an artificial smile across my face, so no one would know what I was thinking. Though a part of me agreed with Paula to some extent, I also hated it when Paula placated her children like they were five years old and deserved credit for accomplishing anything. The implicit message was that she expected very little of them. The truth was it was impressive that Jeannie had finished college as she was only the second person—after Clint—in her family to do so. But I feared Paula's you-did-just-fine attitude undermined Jeannie's confidence.

Paula stared at me, possibly noting the fake grin displayed on my face, but more than likely believing it was real. "Well, let's get you something to eat," she said.

Though we've never really mastered the art of eating crab, the truth is we had a good time that night. Paula finally found us a place to sit—in the middle of a row of tables among people we didn't know—and Jeannie cleared the discarded crab shells that were piled into a giant mound on our table like a mass grave. After we ate, Paula introduced us to her friend who'd had the sick twins I'd heard so much about years before, and, not for the first time, I was surprised by how interesting and intelligent one of Paula's friends seemed. For his part, Clint appeared truly content, and Amy was adorably giddy. I was relieved to see that he was starting his life with someone who was proud to be by his side rather than with someone who wished she could do better. And when the sun finally did set, the sky became an even more brilliant orange, casting an ethereal glow over the festivities, a lucky coincidence I took as a good sign for their marriage.

It was an evening that was remarkably similar to one we'd shared with the Tuckers nearly seven years before, but it couldn't have felt more antithetical. Something had changed, the oppressive veil that had clouded our interaction with each other had miraculously lifted. All of the kids—Willie, Clint, Wade, and Jeannie—were relaxed, and Dave and I were finally comfortable with the Tuckers, in their world.

We finally felt at home.

And, most importantly, Paula was happier than I'd ever seen her. She had gotten what she'd always wanted: all of her children together, celebrating what was to still to come.

The wedding the next day wasn't quite as laid back as the rehearsal dinner, but it was still pleasant. As soon as we entered the church, we could tell things were more tense. We must have arrived early because most of the pews were still empty when we got there. It was an old church—much like the ones that populate Cincinnati— with tall, imposing stained glass, a massive rotunda, and elaborate paintings on every wall. The stained glass meant that not a lot of light entered the space, the darkness making it feel more like we'd gathered to mourn a loss than to celebrate a union.

Like most weddings, people appeared to be worried about everything going as planned, about following the steps that had been clearly outlined for them, and I could see that Paula's smile was as forced as mine had been when we'd arrived in Annandale the night before. Though Paula often looked out of sorts, I couldn't remember a time I had seen her so miserable—both emotionally and physically—and I felt for her. She was wearing a long black gown with an intricately beaded black and silver jacket, which appeared as heavy as a coat of chainmail. Her hair was blonder than I'd ever seen it, dyed an extremely bright shade that would have looked unnatural on a young person and seemed painfully out of place on someone Paula's age. I couldn't believe she was comfortable. Not only did her jacket look heavy, her outfit also didn't fit the Paula I knew—the Paula who lived in t-shirts and shorts, the Paula who wanted everyone to see her as the go-with-the-flow, down-to-earth mom, the mom who wanted to be everyone's friend. On top of that, Paula, like me, has horrible posture, and her shoulders were slumped over even further that afternoon as if weighed down by both her attire and the enormity of the day.

Only Jeannie—in a cream-and-black floor-length gown—was all smiles as she entered the church, not yet suspecting it was a day she would, in the not-so-distant future, look back on with regret.

Even Clint and Amy, though obviously elated, initially looked nervous on the stage of their biggest show. But by the time they'd tied themselves together and begun their long walk back down the aisle, their faces conveyed nothing but pure joy.

The night before Jeannie had confessed to us, in an awed voice, that the reception was going to be extravagant, and we were not disappointed. Clint and Amy had rented an historic mansion in the Shenandoah Valley frequented by presidents and luminaries called Rosemont Manor. The ballroom was cavernous—with wood walls the color of well-worn saddle leather and an exposed ceiling showing off hundreds of whitewashed barn beams. Throughout the rest of the space, tiny string lights, globe pendants, and a breathtaking glass chandelier washed the proceedings in atmospheric light. And when guests walked out to the massive columned portico, they were treated to a majestic view of the Blue Ridge Mountains in the distance. It was the kind of venue often featured in movie weddings, but rarely seen at real-life nuptials by those of us who don't turn in the same circles as the Caroline Kennedys and Will Smiths of the world.

Not only was the location impressive, but so was the reception itself. I knew from experience the Tuckers knew how to put on a party, but even I wasn't prepared for the rowdiness that ensued. The evening started out normally enough—with Clint and Amy sweetly sashaying through the first dance after everyone ate—but once that formality was finished, the night got a little out of hand.

Though I barely remember it, there is a picture of the bride on the dance floor that always takes me back to the hilarity of the evening. In this photo, guests ring the dance floor, and Amy is seen pulling up her wedding dress, so she can kick her legs to the music can-can style, allowing everyone in the room to glimpse the flip-flops she had donned after the ceremony and the flesh-colored Spanx that ran from her knees to her torso underneath her gown. Not long after that, Jeannie jumped into the circle, launching herself to the floor, so she could do the worm in her floor-length bridesmaid's dress. Later Jeannie dragged Kalea out on the floor and bent her cousin over like a ragdoll, so Jeannie could smack her behind, acting out some kind of frat-boy fantasy for all the guests to see. The rest of the night was spent in a similar style—with spanking and grinding and pelvis shaking that would've made my own parents run from the room with their eyes covered.

At one point, nearly out of people to humiliate, Jeannie rubbed her pelvis against an elderly woman in a wheelchair, pushing the events of the evening to the point of ridiculousness. I couldn't help but think of the night I'd seen her mother croon the words, "I got a piece of shit car" to a room full of drunken bikers. But rather than be horrified by Jeannie's performance, as I had been by Paula's, I just laughed. Because no longer did I fear I would be defined by the Tuckers or have my identity overshadowed by theirs. They were their own people. And, yes, there was a part of them in me. But it was a small part, the part that now gets me up on stage at a reading and allows me to sing a few notes of Adam Sandler myself, the part that lets me stand in front of a classroom full of college kids and make self-deprecating jokes to keep their attention.

Still, the most significant part of me is McCaffrey, the part that keeps me working until ten o'clock most nights and the part that doesn't allow me to begin my meal until everyone else at the table has theirs. That's who I really am. That's who I will always be.

Once I figured that out—and once Paula understood it too—we were able to co-exist in a much more peaceful way.

And knowing that is what allowed me to participate in such an important event with the Tuckers and three hundred of their closest friends and family that night. It allowed me to dance with them—albeit a tad more conservatively—and drink with them and laugh with them all night long. It allowed me to be paraded from table to table by Paula, who still enjoyed showing me off as if I were a trophy, without feeling as uncomfortable or self-conscious as I had when she'd done it seven years before. It allowed me to pose publicly with Paula and my four biological siblings for a photo I probably couldn't have tolerated seven years before.

That photograph happened just as the night was ending. We had said our goodbyes and were about to leave when Paula stopped me.

"You can't go yet," she said abruptly.

"Why? What's wrong?" I was suddenly worried Paula had gone back to her old ways, wanting to ask more of me than I could give.

"We need a picture," Paula pleaded. "A picture of all of us."

She didn't say whom she meant by "us," but I instinctively knew—she wanted a picture of all of her children together, all of us in one place. It was something I couldn't deny the woman who had given me life.

"All right," I said, not sure what to do next.

"Just let me get everyone," Paula said, and then she yelled across the dance floor. "Jeannie!"

Jeannie turned in our direction. Her skin was flushed a feverish shade of pink, and her forehead gleamed with sweat. She'd been dancing all night.

"What, Mom?" Jeannie, always the lady, shouted from across the room.

"Come here," Paula said insistently, waving her toward us.

Jeannie skipped in our direction. "What's up?"

"We need a picture," Paula said.

Jeannie glanced at me and then turned back to her mother. "A picture?" She hadn't yet figured out what Paula was saying.

"Yes, a picture," Paula said.

"Okay, I'll get the photographer."

"No," Paula said, "I mean of all of us."

"All of us?" Jeannie asked, her mouth open. She was going to make Paula say it, she was going to make her put her desire in words.

"Yes, a picture of you, me, the boys." Paula paused before she finished her thought. "And Molly."

"Oh," Jeannie said, allowing her mouth to stretch to a large O as she finally put it together. "I get it. Okay, I'll go find them."

Wade was sitting right behind us, at the same table where he'd been stationed all night, the cleaned-up addict not looking for trouble. Jeannie barely stopped there on her way to find the others, instead yelling at her brother with hands on either side of her mouth like a megaphone: "Wade. Picture."

Predictably, Wade didn't respond, and Paula started toward him while Jeannie went searching for Clint and Willie.

I looked at Dave. "Do you think this is a good idea?"

"Sure," he said, waving away my concerns as he so often did. "It'll be fine."

And it was. It took a while to find Willie, who was out on the portico drinking with his friends, but once we were all assembled, the whole thing felt natural. We lined up by the entrance to the ballroom, putting our arms around each other and smiling for the camera like we really were a family. And for that one single moment in time we were closer than we had ever been before.

The photographer began taking photos of the six of us, telling us how to stand and which way to look while releasing the shutter over and over, and then, suddenly as if an emergency alert had gone out to everyone around the room, the other guests made their way to our side of the dance floor, drifting toward us unconsciously—like followers in a cult—and beginning to snap their own pictures. And within just a matter of a few minutes, something strange happened. The whole room was completely overcome with flashes, hundreds of flashes, blinding me with their charged white light. It was as if we were celebrities they wanted to capture on film and take home for themselves.

I squinted into the darkness, spots appearing on all sides, and wondered what it was they all thought they were seeing. Were they thinking it was something incredibly rare, the six of us together—like a comet or an eclipse—a phenomenon they might never see again? Did they think they were seeing the joyful reunion of a family that had been broken apart by an unfortunate circumstance so many years ago?

Or did they know the truth?

Did they know we were still strangers to each other? Did they know we would always be strangers? But we were strangers who understood that, despite our differences, our distance, there was a tiny part of us that would remain forever connected.

PART SEVEN
THE STORY ENDS

JULY 2011

As I finish this book—in the spring of 2015—it's been nearly eight years since Clint's wedding and just over six since I started putting our story into words. All along, Paula told me I should write about what had happened, about what it was like to be adopted and meet my biological family so many years later.

And I started getting it all down the same day Paula flew back to Virginia after she visited us in Ohio, her first and only trip to see me. Honestly, I couldn't *not* write about it. But when I showed it to Eric Goodman, one of my grad school professors, he said, "It's too soon. You need time." He was right, of course, but that first piece I wrote about Paula kept calling me back to it.

For many years—especially the years when I disappeared from Paula's life—I didn't want to return to writing about the Tuckers. It was too painful, too raw. I felt too much guilt—about the Tuckers and about my parents. But when we reconciled, I started to consider it again. Could I write about what had happened? Would it be a good story? It was a story I frequently told at parties, and I had noticed that people always listened to it with rapt attention, like it was the most fascinating thing they'd ever heard. For years, I thought it was just that: a good story to tell at parties. But then, right after we finished our first semester at WKU, I thought it should be more than that and started the book in earnest over winter break.

Almost immediately, I told Paula what I was doing. She was thrilled. I still remember what she said: "I knew you would write about us." And her pleased tone told me she felt as if it vindicated her decision to let me go, like writing the book finally made everything all right. And though things were already good between us, they got even better. We didn't talk often, but when we did, it was easy. I would ask her questions to help me remember things about her or L.W.'s past, and she would go on and on, lost in her memories.

But there were still signs of trouble.

At one point, I was asking her questions about the time when she had dated L.W.'s brother, Roy, and she stopped me mid-sentence.

"You're not going to put that in the book, are you? About me and Roy?"

"Well, I have to," I said. "It's part of your story."

"No, just leave that out," she said. "You can't put that in there. No one can know about that."

I didn't tell Paula the truth—that I couldn't write the book without including how she'd met L.W. and how their relationship had affected the two brothers. So I hoped she would simply forget she had asked me not to include it.

Other than that, Paula was incredibly supportive. I think she was secretly thrilled someone was writing about her, that I had deemed her life book worthy.

My parents were a different story. The idea of someone writing a book about them—especially their own daughter—horrified them. They repeatedly asked me to reconsider or use a pseudonym or take my husband's last name. These comments were always made as jokes, but I also knew they would be relieved if I ever decided to take them up on their suggestions.

But, of course, I didn't.

Instead, I labored through the most difficult writing project I had ever taken on. During the time I spent on it, I heard a well-known writer say that writing memoir was easier than writing fiction, and I was aghast. Every day I spent writing this book—from the first page to the last—was a trial for me. I remember clearly that on the very first day I started it, in December of 2008 while visiting my parents in Florida, I felt really angry. I was angry it had been so difficult to make things work with Paula, that it had taken so long to get to the point where we finally understood each other. I was angry that she had initially asked so much of me and put me through so much misery and guilt.

I was so angry that I actually started yelling about it.

"Why am I doing this?" I said to Dave the first day I worked on the book and many days after that. "Why am I putting myself through this all over again?"

Reliving those memories was that painful for me. That author who'd said writing memoir was easier than writing fiction clearly wasn't writing about the most difficult part of her life. Or maybe her life just hadn't been that difficult. I can't even imagine what it's like for someone who has suffered a real trauma to write about it, to go back in the past and face those truly awful memories all over again, because it was so hard for me to face my merely regular ones.

But I did it.

I faced them—every winter and every summer when school was not in session—for five years. And every time I thought I was about to finish and told everyone I was going to finish, I didn't. That was because every paragraph hurt. If I normally could write a thousand words or more a day, it was hard to write even three hundred about the Tuckers. At more than one point I thought about giving it up, but Dave kept after me the whole time. "Trust me," he said. "It's worth it. This is a good story."

A good story had always been what I wanted to write, so I stayed with it until, one day, I realized I had only a dozen pages left to write and three months to do it. At that point, I knew I had to finish or call the whole project a failure. So I did what any McCaffrey would do: I finished.

But before I could finish, I had to make sure I had all the details right. So I planned a trip to Virginia to do just that. Now that we were both fully ensconced at Western Kentucky, we were eligible for faculty research grants, and I applied for one to make the trek east and fill in the gaps of our story.

That was the summer of 2011. I hadn't seen any of the Tuckers since Clint's wedding four years before. We had kept in touch more often and with more good will than ever before, and there was always talk of visits. But we had moved to Kentucky in July of 2008, a year after Clint's wedding, and spent the next two summers focusing on family and work. Dave's dad had been diagnosed with a terminal illness that was causing him to slowly lose control of his physical faculties, and my paternal grandfather died suddenly, just weeks before his ninetieth birthday. Those two things meant we spent as much free time as possible in Ohio. We had also lost money selling our house in North Carolina and had to teach one summer to catch up on our finances. At the same time, Dave was in the process of selling a book to a New York publisher for the first time. All of those things kept us close to home.

But after Dave's father succumbed to the effects of the disease and his new book deal was inked, there weren't as many impediments keeping us away from Virginia. And that's when we planned a two-week trip to visit the Tuckers.

Right away we had reservations.

Two weeks was a long time to spend with the Tuckers, a lot of time for trouble to ensue. We had never spent more than three days with them at any given time, and we worried we wouldn't be able to keep up the pretense necessary to keep the peace that long. We'd also learned over the years that we weren't the kind of people who like to spend twenty-four hours a day with other people. Downtime and space are crucial to our happiness when we travel and visit friends and family. But we worried—rightfully so—that Paula would be offended by that. Still, we told ourselves we had a built-in excuse: the university was sending us there to write, so we couldn't spend all our time with the Tuckers.

And for a while, that worked.

Until it didn't.

We arrived in Virginia on a Sunday, having just left New York, where Dave had met with his editor and been a panelist at a conference. After giving it some more thought, we had decided to stay in nearby Annapolis to give us a bit of breathing room. We figured it would be harder for Paula to stop by if we were staying nearly an hour away rather than just a few minutes down the road. And we also found a rental house on Chesapeake Bay that would offer us a peaceful place to write when we weren't seeing the Tuckers.

I'd told Paula we'd be writing while we were there, that the university was paying for us to go there and work, so that had to be my focus. She was still thrilled about the idea of the book and seemed eager to talk more about her past and the family. I suggested we see each other every other night so we could do that and still leave our days free for writing. She happily agreed, presumably because that would mean more time for us to be together than ever before.

But almost as soon as we arrived, she became frustrated with our lack of availability. We called her within an hour of unpacking the car, and she told us she might be not be able to see us that night since she was out riding motorcycles with Jeannie and Jeannie's new boyfriend, Dalton. We'd thought it best not to see Paula that evening anyway since we were tired from our time in New York and the drive down the coast, so we told her that was fine. But as soon as I said it, a tiny sliver of the old Paula returned.

"Well, I was really hoping to see you tonight," she said even though she was the one who'd suggested we put it off until the next day.

"I know. Me too," I said, half lying because I really was too tired to see Paula for the first time in four years. "But you have a lot going on, and we need to unpack."

"We could meet at this place in the District. It's supposed to be a hoot. Jeannie and Dalton love it."

"We've been in the car all day already," I said, feeling like I was losing the argument when all I had tried to do was agree with her in the first place. "We'll see you tomorrow. We can have dinner. It will be nice, and none of us will be so rushed."

"Okay," Paula said, not sounding very convinced.

"I'm here for almost two weeks," I said. "We have time."

And we did have time, a lot of time.

In fact, that first week could not have gone better.

Dave and I went out to eat Monday night in Annapolis with Paula, Jeannie, and Dalton. We spent "Taco Tuesday" with Paula, Jeannie, and Kalea at the Hideaway. We did our own thing the next two nights—going out alone in Annapolis on Wednesday night and visiting friends in D.C. on Thursday. Then Paula, Jeannie, and Dalton came over for dinner at our rental house Friday, and we spent all day Saturday hanging out with everyone in the family at the Hideaway's annual pig roast, which meant we also got to spend time with Charlie, Sue, and even Dominic. And, on Sunday, we made the trip out to the Eastern Shore to see the waterfront house Paula was in the process of buying.

On the surface, everything was going perfectly. But there was an undercurrent of dissatisfaction permeating our visit.

That was because Paula was at war with Clint's wife, Amy. Apparently, the two of them had had a few run-ins over the past several years, and one day that spring, Amy finally lost it, telling her mother-in-law to "fuck off." Rather than move past that unfortunate incident, the whole family had been divided into factions, not unlike a particularly nasty season of *Survivor*. Paula had formed an alliance with Jeannie and Dalton while Amy obviously had Clint on her side. Wade could be trotted out by either team if necessary, but didn't really belong to one of them. And Willie, having gotten his fourth DUI, had basically been kicked off the island. The only question left was whose team would I be on.

In other words, it completely sucked.

But we didn't know about any of that until we had dinner with Paula, Jeannie, and Dalton the night after we arrived in Annapolis. We ate at a mom-and-pop restaurant on the Bay called Cantler's. It was a share-tables-eat-on-newspapers kind of place, and I wasn't surprised Jeannie had chosen it since the food was very similar to the two meals we'd eaten at the Tuckers' house.

That was our first time meeting Jeannie's new boyfriend, Dalton, and initially he was a little standoffish, tilting his blond head away from the table as if still trying to decide what to make of us. Later in the bathroom, Jeannie would tell me he'd been sick and wasn't feeling like himself. I wasn't sure if I believed her, but I liked him right away regardless. He was different from us in superficial ways—he wore a blue work shirt with his name on it, had tattoos running up and down his arms and across his neck like hieroglyphics, and had never spent a day in college—but he had one important thing in common with us: he was a thinker. He was a person who considered the world around him, a person who questioned things. He was also a grown-up with a steady job, a small house, and his own interests, a world apart from the overgrown boys Jeannie had dated before, boys she'd often met through Clint, which was a relief since, by then, Jeannie was twenty-nine years old.

But Dalton belonged only to Jeannie. It was obvious from the way they interacted they had a good thing going—they caught each other's eye when they thought no one was looking and appeared to really listen to one another. Right away I was happy Jeannie had finally found someone mature and interesting enough for her.

Dalton was the first one to bring up the book. "So what's this book you're writing?" he asked me, rapping his knuckles against the butcher paper on the table in a repetitive beat.

"Well, it's about being adopted," I said, trying to be as noncommittal as I could, "and meeting the Tuckers."

"Are you finished?" Paula asked, and when I turned to look at her, the peaceful water behind her made it look like she was sitting in front of a postcard.

"Almost," I said. "I need to fill in some gaps while I'm here and then just write the last part."

"So is everybody in the book?" Dalton asked, still leaning back in his seat.

"Yeah," I admitted. "Everybody." I looked at Paula and thought of her admonition about including Roy, hoping it wouldn't come up again.

"You're not going to put *me* in the book, are you?" Dalton asked with a laugh, and I couldn't tell if he was horrified or amused by the idea.

"Actually, no," I admitted. "The book starts in 2000—when I first met Paula—and ends in 2007 at Clint and Amy's wedding." I was being completely honest. Back then I really did believe that's where this book would end.

Jeannie jumped in: "It does?" she asked, putting her hands on the edge of the table. "Why does it end there?"

I was hesitant to admit the truth and had the sense I was opening myself up for criticism. "Because I felt like that's when we finally had everything figured out. It was when everyone seemed happy."

MOLLY McCAFFREY

"Happy?" Dalton said. "At Clint and Amy's wedding?" Then Dalton laughed loudly—howled really—and, looking back, I realize that laugh should've told me there was trouble ahead.

Jeannie glanced at Dalton, offering him a grin and putting her hand across his back in a protective fashion. I could tell something was making her nervous. "Why did it seem like everyone was happy?" Jeannie asked me. "'Cause there was some crazy shit going on that night."

"Jeannie!" Paula said as if warning her daughter, but her reprimand lacked any conviction.

"What?" Jeannie said to her mother. "It's true!"

"What happened?" I asked.

"Well, for starters, both of my uncles got drunk off their asses and showed up an hour late." Jeannie turned to Paula. "You didn't even speak to Charlie for a year after that, remember?"

"Oh, I remember," Paula admitted, nodding, and I was reminded then what Kalea had told me about Paula cutting her off after one of their fights the year before. It was hard not to wonder if that was how Paula dealt with conflict.

"Really?" I said. "I had no idea. Well, I guess I don't know about *everyone*, but I do know *I* was happy that night." I stopped, but they were all looking at me as if waiting for more of an explanation. I felt like I had no choice but to go on even though what I really wanted to do was walk over to the railing of the deck and study the gentle waves of the water below us. "For a long time, it was hard to know how we were supposed to be in each other's lives. I have my family, and you have yours." I glanced around the table and was happy to see that no one was disagreeing with me, so I continued. "At first, I don't think we knew how to make that work. But by Clint's wedding, it felt like we'd figured it out. We can be there for the big things— like weddings—but we don't have do everything together." All four of them were still watching me, so I turned the conversation back to them. "Does that make sense?"

"Yeah, sure," Jeannie said, nodding. "It's not like you're going to be here at Christmas or anything."

"Exactly," I said, thrilled that Jeannie was articulating what I'd been trying to explain to Paula since the day I'd met her.

"But weddings?" Jeannie asked. "You should definitely come to weddings. Those don't happen very often."

"I'm so glad you were able to come to Clint's wedding," Paula added, patting my hand in a maternal fashion. "It was nice you did that."

Dalton laughed to himself, shaking his head as he did it. I glanced at him, not sure what he was thinking, but he didn't elaborate, instead saying, "So when are Clint and Amy getting back anyway?"

Paula hesitated a second before answering. "Saturday, I think."

"Where did they go?" Dave asked.

"The Outer Banks," Paula said. "In North Carolina."

"Just the four of them?" I asked because, since we'd seen them last, Clint and Amy's family had doubled in size with the arrival of twins, a girl named Hazel and a boy named Ford, two years before.

"No," Paula said. "They brought the nanny with them too."

"They took the nanny?" Dalton asked, the skepticism in his voice too pronounced to miss. "Are you kidding me?"

"Now, Dalton," Paula said as she leaned across the table toward him and put her hand on top of his. "You must know I am not kidding."

"That is so weird," Jeannie said. "Don't they want to spend time with their kids?"

"Maybe they want to spend time with the kids during the day," I offered, "and go out alone at night."

"Who does that?" Dalton asked, basically ignoring my theory. "Who goes on vacation with a nanny?"

It was become increasingly obvious Dalton wasn't their biggest fan.

"Clint and Amy, I guess," Jeannie said.

"That's just bullshit," Dalton said, and no one mentioned anything else about it.

The rest of that first week went smoothly though it become more and more obvious that Paula and Amy were engaged in an all-out battle for control. Neither Paula, Jeannie, nor Dalton ever missed an opportunity to criticize what they saw as Clint and Amy's extravagant ways, so I shouldn't have been surprised when Jeannie and Dalton weren't invited to have dinner with us at Clint and Amy's house on Monday night after they returned home from vacation. But before we went to dinner at Clint and Amy's house, I had to sit through an incredibly awkward interrogation about the book.

Jeannie and I had said all along we wanted to do something on our own, and we finally squeezed in lunch on the Monday of our second week in Annapolis. I met Jeannie at the house she was sharing with Dalton, and she showed me around the place. Though Jeannie still owned her roomy townhouse, she was trying her best to unload it even though the housing crisis meant she would probably take a loss. I had no idea how much money Jeannie was making at that time. She'd quit her job as a mortgage broker when the real estate market went bust. Yes, she was still working plenty of hours—splitting her time between bartending at the Hideaway and coaching the women's basketball team at her former high school—but I couldn't imagine she had as much money coming in as she'd had a few years before. I was worried the bar was more of a disservice than a blessing. After all, as long as Jeannie, or the others, could pick up shifts, there wasn't much motivation to stick with anything else when things got tough.

Dalton's house was a cramped but charming two-bedroom Cape Cod. Immediately, I could see he'd put a lot of time into it—just about every room had been updated in a way that made it look like it could've been in a decorating magazine. The house also had an expansive yard with a koi pond and built-in fire pit as well as a screened-in porch decorated with a gurgling fountain and festive party lights. It was the kind of place where you felt instantly comfortable, the kind of place where you want to kick back with a cool beer on a hot summer night—a perfect match for Jeannie's personality.

Because we'd planned to have lunch alone, I was a little surprised Paula was there when I arrived to pick up Jeannie. Okay, maybe I wasn't completely shocked. After all, Paula wasn't the type of mother to send her kids out into the world on their own. But I was a little irritated. It felt like Paula was keeping an eye on us, like we were ten-year-olds who had to be chaperoned on our playdate.

Still, there was nothing I could do. Paula had moved in with Dalton and Jeannie a few months before—around the time of the blow-up with Amy—because Clint and Amy had been living with her while they saved money to buy Paula's house, a clear sign of how dramatically their financial situation had changed. After Paula's relationship with Amy fell apart, she obviously didn't want to stay under the same roof with her daughter-in-law, but Paula, too, needed to work out some financial issues before she could buy the house she wanted on the Eastern Shore. In the intervening period, she had moved in with Jeannie and Dalton. It wasn't an ideal arrangement, but it appeared to be working.

Nevertheless, it seemed strange to have Paula following us around their house like a needy pet while Jeannie showed me the place. Yes, Paula was living there, but it still felt like she could've given us more space. I couldn't help but wonder what it must have been like for Jeannie and Dalton—and Clint and Amy before them—to cohabitate with Paula full time.

At one point, Jeannie went to the use the bathroom, and while she was gone, Paula grabbed my arm. "Come here," she whispered. "I've got to show you something."

Paula pulled me down the hallway to her bedroom, reaching into the top dresser drawer and—after pushing aside some undergarments—producing a small ring box. "Dalton is going to propose," she said, popping open the lid on a ring that was bigger than my own engagement ring but not so big as to appear ostentatious.

"He is?" I asked her, looking at the diamond with the appropriate amount of interest. "When?"

"I don't know—soon," Paula said. "But you can't tell Jeannie."

"Don't worry," I said. "I won't." At the same time, I was wondering if it was a secret I could keep.

"Dalton told me to hide it," Paula said as she put it back in the drawer, barely sliding it shut before Jeannie appeared in the doorway.

"What are you guys doing?" she said, looking at both of us suspiciously. Her eyes were as wide as I'd ever seen them. She knew something was up.

"Nothing," I said, turning away from her because I knew from experience that I could only keep a secret if my interrogator didn't look me in the eye. "Looking at your mom's pictures," I said, lying at the last second. Though most people don't realize it, I can tell a lie about something inconsequential if I really have to. No, it's not my modus operandi, but when I absolutely have to be dishonest, I can do it.

"Huh," Jeannie said, clearly not believing I was telling her the whole truth.

"Jeannie, are you working tomorrow?" Paula asked, an obvious attempt to change the subject that Jeannie seemed not to catch.

"Yeah," Jeannie said. "Why would you ask me that? You know I'm working tomorrow. You made the schedule."

"I just couldn't remember."

"You are so weird," Jeannie said, laughing and waving her hand dismissively at her mother.

"Should we get going?" I asked Jeannie, trying to get her out the door.

"Yeah, just give me a second. I need to change," Jeannie said. "Why don't you guys wait in the living room?"

Paula and I made our way back to the front of the house and sat across from each other in the living room. The secret she'd told me was sitting between us like a landmine, both of us doing our best not to cause it to explode. So I shouldn't have been surprised when, out of the blue, Paula brought up the book.

"So how's the book going?"

"It's going great," I said even though I hadn't gotten nearly as much work done on the book as I'd hoped. In truth, I'd done very little actual writing though I'd learned much more about the Tuckers since I'd been there—listening and observing all of them—than I'd ever known before, and that information was probably more valuable than any pages I could've written in that time. "You've all been very helpful. I mean, by answering all of my questions and telling me so much family history."

"Well, good," Paula said, staring at me like a riddle she was trying to solve. "I'm glad."

Paula was staring at me so intensely I felt like I had to continue. "I still have some unanswered questions, but I know I'm running out of time."

"Well, you can always call."

"That's true," I said, remembering how easy it had been to talk about the book with Paula on the phone. "You know," I said abruptly, "I keep wondering about Wade."

"What about him?" Paula asked.

"Well, I've been trying to figure out how to describe him."

Just then, Jeannie stepped into the room wearing short shorts and a tank top, her summer uniform. "Describe who? Is this about your book?"

"Yes," I said, suddenly nervous about talking about it with the two of them together, making it possible for them to gang up on me. Despite that, I went on: "I was just saying I'm not sure how to describe Wade. What I mean is, how do I describe his condition? Has anyone ever actually used the word *autism* when talking about Wade? A doctor or anyone like that?"

"No," Jeannie said, her voice a little higher pitched than normal, letting me know I'd said too much. "Of course not."

Paula was shaking her head. "Wade isn't autistic. He's just different."

"Well, what do you mean by that?" I asked even though I probably should've changed the subject. "Do you think he has Asperger's?"

"Asperger's?" Paula asked.

"Yeah, it's kind of like a watered-down version of autism. They call it 'little professor's syndrome,' and people who have it—like Wade—struggle with social skills but tend to be very good at other difficult tasks. And since Wade is so good mechanically, and he has trouble making eye contact—"

"Wade doesn't have trouble making eye contact," Jeannie said. "He makes eye contact with me all the time."

Wade almost never made eye contact with me, but I understood that such an argument probably wouldn't sway his sister and that I was being too objective, too pedantic, for both of them. It was a part of myself I hadn't really shared with them in the past, but my interrogative tendencies were kicking in, and once they got going, it was almost impossible to stop them. "Well, maybe that's not the best example. But, you know, he's not very good with people."

"No," Paula agreed, "but that doesn't mean he's autistic."

"I know, but—"

"You're not going to put that in the book, are you?" Paula said, interrupting me.

"What?" I asked even though I knew what she meant.

"About Wade," Paula said. "About Wade being different. You can't do that. That would hurt his feelings."

"It's true," Jeannie said, nodding. "It really would."

"Well, I think he knows," I said, trying to explain that my sense was that Wade understood who he was. "He knows he's not like other people. He's smart enough to see that."

"Sure," Jeannie said, "he knows he's different, but that's not the same as thinking you've got something wrong with you."

"I don't think there's something wrong with him. I just think he has a behavior disorder."

"A disorder means you have something wrong with you," Jeannie said.

"I know it sounds that way, but it's not really a disorder as much as a difference."

"So why do you have to call it anything?" Jeannie said. "Everyone knows Wade is different. Just say that in the book."

"No," Paula said. "You can't say that either."

"How can I write a book about meeting all of you and not talk about how—" I hesitated, searching for the right word. "How unusual Wade is?"

"That has nothing to do with the story," Paula said. "Just talk about meeting me, about meeting us. And how happy you are about that."

It hit me in that moment Paula didn't know the truth. She didn't know I wasn't completely at peace with my decision to search for her. She didn't understand how difficult it had been for me. She didn't get that if I could do it all over again, I wouldn't. I'd had a similar experience the week before when I'd been at the bar talking to Kalea, who'd said to me, "I always feel so bad about you missing all this, missing growing up here with us. I feel like you really lost something." I didn't have the heart to tell Kalea I felt the opposite way. I felt like I was the luckiest person alive and that nothing scared me more than the idea of having missed the life I did have. And that was exactly how I felt in that moment with Paula. I didn't have the heart to tell her the truth, but I also couldn't lie about something that big.

"Well, I—" I began, not knowing what to say. Thankfully Jeannie saved me from having to stumble through some awkward, half-honest response.

"Just don't say anything about Wade, okay?" she said, and I had to stop myself from letting out a laugh. *How could I write a book about all of us and not "say anything" about Wade?* She looked at her mother for confirmation, and Paula nodded, their eyes locking on each other like two halves of a whole.

I know what other people would have done in this situation. They would have just acquiesced. They would have said, "Okay, sure." And then, later, they would have done whatever they wanted. But I wasn't that person. I couldn't say yes if I didn't mean it. "I don't know if I can do that," I said, shaking my head at the ground. "I don't know if that will work."

When I glanced back up at Jeannie and Paula, they were gawking at me with shocked looks on their faces, their mouths hanging open as if they were baby birds waiting to be fed. Were they finally getting that if Wade was fair game, they all were?

"I'll think about it, okay?" I said, trying to satisfy their need to be heard.

"Yeah," Paula said. "Think about it."

"You don't need to talk about Wade," Jeannie said. "It's such a good story that you don't need to talk about him."

"Yes," I said, "it really is a good story."

Jeannie and I went to lunch at a local favorite called the Vienna Inn after that, and thankfully, the subject of Wade didn't resurface for very long. In fact, our meal was nothing like the conversation the three of us had shared just before it. Instead, it was a cathartic reprieve from all of the messy emotions I normally associate with the Tuckers.

"I'm psyched we got to do this," Jeannie said after we were seated in a wooden booth in the middle of the small space. The Vienna Inn was located on a nondescript section of road, so I wasn't surprised it was a bit of a hole in the wall. Still, I trusted Jeannie knew how to pick a restaurant.

"I know," I said. "Me too. Did your mom mind that we didn't invite her? I felt bad when she was at the house."

"No, it's fine! She's not like that. She gets that we want to spend time alone."

"Good," I said though I wasn't sure Jeannie was right. Nor was I sure she was able to see Paula clearly. I felt certain Paula's feelings had been hurt.

"I think she wants us to get along," Jeannie said, and my mind went immediately to the basketball game in Dayton—when Jeannie had shut me out at what I assumed was her mother's behest. I worried again that my relationship with Jeannie was predicated solely on my ability to get along with Paula.

"So what are you going to get?" I asked as we looked at the plastic-covered menus.

"We should definitely get some poppers for starters."

"Definitely," I agreed.

"And then I'm getting a couple of chili dogs. You should get them too."

"You think?" I said, considering my options as I looked over the menu and discovered the Vienna Inn had as many ways to serve chili as Skyline did back in Cincinnati.

"They were my dad's favorite."

"Really? Okay," I said, not wanting to reveal even a sliver of my true feelings about L.W. Tucker.

"Yeah, he used to bring me here—just the two of us. It was one of the only things we did like that—on our own. I loved coming here with him."

Right then the waitress walked up. Jeannie ordered for both of us. It hit me that she'd brought me to a place that was special to her, a place she had shared with her father. I felt honored she trusted me enough to bring me there, but also confused about how to respond in a supportive way without being dishonest, which I was unwilling to do. But when the waitress walked away, it all came to me very clearly: "It's great that you have those memories," I said to Jeannie.

"I can't believe how much I miss him," she said. "He used to drive me crazy. I mean, it was so hard to get him to talk, but I really miss him."

In that moment, I felt for Jeannie. She'd lost her dad at twenty-five, an age that should be too young to lose a parent. But I also wondered if his premature death was making her remember him more kindly than she should. Still, that wasn't something I'd ever say out loud.

"It must be really hard. I can't even imagine losing my dad. I'm crazy about him." I said this with some confidence that Jeannie could handle me talking about my father without feeling that it reflected negatively on my relationship with anyone in her family. I think she got that the McCaffreys were my real family, but I still wasn't sure. "What do you think he'd say about you now? About Dalton?"

"Oh, I think he'd love him," Jeannie said without hesitation. "They're a lot alike. They're both charming and bullheaded at the same time."

I knew Jeannie was right. Though I'd never seen the charming side of L.W. Tucker, he must have had one in order to have done so well with the bar. "So you buy into the idea that we marry someone like our fathers?"

"Kind of," Jeannie said. "But Dalton is different too. He's warmer and definitely more outgoing."

"I'm not gong to argue with you there," I said, knowing that I'd exchanged more words with Dalton over the past week than I had with L.W. in all the time I'd known him.

"But I wonder what my dad would say about what's going on." Jeannie paused then, clearly choosing her words carefully. "With Clint and everything. Sometimes I think I should just walk away."

"Walk away from what?" I asked at the exact moment I figured out what she meant. "You mean the bar?"

"Yeah, if I did that, things would be so much better. I just don't think I can work with Clint anymore."

Our waitress appeared with our appetizer then, but after she'd left, I asked Jeannie the question that had to be asked. "What would you do? You know, if you didn't work at the bar?"

"I don't know," Jeannie said with a bit of hesitation in her voice. "I think about teaching." But she sounded tentative, unsure.

"At the school where you coach?"

"Yeah," Jeannie said as she dipped a greasy popper into a small cup of ranch salad dressing. "But then I'd have to go back to school, get my teaching certificate."

"How long will that take?" I said, picking up a popper.

"A year or two?" Jeannie asked as if I were the one who would know the answer.

"Do you want to do that?" And I wondered then if Jeannie could have a life away from the albatross that was the bar, a life independent of dealing with all of the Tuckers' family drama on a daily basis.

"Yeah, I'd love it. But what if I went back to school, and they didn't hire me? Then it would all be a waste of time. Not to mention money."

"Sure, but I bet they'd hire you. Don't they like you?"

"I guess," Jeannie said before taking another bite of food.

I knew Jeannie was insecure about her ability to make it in the world outside of the Hideaway, especially in terms of her intellect. She'd been confiding in me about her self-doubts for years. But I also knew those doubts were unfounded. She was smart, and I knew she could do anything she wanted—as long as she believed in herself. So I did the only thing a big sister can do: I told her she couldn't fail in terms she would have to accept. "I know they'll hire you. You're too important to them. You're too good a coach. You've accomplished too much. And you went to school there, so they want you to succeed. They believe in you. You can do this if that's what you want. I know you can."

"Thanks," she said quietly, catching my eye for just the briefest of moments, and then looking down at her food. "It's so cool that we know each other."

"Yes," I said. "It really is."

It was the most honest thing I'd said all day.

Clint and Amy had moved out of their McMansion a few years before, the real estate bust forcing them to downsize. At first they lived in the townhouse Amy had bought before they'd met, but eventually they decided to buy Paula and L.W.'s house. It was supposed to be a win-win for everyone: Clint and Amy would get a good deal on the house, and Paula would get enough money to be able to buy a retirement home on the Eastern Shore. The only problem was it meant the three of them would have to live together—with the twins—while Clint and Amy saved money and started renovations on Paula's house. Needless to say, it was a bad idea from the start.

Everything seemed fine at first. Paula was thrilled to have the company, and Clint and Amy enjoyed the luxury of a live-in babysitter. But they might have enjoyed it too much, often taking for granted that Paula would watch the twins when she was home. As a result, Paula began to feel like a servant in her own home and bristle at the notion that she be expected to babysit if she had no plans. I never got the whole story, but those frustrations eventually led to the confrontation when Amy told her mother-in-law off. After that, Paula moved out of her house and in with Jeannie and Dalton.

Though Paula was still not really on speaking terms with Amy, she was the only other person invited to dinner the night we went to Clint and Amy's, a choice I found surprising, but I figured the two of them had decided it was too risky to exclude her. Or maybe they saw my presence as an opportunity to work things out. For whatever reason, the five of us, plus the twins, gathered on the same deck where four of us—Paula, Clint, Dave, and me—had first feasted on steamed crabs eleven years before.

But the deck was almost unrecognizable once Amy and Clint had taken over Paula's house. Gone was the giant porch swing that had taken up almost half the space, and there was no sign of laundry baskets or moving boxes or beer cartons or plastic lawn chairs as there had been during my previous visits. In their absence, Amy had put the picnic table in the middle of the deck and hung small globe lights around the periphery, giving the outdoor space a spare, clean look and an ambiance that had been missing before.

"Wow," I said after we arrived. "Everything looks so nice. Did you change something? Did you expand the deck?"

"No," Amy said. "It's exactly the same size."

"But it wasn't covered before, was it?" I asked.

"Yes, it definitely was," Amy insisted.

"Huh," I said. "Well, it looks so much bigger. You did a great job." I was aware that I had to be careful not to hurt Paula's feelings, but it was hard not to be enthusiastic about the dramatic improvements Clint and Amy had made just to the outside of the house. I also knew Paula couldn't hear me since she'd gone indoors to use the bathroom.

"Wait until you see the inside," Amy said triumphantly. "It's unbelievable."

"Okay, but I don't want to insult Paula," I told her.

"Are you kidding?" Amy said. "She's so pissed at me she doesn't even notice what anybody else says."

I had only been there five minutes, and Amy had already acknowledged the elephant in the room. It was clearly going to be an awkward evening.

Amy was right, though, about the inside of the house. The renovations were truly unbelievable. The two walls separating the kitchen from the dining and living rooms had been knocked down, creating a huge space for an open-concept kitchen and family room. The formal living room had been relocated to the old master bedroom, on the other side of the stairs that sat in the middle of the house, and the wall between the front door and that room had been taken down as well. Not only that, the entire kitchen area had been remodeled with brand-new appliances and fixtures, and the worn-out carpet had been removed, showing off the original hardwood floors. Clint and Amy had done the impossible—they had made a rundown middle-class house look like a showroom. Luckily, Paula had gone outside as soon as Amy and I came in, so I still didn't have to worry about her overhearing my enthusiastic response.

"My God," I said, "this is amazing."

"I know," Amy said, demonstrating the fact that she wasn't lacking in self-confidence.

"It doesn't even look like the same house."

"No shit," Amy said. "It was a dump."

I didn't want to call Paula and L.W.'s house a dump, but I also couldn't disagree. "I couldn't understand why you two were buying it."

"Well, we got a good deal," Amy admitted, and I wondered not for the first time if they'd lost money when they sold the McMansion.

It hit me then that the last time I'd been in Annandale before Clint's wedding—in 2006—all of my biological siblings had been living better than I was, but five years later, I had finally made good on the promise of my education and graduated to a better life. At long last, Dave and I had traded in our cramped grad school apartments for a roomy house in a desirable neighborhood. No, it wasn't a palace, and we didn't have a fancy SUV in the driveway either. But that was more because we weren't interested in those kinds of material things than because we couldn't afford them. At the same time, Clint and Jeannie had backed off their extravagant lifestyle, ultimately making more realistic choices with their money. I hoped they understood it was better to save than to spend when things were good. It was a lesson my parents had taught me my whole life—always opting for less when they could afford more—but one I was sure Paula's kids had been forced to learn on their own.

"Was it worth it?" I asked Amy, hinting both at the change in their lifestyle and at the ongoing trouble between her and Paula.

"That remains to be seen."

Clint and Amy served us a full meal on the deck—roasted chicken, mashed potatoes, macaroni and cheese, vegetables, and fruit. Even though the food was excellent, the rest of the evening was more than awkward; it was a bloody game of chicken designed to see who would give in first. Clint and Amy tried to act normal, telling us about their vacation in the Outer Banks and asking us about our lives in Kentucky, but Paula sat through the whole meal without speaking. The message was clear: Paula was going to shut out her daughter-in-law until she cracked.

"This is delicious," I said at one point, trying to touch on a neutral subject even Paula could agree on. "Thanks so much for cooking, you two."

"Yes, really," Dave said, clearly playing along. "We appreciate it."

"Not a problem," Clint said. "We love having people over for dinner."

"It's honestly our favorite thing to do," Amy said. Paula still wasn't speaking, so Amy turned to her then and tried to draw her out. "Do you want something else to eat, Mom?" she said. "You hardly touched your plate."

Paula shook her head and kept her eyes on the table, silent as a Trappist monk. By that point, I understood Paula wasn't interested in being the bigger person. In fact, she was acting like a child—an overgrown, spoiled child. It reminded me of Jeannie's behavior at the basketball game in Dayton.

And that's when it hit me that my issues with Paula weren't about me as much as they were about Paula. For eleven long years I'd thought I was the problem in our relationship—that I just couldn't give enough, that I was somehow flawed—but that night I finally saw that it wasn't all me.

Paula was part of the problem too.

She had no idea how to have an adult relationship with another person, no idea how to compromise and work through difficulties like a grown-up or even talk about things. And it all finally made sense to me. Of course, she didn't know how to have an adult relationship. She'd never had one. Her relationship with L.W. had always been about Paula kowtowing to L.W.'s wants and needs. She'd never been allowed to stand on equal footing with him. He'd always had the upper hand, most likely teaching her the only way to get what she wanted was to pout and sulk, to act like a child.

Not long after that, Amy and I fled to the kitchen under the guise of getting dessert. And as soon as we got there, Amy lost it.

"Can you believe this bullshit?" Amy said. "She won't even talk to me! She won't even speak a single word to me!"

"It really is insane," I admitted, but I was more interested in confirming the epiphany I'd had a few moments before than talking about Amy's current frustrations. "I want to ask you something."

Amy nodded at me, so I went on.

"Does Paula act like this with other people?"

"Are you kidding? This is her M.O. She doesn't get her way, somebody speaks out, and that's it—she shuts them out. They might as well be dead to her."

I knew it was true. I'd watched Paula do it with Amy that night, and I knew from the stories I'd been told it was something she'd done with almost everyone: her brother Jimmy, Kalea, even Sue and

Charlie. No one was immune.

"I honestly can't believe it," I said. "I had no idea. All those years—" I started and then stopped, my throat tightening and tears coming to my eyes that I refused to release. I suddenly understood that the guilt I'd felt for over a decade may have been unnecessary, may have even been *caused* by Paula, and the sense I'd had that Paula was always being passive aggressive with me was, in fact, dead on. No, I was by no means without blame in our relationship, but it seemed more and more likely it was a blame we shared. "All those years, I thought it was all me. I thought *I* was the only problem."

"Trust me," Amy said. "It's not you. You're normal. That woman is a fucking bitch."

Amy's words came out a little too loudly, and when I looked out the window above the kitchen sink, I could see that Paula, Clint, and Dave were all looking in our direction as if they'd heard exactly what she had said.

But some part of me just didn't care anymore.

Before I truly understood how bad things were between the Paula and Amy camps, I'd proposed that we all have dinner at the rental house our last night together. We knew we'd be busy packing and getting ready to leave all day Thursday, so I told Paula we wanted to have everyone over on Wednesday night to say goodbye even though we wouldn't drive out of Annapolis until Friday morning. But every time the idea came up, someone balked—whether it was Jeannie and Dalton or Clint and Amy—but I still didn't get the hint. Having the whole family over at once was really not a good idea. Despite that, I persisted. Maybe I had some naïve sense that if I brought everyone together, they would finally see they were a family and needed to work things out.

Even though the temperature was in the mid-nineties and the air was as thick and oppressive as it gets in Annapolis, Dave and I made pasta for everyone that night. Penne a la vodka was one of the few crowd-pleasing dishes we knew how to make well. But once I realized we'd have to sit outside to have enough room for the nine of us to dine, it occurred to me that eating steaming hot pasta on a blistering day was about as appealing as a dip in the River Styx. But at that point it was too late to adjust the menu. We'd bought the food and didn't have anything else to serve. So we went ahead with the plan and made enough pasta and salad for the whole Tucker clan.

Paula arrived first, surprising us forty-five minutes before we expected anyone. If I had thought about it for even one second, I would've realized she was going to show up early since she'd done that just about every other time I'd seen her over the past week and a half. But I hadn't taken the time to think it through, so I had just stepped out of the shower when she knocked on the door, sending us both into a bit of a frenzy.

"Paula's here," Dave said from the kitchen.

"Are you kidding?" I said from the bathroom, where I stood dripping wet in only a towel. "I'm not even dressed."

"Damn it," Dave said. "Fine, I'll take care of it."

Even though I couldn't see her, I recognized Paula's voice as soon as the front door opened. "I brought you this," she said as I eavesdropped from the bedroom.

"You didn't have to do that," Dave said, making me wonder what it was Paula had brought. Was it another elaborate gift? Another factory-made quilt or giant-sized t-shirt? When I finally I threw on some clothes and went to greet Paula, who was now standing in the kitchen with Dave, I was relieved to see there was only a twelve-pack of beer sitting on the counter in front of her.

"Paula," I said. "I told you not to bring anything. We're leaving in less than two days." Was this her way of trying to make us stay?

"I didn't want you to run out," she said.

"We have plenty!"

"Oh, well, you can take it home," she said.

"We're not going right home. We'll be on the road for three days."

"Oh, okay," she said, giving me the beaten-down puppy eyes she used in times when she felt she had no other defense.

"It's fine," I said, taking the box from the counter, ultimately resigned to the fact that we now had more than a case of beer to drink in less than a day and a half. "I'll put it in the fridge."

*

Clint and Amy got there only about twenty minutes after Paula. They'd taken the day off to celebrate their anniversary at the Nationals game in the District and were both glowing—from the sun and the beer—when they arrived. They went right to the living room and plopped down on the furniture like they belonged there.

"This place is amazing," Amy said. "I want to buy it."

"Me too," Dave said though I knew he meant he'd buy it if it were somewhere else, but not that close to Tucker country.

"No kidding," Clint said right away. "This place is killer." He was on his feet then, looking out the window, down to the water.

"But it's a thousand dollars a week," I pointed out, bringing everyone back to reality.

"If I could afford it, I'd do it," Clint said without hesitation. "I'd pack up and move here tomorrow if I could." I didn't remind him he'd never lived anywhere but Annandale his whole life, and that Annapolis, even an hour away, would seem like a whole other planet to him.

"Do you want a beer?" I asked them both, moving toward the kitchen, where Paula was still lurking around Dave while we finished cooking.

As I walked to the refrigerator, Clint stepped up to the pass-through that separated the two rooms. "Hi, Ma," he said, his gaze following her around the room. He had the same eyes as Paula's, and even though I knew he wasn't feeling particularly upset on the surface, I could see that, at his core, he was miserable. He and his mother were not getting along, and it made him horribly unhappy.

"Hi, Clint," she said without looking at him, her voice cracking on the second word. She was as cautious as I'd ever seen her. I glanced at Amy on the sofa and Clint in the pass-through window and wondered what I'd gotten everyone into.

"Can I get you something to drink yet, Paula?" I said, trying to interrupt their standoff.

"No, I'm okay," she said as she started to move toward the living room, which made me even more worried about the evening. If Paula wasn't drinking, something must have really been wrong.

"How about some water?" I asked through the pass-through.

"I'm okay," she said, sneaking a look into my face. She was not okay. The sadness in her eyes told me she was more afraid than I'd realized before.

"Wow, you look great, Mom," Amy said when Paula finally walked into the living room.

"Thanks," Paula said shortly to Amy, staying on the other side of the room—perching tentatively on a dining room chair—rather than sitting near Amy on one of the two overstuffed sofas.

"You really do," I said from the kitchen, trying to engage Paula.

"I've lost twenty-two pounds," Paula said, looking in my direction but avoiding the pleading stare of her daughter-in-law.

"You can really tell," Amy said. "You look fabulous."

Amy was laying it on thick, but Paula just ignored her as if no one had spoken at all.

I felt the need to keep the conversation going, so I turned to Clint and tried to change the subject. "What do you remember about the day you found out about me? What was that like?"

Before he could answer, the sound of a roaring motorcycle outside alerted us to the arrival of Jeannie and Dalton. Paula darted for the door as if she needed to be closer to her allies, and the four of us watched her walk out, equally stunned by her behavior.

"She's not even talking to me," Amy said once Paula was gone.

"Give it time," I said. "Things will get better."

"They have to," Clint said emphatically, "because they couldn't get any worse."

Paula came back inside a few minutes later. "Where are Jeannie and Dalton?" I asked her, glancing to Clint to search for signs of discomfort on his face.

"They're outside," Paula said, making me wonder for a moment if they were refusing to come in because of Clint and Amy. "They're showing Willie and Wade something on the motorcycle."

"Willie and Wade are here too?"

At the exact same time the words came out of my mouth, Wade appeared through the floor-to-ceiling windows along the front of the house, walking purposefully across the lawn as if heading for some destination I couldn't see.

"What is he doing?" I asked, knowing immediately that anything Wade might do with such resolve could be dangerous. He was supposedly clean by then, but still completely unpredictable.

"Oh, nothing. He just brought some fireworks," Paula said casually. "Roman candles, I think."

"What?" Dave said from the kitchen, his voice rising louder than normal.

"We're not allowed to set off fireworks," I told Paula as I kept my eyes on Wade, who had stopped in the middle of the lawn and appeared to be inspecting the ground around him. "We could lose our security deposit."

"Howard isn't even here," Paula said.

"How do you know?"

"His car is gone." Her voice was still too casual for the situation at hand. The week before, unbeknownst to us, Paula had introduced herself to Howard, the owner of the house where we were staying, asking him to lift his no-pets policy after we'd explicitly told her that Jeannie could not bring her injured dog to dinner. Paula's willingness to go over our heads had infuriated Dave, and he'd asked her, as politely as he could, not to talk to Howard anymore and simply obey the rules of the rental—no pets, no smoking, no fireworks—since we didn't want to lose our deposit or have our behavior reflect poorly on the university. But a week later, she still didn't seem to get it.

"Somebody has to stop him," I said as I watched Wade crouch down in the grass. The sun was just starting to set, and Wade's form was silhouetted against the bright blue sky in the fading light. "Clint?"

"I'll take care of it," Clint said, moving toward the sliding glass door in the middle of the room. "Wade, put that thing away," he yelled across the yard as he slid the door open.

But as soon as Clint spoke, Wade turned to look at his brother for only a second before standing up. And then a few tiny sparks began to fly from the torch he'd set up in the middle of the yard.

"Goddamn it!" Dave said. "Stop him!"

"Wade!" Clint yelled again at his brother as he stepped outside and moved toward him. "What the hell are you doing?" Even from inside the house, I could hear Clint scolding his brother.

Willie, Jeannie, and Dalton showed up at the side of the yard just then, apparently having heard the commotion, and the three of them pulled Wade back from the place where he'd been standing. They weren't even ten feet away when the Roman Candle erupted, shooting electric sparks into the air only a few yards in front of the house. From inside, the brilliant rays appeared against the fading sunlight, creating a halo of colors around the four of them as if the explosion had emanated from somewhere deep inside their bodies.

I glanced at Dave, who was standing in front of the windows too, and saw that he was shaking his head at them, clearly disgusted.

It was going to be a long night.

After Wade and his fireworks had been corralled, everyone came inside to get dinner.

"Wow, this looks awesome," Jeannie said, appreciatively surveying the spread of antipasto, penne, and bread we had put out in the kitchen. "I can't believe you did all this."

Amy jumped in before I could respond: "I bet it's going to be delicious."

"I want to eat it all by myself," Jeannie added enthusiastically.

I was pretty sure they were trying to make me feel better after Wade's behavior in the yard, but I was also happy to see everyone getting along for the time being, even if they were merely pretending for my benefit.

"Make sure you get a lot because we won't be able to take it with us," I told everyone, knowing full well I sounded just like my mother. But it was one of the only ways I knew how to show people I cared— by feeding them.

Though it was still hot enough to melt the fresh parmesan I'd put on the table, the nine of us sat outside to eat. We'd pushed two picnic tables together for the occasion, decorating them with blue-and-white checkered tablecloths and a handful of tiny white candles. Paula, Jeannie, and Dalton were at one end, and Clint and Amy at the other, putting Willie, Wade, Dave, and me in the middle to serve as a human buffer. No, the two warring factions didn't speak to each other, but for the rest of the meal, everyone seemed content, eating and making small talk about things that didn't matter. And, for a short time, I thought maybe everything would be okay.

Once dinner was over, Willie and I went down to the pier to

check the trap Dave and I had lowered into the water after we'd arrived. It was the first time the two of us had spent any time alone during that visit. He'd been at the pig roast at the bar a few days before, but had been kicked out by Paula when he got so drunk he couldn't walk. I knew Willie was having a rough time. He hadn't found out yet what the courts were going to do—there was even a chance he'd go to prison—as a result of his fourth DUI, and Misty had left him for another man, a man she'd already married and whose baby she was about to have. And, of course, she'd taken William Jr. with her, so he only got to see his son from time to time. All of that was in my head as we walked down to the water, making me wonder if he'd say anything about the state of his life.

When he pulled the metal cage out of the water, there was still nothing inside but weeds even though we'd been there for eleven days at that point.

"You forgot the bait," Willie said.

"I didn't know you were supposed to do that," I said as I watched the cage soaking the pier.

"The crabs won't crawl inside if you don't put dead fish in there," he said, pointing at a compartment near the top.

"I'll have to take your word for it," I said.

"You don't know *anything* about crab pots, do you?"

"I didn't even know it was called that, much less how to use it."

Willie laughed softly. "Well, I guess you wouldn't. Living in Kentucky and all."

"Right," I said as Willie lowered the trap back into the water.

"It's a nice view here," he said as we started the walk back up to the house, Willie glancing over his shoulder back at the Bay. When we got to the top, he turned to me and said, "I could just sit here all night, looking at the water."

"Me too," I said.

And then he did sit—on the top step of the stairs—so I sat next to him. We spent the next fifteen minutes enjoying the view and talking, not a serious discussion about the problems he was having or anything else important, but just small talk. And before we ran out of things to say, the sky had become completely dark.

*

We had brownies and ice cream for dessert, and not long after that, Willie mentioned he had to get going. He hadn't had very much to drink, and I knew he'd hit the wall with family time. I knew because—like him—I had too. As soon as he said it, Paula, Dalton, and Jeannie stood up, claiming they also needed to leave. I suspected they didn't have anywhere to be, but wanted to get away from the tension with Clint and Amy as soon as they could.

"Wade," Paula said. "Are you going with us?" I knew her question was more loaded than it seemed. She wanted everyone but Clint and Amy to leave with her, sending the message they were all on her side.

"No, I think I'll stay," Wade said, scratching his ear as he spoke. He was clearly not getting what Paula was really asking him. It was so obvious to everyone else that I wasn't at all surprised when Amy jumped in, giving him an excuse to remain put.

"We can drive him home, Mom."

Every time Amy called Paula "Mom," I felt more and more uncomfortable. Couldn't she see her transparent attempts at being familial were only making things worse?

"Yeah," Wade said, still clueless about the battle that was being fought between the two women. "I'll just ride with them."

"Okay," Paula said, staring at Wade—possibly trying to catch his eye and convey that she wanted him to go with her—and not sounding at all convinced that his staying was acceptable.

But Wade, as usual, was oblivious to social cues, so rather than follow his mother's lead, he headed for the kitchen and more dessert.

I walked to the foyer with Willie, Jeannie, and Dalton, giving each of them a long hug goodbye.

When I turned to give Paula her hug, I was surprised by what she said.

"Are you coming to the restaurant tomorrow?"

"No," I said. "We have to pack, remember?" It was a word I felt like I was always saying to Paula. *Remember? Remember? Remember?* She often seemed incapable of remembering anything I said to her, especially the important things.

"Oh, that's right."

"We have to do laundry and pack and clean and do the walk-through with Howard, and I told you—I really want to go into

Annapolis to see the house I used to live in. It's going to be a long day, and I'll be lucky to have time to do that. And then we have to drive all the way to Ohio on Friday, which is going to be exhausting."

"Well, I could come here," Paula offered.

"There's too much to do. I won't get anything done with you here. Remember we were going to say goodbye tonight." *Remember, remember, remember.*

"Oh, yeah," Paula said, and I went to hug her before she could find another reason to object.

I felt a huge wave of relief wash over me when I shut the door behind Paula. I'd made it through our visit without any major damage.

Or so I thought.

Because almost as soon as Paula walked out the door, Amy started to unload on her. She had gone to the kitchen to get another beer, and I followed her there, starting to clean up some of the dishes.

"God, I can't believe she wouldn't talk to me," Amy said. "None of them would even speak to me. What the hell is their problem?"

We all know what their problem was. Amy had not only challenged Paula, she'd insulted her. She'd cursed in her face, a high crime to commit against another family member, especially a strong-willed matriarch, and one Paula—and Jeannie and Dalton—were not ready to forgive, but instead would continue to punish for the foreseeable future. But none of us mentioned that to Amy. She knew as well as we did what they were angry about, and from my way of thinking, she just needed to blow off a little steam. I'd felt the same way many times after seeing family, so I figured it was best to let her get it out.

And get it out she did.

While Dave, Clint, and Wade sat in the other room, Amy raged about Paula for at least twenty minutes without interruption—about Paula's passive aggressiveness, her controlling behavior, about Jeannie's blind loyalty to Paula. About how Paula ran the bar, about how she decorated the bar, about how she told all their problems to customers, about how she didn't want to babysit the twins anymore. At some point, Clint came out to the kitchen and stared at his wife, her arms flailing about like someone who was drowning. While he watched her, he kept drinking, pretty quickly emptying the beer he was working on and going to the fridge for another. And when he did, Amy held out her hand, sending the message that she too wanted another, which he gave her without comment.

Finally, Amy moved on to Paula's drinking, which was something everyone—including Jeannie and Dalton—had been talking about the whole time I'd been there. The doctor had told Paula to cut back because of her high blood pressure, but as far as we could all tell, Paula seemed to be continuing with her regular habit of having several drinks a night.

"She's got a drinking problem," Amy said. "She drinks all night, and then she starts going off on me to anyone she can find."

"I think we better go," Clint said suddenly, his voice flatter than I'd ever heard it, but Amy ignored him, instead taking another long swig of her beer. He'd been silent until that point, and I was shocked by his emotionless comment. Normally, he was a lively force, so much so that I half expected him to join Amy's tirade. But his comment made me wonder if I'd done something wrong or if he was uncomfortable with what Amy was saying about his mother. Paula's behavior over the previous week and a half jibed with everything Amy was saying, and he must have known it even though I wasn't sure it was fair to imply that Paula drank all night every night.

"You don't think she drinks that much, do you?" I asked. "I mean, I see her have a few beers, but that doesn't seem awful."

"A few beers," Amy said, lifting her own bottle to her mouth. "She puts away a twelve-pack a night!"

Initially I found that number hard to believe, but once I thought about it more, I had to admit to myself that Paula had never shown up at the rental without that much beer and that she easily drank three or four bottles to my one.

"You really think so?" I asked.

"Yes, I do," Amy insisted. "She's an alcoholic."

"That's enough," Clint yelled suddenly, interrupting his wife for the first time that night, but Amy continued.

"She is," she said, ignoring Clint. "She's a drunk."

"I said, that's enough!" Clint yelled again and then just as suddenly threw the sunglasses he held in his hand across the kitchen. Dave and Wade had come to the pass-through and were watching, audience-like, as Clint's glasses smashed against the far wall of the kitchen and broke apart into three pieces. I had never seen anyone in my family throw something in anger, and I was so shocked I couldn't speak. I looked to Clint to see what he would do next. "You're the one who's drunk," he said, pointing at Amy with a beer still in his hand. "How much have *you* had to drink today?"

"Oh, shut up," Amy said casually as if his words didn't concern her at all.

"I'm leaving!" Clint yelled again and grabbed his keys from the table.

"Don't go," she said blandly, but made no move to stop him, instead letting Clint walk out the front door and slam it behind him.

"Everyone in this family has a drinking problem," she said to me, but I was still speechless. Her husband had thrown his sunglasses across the room, stormed out of the house, and she was still standing there talking to me.

"Don't you think you should go after him?" I asked. "What if he leaves without you?"

"Oh, he's not going to leave without me," Amy said. I half-expected her to say, *he doesn't have the balls*. But she didn't. Instead she just waved her hand at me like I was being silly. Clearly, his behavior did not strike her as alarming, which made me question if it was common.

"Still," I said, "you should go check on him. He's in no shape to drive."

"Fine," Amy said, picking up her purse and moving noisily toward the door. But before she got there, she turned around. "I don't know if I'll see you again. Give me a hug." I was completely floored that she was taking the time to offer me a heartfelt goodbye, but I acquiesced, hugging her in the same foyer where I'd embraced her practically estranged mother-in-law only an hour before.

"I hope I get to see you again," she said. "I want us to be friends. And thanks for everything. Dinner was delicious."

It was one of the strangest goodbyes I had ever experienced.

Once she was out the door, I turned back to Dave, who was still standing next to Wade in the living room.

"Wade?" I said. "You're still here?"

Dave looked at Wade then, too, as if seeing him for the first time. "Don't you have to go?" Dave asked him, barely hiding his desire to get Wade out of the house.

"I was supposed to ride with them," Wade confessed.

"Well, you better get going," Dave said. "You can't miss your ride."

"I could just stay here," Wade said, inspecting the space around him. "Sleep on the couch."

"Oh, no," Dave said, no longer hiding his intentions. "You're going with them. Didn't you come with something? A backpack?"

"It's outside," Wade said in a resigned voice.

"I'll go get it," Dave said. "I'll meet you outside. Go out to the car now, Wade. Now!"

As Dave went out the sliding door to the yard in search of Wade's backpack, I led Wade to the door.

"I'm sorry things ended like this, Wade," I said.

"Me too," he said.

"Can I have a hug?"

"Yes," he said formally, leaning in to me and putting his hands awkwardly on my arms.

"Don't let Clint drive if he's drunk, okay?"

"Okay," Wade said automatically.

"You're not drunk, are you? You could drive."

"I could drive," he said.

I opened the front door, and Dave was standing there on the front steps, clutching Wade's backpack of illegal fireworks and God knows what else.

"Come on, Wade," he said. "Let's go!"

Clint's giant SUV was idling in the road behind them. With the dark windows rolled up and the grill gleaming in the dark, it looked like a modern chariot of death, waiting to take two of my biological brothers to what could be their final destination.

As soon as they'd pulled away, we shut the door and flipped the deadbolt.

"We need to lock everything," Dave said without hesitation, and I nodded. "I don't want any of them coming back tonight."

"The windows in the back are still open," I said.

He moved toward the rear of the house, shutting windows and turning out lights as he went. I followed him, geisha-like, from room to room.

"Do you think they'll be okay?" I asked him. "Clint had a lot to drink."

"Are you kidding?" Dave asked with a laugh. "He was shit-faced."

"Amy too," I admitted. "I didn't realize it until Clint said it."

"They'd been drinking all day."

"I know."

Then he turned and looked at me.

"We have got to get out of here," he said. "We've got to pack up our shit and get the hell out of here. These people are crazy."

In the past I might have defended the Tuckers. I might have encouraged Dave to be patient, but not that night. "Yeah," I said. "I know."

New Message from Molly McCaffrey to Clint Tucker
9:12pm July 20, 2011

I'm sorry about tonight. Let me know when you guys get home safely, okay?

New Message from Jeannie Tucker to Molly McCaffrey
9:13pm July 20, 2011

Thank you so very much for tonight. Dinner was delicious. I'm so happy you came here for this week. Means a lot that you got to spend time with all of us. I will miss you

New Message from Molly McCaffrey to Jeannie Tucker
9:36pm July 20, 2011

You're very welcome about tonight. I really appreciate you and Dalton (and Paula) coming to dinner with Clint and Amy even though things are rough right now. I know it was hard for all of you, so it means a lot to me.

And, yes, I'm glad I came to visit too! I wish we could see each other more. I'll definitely miss you too! And I'm so glad I got to meet Dalton—he's a keeper for sure. Please thank him for doing the dishes, okay?

Clint called me the next morning. He seemed to want to

apologize and confer over what had happened. He was completely calm and, as usual, easy to talk to. And we probably had the longest conversation of our lives. Despite that, it felt like the most normal thing in the world—to talk to him about his problems and to try to offer some words of encouragement. That was the weird thing about Clint and his siblings. It always felt easy with them, as if we didn't even have to try to get along. It just happened naturally. As if our bond was greater than the forces that had tried to keep us apart.

Though Clint seemed much calmer twelve hours after he'd lost his temper and stormed out of our rental house, he also seemed unhappily resigned to the massive struggle going on between his wife and his mother. It was obvious they still had a long way to go before all of their wounds would be healed. I felt for *all* of them, but I felt the worst for Clint, understanding he was caught in the middle and desperately wanted to have a good relationship with both of them.

"You can always blame it on me if you have to," I said before we hung up.

Clint laughed. "You think that would work?"

"Maybe," I admitted, knowing full well that if he ever took me up on the offer, he could easily re-direct Paula's anger in my direction. At the same time, I also knew he was too caring, too ethical a person to dump his problems on someone else.

Not long after I talked to Clint, Paula called.

It was obvious from the minute I answered the phone she was fishing for information. She asked me how I was doing, but before I could finish answering, she was onto another question, probably the real reason she'd called.

"How'd everything go after I left?"

It wasn't the kind of question you asked unless you already knew things had not gone well.

"Great!" I said with artificial enthusiasm, not at all uncomfortable lying to her about what had happened since I knew it wouldn't be a good idea to get involved in the Paula-Amy feud.

"Really?" she said.

I knew she didn't believe me. I knew she was aware more had happened the previous night than I was letting on. I could hear it in her voice. Normally, Paula's words were slow, casual, her sentences reluctant to form, but that day she was rushing to get her message out as if there were an emergency on the other end of the line.

"Yeah, it was fun," I said in the faux happy voice I had learned from Dave to use on such occasions. "I mean, unless you're worried about Wade eating too much ice cream."

"What?" Paula said, disbelief still in her voice.

"Yeah, he ate almost a whole carton of ice cream. I figured he'd be up in the middle of the night with a stomachache like a ten-year-old after a day at the amusement park."

I half-expected Paula to call me on my lie. To say she didn't believe me or ask me if there was something I wasn't telling her. But, for some reason, she let me off the hook. Instead she asked me about packing, and I lied again, like I was a natural at it, telling her it was going well even though I'd spent the morning on the phone rather than doing anything productive.

New Message from Molly McCaffrey to Clint Tucker

1:02pm July 21, 2011

Good to talk to you today, Clint. I realize that you are suffering the most because you're in the middle. Try to take it one day at a time. I truly believe you can all work this out.

I want to let you know I just talked to Paula, and she asked me directly how things went after she left last night. I told her things went great (so, in a sense, I was dishonest), and that Wade ate a lot of ice cream. If you decide to tell your mom what we talked about last night, that is completely your call. But please tell her that I wasn't honest with her only because I thought it was your decision to tell her, not mine. And if you don't ever tell her, that's fine with me!

New Message from Clint Tucker to Molly McCaffrey

7:37pm July 21, 2011

Thanks Molly. I did enjoy spending time together and I hope we get to again soon. It would be very nice.

New Message from Jeannie Tucker to Molly McCaffrey

11:03am July 21, 2011

Hey Molly,

I wanted to say thanks for dinner again. And before you leave, I want to write to you about the book.

I just want to make sure my moms feelings are taken into consideration. I know that this was an extremely hard and crazy experience for you. And I have no clue how you or her feel. But I do know, giving you up was the hardest thing my mother has ever gone through. Even harder than my fathers death. I know this because she has said it.

As her best friend and daughter, I just want you to know that its challenging for her to listen to my brothers responses regarding the matter. And I'm sure that's why she kept stepping outside last night.

I think she is coming to see you today. It's very hard for her to talk about all of these emotions. I dont think she wants to let you down again or disappoint you.

Even though I havent even read the book, I guess I just wanted to put in a word to you to kind of protect her feelings. If that makes any sense at all. I hope it does and is taken the way I've intended it.

I really hope I didnt upset or offend you.

Be safe in your travels back home. I will definately miss you!

New Message from Molly McCaffrey to Jeannie Tucker
12:59pm July 21, 2011

Hey, Jeannie,

Thanks for writing. You are not offending me at all. I'm glad you mentioned it, and I especially appreciate that you feel like you can tell me this. My parents have said the same thing many times—that I have to be careful that I don't hurt people's feelings with the book (their feelings, Paula's feelings, everyone's feelings). I have to say that the whole thing is very hard—it's hard to be honest in the book, but also not hurt anyone's feelings. This is going to be the next thing I have to worry about. I plan to have a draft of the book done by the end of August, but then I have to go back through and see what needs to be changed or cut so the book doesn't hurt anyone. For instance, I talk very honestly about Wade, and I think I'm going to have to scale that back. I know I need to do it, but I'm not going to think about it until the draft is finished. I don't think I will be trying to sell it until December, so there is still time to cut things out that need to be cut. It's so hard to balance diplomacy and honesty!

I actually just talked to Paula, and if you have an iota of time or energy, if you could help make sure she's not upset about today, I would really appreciate it. She said she was on her way here, but I told her that we need some alone time/downtime/work time today. This is especially true because we are going to be with family for the whole weekend, and then my sister is coming back to Bowling Green with us (with her whole family) on Sunday. That means we won't be alone again until Wednesday. As I told Paula, we are used to spending a lot of time alone, so we need to mellow out today to prepare for what is to come this weekend. I really, really hope I didn't hurt her feelings. It is not personal, but we just have to balance our alone time with our people time. Maybe we're just no fun, but that's just how we are. I hope you all understand. If there is anything you can do to reinforce the message that this is not about Paula, but about us, I would really appreciate it. Things have gone so well, and I don't want to leave on a bad note.

I did tell Paula we'll stop by the Hideaway tomorrow morning on our way out of town to say goodbye. We have to drive right through Virginia, so it's not out of the way or anything. I just hope she's okay with not seeing us today.

Again, I really appreciate you being honest with me about the book. I'll have your thoughts in my head as I revise the book.

Thanks!

Molly

New Message from Jeannie Tucker to Molly McCaffrey
1:05pm July 21, 2011

I do not know if she will be ok. But I will try to talk to her to make sure she is alright. I think she had some things she wanted to talk to you about before you left. And she wanted to do them face to face.

I'm sure she understands though.

I'm eating your pasta as I type!

New Message from Jeannie Tucker to Molly McCaffrey
1:17pm July 21, 2011

And I do think some things regarding my mom, should not come up. I just think that there are things that should be sacred and protected. That's all.

New Message from Molly McCaffrey to Jeannie Tucker
3:06pm July 21, 2011

Oh, I didn't know she wanted to talk. She just said she wanted to give me a Tucker's sweatshirt—I can try to come to the Hideaway earlier in the morning

*on Friday then, and Paula and I can take a walk out back to be alone. Still
doing laundry! Hope you like the pasta!*

Paula called that night while we were at a copy shop in Annapolis
printing maps. She immediately asked where we were. She said it in a
mocking tone as if doubting my assertion that I didn't have time to
see her that day. When I told her where we were, she seemed
surprised, like she'd never believed anything we'd told her. And that
may be why she launched into another interrogation as soon as her
first one was finished.

"I thought you said that everything went well last night," she said.

"Things did go well last night."

"Well, Wade told me that Amy was complaining about me after
I left," she said, sprinting right to her point.

"Wade said that?" I asked.

"Yeah," Paula said. "Is it true?"

"I don't think you should be asking me about this, Paula," I said.
"I think you need to talk to Clint."

"Is it true?"

She clearly wasn't going to let it go, and since I felt guilty about
not seeing her that day, I decided to answer her question without
saying anything I shouldn't. "Yes, it's true that Amy was talking about
what's going on between the two of you, but she didn't tell me
anything you haven't already told me yourself."

"What did she say?"

"I am really not going to discuss this with you, Paula."

"But Amy talked to you about it?"

"Sure, she talked to me, but she was just trying to figure out how
to get past it. She wants to work things out with you." Though I
wasn't being entirely forthright, it was true that Amy wanted to make
peace.

"Did Clint storm out because Amy was complaining about me?"

"Oh, Paula," I said, not sure how to continue. It was clear Paula
wanted to lay all the blame on Amy for a problem that was about all
of them, not just her daughter-in-law. And she was fishing for
evidence that might help her convince everyone it was simply Amy
who was the problem, but I wasn't going to help her close Amy's

coffin. "I really think you should ask Clint, not me."

"I just wish you hadn't talked about this with them," she said.

"I *didn't* talk about it," I insisted, becoming frustrated by Paula's implication that I should only be there for her. "I just listened."

"Well, I wish you hadn't done that either."

I can't remember what I said after that. I was so angry that the entire rest of our conversation was erased from my memory. Paula wanted me to shut out Amy—and maybe Clint—because she was angry with her. She wanted to send the message to Amy that if she didn't get in line, she would be cut out. It was the same message I'd gotten from Jeannie ten years before.

Though the conversation didn't get much better after that, I did manage to get Paula to focus on the positive. We had changed our minds and decided to stop by the bar to see her the next day before we drove to Ohio. At least I thought that was good news, something that would make Paula happy, but she seemed more resigned than grateful.

New Message from Molly McCaffrey to Clint Tucker

8:24pm July 21, 2011

I want to apologize for continuing this further, but I do want to tell you that Paula called about thirty minutes ago (while we were out printing maps for tomorrow) and asked me what happened last night. Apparently Wade had mentioned something to her about Amy complaining about her after she left. I told Paula she should ask you about it, and she pushed me, and like a total wimp, I folded and told her that we all talked about the problems you've all been having. On the bright side, I did not tell her details and tried to focus on the positive. Wade had told her that you walked out because you were mad about what Amy was saying. I told her most of our discussion was about moving past all this trouble. I also told her she was giving Amy the cold shoulder, which might have been what pushed Amy last night. Anyway, I hate that I inserted myself, but to be honest, I feel guilty about not seeing Paula today, so when she pushed me, I was unable to stand up to the pressure.

Anyway, I did have fun seeing you guys and meeting the kids. Come visit whenever you want.

I really hope this works out for all of you, and I'm sorry any of you are suffering.

I probably shouldn't have been surprised when we showed up at the Hideaway the next morning, and neither Paula nor Jeannie seemed pleased to see us. But the truth was I was more than surprised. I was flat-out shocked.

The second we walked in the door, there were no greetings, no how-are-yous, nothing. Paula was behind the bar, and Jeannie was sitting on a stool in front of her. Instead of saying hello, as soon as we set foot inside the Hideaway, Jeannie glanced up from her laptop and asked us, "So how was the walk-through?" Her voice was just like her mother's the night before—mocking, disbelieving. Jeannie had never acted like that with me before. Yes, she'd been distant and cold at the basketball game in Dayton, but this was something more pronounced. Her tone that morning was openly hostile. She was pissed. I thought about calling her on it, about asking her what her problem was, but instead I kept it civil. I didn't want to start something I had no intention of finishing.

"Actually," I began as Dave lofted a half-empty twelve-pack onto the bar, "Howard called and said he was out of town. He couldn't do it. I hope we still get the deposit back."

"Oh, we'll get it back," Dave said.

"Huh," Jeannie said. "That's really interesting." Again, her tone was mocking and insincere: it was obvious what she was saying—that she and Paula had never believed we were supposed to have a walk-through, that they thought we'd been intentionally dishonest with them. I could also tell that no matter what I said, they wouldn't believe me, so I didn't even bother trying to convince them. And as soon as Jeannie's judgment had landed on me, like a cloud of disapproval, she turned back to the laptop that was sitting in front of her on the bar, acting as if we'd already left.

"Paula," Dave said, forcing Paula to look him in the eye for the first time since we'd arrived, "I brought you the leftover beer."

Normally Paula would have argued with him, saying something about how we should take it with us. But there were clearly going to be no more offers of generosity. "Thanks," Paula said without any emotion. "You don't want anything to eat, do you?" Paula's voice was normally pleading—*please, let me in, it said*. But that morning, she sounded like she couldn't care less whether she was a part of my life or not. And though she was technically offering us food, the message was clear: *I'm only saying this to be polite. I don't really want to feed you.*

"No, we're fine," I said. "We ate before we left. But I do have to use the bathroom."

"You know where it is," Paula said flatly.

"Yeah, me too," Dave said, and though he was probably being honest, I also knew he didn't want to be left alone with the two of them.

When I returned, Paula had a Tucker's sweatshirt and t-shirt folded up in her hands, and she handed them to me in a rushed manner, more like they were rations than gifts. "Here you go," she said.

"Thanks," I said, though I wasn't sure what she was more interested in—giving me something or getting me out of there. She certainly was in no mood to talk even though Jeannie had told me the day before Paula wanted to discuss something with me, and we'd shown up early that morning to allow time for that. And when I glanced at Jeannie, I saw the same was true of her. She was wrapped up in something on her computer screen, ignoring us altogether. The message was clear. They wanted us out of there. They wished we were already gone.

"Well, I guess we should get going," I said even though we'd expected to be there at least thirty minutes before we could leave without hurting anyone's feelings. Dave was just coming out of the bathroom.

"Yeah, you've got a long drive ahead of you," Paula said, and I wondered, yet again, if she believed anything we'd told her over the past twenty-four hours.

"Yes, we do," I said, and I heard my voice betray the tiniest bit of suspicion. *Why was Paula behaving like this? Why was she so anxious to get us out of there?* It just wasn't like her. "Listen, I'm sorry about everything with Clint," I said, hoping to heal whatever wound had been opened before we left town. "I didn't mean to get involved, and I feel bad about that."

"It's fine," Paula said, but she didn't look at me when she said it. And Paula always looked at me, her eyes forever probing me for more. "It's all good."

"I hope so," I said because I really did hope everything would work out between all of them.

"Well, you better get going," Paula said abruptly.

I couldn't believe how she was acting. She wasn't physically pushing us out the door, but she was doing everything else she could to get rid of us.

"Okay," I said, reaching in to give Paula a hug. "Goodbye," I said, glancing at Jeannie, who was still sitting at the end of the bar working on her computer. "Bye, Jeannie," I said with a wave.

"Yeah, bye," she said without getting up or looking in our direction.

Paula and Dave shared a forced hug, and then we moved toward the door.

"Drive carefully," Paula said quickly, and for the first time in my life, I honestly wondered if she meant it.

When we were safely in the car, I turned to Dave and said, "What just happened?"

"I have no fucking clue," he said as he backed out of the parking lot in an uncharacteristically hurried fashion. "But I have to admit this is the most I've ever looked forward to an eight-hour drive in my life."

"No kidding," I said, looking out the window and studying the bar as we pulled onto the roadway. Even though the inside had been renovated, the exterior looked exactly the same, and I half expected to see L.W. walk through the glass door to the outside bar, wiping his hands on a rag and surveying the scene before him.

"And," Dave said, jarring me out of my thoughts, "it really seemed like they didn't want us there."

"That's what I was thinking," I said. "It was like they'd decided they were done with us. Just like Amy."

"Exactly," Dave said.

"I don't get it," I said. "We weren't even supposed to stop by today. Paula was the one who insisted on seeing us again. And then she acted like she didn't want us around."

"It's very strange," Dave admitted.

"Have you ever seen Paula act that way with me before?" I asked. "She was so cold, so distant."

"Never. At least not with you. And what's weird is that, all those years, Paula was so needy that she never held anything against us. Any time you called or visited, you were always worried she'd be angry with you for being out of touch so long, but she never really was. She was always just happy to hear from you. And now—"

I interrupted him and finished his thought: "Now she's acting like she doesn't want to ever hear from me again."

"Right."

"So what happened?"

"I have no fucking clue," he said a second time, leaving me to wonder if he was right.

Of course, we did have a clue. We knew Paula was angry I hadn't made time to see her the day before—though that wasn't something she'd complained about in years, so I didn't believe that was the real issue. Nor did she have any right to complain about how much time I spent with her given that I'd taken the time and energy to come see her for almost two weeks and had told her all along I wouldn't be able to see her every day. I'd stuck to that promise too, spending six of the twelve days we were there with her, which was more time than I'd ever spent with her in my entire life.

No, it wasn't that I hadn't spent enough time with her.

It was something bigger than that.

I also knew Paula was angry with me for talking to Clint and Amy about what was going on between them, for what I assumed she saw as me taking their side. But I had the sense that was just a temporary frustration, not something that had any real staying power. In six months, the whole thing would be over, and I believed Paula knew that too. Still, I wasn't surprised when, a few days later, I heard from Jeannie about it one more time.

New Message from Jeannie Tucker to Molly McCaffrey

9:53am July 25, 2011

Hey Molly:

Hope you guys had fun this weekend at the wedding and are traveling saftely.

Just wanted to touch base about the dinner at your house. I'm a littel upset because I'm hearing bits and peices of things that came up after I left. I dont even know why anything came up because it did go so well. and like you said to me at the Hideaway before you left, I hardly told you a thing.

It seems a lot of unneccissary things came up in discussion and I dont really know why. I went to dinner because I wanted to and thought it would be a good idea. If I didnt want to attend dinner because of other people being there, I wouldnt have gone. It appears a lot of emotions were stirred.

I wish nothing came up.

I had mixed emotions to write you about this...thought I would just let it go. Hope you can understand and appreciate that I did write.

Jeannie

New Message from Molly McCaffrey to Jeannie Tucker

11:35pm July 25, 2011

Hey, Jeannie,

I'm glad you wrote. I'm not sure anything was said that you haven't already heard, and you're right that I still have no idea what is really going on or what has happened. I feel awful about what's going on with all of you (and that anything came up at all the whole time I was there), and I'll do anything to help that I can.

The wedding was fun and now my sister and her family are visiting, which means things are still crazy for us for another thirty-six hours. Back to normal life on Wednesday.

Molly

It's hard to admit this, but that was the last correspondence I ever had with Jeannie, and I only heard from Clint one more time after that. More than a month later, when he and Dalton became friends on Facebook, I wrote to him and asked if that meant things were improving. And he said, yes, thankfully they were.

I told him I was happy they were moving forward, that he could throw me under the bus if he needed to. The whole time I was in Annapolis that summer I'd thought if they all needed to direct their anger at me to find some common ground, that would be fine. And now I can't help but wonder if that's what they've done. I wrote to Jeannie not long after talking to Clint and asked her if everything was okay between us, but she never responded.

Since then, my forty-second, forty-third, forty-fourth, and forty-fifth birthdays have come and gone without any correspondence from the Tuckers, and I was not invited to Jeannie's wedding the summer after our visit though I saw the pictures on Facebook. Fifteen years after I met my biological siblings and eight years after Clint and Amy's wedding—and the precarious but happy peace we had all found—it seems that our relationship is finally and irrevocably over. On the one hand, I'm relieved. Not having to worry about how to fit them in my life means a huge burden has been lifted.

But I can't help but feel like I've lost something. I've lost the only four people in the world with whom I share my genes. Despite our differences, I grew to care about them deeply. Maybe I even love them. I'm not sure why I feel so connected to them, but I do. In fact, my relationship with them feels natural and innate in some ways, just like real family. But they are family who are lost to me now. Because I believe I will never again have them in my life and will feel that loss for years to come.

I can't explain why, but I just know I'll never get them back.

If, as I suspect, things finally did improve between the Paula and Amy camps, that only left one thing that could have made Paula act so cold with me that morning at the Hideaway: the book.

By the time we left Virginia, I knew with certainty Paula was unhappy about the book. Jeannie had said as much the day before we left when she asked me to protect Paula's feelings as I finished it. But, at the time, I hadn't thought Jeannie's request was that big of a deal or demonstrated anything out of the ordinary. It's not unusual for people who are the subject of a piece of writing to ask for that kind of consideration.

But after seeing Paula's and Jeannie's behavior that morning—after watching the two of them act as if I were dead to them—I finally understood how much the book scared them, how worried they were about what I would say. I'd told them I was determined to be honest about Wade, so they might have been wondering what else I would include. And there can be no doubt they finally understood

I was going to tell the whole story.

The truth is that all I have ever wanted was to do our story justice, to tell it as it really was. Which is why I have to admit that, after we left the Hideaway that morning in July of 2011, I never talked to or heard from Paula again.

Never.

After years of begging for more from me—more time, more phone calls, more letters, more visits, more connection, more love—Paula Tucker had decided she no longer wanted me in her life. That she was simply and completely finished with me.

It had taken her forty-one years to do so, but my biological mother had finally let me go.

Epilogue

The night before we left, Dave and I followed through on our plan to visit the first place I had ever lived with my parents: a small townhouse on the base of the Naval Academy.

Dave and I had fallen in love with the area during our trip that summer. It wasn't the first time I had swooned over Annapolis, but seeing it with Dave was somehow more meaningful. And during our last drive into town, it felt bittersweet to be leaving it all behind—possibly forever.

We drove through the lush hills outside the city, past million-dollar houses and quick glimpses of the Bay, until finally making our way to the bridge that spanned the Severn River. From the far side, the Naval Academy loomed in the distance like a magical glimpse into the past—with patina-colored rotundas, gothic chapels, and giant limestone dormitories. It wasn't hard to understand why Dad had asked to be stationed there. Of course, after spending two years at sea, he'd made that request so he could spend more time with Mom. Though I'm sure he didn't say it to his superiors—that wouldn't be his way—they were trying to have a baby, and there's no doubt the idea of living under the same roof for more than a few days at a time would have facilitated that process.

My parents lived at the Naval Academy from 1968 to 1971, and we'd visited Annapolis as a family a handful of times while I was growing up. Of course, I have no memory of the townhouse where they first brought me after leaving St. Jerome's. Mom and Dad had only driven me past there one other time—when I was living in D.C. in my twenties. Unfortunately, it had all gone by way too fast that day so many years before. The two of them were showing me around the whole Academy, and there was so much to see that I never made a clear imprint of the place where we lived in my memory.

But Dad never forgot anything from that time in his life, so I called him while we were in Annapolis that summer and asked him where the townhouse was located. Without a moment's hesitation, he told me the address: "1-D Badger Road," he said as if he'd lived there just the year before.

So after we finished packing, Dave and I set off for one last trip into Annapolis, to the first place I had really called home.

Back in the late '60s and early '70s, Badger Road was home to the Academy's married officers, and my parents quickly made friends with everyone in the neighborhood, the wives sharing recipes and covered dishes as easily as the husbands traded stories about their time at sea.

When Dave and I arrived on Badger Road that hot, humid night more than forty years later, we were greeted by three dozen identical townhouses, all of them with bright American flags flying crisply from their front porches, a tribute to the American dream.

My parents had big dreams when they lived in Annapolis. They'd dreamed of owning a home some day, they'd dreamed of being financially secure, and, most importantly, they'd dreamed of having children. I imagine, in that sense, not much has changed in that tiny little neighborhood.

Everyone on Badger Road was having children back then, so when, after five years of trying unsuccessfully to get pregnant, the two of them finally came home with a baby of their own, the whole neighborhood gathered to celebrate. If any of them saw me differently because I was adopted, they didn't let on to my parents and, from all accounts, welcomed their friends' new arrival with true happiness and warmth.

During my childhood, we would often reunite with some of the people who were there the day my parents brought me home, and each time they would recount, with glassy eyes, the delight they felt that warm May afternoon in 1970, six weeks after I was born.

And thinking about all of that—about Badger Road, about my

parents, and about everything that's happened since the day I was born—has made me realize that this is the life I was meant to live.

A life that started at 1-D Badger Road.

A life that began with joy and gratitude.

Not a life overwhelmed by sorrow and regret.

And as long as I remember that, I will know who I really am. After all, the only name I have ever answered to is Molly, a name my father loved so dearly he wanted to give it to my sister as well.

And though it requires great discipline to do so, when I think back on the trip we took to Annapolis in the summer of 2011, I am fully committed to remembering not all of the distrust and animosity we experienced during our visit, but rather the wonder and relief I felt when I returned to Badger Road for my true homecoming.

I will remember the red-white-and-blues waving at me under a picture-perfect sky as if they were as delighted about my return as I was. I will remember the connection I had with a place I can't technically remember but somehow still feel is a part of me. It's a feeling not dramatically different than the one I experience every time I look at the photo of the first moment I was in my mother's arms, her giant white hat unable to dwarf a smile nearly as big, my father's tousled hair adding to the sweetness of his shy grin.

In that picture, my parents took no notice of the camera. Instead their eyes were trained only on me—as if I was too precious for them to look away.

That is what I will always remember.

That is who I will always be.

SPECIAL THANKS

Yet again, Scott Douglass has offered me a home for my work. Scott, I am forever indebted. Truly.

I also have a special place in my heart for my early readers—Kristie Lowry, Lee McMichael, Katie Pickens—who put their all into helping me edit this book. Also a big thanks to Eric Goodman who saw this book in its very earliest form and then told me to wait. I guess you were right, boss.

And to the other writers who have helped me on this journey—Laney Becker, Joe Blair, Beth Browne, Lee Martin, Mary Ellen Miller, Josip Novakovich, Jane Olmsted, Jim Reiss—your support means more than I can say.

A word of appreciation to Samantha Starr, Samantha McAllister, Barrett Griffin, and Marianne Hale, who carried me through much of this process: you are all amazing.

There were also some people who lent their personal and professional expertise to this book, and I must thank them too: Jacqueline Adams, Kenly Ames, Pam Eisert, Jill Higgins, Jeong Oh Kim, Craig Losekamp, and Jeff Weems.

Can a girl ever have too many friends? I really don't think so. But that doesn't make me appreciate any of mine any less. Thank you all for standing by me even at my most difficult: Angie Alexieff, Laura Bain-Selbo, Al Bardi, Tomitha Blair, Cyndi Crocker, Kristin Czarnecki, Peggy Davis, Julie Ellis, Sherry Hamby, Rachel Hardwick, Kim and David Jones, Linda King, Misty Like, Meredith Love, Sandy McAllister, Chrystal Mills, Leslie Nichols, Tina Nemphos, Kelcey Parker, Donna Schulte, Jen Sheffield, Kara Thurmond, Jen Vanderpool, Fleur Whitaker, Michelle Zimmerman, and last but never least Tracy and Craig Williams.

An enormous thank you to my family—Mom, Dad, and Katie—for not only supporting me through this process, but also for dealing with the frightening reality of having their lives appear in print.

And, finally to Dave—what could I possibly say after everything we have been through that would suffice? No words can convey how I feel, but I can say this: thank you for letting the wild be.

Molly McCaffrey is the author of *You Belong to Us* (memoir) and *How to Survive Graduate School & Other Disasters* (stories). She received her Ph.D. in literature and creative writing from the University of Cincinnati and lives in Bowling Green, Kentucky, with her husband, novelist David Bell.